Greg McEnnally trained as a science teacher, teaching for a number of years in Australia before teaching in Papua New Guinea. Subsequently, he switched to teaching English, training in TESOL (Teaching English to Speakers of Other Languages) with Cambridge University. He moved to China in 2002, teaching there until 2014. The final three years were spent teaching at SISU (Sichuan International Studies University) in Chongqing. This book is the story of those years: the land, the people, the culture as seen through the eyes of a westerner.

This book is dedicated to the ordinary people in China, people who are not responsible for the political system under which they live. These people accepted me, shared their lives with me and made me welcome. This especially includes my students. Thank you.

Greg McEnnally

TEACHING IN CHONGQING

AUSTIN MACAULEY PUBLISHERS™

LONDON • CAMBRIDGE • NEW YORK • SHARJAH

A CIP catalogue record for this title is available from the British Library.

ISBN 9781398467934 (Paperback)
ISBN 9781398467941 (ePub e-book)

www.austinmacauley.com

First Published 2023
Austin Macauley Publishers Ltd®
1 Canada Square
Canary Wharf
London
E14 5AA

As usual, I received invaluable assistance with the maps and graphics in this book from Greg Tait. Some of my friends in Chongqing during our discussions gave me important insights into China, especially Michael. To these I am deeply indebted.

Table of Contents

Introduction   **17**

Chapter 1: Chongqing   **22**

1.1: Nomenclature   22

1.2: Climate   24

Autumn   25

Winter   25

Spring   27

Summer   29

1.3: Jie Fang Bei   30

1.4: Chao Tien Men Square   32

1.5: The Three Gorges Museum   37

1.6: Stilwell Museum   39

1.7: Nan Shan   42

1.8: Rong Hui Hot Springs   44

1.9: Ciqikou   47

1.10: A Chongqing Walk   50

1.11: Thanksgiving   52

1.12: Transport   54

Introduction   54

1.12.1: Trains   54

Red line 60

Blue line north 60

    1.12.2: Buses 62

    1.13: Food 62

Chapter 2: Sichuan International Studies University **65**

    2.1: The Name 65

    2.2: Location 68

    2.3: Lower Campus 70

    2.4: Words OF Wisdom 73

        Education 73

        The Future 75

        Language 77

        The Meaning of Life 78

        Miscellaneous 80

    2.5: Upper Campus 83

        2.5.1: Layout 83

        2.5.2 The Military 85

    2.6: My Apartment 89

    2.7: A Tale of Tongs 94

    2.8: Rudolf 98

    2.9: Christmas 101

    2.10: Sport 103

Chapter 3: SISU Surrounds **109**

    3.1: Gele Shan 109

    3.2: Zhazidong Prison 111

    3.3: Lieshimu 113

    3.4: The Law University 117

3.5: Shapingba   119

3.6: Coffee Shops   122

Chapter 4: Outside the City   **126**

Introduction   126

4.1: Dazu   126

4.2: Zunyi   130

    4.2.1: Christmas 2011   130

    4.2.2: February 2014   135

4.3: A Wedding in Qian Xi   143

4.4: Daying   156

Chapter 5: Some Happenings   **163**

5.1: National Day   163

5.2: Awards' Night   166

5.3: The Intercontinental Hotel   169

5.4: ANZAC Day   171

5.5: Acting   175

5.6: Phoning Home   176

5.7: A Scungy Mao   178

5.8: Earthquake   181

5.9: Thrills and Spills   182

5.10: Daddy   186

5.11: Nationalism   187

5.12: Miscellaneous   189

    5.12.1: A glowing toe   189

    5.12.2: Buying wine   189

    5.12.3: Beggars   190

    5.12.4: Information   190

Chapter 6: Entertainment   **192**

    Introduction   192

    6.1 Television   193

    6.2: Alliance Francaise Auditorium   194

        6.2.1: A Baroque Concert   194

        6.2.2: A Short Film   195

        6.2.3: A Ballet   195

        6.2.4: A 7th Birthday Concert   196

        6.2.5: Down Town   199

    6.3: Chuan Opera   200

    6.4: New Year Concerts   204

    6.5: German Boys' Choir   207

    6.6: A Teachers' Concert   209

    6.7: Towel of Babel   211

        6.7.1: May, 2013   211

        6.7.2: May, 2014   216

        6.7.3: Conclusion   218

    6.8: A Tchaikovsky Feast   219

    6.9: Impressionism   222

Chapter 7: Going to Church   **225**

    Introduction   225

    7.1: Shapingba   225

    7.2: The Cathedral   227

    7.3: Our Third Church   230

Chapter 8: Education   **234**

    Introduction   234

    8.1: First Semester, Autumn 2011   235

8.2: The Second Semester, Spring 2012   238

    8.2.1: The first week   238

    8.2.2: The second week—confusion continues   242

    8.2.3: The fourth week   244

8.3: Third Semester, Autumn 2012   246

8.4: Fifth Semester, Autumn 2013   247

8.5: Daily Schedule   251

8.6: The Lancaster and Newcastle Programmes   252

8.7: Adult Classes   262

    8.7.1: Business English   262

    8.7.2: Sinopec   265

    8.7.3: Visiting Scholars' Class   266

8.8: Academic Writing   271

    8.8.1: Introduction   271

    8.8.2: Plagiarism   272

    8.8.3: Independence   273

8.9: Intermediate Class   276

8.10: Speech Contests   280

    8.10.1: 2012 Speech Contest   280

    8.10.1: 2013 Speech Contest   283

Chapter 9: Students' Work   **286**

Introduction   286

9.1: Listening, Speaking, Reading   286

    9.1.1: Listening   286

    9.1.2: Speaking   286

    9.1.3: Reading   287

9.2: Writing   288

Example 1: Marriage   288

Example 2: Success   290

Example 3: Grandparents   292

Example 4: Friendship   295

Example 5: Rainbows   297

Example 6: A Touching Moment   300

Example 7: A Sunrise   303

Example 8: Sport   305

Example 9: A Thunderstorm   310

9.3: "Mao's Last Dancer"   315

Chapter 10: Extra-Curricular Work   **319**

Introduction   319

10.1: Hewlett Packard   320

10.2: Doctors   327

10.3: IELTS   335

10.4: Cambridge Cup   337

Chapter 11: Farewells   **340**

Introduction   340

11.1: End of Semesters   340

11.2: Farewell to Fujian   346

11.2.1: To Luo Yuan   346

11.2.2: Luo Yuan   349

11.2.3: Final visit to Fuzhou   352

11.2.4: Return to Chongqing   355

11.3: Farewell to Guizhou   358

11.3.1: Guiyang   358

11.3.2: Zhen Yuan   361

11.3.3: Shiqian 364

11.3.4: Sinan, De Jiang, Guiyang, Chongqing 368

11.4: Farewell to Erica, Sunny and Amy 373

11.4.1: Chongqing to Na Yong 373

11.4.2: The wedding 375

11.4.3: Na Yong 381

11.4.4: Return to Chongqing 384

11.5: Farewell to Chongqing 390

11.5.1: End of Semester 390

11.5.2: Expo Gardens 391

11.5.3: Return to Australia. 26thAugust 394

Introduction

From 2008 to 2011, I taught at Tongren University, Guizhou Province, as related in Book 6 of this series, *A Teacher in Tongren*. They were wonderful years, not because of the university, nor even because of the town, pretty though it is, but because of those warm, friendly students.

The university kicked us out—both Greg McCann and myself—not because of anything we had done, and not because of anything we had not done—but because it was adjudged that we had passed our use by date, which that poorest of provinces had set at 60 years of age. Where would I go? Especially since I was not yet ready to leave China. It did not take long—less than a day—to find a vacancy in Sichuan International Studies University in Chongqing, where in theory the use by date was 65 years old, which is still far too young. The truth of the matter, however, is that we native English speakers had taught millions of Chinese, who could now take over our role, albeit imperfectly. Nationalism dictates that Chinese teachers must supplant foreign teachers.

On a Tuesday night in mid-July 2011, Tongren University, in its benevolence, decided to farewell me with a formal meal, where the head of the Foreign Affairs Office presented me with a very nice grey summer shirt as a farewell gift, and a promise to pay my train fare to Chongqing when I did move, which I told them, would not be until mid-August. He kept his promise too, much to my surprise, as it would be easier to get blood out of a stone than to get money out this revered establishment.

In the intervening month, I had other plans.

In the first place, there was the need to travel to Hong Kong in order to renew my visa, which was due to expire on 20 July. This turned out to be quite a drama. Then followed a two-seek teaching stint in a Guizhou town called Meitan. After this I needed a holiday, for which I travelled to Tian Men Shan in Hunan Province with two students. All of this has been related in Book 1, *A Traveller in China* (Austin Macauley, 2014), sections 52 to 59.

Back in Tongren, students helped me pack up for the move to Chongqing. A friend told me of a company which would take most of my luggage, so Erica and I went there to check it out. They would even pick it up from the university. It would cost 50 Yuan to send my "stuff", but it was worth it, especially if the university at the other end were going to foot the bill, which in fact they did.

The last few nights in Tongren were spent in celebratory farewell meals.

Sunday night was special. My favourite restaurant in Tongren is called "Royal Coffee", situated on the 20th floor of a corner building in Walking Street, overlooking the river. There were just four of us: Erica, Kim and Cindy. I had brought a bottle of Australian wine from Sydney the previous May, reserving it for a special occasion. This was that special occasion. And it was so nice: everyone enjoyed it. One of the things scarcity has taught me is to really value what we have. That wine was savoured: every single drop. We talked, we toasted, we reminisced. After the meal, and many photographs, we went to a Karaoke bar, where Tina and her boyfriend joined us. We had a great night. At 11.00 p.m. I called a halt, as I still had things to do.

On Monday, 22 August, I left Tongren accompanied by my lovely "daughter", Erica, with Kim, Sunny, sweet Lemon and two Cindys coming to see me off—right onto the train itself. They are very kind and I miss them dearly. The train, as usual, was crowded. I had heard nothing from Chongqing, so really did not know if anyone would meet me, or even if I would have an apartment. "I may have to sleep on a park bench," thinks I. Life can be like that. The past is gone, the future uncertain, the now is a journey—not just a physical journey, but a journey of the spirit, where we really entrust our lives to the Lord who is looking after us. I was conscious that I was making this change in response to God's call, but had no idea what was awaiting me. It was limbo.

There was an innovation on this train: a TV screen. Oh no! not more noise or maybe films of unrelenting, mindless violence. What is wrong with silence?—not that you get much of that on an overcrowded train, with people talking loudly, attendants pushing trolleys of food through, others selling baubles, like the necklaces being pushed under my nose, and particularly the mobile phones, where males seem to think they will not be heard unless they shout. I settled down to write, with people looking over my shoulder, trying to read it. They had Buckley's, both because of the language barrier and also because of the illegible state of my scrawl, which I can hardly read myself at times.

Meanwhile, Erica wanted to read my Prayer Book, which she calls my Bible, which it largely is. I made a note to get one for her, as she had become very interested, asking me to tell her Bible stories. The train stopped; naturally, there is no explanation. This is common. On this trip, we would stop three times, for 70 minutes, 20 minutes and 50 minutes respectively. No information was given and none asked. People simply sit, waiting patiently. Would travellers put up with this in the West?

At 4.30 p.m., we arrived at Chongqing North railway station. I still could not figure this out, as we had come up from the south, learning later that the train does a loop. We were intending to be here for a short while, so my first priority was to store my baggage. Here however, they do not call it "baggage claim" but "left luggage". I find some of these minor differences to be intriguing. Another is the "free duty" in Hong Kong, rather than "duty free".

Here, we met the lovely Lisa, with whom we had planned to spend most of the day. She was busy packing herself, because she was heading off to spend some time at home before travelling to Trinity College, Dublin for post graduate studies. For the past couple of years she had been working for the British Council, which, amongst other things, supervisors IELTS (International English Language Testing System). Greg McCann had been an IELTS examiner for years, so Lisa was his boss, which is a little ironic, as she had been his student. We had our evening meal together, railway dumplings, which were just so-so. In fact, for the next two days, I would be suffering from an upset stomach. First resolve in Chongqing: never eat railway dumplings.

After saying goodbye to Lisa, we collected our baggage and caught the 812 bus from the station to SISU. Luckily it dropped us right at the front gate, after 23 stops and about 50 minutes. It could not be more convenient. Finally, I managed to get in contact with Mr Ma, head of the Foreign Affairs Office, arranging that we would be met at the front gate and taken immediately to my new abode—and very nice too: clean and spacious. The electricity even worked, so already it was two steps ahead of my Tongren abode. One drawback was that it had no plates, cutlery, pots, pans, utensils of any sort. We know what happens. When someone leaves, the apartment is ransacked by the locals. It is a racket. Each new resident must spend a deal of money getting it restocked, which the locals collect when it is time for he/she to leave.

Thankfully, I did bring some things with me, while a few other items which I had left behind in Tongren belonged to me and not to Tongren University. I would be returning to Tongren at some stage, so could pick them up then. These included a pair of metal tongs, very useful for cooking, but as scarce as hen's teeth. More of this later.

My new apartment boasted a spare bedroom, but it was locked, so I never went in—like never, over the whole three years I lived in this apartment. Something was being hidden away there—dead bodies perhaps? Dear Erica remained with me for some days. Since I could not give her the spare bedroom and nor would she take my bedroom, so perforce she slept on the couch. She told me it was quite comfortable, but I assure you it was not, as when I had other guests, I would offer them my bed, while I slept on the couch—or tried to. We cleaned the apartment, stocked up with food and explored the neighbourhood. My goods arrived by truck from Tongren with the university maintenance men helping me lift them—before they asked for 10 Yuan. Erica helped me unpack and furnish the apartment.

It was good to spend time with her, while settling in. getting to know the surrounds and the neighbours. After a couple of days dear Erica needed to return, while I needed to work on class preparation. The university provided me with a number of meal tickets which I would use in the Teachers' Restaurant, situated only about 10 metres from our residence. This did for my evening meal for about a week—wonderful.

I was to learn a little more about this university. I fronted up to the Foreign Affairs Office to introduce myself and settle a number of practical matters. I had brought various papers and receipts with me, because I had been told they would pay for the cartage of my luggage from Tongren: no problems. Mr M noticed my air ticket from Hong Kong, where I had gone to obtain my visa. "We can pay for that," he volunteered. I was flabbergasted. For three years in Tongren I had been dealing with an administration which was miserly in the extreme, having to fight to get any pay at all; yet here in Chongqing SISU was actually volunteering to give me something. Wow! I was impressed.

I thought that I would really enjoy my time here—and I did.

Map 1: Chongqing's Position Within China

Map 1 shows the position of Chongqing in relation to the rest of the Chinese Empire and Taiwan. The star to the north-west indicates Beijing, the capital.

Chapter 1: Chongqing

重庆

1.1: Nomenclature

Chongqing is the city where I would be working, but it is also a municipality. Both of these concepts are confusing. For us Australians, municipalities are areas of local government within a city. I come from the city of Sydney, which is divided into a number of smaller administrative regions called municipalities, plus one shire. The term "shire" generally refers to a rural district, but in Sydney one outer region decided to retain this nomenclature, now proudly referring to themselves as "The Shire". Whether this makes them better than anyone else is a moot point, but it certainly gives them cohesion.

In China, however, the term "municipality" means something else, although the leader is still called "mayor". The empire boasts some truly massive cities, big enough to be countries in their own right. Four of these have been given their own administration, rather than be considered part of some province. These are Beijing, Shanghai, Tianjin and Chongqing. The latter used to be part of Sichuan Province until 1997. This system also enables the central government in Beijing to keep stricter control, especially in the case of Chongqing, which was China's war time capital under the Kuomintang, the Communist Party's enemy during the civil war. Hence the Party has looked upon the city with some distrust.

The city hit the international headlines in 2013, with the trial of the mayor, Bo Xilai. He was a big man with even bigger ambitions, but politically an adversary of the ruling elite. This would not do. They would have to get rid of him. But how? Their chance came when Bo's wife, Gu Kailai, was accused of murdering a British businessman—and she probably did. Bo was accused of covering up the crime. He was also accused of embezzling some 4 million Yuan when he was governor of Dalian—and he could well have done so, as many officials do the same. He was subjected to a show trial, whose verdict was a foregone conclusion. "Justice", Chinese style, was served.

We in the West cannot feel too smug, however, as we too have our sham trials. We too have people being picked on by the Press and others and publicly vilified. We too have people who are not the least bit interested in true justice, or in truth, but only in finding someone guilty, whether he is or not. A case in point is accusations of child molestation: if you want to discredit someone you simply accuse him of molesting you. Whether he is guilty or not, he is considered to be guilty until proven otherwise, which is not the case in other areas of Law.

I was living in Chongqing towards the end of Bo Xilai's tenure, and he was a popular figure. Under his governance, much was done to root out corruption, crime levels dropped and people's incomes soared. Life had never been so good. I found it interesting that when Xi Jinping became China's ruler (read "emperor"), he made the rooting out of corruption a major priority. You have to say the right things. He has done much too, but—as the Bo Xilai case emphasises—you do not want to root it out completely, as it remains a useful tool in getting rid of one's rivals.

Chongqing's municipality covers a massive 80,000 square kilometres, which is bigger than some countries. The population is also huge at around 32 million. The largest urban centre within this is also called Chongqing—confusing. It is always difficult to give the population figures for Chinese cities, because these often include surrounding districts. In this case, the city's core stands at around 8 million, while the urban population, including those districts, make it around 18 million. Gazing over the city from Ge Le Mountain, one is met with a panorama of high rise buildings, 30 to 40 stories, for block after block. Yes, the city is huge. Cf. photograph 19.

Perhaps related to nomenclature are mottoes. Police cars often have mottoes on the side panels. In Chicago, for instance, I was rather taken with their motto, which I like very much, to wit, "to protect and to serve". This is what the police should in fact be doing. Down in our shopping centre in Lieshimu I saw a local police car, with its motto also on the side. In this instance, however, I was not so much taken with it, as taken aback. It had: "to punish and enslave". My goodness!

Scale:

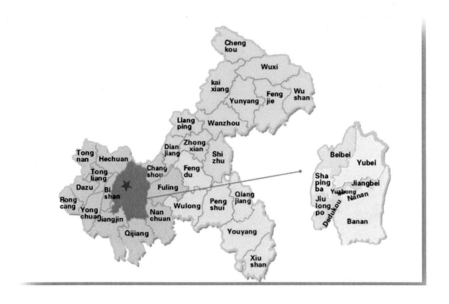

0 50 100 km

Map 2: Chongqing Municipality

Map 2 shows the Municipality of Chongqing, divided into 37districts, with nine of these lying in what we might call the city limits, the area in orange. The district where I was living at SISU is Shapingba.

1.2: Climate

Chongqing is a mountain city, its altitude beginning at a mere 244 metres ASL, rising to over 1700 metres ASL. Its location marks the end of the navigable section of the Yangtze River. Further upstream, the landscape rises up to the Tibetan High Plateau. In summer the temperature range is from around 24 to 33 degrees. Many days can be over 40 degrees.

Each season of the year has its own attractions. It is good to experience variety, both warmth and cold, rain and sunshine, wind and calm, although extremes can be difficult to cope with, whether bitter cold or stifling heat, especially when these last for a long time. I am so glad I grew up in Sydney, with its mild climate and abundant sunshine. If you ask people which season is their favourite you will get different answers, but I bet that for most people it is spring.

I too like this season, but in Sydney I really like early autumn because of its settled weather, its warmth and sunshine, especially the month of March.

In the Northern Hemisphere, of course, the seasons are reversed, something the Chinese are intrigued by, even finding it a little difficult to comprehend. I always have to be clear when I am asked when I shall be returning to Australia, in the summer or in the winter: whose summer? Whose winter? Personally I do not like the cold, so getting out of China's winter was appealing, especially knowing that back in Sydney I could walk down to Coogee Beach for a swim. It is also appealing to get out of Chongqing during its long very hot summers. Then Sydney's mild winter temperature of around 15 to 18 degrees is quite attractive.

Autumn

The academic year begins in autumn, so let us begin with this season. It is a short lived season, as the heat of September quickly turns to the cold of November. Leaves fall all year round, with the trees mostly being evergreens so that China has autumns not falls, as the Americans have with their deciduous trees. In fact the leaves tend to fall mostly in the spring. The month of October really is autumn, with the weather no longer hot, but without the chill of November.

Winter

Officially, winter begins on 1st December, but it really begins much earlier. In the depths of Chongqing's winter I needed to rug up. This meant wearing long johns, winter shirt, jumper and heavy coat. When going out, this would be augmented with scarf, gloves and beanie, but only on the coldest days. It never snowed—as it had done in Tongren. I had a heater in my room, which I would turn on at night time while working. My laundry would be hung on my balcony, but often it would takes days to dry; I would also place them around my room, when the heater was on.

Winters can get some people down, but people are not the only ones who can sink into depression, as the city itself is in a depression at the foot of the mountains, which climb up to Tibet. Into this depression the mist settles as does the polluted air. Over the summer vacation one of our students actually rode his bike into Tibet. Wow! Cold moist air sinks into this depression, resulting in much fog. Now of course, with much pollution, we have smog. Sunny days can be a rarity, even in autumn. Each day we can have grey leaden skies, with lots of drizzle and rain nearly every day, the temperature ranging from about 6 degrees to about 10. I was lucky to have an apartment on the second floor, but on the ground floor(s) your floors stay wet. Let me explain. Half of our building begins at a lower level, so that rooms 1, 3, 5, and 7 on the left hand side are half a level lower than rooms 2, 4 (mine), 6 and 8 on the right hand side. The wet settles at the lowest level. The same thing happened in my apartment in Tongren, where I did have a ground floor room. In this kind of weather, the floor was perpetually wet, so that I had to be careful in walking on it and kept mopping it. Even the locals can get depressed here: at the end of 2012 we had only one sunny day in six weeks.

The high rise buildings in winter often have their tops enveloped in cloud, as can be seen in photograph 1.

Photo 1: head in the clouds

Winter is also dry, apart from the mist, and the dearth of rain affects the rivers, with both our rivers—the Jia Ling and the Yangtze—very low indeed.

There is not much that we can do about the weather, so you just put up with it. Anyone want to visit CQ in winter?

Spring

Officially spring begins on 1st March, and indeed soon after that date there is definite improvement in the weather, which begins to warm up quite noticeably. Winter clothes start coming off, to be replaced by fewer and lighter clothing and the people are glad. The following is what I wrote about spring in Chongqing in May, 2013:

"Currently here in Chongqing summer has just begun, after spring briefly made its appearance, lasting only a month or so. The weather is now hot and should remain so till October. There is little rain, and most of this comes at night, often in the form of a thunderstorm, when one can be woken suddenly by the nearby crash of thunder, with one's room illuminated by a bolt of lightning. Most days are overcast, but sometimes the days are sunny, although of course here in this highly polluted city, it is always hazy, the sky never bright blue.

Springtime also heralds the return of life. Butterflies flit amongst the trees, seeking the flowers which are now blooming. Dragonflies hover over water or close to water. Water striders abound on our local pond, while at night time one can hear the call of frogs. I found a beautiful beetle, with a back of iridescent emerald green. New leaves are sprouting: the tree next to my apartment has grown considerably over the past month. These new leaves push out the old ones, so that leaves are falling all the time, in March and April. People are perennially sweeping up the leaves. Why not leave (!) them?

And we have the birds.

Around my home in Randwick, Sydney, there are some thirteen species of birds which I have identified. You do not get so many here: there are fewer species and fewer individuals. But there are some, and now they are announcing themselves. I love the chatter of small birds in the trees, as if rejoicing in life, thanking God for their existence. My bird identification book had been left in Sydney, so I do not know the names of most species here, but I do know some. Doves call to each other with their cooing. I have heard the cuckoo, a good example of onomatopoeia, its name echoing its sound; in Sydney we have the kohl, which is a species of cuckoo. There are no large birds here, although there are cranes elsewhere in China. I think the small birds are probably chats, as well as the ubiquitous sparrow. Sadly sparrows have disappeared in my part of Sydney, their eggs having been eaten by the kurrawong, a species in the crow family.

There is, however, another bird which deserves special mention. I do not know what it is, but it has a very distinctive sound, like "oo-ooo, oo-ooo", a little mournful. Possibly it is an owl. It is not, however, very popular, especially with the gentleman living below me. There are two reasons for this. The first is that its sound is quite loud, while the second is that it starts up around 4.15 a.m. Who needs an alarm clock? I have been searching for him using my torch, but he is lost somewhere in the foliage of the trees which surround our building and I have not been able to spot it. I do hope my neighbour does not find it, as he is may be tempted to throw a rock at it. I did see a man recently with a slingshot around his neck, so maybe he was looking for it too. I hope he does not find it.

Some of the locals, I am sorry to say, seem to show scant respect for our fellow inhabitants on this planet. Fish arrive for the wet market in enclosed water trucks. They are then fished out with a net into a large bucket of water; there is absolutely no attempt to treat them gently. This bucket is suspended from a pole and carried by two men, staggering under the weight. You will find these fish in the market packed into small basins, with barely enough room to move. One can see from the movement of their gills that they are having difficulty breathing. Sometimes they are floating upside down. Not good. I once bought a live fish to cook, and asked the man to scale and gut it. He did, in that order, without first killing the fish. It was still moving as I was carrying it home. So cruel. I have also seen chooks treated very roughly before they are killed in the restaurant trade. I do not like this.

There is one animal, however, that I have no compunction whatsoever in killing whenever I can, wherever I find it: the … mosquito. Getting malaria in Papua New Guinea did not exactly endear them to me, although—perhaps surprisingly—the worst place in my experience was Melbourne, where I would commonly kill 100 a night. So far about a dozen of the little beasties have managed to find their way into my apartment, even though my windows are protected by screens. There is a pond nearby, so possibly that is where they breed. The pond is stocked with fish, so I presume most of the wrigglers have been eaten by them. You do not notice them until about 2.00 a.m. The whine wakes me. Immediately I close the bedroom door and go hunting. The aim is find it and swat it. Then I can go back to sleep, but this may take time: 2 ½ hours on one night. But I got it. When—OK, if—I get to Heaven, I am going to have words with Noah. Why didn't he swat those two mozzies when he had the chance?"

That is what I wrote in 2013. Spring is the time of new life. It is also the time of much death, as many young animals do not make it adulthood. With the warmth also comes the rain, if you could call it that. It almost never rains heavily in this city, with rain coming at night, Camelot style. The rain is usually no more than a fine mist. If you are out in it for a short space of time you really do not need an umbrella; it is only after you have been out for longer that you notice how wet your clothes have become. The two rivers, at low ebb during the winter, now begin to rise. This is partly due to rainfall, especially in the mountains, but it is mainly due to melting snow.

Summer

Spring is short, so that by May we are entering· the hot months of summer, even though officially summer does not begin until 1st June.

From May until the end of September we have summer, and in Chongqing it can get hot, with at times temperatures exceeding 40 degrees. Perhaps I should clarify that. If the temperature officially exceeds 40 degrees, then people are not obliged to go to work. But—and isn't this strange?—the official temperature never exceeds 40. While my thermometer might be reading 42.5, the official temperature is a mere 39.5. I know of nowhere else where the government controls even the temperature!

On the hottest days in summer, I would be wearing as little as possible, and again would turn on the reverse cycle air conditioning only when absolutely necessary. On the hottest days, I liked to walk across to the Alliance Française building which had an air conditioned café. There I could work in comfort while sipping on a cold drink. Wonderful.

This completes the cycle of Chongqing's seasons.

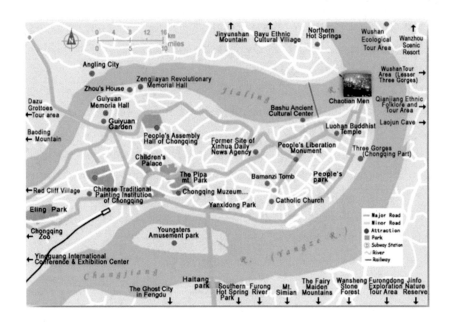

Map 3: Central Chongqing

1.3: Jie Fang Bei

Some cities have a recognised centre, while others not so. Los Angeles, for instance—at least to my way of thinking—just spreads out without a single centre. The harbour is the focal point for Sydney, although these days, with the population exploding, other centres are being developed at Parramatta, Campbelltown and Liverpool. In Chongqing the centre is on the peninsular close to the junction of the Yangtze and Jialing Rivers. The Yangtze comes up from the south, while the Jialing comes down from the north. Both hit a high rocky plateau, running along it for about 20 km until they meet at Chao Tian Men. This peninsula is a mountain ridge, and is quite high, so the city is hilly. Our university, SISU, is situated about 15 km to the west, close to the Jia Ling River.

Photo 2: Junction of the Jia Ling and Yangtze Rivers

Photograph 2 was taken from Chao Tian Men. It shows the green Jia Ling River coming in on the left and the brown Yangtze on the far right. In the foreground cruise boats are tied up, while opposite can be seen the Grand Theatre, the squat building just to the left of centre.

Not far from the point is a square with a 20 metre high octagonal clock tower in the centre. Cf. the cover photograph. While the city does have many regional centres, if any place can be considered to be the heart of the city then it would have to be Jie Fang Bei, which literally means Liberation Monument. Cf. map 3. This is the clock tower. No doubt when first constructed it was of no mean height, but these days it is dwarfed by high rise buildings surrounding it on all sides. The monument celebrates the victory over Japan in the Second World War, although this is not the way the Chinese express it. For them it is the "Anti-Japanese War", a war of resistance against Japanese aggression. It is quite a beautiful clock tower: it is just a pity it has been politicised.

This is Yuzhong District, the commercial heart of Chongqing, with tall buildings around the square featuring high class shops—designer labels and all that. So if you want a handbag to put your money etc. in, you can get one cheaply from anywhere, but if you want the bag to be worth many times the value of its contents, then you can buy one here. Gosh, they both carry your possessions equally well.

Nearby is the Art Gallery with its extraordinary roof beams. It is a wooden building in traditional Chinse architectural style, as befits its purpose. I rather like it. There are also high class restaurants and hotels.

Photo 3: Art Gallery

1.4: Chao Tien Men Square

There is a museum, called the "Three Gorges Museum" situated not all that far from Jie Fang Bei and on Saturday 5th November, 2011, Pat—another teacher at SISU—and I decided to pay it a visit. At this time, still early in my time in Chongqing, I was in no way familiar with the geography and this is very large city. We were told that this museum was opposite the Opera House, which we had been to before, albeit being driven in the university bus. It had also been at night. However we were told to take bus 265 for about 30 minutes, then look for the Opera House. Sounds easy enough, but life is never that easy.

We did not see the Opera House, and we kept going and going. What do we do? I had a brochure which told us that the 262 bus also goes there, and I happened to notice a 262 going the same way as we were going. "Follow that bus!" Well, we did and found that both buses ended up at the same terminus, which is simply a stop on the side of the road at Chao Tian Men Square. There are lots of "Tian Men"s in China . It means "Heavenly Gate", and in this case the gateway is a peninsular, V-shaped promontory, with the Jia Ling Jiang (Jia Ling River) on the left hand side and the Chang Jiang (Yangtze River) on the right; it is here that they meet. "Let's stay here. I'd love to look around." So we did.

We had not gone far—in fact we had not gone anywhere—before we were accosted by a lady trying to sell us tickets for a sail down river to the Three Gorges. Right below us in the Yangtze was a large boat which would be heading that way. I had already been there, some six years previously, although on that occasion I had boarded from the other side of this peninsular, i.e. on the Jia Ling River. It was a wonderful three day cruise. On this occasion we graciously declined. At that time the river was a lot lower than it is now and I was able to see towns before they were flooded, ghost towns, because by then the populations had been evacuated. Since the construction of the Three Gorges Dam, the water level has risen an amazing 175 metres.

We walked on up to the point, which is an open plaza—thronged with people of course. And there were the usual vendors hawking knick-knacks, food and especially maps. Some people were flying kites—a Chinese invention, incidentally—which provided a welcome colourful addition to an otherwise drab, grey sky. A sign advises motorists to exercise caution, due to Chongqing's wet and foggy weather. Indeed. It was good to get a panoramic view of the two rivers joining, not that you can see the meeting of the waters, as they were both the same mud brown colour on this day. At other times, they are of different colours, so that one can see the two rivers flowing side by side for some distance before they gradually intermingle.

Underneath the concourse we found a museum, dedicated to preserving Chinese art forms. This seemed interesting, so we wandered in. We had only got as far as the first display room before the woman looking after this section came up to us and spoke in English. For the next 20 minutes she proceeded to be our guide. She was great.

Bamboo is a most wonderfully versatile wood, being used for virtually anything from the humble building scaffolding to the finest artwork, which is what we had here. The outer layer can be stripped off in long thin fibres, just like any thread, and hence, just like any thread, it can be woven. This lady proceeded to demonstrate on a loom how these threads can be woven into a sheet. There is a village called Liangping, some 200 km from Chongqing, where inhabitants during the Northern Song Dynasty (AD 960—1127) started using bamboo to make curtains. You bind the thin strips together and hang them, and since they are flexible, you can roll them up and down. Much later, Fang Bingnan (1880—

1920) started to paint on them, with great success and another art form took off. Later, other artists began to embroider designs onto the curtain. They look really beautiful. The processes involved here are quite lengthy—a little more complicated than I have presented them; it takes about three months to produce one hanging. The art of embroidery in China, called Shu Embroidery, dates from the Han Dynasty (206 BC—AD 220), so has been around for about 2,000 years.

Photo 4: embroidery on bamboo

In this same room were very delicate paintings done on—believe it or not—banyan leaves. The leaves are left to dry before being painted on. For this type of painting you need to use the thinnest of brushes, using just the tip. They are quite fragile, so need to be well mounted. There are other brushes which are even thinner, illustrated in another section of this museum where there is a display of miniature paintings. A whole painting, or a script of about 50 characters, is the size of a fingernail. Amazing.

Another display showed Purple Robe Jade carvings. This kind of jade only comes from Fan Jing Mountain, which just happens to be in Tongren County, Guizhou, where I had been living for the previous three years. It is formed from the metamorphosis of the overlying rock by an upwelling of molten granite. The pieces on display here show how skilful the artist was in using the natural colours of the rock.

The next display showed batik, another ancient craft. The technique basically involves using wax to cover one section of the material, while the rest is painted. You do not usually have many different colours in batik, as this would really take a long time and in fact—although I am no expert—may not be feasible. Indonesia is another country which produces excellent batik. In fact I suspect that the word "batik" is itself a Bahasa Indonesian word.

The final section showed traditional Chinese lacquer works. This really is ancient, as it has been in existence for at least 7,000 years, no doubt due to the abundance of lacquer trees, especially around Chongqing. It was a highly developed art form as early as the Shang Dynasty (1600—1046 BC). The red sap of the trees proved ideal for painting and then fixing through firing. The result is eye catching to say the least. The lacquer here has been embossed onto plates, so that they are for decorative purposes only. Eating from them would be impractical, raised as the decorations are.

So there you have it: a truly wonderful exhibition of traditional Chinese art forms. I am so glad we did not get to the Three Gorges Museum, which could wait for another weekend. On the way back in the bus, we actually found the Opera House. It was on Pat's side of the bus. "How come you did not see it?" I complained, although secretly I was glad he did not. "The bus was too crowded; I just could not see." Likely story! It had been a wonderful Saturday afternoon.

In this district there is the Hongya Cave hotel, where I stayed for one night in November of 2011. I have described this hotel before in "Journey to Beijing", but it is worth a mention here. It enjoys at least a four star rating, possibly five as it was certainly very comfortable and is extraordinary, irrespective of whatever star rating it has, due to the fact that it is built onto a cliff face. I have told you that CQ is hilly. You actually enter at the 11th floor; and we are at street level. Our room was on the 7th floor, with not the most exciting view in the world, as we gazed out at the cliff face. The other side of the hotel has water views, as it is situated on the bank of the Jia Ling River, not all that far from its junction with the Yangtze, which of course is at Chao Tian Men Square. The dining room is on the 6th floor.

This is confusing, as we are used to entering any building on the first floor, not the eleventh. When trying to exit at the river side I went the wrong way, being somewhat disorientated, as what should be up is down, and what should be down is up. Normally, the 11th floor is up in the air, not at ground level. Eventually, I asked a lady also in the lift. *"Wo yao chukou; ni zhidao zai nali?"* Kindly she told me to go to the 4th floor. How silly of me! Of course the exit would be on the 4th floor! Here there are shops, seemingly catering mostly for the tourist trade. I continued to walk down steps, past an attractive water feature, to another street level, this one along the riverside, but still high enough above the surface of the water. From here the hotel looks very pretty, both because of its lighting and its architecture, in traditional Chinese style.

From the river, the hotel looks very attractive at night, as it is lit up, the lights cascading down the cliff face.

Photo 5: Hongya Cave Hotel

1.5: The Three Gorges Museum

In the spirit of "if at first you don't succeed, try, try again," Pat and I decided to have another go at finding the Three Gorges Museum on the following Saturday, 12th November, since we now knew where to get off the bus. And we succeeded.

We took the Opera House as our reference point, since the museum is opposite. This gave us an opportunity to see the outside of the Opera House by day. It truly is beautiful, reminding me of the Temple of Heaven in Beijing. It is perched on the side of a hill—as nearly everything is in this city—with the museum facing it from the opposite hill. In between is a traditional Chinese gateway. I do love these gateways, a high point in Chinese architecture. Outside the museum, we could look back at the Opera House for a great view. Apparently others think so too, as a group of primary school students were busy sketching it.

Photograph 6 shows the Opera House by night.

Photo 6: Opera House by night

The museum is itself a beautiful building, with a curved façade, curved sides, but with a straight rear, square rooms and a circular atrium, thus combining yin and yang rather well. Its focus is on objects d'art, the 56 minority groups, and some history. Let me say at the outset that I was a little disappointed, not because of what was displayed, but because of what was not there. I had thought that there would be a lot about the Three Gorges, and I was particularly keen to learn something of the Geology. Sadly "Three Gorges" is just a name, one I think they should change to something more realistic, but as always in China, the façade is more important than the reality. There are four floors; we decided to begin at the top and work our way down.

The first hall we visited has a display of porcelain. This I really like. Porcelain began in China, and many of its examples are simply exquisite. One can but admire the artistry of form in shaping pots and dishes, together with the colours and workmanship of the designs. Curiously, some of the naming cards were incorrect. I think that possibly some attendant inadvertently swapped them.

One hall was given over to currency, showing different coins down through the ages. You are probably familiar with the shape: round, with a square hole in the centre, stemming from the Qin dynasty (221—206 BC). The earliest coins appear to have been shells, especially cowries, dating from the Shang dynasty (1700—1100 BC). Shells have been commonly used in various cultures around the world for currency. In PNG their currency today is called the kina, named after the large shell they used to use. Paper money, which began here in China, appeared much later in the Song dynasty (AD 960—1279). There is quite an extensive display here of Chinese paper money down through the ages. Most is in really good condition too. Today most countries still use paper money and coins too of course, although the metal has changed. In Australia the paper has been discarded in favour of plastic, which is longer lasting and harder to counterfeit.

The history section proved interesting. The first segment went right back to the first appearance of humans in the region. I am very interested in this, but unfortunately (for me, that is) it was all in Chinese. However, I did notice that early bone and teeth fragments came from Homo Erectus, but of course there were other hominids as well. Of recent years there have been a lot of new discoveries in this area. One of the first migrations of Homo Sapiens out of Africa, around 70,000 year ago, ended up in Australia where the aboriginal people still live today, thus making them the oldest continuous civilisation on Earth.

There was a lot on the Ba Yu peoples, the first inhabitants of Chongqing, who had a thriving culture until overrun by the advancing Han people. They fought vigorously for their independence, but lost. They are now extinct as a group, although their culture and probably their descendants have been absorbed into the Han, partly shaping today's Chinese culture, and it was good to see this acknowledged. In fact all of the minority groups today were at some point of time invaded and conquered by the Han. The Chinese have shown that the best way to expand your territory is to fill it with your peoples, which is exactly what they have done in southern China, in Manchuria, in Inner Mongolia, in Taiwan and now currently in process in Eastern Russia, Mongolia, Xinjiang, Mongolia and the "Stan" countries.

Coming to more modern times, there was—predictably—a section on "The Anti-Japanese War", which is still being waged today. The Chinese people like to keep alive their hatred for the Japanese. They do not really want any amount of apology, so far as I can judge; what they want is revenge. They may get it too. Whether that will make them happy is debatable. Chongqing, as you would know, was China's wartime capital, and so was heavily bombed. I had noticed many caves dug into the hillsides of this hilly city, and I have no doubt that they date from WWII.

We were working our way downstairs, with me looking forward to the Three Gorges section as the pièce de résistance. I was judging my timing so as to allow a good half an hour in this exhibit before the scheduled closing time at 5.00 p.m. It was on the first floor, or so our brochure told us. Alas, such was not the case, as half of the first floor was not open. What a pity. In any case, I doubt that I would have learnt much about Geology, as this is a prohibited subject. In other countries I have had no trouble in purchasing geological maps, but here you cannot do that, as they are considered state secrets. Why? Why indeed. Nevertheless, what we saw was excellent. I am glad I came—eventually.

1.6: Stilwell Museum

In June of 2012 one of the students decided to take me under his wing and show me some of the attractions of his fair city. This included a visit to the Stilwell Museum. Who was this man? And what was his importance such that he has a museum dedicated to his honour?

It is not my purpose to give his biography, which in fact I have read, but some salient points should make clear why this museum is here.

Joseph Stilwell was born in New York in 1883. Deciding to pursue a military career, he graduated from West Point in 1904. In 1911 he came to China for the first time. In World War 1 he served in France, but it was after the war when he really became interested in China, being posted with an engineering corps to help build roads. He served for quite some time in China, becoming interested in Chinese history and culture, making many friends and becoming proficient in the Chinese language, which is no mean feat; he had earlier exhibited a penchant for languages.

During the Second World War he was posted back to China as liaison officer between America and China. In particular he was responsible for Lend-Lease supplies and ostensibly Chief of Staff to Chiang Kai-Shek. I say ostensibly, because while he was nominally in charge, Chiang kept going behind his back: it is unconscionable to have Chinese troops taking orders from a foreigner. He was also US commander in the Burma theatre, again pushing stones uphill.

His relationship with Chiang Kai-Shek was very rocky and indeed it would be hard to imagine two more different characters. Chiang was interested first and foremost in beating the Communists under Mao Zedong, with beating the Japanese as a secondary objective; in fact much Lend-Lease materiel was being stockpiled to this end. His manner was circuitous and evasive, contrasting to Stilwell's approach of calling a spade a spade. His comments were often caustic and hardly diplomatic, earning him the soubriquet of "Vinegar Joe"; rather than being offended by this he was proud of it. His abrasive attitude often put him into conflict with others, including his second in command, Claire Chennault. From Stilwell's perspective, all would be well if only he could have a free hand to get the job done—and he was right. Chiang Kai-Shek and his cronies were also corrupt, while Stilwell was honest.

The Japanese occupation of Burma cut off supplies, resulting in the necessity to fly these in over the Himalayas, which were nicknamed "The Hump"—a rather hazardous undertaking. Much of these supplies landed in the Chongqing area. Chennault became famous for organising the "Flying Tigers", a group of American airmen who "had been" in the US Air Force and whose job was to begin a Chinese Air Force. They were successful to the point of reaching legendary status. Opposite the Stilwell Museum is another museum dedicated to this force. I will have more to say of them in section 1.10.

In October 1944, Stilwell was relieved of his position, returning to the United States, filling various military roles until he died two years later from illness.

The museum itself occupies the site of his residence, on the northern side of the peninsular overlooking the Jialing River, a few kilometres from Chao Tien Men. Inside there are several plaques, indicating why this museum is important. In part one plaque reads: "During the World War Two the Chinese and American peoples fought shoulder to shoulder against the Japanese Fascists and they defended the world peace with all the peoples around the world." Another plaque reads: "The friendship between the peoples of the two countries is precious. The Chinese people, and especially the people of Chongqing, have great respect to the American friends for their contributions to the Chinese people's course of national liberation. The valuable friendship will live forever in the hearts of the Chinese people."

The English could be improved: Chinese have always had some difficulty with both the use and pronunciation of "th". There is more about the friendship between China and the United States, which is rather fitting for today's world, but how much of it is real? What was speaking volumes to me was the neglected state of the museum, with precious historical photographs allowed to deteriorate. What a pity. In my opinion this should not be allowed to happen, for two reasons: 1) Joseph Stilwell was a great man, and he did make an enormous contribution to the war effort. 2) He stands as a symbol of much assistance given to China, something the Chinese should never forget.

A bust of this great man stands in the grounds. Cf. photograph 7.

Photo 7: General Joseph Stilwell

1.7: Nan Shan

"Nan Shan" literally means "South Mountain", which is exactly what it is: a mountain bordering the city to the south. Chongqing is a mountain city within a depression and this particular mountain blocked a major route out of the city, so that in times past this mountain had to be scaled if one wished to trade or simply travel, at least in one direction. It stood astride an ancient caravan route.

Another teacher at SISU, Anne, and I were invited by a friend, Michael, to join him with a group of students to climb it. Hence on a Sunday morning in late 2013, we met Michael at 8.30 a.m. and were driven to a rendezvous with the students, a delightful group of fifteen. We got on well. Initially our climb led us through suburban streets, steep in places, narrow, yet with people lining the sides selling their wares. Chinese are really good at this. Their produce consisted of household goods, fruit, vegetables and herbs, the latter being used for medicinal purposes. At one point a major road crossed our path, but not to worry, as there is a tunnel leading beneath it. Then we were into a forested area, as the houses dropped away. Soon we were back into houses. There is even a cave house, but I do not know its history. There is also a church, of the Protestant variety, with a service going on at the time. The path, as usual, was cement with many steps. I have remarked before how in this country, enormous labour goes into building steps, where we in Australia would simply walk on the earth. I did not count the steps, but I would hazard a guess at around 2,000, to give you an idea of the height of this mountain.

Photo 8: climbing Nan Shan

In due course—less than two hours—we arrived at the summit, marked with a pagoda. You have no view, as trees obscure one's sight, and in any case, the pollution means that you would not see much anyway. Not to worry. I saw one young lady at the top, dressed really stylishly, including high heel shoes. True: she climbed this mountain wearing high heel shoes. Goodness, the climb down would have been challenging for her.

Not far from the summit is a mansion. What is this doing here? Apparently it used to be the German embassy, and in time past commanded a view of the Yangtze River below. The house was being guarded by two dogs, tied at each end of the building. One did not appear to be particularly fierce, but the other did. We left them alone. What we went to see was a grave: one of the ambassadors died here, with his gravestone indicating that his name was one Dr P. Assmy, born 1869, died 1935.

By now it was early afternoon and people were starting to feel a mite hungry. It was time to eat. Back down we went, but not via the same route. On a main road, we piled into two mini buses, squeezed in like sardines; around here they do not worry too much about how many people are jammed into any public conveyance, whether bus, train, or indeed taxi. Michael, our worthy guide, had already chosen a restaurant. He does a lot of work in the tourist trade, so is used to organising details. The restaurant chosen had an attractive ambience and was very popular, with seating both inside and out. There was a little trouble finding a couple of tables which would accommodate our large group, but two were found. The meal was worth waiting for.

After sating our hunger, the students remained to play some games, but Anne and I had to get back. This proved no easy task, as in this neck of the woods there were few taxis and few buses. We actually walked for some time before we finally got a taxi, which dropped us at the nearest metro station. Good: getting home by train was not a problem. So long as there is a metro station, one can go anywhere in Chongqing.

1.8: Rong Hui Hot Springs

Wow! Whatever happened to good old penance? As Christians are we not supposed to be disciplining our bodies to bring them into subjection, rather than hedonistically soaking oneself in a hot spring? Yet what penances did Jesus do? Is there any record of him flogging himself, either literally or metaphorically? No there is not, yet Jesus did suffer—intensely—and we suffer too. My theology is that there is no need for us to go out of our way to punish ourselves: life has its inherent sufferings; we do not have to seek them out. I would much rather be grateful and thank God for the gifts He has given us and ask God to help us bear the sufferings which come, hopefully using them for the benefit of others.

With that as my excuse I had indeed been pampering myself. It had been a particularly busy semester, one in which I had been teaching nearly a double load, so the beginning of January 2014 was time to relax.

Chongqing has a number of hot springs. I do not know why, as it is not a volcanic region, nor even an earthquake prone region, though it is not far from what is called "the dragon's tail", a seismically active arc, which curls around the Qinghai plateau. Maybe there is a connection. I would love to be able to get hold of a geologic map so that I could check, but of course that is not possible. As I have explained before, this country, whose entire history has been laced with invading other territories, is nevertheless paranoid about security. It is heavily militarised. Consequently it is afraid and has a government based upon fear. Much military hardware is underground, and they do not want "foreigners" knowing. Nor do they want them knowing about mineral resources. In fact the government wants its own citizens knowing as little as possible.

Not far from SISU, only about ten minutes by taxi, there is a hot spring called Rong Hui. None of us had been there before, but to celebrate the end of semester, three of us hopped in a taxi and off we went. Actually "hopping in a taxi" was not quite so simple, as the first taxi driver did not want to take us, and nor were we too keen to go with him, as he was smoking. The second driver was better, after we gave the name of a hotel—Radisson Blu (sic)—which is near the location.

The entrance fee to the spring was at this time 139 Yuan which gave access to most of the facilities. I must say the place is beautiful: well laid out, clean and with many staff on hand. The male changing area has some 2,000 lockers, and I imagine the female change rooms are similar: 4,000 people? If that many people did come, I do not think the facilities would be adequate, as the main pool could only hold maybe 200.

You are issued with a wrist band, which opens your allocated locker. All you need to wear is swimming trunks, have a shower then hop into the main pool: heavenly, so warm. I do not know what the minerals are in the water, so one lives by faith that whatever they are they are doing some good. The pool is shallow, but just deep enough to swim if you feel so inclined. We did, but of course the locals did not. I noticed they were looking at me in amazement as I swam past. "*Laowai*"—foreigner. There are points around the pool where one can access jets of water to get a kind of massage—very pleasant. I liked the chair, with nozzles squirting water onto your feet. Ahhh! Another area has a flat table that you lie on while a high pressure shower pummels your back. Who thinks of these things? There is an adjacent pool with much hotter water in it.

You are issued with rubber thongs to wear around when not in one of the pools, and there is also a supply of large towels. People wrap these around themselves when they get out of the pools: we did the same.

Oh the hardships of life!

Photo 9: main pool, Rong Hui Hot Springs

After some time we walked outside to discover more hot pools extending up a hillside, all kinds of shapes and sizes, some large, some just for a couple of people, and some wooden tubs for just one person. There is a wading pool paved with pebbles which massage your feet as you walk up and down. The pièce de résistance, however, is another pool into which you dip only your feet. A school of small fish then swims up and proceeds to eat you. True. Well, they do not draw blood, but they are actually eating the dead cells which form the outer layer of our skin. They do not hurt: they tickle. One in our group—admittedly something of a wimp—could not stand it. No not me: I liked it. Maybe that is because I am more insensitive than others.

After all of this, we did try a sauna, but it was not so good, being far too cool. So we got dressed again and headed for one of the dining rooms for lunch. I should say JC and I got dressed, but not A, our third member, who was given a special outfit. Others were wearing similar loose fitting gear. The idea is that after lunch you can then easily dive back into one of the pools. The meal was really nice, a set affair: for me it was beef, rice, vegetables and soup and at 39 Yuan quite reasonable.

After our repast, we did not dive back into the pool, but judged that the several hours we had been there was enough, so we headed back home feeling relaxed and at peace with the world. We were very impressed with facilities and—surprise, surprise—were not being jostled by 50,000 other people, rather unusual in this country. We went on a Tuesday, so maybe they are busy on weekends.

Do I have a guilty conscience? Nah. In any case my birthday was coming up in a couple of days, which is as good excuse as any to pamper oneself.

1.9: Ciqikou

Only about 20 minutes' walk from SISU lies a delightful ancient town, called Ciqikou, which happens to be the Number One tourist destination in Chongqing. It is hundreds of years old, dating from the Ming and Qing Dynasties—well the town is, although the individual buildings have been renovated, some very recently. Nevertheless the feel of the town is still evocative of a look back in time. It began as the major port hereabouts, due to the fact that the hinterland is not as steep. The modern port at Chao Tian Men lies at the tip of the peninsular where the land rises steeply. Ciqikou would be 20 km upstream on the Jialing River, in the Shapingba District, where our university is also located.

The streets are narrow, lined with shops, mostly for the tourist trade. I became friendly with a lovely young lady named Reine who had become a Catholic the previous year. Her family owned a coffee shop, while she made and sold knick-knacks, which she would sell in the doorway of another dwelling, as can be seen from photograph 10.

Photo 10: selling knick-knacks, Ciqikou

Various foods are sold, the most popular, surprisingly, being a type of Indian bread. There are many restaurants, as one would expect, some with good views over the Jialing River.

I do love this style of architecture. On top of the hill is a Buddhist temple and these temples always provide classic examples of Chinese architecture, with wood as the principle construction material.

There are plenty of stairs too, as the town rises in levels from the river. This river can flood, especially in spring with melting snow feeding the headwaters. I have known it to rise as much as ten metres, flooding the wharves and lower parts of the town. In photograph 11 all of the esplanade had been covered with water, including the bole of the tree on the left. Months afterwards one could still see the watermark high on the wall of the police station.

There was one particular reason I liked to go to this town: Mr and Mrs Ling. They ran a foot massage business and ran it very well. For 60 Yuan, they would first soak your feet in very hot water—a bit too hot to start with, until your feet became accustomed to the temperature. They would pare off any loose skin, cut the nails, attend to any bunions or ingrown toenails and massage. The theory is that the feet are linked to other areas of the body, so that relieving tight muscles and nerves calms other areas of the body. The whole treatment lasts for over an hour, after which one would more or less float out of their shop. Marvellous.

A word of warning, however: avoid Ciqikou on the weekends. On weekdays, it is OK, but on the weekends, half Chongqing seem to be there and you can hardly move. As I said, this ancient town appears to be the chief tourist attraction in the city.

Photo 11: Ciqikou port

1.10: A Chongqing Walk

There is a real estate agency in China called Maxxelli. Apparently they specialise in helping overseas companies and expatriates find accommodation, not everywhere, but in some of what they call, China's "second tier" cities. Chongqing, however, is a first tier city, yet here they are. Apart from the roughly half a dozen massive urban conglomerates of more than 10 million inhabitants, there are a further 170 cities which have more than a million people. Australia has just five. In May, 2013 Maxxelli, in association with the Intercontinental Hotel decided to hold an explanatory walk around old CQ for anybody interested. I was—most emphatically—and nor was I the only one, as some 70 people, from various countries around the world, turned up.

At around 9.30 a.m. on a warm, sunny Sunday morning, we gathered at the Intercontinental for registration. Some of the walkers I had met on previous occasions, such as at Thanksgiving the previous year, or ANZAC Day this year. It was good to meet again. At around 10.00 a.m. we set off.

Not far from the hotel is the town square, Jie Fang Bei. We could see the new arts centre, still under construction, looking like red Lego blocks. Cf. photo 3. Nearby is a flower market, very colourful, although also very crowded due to a combination of many people and narrow alleyways.

The next attraction was the old wall, built in the 13th century to keep the Mongols out. It didn't. One of the extraordinary things I have noticed in history, anywhere, is just how often walls have been breached, from Jericho to Megiddo, from Harfleur to the Great Wall. With regard to the latter, the Mongols went around it, while the Manchus were let in by a Chinese general, and later the Chinese themselves simply walked through on their way to invading Mongolia. We walked beside this wall for some distance, noticing the murals, bas reliefs both in stone and bronze, the latter celebrating the victory of the Communists over the Kuomintang during the civil war.

Not far along we came to an entrance dating from the 1920s to a hospital, run by French Catholic nuns. It is extraordinary that wherever the Church has been, it has brought healing, to the body, the mind and the spirit. Even today in China, hospitals are still marked with a cross, although I doubt if anybody realises the significance. We entered through a gateway to find a ruin, an open area full of weeds, a few walls and doorways. I tried to imagine what it would have been like in its heyday. What happened? Was it bombed during the war, either by the Japanese or by the Communists? I do not know. Certainly after the latter took over, overseas missionaries were forced to leave. What a misunderstanding, with fault on both sides. Nearby there is a Catholic Church, but it was not on our route for this day. It is one we often went to for Sunday Mass.

We continued through this overgrown ruin to a magnificent lookout atop the old city wall, overlooking the Yangtze far below. The ridge between the two rivers is quite high, at least 100 metres, maybe more. A stone archway leads to a viewing platform. One can also walk up more stairs to the right to climb further up onto the wall. From here one could see something really worthwhile, and to see this was my major reason for coming on this walk. To understand its significance, we need to go back to the Second World War.

Before America even entered the war after the bombing of Pearl Harbour, they were helping China against the Japanese, albeit unofficially. They supplied three squadrons of fighter planes under the command of General Claire Chennault, with all of the crews American service personnel, who had been "discharged" from the armed forces. Against better Japanese planes, Chennault devised new tactics, which worked, resulting in a significant kill ratio advantage. They fought in many areas, not just CQ, but especially here because this city was the wartime capital. What I was interested in was their airfield: where did they land in this mountainous city? Now I know: there is a flat island in the Yangtze River, at least a kilometre long, and this was their landing strip. From our vantage point up on the heights, we had a good view of this long narrow island. I must say that landing on it today would be even more hazardous than in wartime, as in the intervening years, several bridges have been built across the river.

Photo 12: island in the Yangtze River

From here we continued our walk along a wooden walkway down outside the old walls. The houses to our left are themselves quite old, even if not as old as the wall. Eventually one comes to a stone gateway leading back into the city, with more old houses. On one of them is a plaque, riddled with propaganda, and I quote: "During the Anti-Japanese War period, a great many government officials (sic), warlords, comprador, landlords etc (sic) also flocked in (sic) in the war time capital, because of the transfer of the reign centre of the Nationalist government to Chongqing. They began building mansions here. Although the buildings are not in large number, it made a sharp contrast with residences of local ordinary People." Well, thank goodness the CP officials today live such basic, simple lives! Note too, that it is always the "Anti-Japanese War", never WW II, and it is the Nationalist government, not the Chinese government.

There is a seat against the wall here, and one old lady was sound asleep, oblivious to the invasion of 70 "foreign devils" (*yanggizi*) tramping past her. One small family restaurant we passed caught my eye, as it is decorated with used beer bottles, hanging from a roof beam: quaint. Next we sauntered through a market area with all kinds of goods for sale, ranging from trinkets to clothing. This was our second market area. Here the contrast between these old, low buildings and the modern high rise is evident. Some of these older ones were being pulled down, a process going on all over the city, to be replaced by yet more thirty storey structures.

And so we returned to the Intercontinental Hotel to be greeted by the staff with a welcome bottle of water. This was followed by lunch. It was a Western buffet style of "eat as much as you can" of really delicious food for 150 Yuan, laid on by Sharon, our gracious hostess who had been a party to organising all of this.

What a great way to spend a couple of hours and what a great way to explore the city: a big "thank you" to the organisers.

1.11: Thanksgiving

Thanksgiving is not a Chinese festival, and nor is it Australian, but it is American, tied to part to their history. If I have got it right—and my American friends can correct me on this—I think it dates from the Pilgrim Fathers. It is not easy to adjust to a new land. Farming techniques which worked well in England may not work quite so well elsewhere, as in America or indeed in Australia. Certainly early settlers to Australia made many mistakes, and we are still feeling the effects 200 years later. Both the Pilgrim Fathers in 1620 and the First Fleeters in 1788 found themselves in desperate straits due to shortage of food. In Australia, they gradually learnt how to work the land, and were initially saved by the timely arrival of the Second Fleet. In America, the Indians helped feed the starving settlers, and they shot turkey, the local wild bird in the bush. Hence Thanksgiving is a festival to thank God for God's bounty—and for turkeys, which have become the traditional fare, garnished with cranberry sauce. Presumably they also thank the Indians. It is held on the second last Thursday in November.

Now there were not many Americans in this neck of the woods, but why let that deter us? The local International Hotel had, for the previous few years, been putting on a dinner for expatriates around town. It is an excuse to get together, even if we are not Americans. This year the traditional day was not suitable for us; hence in 2013 we had our meal on the following day. The cost was 220 Yuan (about $45), which was very expensive for me, although it was a really, really nice meal. However I had been invited by the manager of the hotel, so as her guest the meal was free for me. Was that why I really savoured it? The manager, Sharon, happens to be a Kiwi, so just as well Australia's defeat of New Zealand in the Rugby League World Cup came later!

It was a great opportunity to meet other expatriates from different countries. I found myself chatting to many, even some Aussies. One family came from Geelong: great people, except for one rather serious flaw: they barrack for Geelong in the footy, and of course, the only team is Collingwood. For the uneducated, "footy" equals Australian Rules Football, which is, in my humble opinion, the greatest of all the football codes. Just watch it. Not long before, while teaching a student working for HP (Hewlett Packard), I showed him a video of Aussie Rules. He was so enthralled that he decided to do a presentation on it. The game is so fast, so skilful and so spectacular, without the hooliganism of soccer. It is also fairer, as one goal is not the end of the world. I have heard soccer commentators lose their minds after a goal has been scored; and the fans riot. No, go for Aussie Rules.

I also met some truly beautiful children from a local orphanage, who were being supported by the hotel. I love this—wonderful, as indeed are the children. They are God's own, and I for one thoroughly enjoyed their company.

At our table, I found myself sitting next to the Danish consul, a delightful lady, with her two teenage sons. Some consulates are located in Chongqing, though not the Australian, the nearest one being in Chengdu, which is only a couple of hours away by fast train (300 kph). The hotel manager, was on the other side of me. It was great meeting people, not just around our table, but those on other tables as we wandered around, collecting the next course. Thank you Sharon: it was well done.

1.12: Transport

Introduction

Like any city, Chongqing has various modes of getting around, yet every city is peculiar. One of the peculiarities in Chongqing is its hilly nature, thus precluding bike riding. It was quite a contrast to notice the paucity of bikes in this city compared with other places in China. Buses and trains form the backbone of public transport, together with taxis. These modes can be found in most of the world's cities—including Sydney.

1.12.1: Trains

Sydney is my home town, so naturally, everything that comes from Sydney is the best in the world—except that it isn't. The rail system is a case in point. When you read the paper—a Sydney paper that is—you may think that Sydney's rail system is the worst in the world, as journalists never seem to be able to say anything good about it. Well, it is not that bad, but the system in Chongqing—in my humble opinion,—is definitely superior.

Chongqing is decidedly hilly, whereas Sydney, apart from the coastal fringe and the far western suburbs, is largely flat. Chongqing has an urban population of some 17 million people, compared with Sydney's 5 million. Both of these factors influence the rail system. Sydney's rail is mostly above ground, whereas Chongqing's is mostly underground or if it is above ground it is elevated. It can be strange sitting in a carriage, looking down on the Jia Ling River, when suddenly we are underground, and when we get off at a station, you find that we are quite deep underground.

One major difference is in the frequency of trains: comparatively infrequent in Sydney, yet here one seldom has to wait more than five minutes for a train. The platforms are also different. Here there is often a barrier between the platform and the edge, complete with its own set of doors, which open automatically when the train arrives. In Sydney the trains pull up anywhere, but here the train doors are exactly aligned with the platform doors. This system is just beginning to enter the Sydney system.

Apart from peak hour, one is usually assured of a seat in Sydney, with the some five seats across the carriage, with a central aisle; these seats usually nicely covered. This is changing in Sydney due to rapid immigration: more people are streaming into Australia than can be absorbed with the vast majority of these settling in Sydney or Melbourne. Building new infrastructure is struggling to meet current demand, let alone building for the future. In Chongqing there are no forward facing seats. Instead, each side of the carriage has a row of aluminium inward facing benches. These can be quite slippery, so that if the train accelerates or decelerates rapidly, one finds oneself sliding up and down, or pushing up against one's neighbour. This may not be too bad if you happen to be sitting next to a pretty girl! Most people stand—at any time of the day, not only during peak hour—holding on to rails.

Respect for the elderly is an endearing aspect of traditional Chinese culture, and it is great to see young people standing up to offer their seats to someone older—like me, for instance! This does not always happen. It is extremely rare to see children do it; in fact I can remember only one instance. Many teenagers also do not bother, usually engrossed in their mobile phones or iPad. This behaviour is not, of course, limited to China. If someone is talking on their phone, especially if this is a man, they shout—really shout. I keep thinking, "Goodness, they hardly need their phones, as they can almost be heard in Beijing." I have no idea why they do it. I wonder how much the One Child Policy has contributed to selfishness amongst the young, producing a "me generation".

Photo 13: inside a carriage

Carriages are equipped with TV sets, for those who may be bored. Electronic displays tell passengers what the next station is. There is also a route map, listing all stations on the line. None of this is to be found in Sydney trains. Information is broadcast throughout the trains in both Chinese and English. A typical announcement goes like this. "Dear passengers …" It is all very polite and gentle, with the voice of a young woman. "…We are arriving at Shuanbei. To avoid clipping, please do not touch doors before opened. Doors will be opened on the left." Goodness, what is clipping? Sometimes it sounds like "trapping". I assume it means: "Do not get your finger trapped in closing doors."

On the platform too, there are announcements. You may, for example hear: "Attention please, the train is arriving. Do not lean on the screen door. Please queue and take care of children and elderly people beside you." Nobody seems to pay any attention to this, as there is usually a bum rush to get on the train, without waiting for the passengers on the train to get off first. The platform has arrows which light up when the train is approaching, indicating that passengers are to enter from the side, leaving the middle free for disembarking people. It is a good system—except that people often take no notice. Once aboard too, there is often a scramble to get a seat before anyone else.

Photo 14: stairs and escalators

Stations are often attractively decorated, with, for example, paintings of flying birds on the ceilings. I liked them. Naturally, many stations are to be found underground, but not all. Trains tend to run along nearly horizontal tracks, not steep inclines, meaning that in this mountainous city one could be travelling underground for part of the journey, but above ground for the rest of it. What I like about the former, is that the tracks are built on pylons, generally running down the middle of roadways. Stations too are built on above-ground platforms. The advantage of this system is that the rail is some 10 metres above the roadway, thus not interfering with traffic flow, and freeing up more roadway for cars. I wish in Sydney we had built the light rail network on pylons, instead of adding to traffic congestion. Cf. photograph 76, showing Weidianyuan station.

Since many stations are deep underground, there are stairs and escalators to get people to the surface and vice versa. Sometimes there are stairs only. Sometimes the escalators go up but not down. These too are attractively decorated, as in photograph 14. Here too there are announcements, using the same calm voice as before. "Dear passengers, when you take the escalator, please hold tight the handrail." Note that the grammar is not quite correct: "tight" is an adjective, not an adverb. Of recent days there has been a variant on this, to wit "Please stand firm and hold the handrail." Maybe somebody drew their attention to the grammar. "Stand on the right side to leave the left side as a passage." Needless to say, this is only observed when there are few passengers. "Do not play around at the escalator"—now what exactly does that mean?—"or walk in the opposite direction."

Map 4: The Metro System

Map 4 shows the metro system, somewhat stylised. The thick blue line represents the rivers, the Jialing to the north and the Yangtze to the south, before they meet at Chao Tien Men. There is a rocky peninsula about 20 km long running east-west, which forms the heart of the city. There are six metro lines, both numbered and also colour coded. One interesting feature is that light rail is combined into the system. Some stations mentioned in the text are as follows:

Red line

1: Xiaoshizi: the start of the line, close to Chao Tien Men

3: Lianglukou: junction with the blue line, which runs north-south

6: Daping: junction with the green line.

13: Shapingba: major centre.

15: Lieshimu: the suburb in which SISU is located

16: Ciqikou: old town, major tourist attraction, close to SISU

20: Weidianyuan: location of Hewlett Packard, where I did some work

22: Daxuecheng: or University Town, where many universities are located.

Blue line north

1: Lianglukou: junction with the red line.

4: Guanyinqiao: where I did some teaching of doctors.

10: North Intercity Railway Station

16: Expo Gardens

22: Jiangbei Airport

Blue line south:

4: Sigongli: cf. section 10.2 on teaching doctors

In 2014 there were in excess of 100 stations in the network, spread over four lines, numbered 1—the red line, 2—the green line, 3—the blue line, and 6—the pink line. Lines 4 and 5 were under construction. These lines crisscross so that you can transfer from one to the other. It is quite convenient. It is quite fast too, taking on average less than three minutes between stations. To get from my apartment to the international airport, for instance, would take two hours: 10 minutes to walk to Lieshimu station, then 11 stops on line 1 to Jianglukou, where you change to line 3; then it is another 22 stops to the domestic terminal. From there you can either take the free shuttle bus to the international terminal, or walk for ten minutes.

To pay for your journey you can either obtain a ticket from an electronic machine or use a card. If you choose the former, you punch in your destination on the grid map which comes up, then put in cash for the required amount. If you choose the latter, you pay 25 Yuan for the card, but then get a 10% reduction on your journey. Machines read your card and tell you how much credit you have left at the beginning and end of the trip. The same card can be used for buses, which cost 2 Yuan for any distance or 1.80 Yuan with the card. The bus and train are also co-ordinated. Once I got caught in the rain, so instead of walking to the station I took the bus, followed immediately by the train. My train journey cost me 2.00 Yuan, instead of 3.60 Yuan, thus the bus trip only cost me two jiao, or 0.2 Yuan (about four cents). These days people can pay using their mobile phones, as China races towards becoming a cashless society.

In class we were looking at various systems of government, comparing a one party system with one which has numbers of parties. Each system of course has its advantages and disadvantages. The one party system, as China has, does have the advantage of efficiency. They want something done, so they just do it. Currently throughout China, many metro systems are being built, to the tune of nearly one whole line being opened each year. Compare this with Sydney, which argues for decades about extending the rail line into the Eastern Suburbs, or up to Palm Beach, or up into the Hills District. What happens? Very little. We talk, talk, talk, but little gets done. We somehow lack the will to make hard decisions, especially when individuals will be inconvenienced for a period of time. What a pity. Perhaps we can learn from China. On the other hand, the light rail built recently in Sydney did result in serious disruption to many businesses, with the foreign company, which had been given the contract, some four years past the contracted finishing date. This resulted in great financial hardship to the point of bankruptcy, with the company, paying nothing by way of compensation. This is not right.

When I arrived in Chongqing in August 2011, the nearest station was at Shapingba, some 15 minutes away by bus. It was not long, however, before line 1 was extended to Lieshimu, the suburb in which SISU is located, with the station less than 10 minutes' walk away. In quick time the line extended station by station further out. I often used this line; it was so convenient.

At train stations in the early morning you will find newspapers, which are free. Commuters pick them up to read on the train. Or, if you prefer, you can watch the TV monitor. The other alternative, of course, is to spend your time in deep contemplation of the Almighty. Most people read. When they get off, they simply drop their paper at the station of their destination for someone else to pick up. It is a good system. On one occasion I was on a train—lost in contemplation, of course—when I noticed that nearly everyone on the train, or at least near me, had their head buried in a newspaper. We came to a station; the doors opened; a little time passed; the doors closed, just as a young man let out a yelp and dived for the doors—too late, much to the amusement of his fellow passengers. I guess he just had to get off at the next station and return on the next train.

1.12.2: Buses

The bus network in Chongqing is much the same as in most cities, except busier than most. In Shapingba, for instance, some 17 different bus lines would be converging at the same stop. Even so one never had to wait long for one's bus.

One surprising feature is the time at which bus routes shut down. On more than one occasion I found myself without a bus because I was out too late. Some buses would begin their final run for the day from their depot at the early hour of 8.30 p.m. I have no idea why this should be so.

Another surprise concerns the Concert Hall. You would think that such an important cultural venue would be richly serviced by public transport: not so. The nearest bus route is still a long way from the hall, necessitating a walk of at least a kilometre—or you hail a taxi.

1.13: Food

Many areas of the world have their own cuisines, sometimes found nowhere else. It might be a particular food—such as frogs' legs—or it might be a particular way of cooking—such as mumu, the in-ground cooking of Papua New Guinea, or it could be a combination of factors. In China people eat almost anything which swims, walks, glides, flies, runs, slithers or just sits. Of recent days we have seen a consequence of this with the rise and spread of the corona virus, beginning in Wuhan in January 2020, before spreading worldwide. Each region, however, has its specialties. Potatoes, for example, are not usually associated with China yet the empire produces and consumes more of this particular vegetable than anywhere else in the world. Cool mountain regions have villages which pride themselves on their own presentations. Fuzhou in Fujian Province has fish balls as a specialty, while Tongren in Guizhou Province has fried eggplant.

So what does Chongqing have? Hotpot or *huoguo* (火锅), which means "fire pot", a dish particularly suited to the region's cold, moist winters.

This particular method of cooking did not originate in Chongqing, but was used in other regions of China, sometimes extensively. It was the favourite dish of the emperor Qianlong (1711-99) during the Qing Dynasty. Nor is this method restricted to China, as many other countries have also cooked food by dropping ingredients into boiling water. Chongqing, however, has its own unique style, due both to the ingredients used and to the hot chilli pepper. The "hot" refers not only to the boiling water but also to the chillies.

The city has been declared by China's Cuisine Association to be China's hotpot city. Quite possibly this began with the boat haulers and peasant farmers. Basically you gather whatever you have and drop it into boiling water together with hot chilli peppers—not exactly haut cuisine one would think. It really became popular when Chongqing was China's capital under the Kuomintang during the Japanese occupation; capitals do attract people from far and wide. Hotpot restaurants began in the 1930s with the subsequent need to enrich the menu and make it desirable, especially by adding delicacies, not just herbs from the hillsides. The essence, however, is the chillies.

I have had many hotpot dishes, with the favourite ingredients including lettuce, lotus root, potato, blood, pork, chicken, tofu, garlic, spring onions, various meats and of course chilli. Broad leaf vegetables can soak up sesame seed oil. In Chongqing, situated far from the sea, there is not much in the way of seafood. In any restaurant, you choose from the menu what ingredients you wish to add to the boiling water; the more people you have the more ingredients you choose. Hotpot is therefore great for groups, rather than for individual serves. Usually, a large pot is placed in the centre of the table, often round, with all the diners feeding from it. This continues to simmer throughout the meal and you add ingredients as desired, so that it is not all cooked at once; you also add more hot water as required. The pot may have two sections: one with chilli and one without. Sometimes, however, each diner has his/her own pot over a small stove, so that you cook your own.

There is yet another variant, which I sampled for the first time in March, 2014. The restaurant we visited has a central U-shaped table. Diners sit on each side, facing the table on the inside of the U, or at separate tables on the outside of the U. Each setting has its own stove and each diner has his own cooking pot plus another bowl, into which various spices are added according to taste. Now here is the real difference: the U shaped table has a conveyor belt, on which dishes are placed containing many different kinds of foods, such as fish, bivalves, various meats, animal intestines, tofu, noodles, quail eggs and various vegetables. The meats are usually in balls, mostly pork or perhaps some beef and there are also fish balls, a specialty of Fujian Province, and a favourite of mine. Chicken was absent except for chicken feet. You could also augment your meal with a drink: we opted for beer. It was all very nice, to the extent where I would have to say that it is the best hotpot I had experienced up to that time. There were seven of us altogether. To make our night even more memorable the weather was balmy with the temperature reaching 20 degrees on this day, the sky clear and a full moon beaming down on us. God is good.

This restaurant is located in a district known as Da Xue Cheng, which literally means "big school town", or University Town, as it is here that many universities are located. Indeed Chongqing Normal University is close by the restaurant. This district is new, with this being the first time I had been there. Three years before it consisted of empty paddocks, but now it is urban. They build so quickly. The Da Xue Cheng station was then the terminal station of line 1, which is the one we were on at Lieshimu, so that it is easy to get to. Work meanwhile was continuing to extend this line still further, the rail tracks having already been completed, sitting atop huge pylons, which look solid enough to last centuries.

There is also dry pot, where the food is cooked in just a little oil or water. This tends to be better if you are eating alone. Another local dish consists of loads of chillies with just a little bit of chicken: too hot for me.

I must confess that when I first tried these hot spicy dishes I was not exactly partial to them; or perhaps they did not like me. I called the chillies "red torpedoes", because they exploded after entry. The effects can be almost volcanic, with smoke pouring out of one's ears, fire from one's mouth and tears streaming down one's face; well, almost. Over the years, however, I not only grew accustomed to it, but began to like it, so that now I like to add *lajiao* to my own meal every day. Try it.

Chapter 2: Sichuan International Studies University

2.1: The Name

SISU began life in 1950 just after the Communist takeover of China, and at a time when China and Russia were bosom pals—more or less. It was established by Russia as a military training facility, glorifying in the name of "The People Liberation Army's Russian Training Corps of Southwest University of Military and Political Sciences"—which is quite a mouthful in any language. Remnants of this history are still in evidence today, with the university next door being called: "The Southwest University of Law and Political Sciences". Chongqing, of course, lies in the southwest of the empire. SISU was renamed in 1951, 1952, 1953 and 1959, when it became known as "Sichuan Institute of Foreign Languages", which is more recognisable, not that this lasted long, as the following year it took its current name, "Sichuan International Studies University" (四川外语学院) or SISU for short or Chuānwài (川外). If one was getting a taxi back to the university from somewhere around town, it would not do to ask the driver to go to SISU as all you would get would be a blank stare and a "Eh!"—which expression appears to mean much the same in any language, but everyone knows Chuānwài. Chongqing used to be part of Sichuan Province, until separated off by the central authorities in Beijing in 1997, but the university continues to have "Sichuan" in its name.

The name does suggest an international focus, which I found to be rather refreshing after the insular thinking of previous places where I had worked, where students had shown an appalling ignorance of China's position in the world. Indeed they did not even know the location of other countries, apart from Australia, which does stand out as the only island continent occupied by a single nation. The more knowledgeable seemed to think that The United States was somewhere near Brazil; Americans would not be pleased.

Total enrolment of students was around 12,000, with about 100,000 having graduated over the years. The accent is on international studies, including trade, commerce, international relations and law. It also includes languages, running courses in Chinese, English, French, German, Italian, Japanese, Russian, Spanish amongst others. Some countries have established language centres, viz. Alliance Française (French), the Goethe Institute (German), the Cervantes Institute (Spanish), the Russian Language Centre (Russian—obviously), and the South Korean Centre. Altogether there were 23 different academic courses, including two in English—English language and English literature. Most courses are under-graduate, but there are post-graduate courses as well. The university enjoys an excellent reputation. There are similar universities in other parts of China: BISU (Beijing International Studies University), and another SISU (Shanghai International Studies University).

This SISU operates in partnership with some middle schools, thus tapping into sources for future students. There are many exchanges with other tertiary institutions around the world and I was involved in programmes to prepare students for overseas studies, principally to Lancaster University in England and Newcastle University in Australia.

At our opening ceremony for my first semester, I was asked to give a speech. I told the audience of about 150 how delighted I was to be here, since in my opinion, we are coming out of the age of Nationalism evident over the past few centuries, into an International age. For the future we should not be putting the welfare of my own country first, but rather the welfare of the planet as a whole. We still have a long way to go. I also quoted G.K. Chesterton: "What does he of England know, who only England knows." If all we know is our own country and culture, then we really have not sufficient perspective to understand even our own country and culture.

This is all very well, but I had an ulterior motive. In China Nationalism is extreme, to the point where the empire is a threat to the whole world. The Chinese consider it their right to take over any territory they choose, their right to dominate and control the entire planet. And it does not matter how they do it.

I am impressed with the way this university looked after us. My previous book, "Teaching in Tongren", told of the problems we had with Tongren University, so I was coming off those experiences. In Tongren, when a problem developed, one would bring it to the attention of the *waiban*'s assistant—and wait. Usually something would be done—eventually—but sometimes nothing would be done. There was a classic case of this with my friend, Greg, getting a new gas cylinder, because the one he was using had developed a leak. A call to the *waiban*'s office elicited a less than enthusiastic response. Upon being told that something needed to be done, the reply was: "We will send someone around tomorrow."

"No. I have a gas leak. This is dangerous. All you need is a spark and my whole apartment, with me in it, could go out in a big bang."

"Oh, yes, oh, I see. OK, we'll send someone around now."

I had water leaking into my apartment from above, which covered half of a living room wall with mould and cut off electricity to my kitchen and shower room, including my washing machine. It was never fixed.

At SISU, by contrast the administration did not wait for something to go wrong before they did anything. Two men, for example, came to my apartment to check both gas and electricity and indeed they found a potential problem with my water heater, requiring the services of an expert to fix. A few days later they returned with their expert, the heater was fixed and everybody was happy—me especially.

Drinking water, by contrast, was easier to get at Tongren. When my bottle ran out, I would simply ring the supplier, tell him what I wanted, my name and address and it would be delivered within five minutes: very impressive. That man deserves even more credit, in that he could understand my Chinese!—and he would charge only 6 Yuan for a ten litre bottle. At SISU I would take my empty bottle to the workmen downstairs, and they would ring the supplier, who would deliver it sometime later, generally some hours later, and he was charging 10 Yuan per bottle. Furthermore it was incumbent upon me to open and upend it: yet it is both heavy and awkward. On one occasion I was told in the early morning that the delivery man would not be here before 8.00 p.m. I remarked on how late that was. Later that morning one of the workmen delivered it. What happened? Did he ring the supplier and say that the *laowai* was not happy? I do not know, but I got my water. I was happy.

At the end of my first semester my final piece of work was to conduct IELTS practice interviews. On the final Monday, I went all day, even though I was limiting each interview to around ten minutes. The department looked after me well, however, during the day, having the coffee shop bring up both morning and afternoon coffee, plus providing lunch. On Wednesday I had 15 more interviews, taking about 4 hours. Then I was finished. On Thursday morning I left after breakfast for a holiday back in Australia, via Guangzhou. What was pleasing was how well the department had looked after me. Thank you.

2.2: Location

SISU is situated about 20 kilometres to the west of the city centre, at the end of Chongqing's peninsular which is its defining feature. The city is divided into districts, this one being called Shapingba, referring to a sandbank in the Jialing River, which forms the northern border. The Yangtze is not far away either, to the south. The suburb is called Lieshimu, or "Martyrs' Tombs", since there is a park jutting into the university campus which contains the graves of quite a few people killed by the Kuomintang. You have to get the terminology right, by the way: anyone killed by the Kuomintang is a martyr, while anyone killed by the Communists is a criminal. They do not, however, have this nomenclature all to themselves, as it appears that if a Muslim terrorist is killed he is ipso facto a martyr, goes to Paradise and gets 72 virgins. Talk about sexist—apart from everything else.

In area the university covers 77 ha; it has three gates: two on the north side and one on the east. There is none on the south side, which abuts the Law University and there is none on the west either because you run up against a mountain, Gele Shan. In fact the upper campus is on the slopes of this mountain. The main gate is the east. For some time there were boom gates across one north side entrance, the one going to the upper campus, and also across the east side entrance. Over the summer holidays in 2013, two changes were made. Boom gates were also constructed across the third gate, while the east gate had its boom shifted a whole 10 metres up the road. I have no idea why. Soon afterwards these gates were demolished and then rebuilt. What is going on? It sounds a bit like one way to solve unemployment: you have one man dig a hole, while another fills it in. Once again, confusion abounds: situation normal.

Thankfully, my accommodation and all my classes were on the bottom campus, but others were not so lucky, necessitating the climbing of many steps each day: there are something like 300 between the two sections. During my time construction began on yet another section, further up the mountain—yet more climbing. It certainly keeps one fit. I used to walk all over the campus for exercise in the afternoons, but I would not want to be doing it just to get to class. I found it to be so interesting, with its pathways, steps, views and all the time the bustle of young people.

The lower campus is divided from the upper campus by—surprisingly—a railway line. This ceased to function the year before I arrived, but the tracks remained for some time before being gradually cleared. It made for interesting walking, as one had to keep concentrating on placing one's feet on the sleepers, and just to make life even more interesting, the width between the sleepers varied. One did have to be careful. To the north the tracks led to a lovely wooded trail, seemingly far from the city, at one point diving into a long dark tunnel: torch needed here, even on fairly bright days. To the south the tracks led past the Law University next door, then through an army barracks, where one needed to be careful, as there were always armed guards: I would not want to mess with them. There was yet another barracks not far away to the north. If you continue following the tracks there are many possibilities—all interesting. Going straight ahead one comes to a goods yard, with engines shunting up and down. One can continue through here to climb back over Gele Shan, re-entering the university via the upper campus. Or you could follow a branch line to the left, running on trestles over a valley, the valley floor some 50 metres below: very exciting. In my final year metro line 5 was being constructed over this same valley, necessitating dodging the construction. Great fun.

Photograph 15 shows this disused railway line.

Photo 15: disused railway line.

2.3: Lower Campus

This is where I lived and worked. The east gate is the main point of entrance and egress. As you enter, those graves I mentioned are on the left hand side. On the right is a delightful pond, which I loved to visit, especially in springtime with the lotus in bloom and tadpoles swarming in the shallows; actually the whole pond is shallow, being no more than knee deep: you are not going to drown in this pond.

Continue walking and you come to a six storey classroom block on the right. Behind this is our compound, where most us overseas teachers lived. There are two four storey blocks. My apartment was located on the second floor, facing a tennis court, where I would play from time to time. On the left, opposite this court is a restaurant, called the Teachers' Restaurant, where we would eat on special occasions.

Many sporting facilities are to be found on this lower campus: more tennis courts, basketball courts and badminton courts. They were used too—often—and it was good to see the students getting some exercise, and indeed some of the staff as well.

Past these courts, on the left hand side, is the area where I did most of my teaching, viz. the International English Department, consisting of two buildings: the first was new, seven storeys high, while the one behind it on a higher level was much older and five storeys high.

One could look out over the Law University next door.

Photo 16: pond behind our apartment building

The modern seven storey building is built around a central courtyard—very pleasing—with classrooms mainly on levels 1 and 3, with some on 6 and 7. Level 2 is administration, while the rest are given over to accommodation, often with four students to a room. The top floor on the western side provided living quarters for the caretaker and his family. A lecture theatre occupied the western

71

side of the second floor. On the second floor there is also a café and a most pleasant place it was. I liked to spend time here. It was also used for formal functions, catering for up to twenty people.

Behind this building is the major dining room, where official dinners for all the staff would be held. On the floor below is the students dining room, where sometimes, but not often, I would share a meal with students. For a set amount of money you could get a set number of dishes, depending upon how hungry you were. There was always rice and seaweed soup, which you collected yourself. The rest was ladled out by the staff. You collected your own chopsticks from a hotbox. The meals were palatable, but hardly cordon bleu.

Heading west from here is a collection of shops for general supplies. A photograph shop supplied those essential ID photographs, while another shop supplied USBs and the like.

Continue heading west and you come to a series of high rise buildings for accommodation, administration and classrooms. Also here there was the swimming pool. I say "was" because unfortunately it was demolished in my final year. Prior to that, it was a good place to go to on a hot summer's afternoon to get some exercise. Many buildings in this area and to the west of the courts were being demolished to make way for new constructions, resulting in much dust choking the already polluted air.

Photograph 17 shows part of this lower campus. The building immediately to the west of the courts and bordering the road is the Alliance Française building, which contained the hall, as well as a café and classrooms for French teaching. On the northern side of the road are more accommodation blocks. In the background, right Gele Shan can be seen, the mountain on whose lower slopes the university is built.

Photo 17: lower campus

2.4: Words OF Wisdom

The Chinese love slogans. They use them to link people to the past. They use them to rally mass support. They use them as motivation for greater endeavours. Traditionally they have been hung on banners across streets or put up on walls. One can see the attraction, as much can be expressed in a few words. This also aids memory, in a society where memory is so important in the learning process, beginning with learning each Chinese character, one by one. These slogans can also tap into the wisdom of wise people of the past, or indeed of the present. Slogans on the walls of educational institutions are thus not surprising, and this university is no exception, being a feature of all three places where I have worked in China. The International Building, where I did most of my teaching, had them on the walls outside classrooms. There are others found inside the walls of classrooms and in other buildings. Here are some examples.

Education

Since this is an educational establishment, let us begin with education. As one enters the foyer, we find no less than eight slogans: two in Chinese, two in Italian, one in Russian one in German and two in English. The English read as follows:

1) Ignorance is not innocence but sin. Robert Browning.

I think of the enormous damage done to Australia's environment by ignorant Europeans who came to our country bringing their animals, especially rabbits, foxes, toads, cats and carp to name just a few, not to mention the plants.

2) To learn without thinking is blindness, to think without learning is idleness. Confucius.

Are terrorists blind? They learn to kill because they have been brainwashed—no thinking involved here. Thinking can reinforce what one already knows, but can also lead to innovation, expanding one's horizons. Learning is needed to provide the groundwork for thinking.

3) Education is what remains when one has forgotten everything he learnt at school. Albert Einstein.

I like this, as education is what happens within oneself, not what is imposed from without. Education should therefore be a lifelong process, not ending the day we leave school.

4) Genius, in truth, means little more than the faculty of perceiving in an unhabitual way. William James (1842—1910).

"Unhabitual" is an unusual word, and one wonders if he means that the genius differs from everybody else. Does that make me a genius? It certainly does apply to someone who comes up with something very original. Nothing is entirely original, in that we keep building on the shoulders of those giants who have gone before us.

5) If you think education is expensive, try ignorance. Derek Bok.

I like this one. A little bit of education in the 19th century might have saved Australia billions of dollars in damages, caused by the rabbit alone. In Pakistan ignorant extremist Muslims are killing doctors and nurses who are inoculating children against polio. They are also trying to prevent women from being educated.

The Future

Most of the students here are young people, although some are middle aged, including scientists, doctors, university lecturers etc. who were wishing to improve their English. Even for them, their outlook is towards the future. We study for what is to come, to improve our own lives, and—as is often the case in this country—to make China strong and powerful.

1. Learn from today, hope for tomorrow. The important thing is not to stop questioning. Albert Einstein.

I see questioning as being at the heart of education. You do not simply read words in a passage, for instance, without asking yourself a whole series of question. Firstly, what does this mean? Then how does this gel with my own experience? Do I agree with it? What does it lead to? Etc.

2. You see things that are and say "Why?" I see things that may be and say "Why not?" George Bernard Shaw.

If I remember correctly, this quote was used by Robert Kennedy when he was on the campaign trail. We do need to dream of a better world if there is going to be any hope in bringing it about. What do we want? What world do we want for our children?

3. I never see what has been done: I only see what remains to be done.

There is no author given for this quote. I would delete the word "only". We do need to see what has been done, in my opinion, as part of the process of forming the future.

4. Success is the sum total of small efforts repeated day in and day out. Robert Collier.

If you will, a journey of a thousand kilometres begins with a single step. It may take millions of bricks to build an edifice: one by one, however, they are applied and eventually, the job is complete. The secret, I suppose, is to keep putting in those small steps daily.

5. Don't lose hope: you never know what tomorrow will bring. Today—a caterpillar; tomorrow—a butterfly.

Whenever we speak of the future, inevitably our hopes play a major role. Deep down inside of us, we know that all will be well, in fact much better than the present.

6. Twenty years from now, you will be more disappointed by the things you didn't do than by the things that you did. So throw off the tow lines; sail away from the safe harbour; catch the trade winds in your sails. Explore, dream, discover. Mark Twain.

Mark Twain, of course, spent some time on the Mississippi River, and hence his nautical analogy. In fact he took his pen name from there, throwing a lead weight from the prow of the boat in shallow water, to make sure that there was sufficient draught, the linesman calling out the depths: "By the mark, four; by the mark, three; by the mark, twain"—the "mark" of course, being the knots in the rope to mark off the depths in fathoms. So don't delay any longer in doing what you have always dreamed of doing.

7. I have a dream … that my four little children will one day live in a nation, where they will not be judged by the colour of their skin, but by the content of their character. Martin Luther King Jnr.

The dream theme continues. King's dream has come from the past, and the sad reality of people not treating each other as equals. We still do not do so, more than forty years on, but things are a lot better than they were, in large measure due to King's stirring speech.

Language

This building, as I have stated, is given over to international studies, including various languages, not only English. The Goethe Institute from Germany was hiring several rooms on a permanent basis. I was actually assigned some classes there, but the German guy came in and told me off, so we had to shift our classes to the café. But let us get back to those words of wisdom.

1) Language is the dress of thought. Samuel Johnson.

Well, yes: but it is a lot more than that. Dress is on the outside. Dress is not who we are, but it can be an indicator of who we are. Language is more than an indicator of our thoughts: it also shapes our thoughts. The way we think depends upon our language. Thoughts and language mutually shape each other.

2) My words fly up, my thoughts remain below. Words without thoughts never to heaven go. Shakespeare. Hamlet, Act 3, Scene 3.

Hamlet is planning to kill his uncle, King Claudius, but finding him at prayer, decides not to, as the king's soul may go to heaven. He will wait for another opportunity. Meanwhile, the king is not succeeding in his attempt at praying. Too often we use empty words, thoughtless words, or in the case of Claudius, we do not mean what we say. He had seized the throne by murdering his brother, Hamlet's father, but ipso facto had virtually destroyed himself.

3) The sum of human wisdom is not contained in any one language. Ezra Pound (American poet).

No it is not. This links in with the previous saying. People who speak a particular language, which is embedded in a particular culture, see things one way. I am beginning to see how much language, culture and even religion are bound up together. We can get into trouble if we do not delineate these clearly enough.

4) A different language is a different vision of life. Federico Fellini.

This backs up what we have just been saying.

5) Language is not an abstract construction of the learned, or of dictionary makers, but is something arising out of the work, needs, ties, joys, affections and tasks of long generations of humanity and has its own bases, broad and low, close to the ground. Walt Whitman.

It is people who shape language in everyday life, not academics or dictionaries. We tend to look at dictionaries as authorities on what a word means but really a dictionary is only a record of what people say it means. Let us look at an example. The word "decimate" comes from the Roman army, where one man in ten was executed when there was a rebellion. Note this: one in ten. Now we find sports writers saying something like: "The cricket team has been decimated by injury." Do they mean that one player is injured, or—heaven forbid—executed? No: they mean four or five players are out injured. The situation is far worse than "decimated", yet this is the term that is now acceptable.

Let us look at another example. In a supermarket one finds a fast lane for those shoppers who have "ten items or less". This is bad grammar, as "few" refers to number, not "less", which refers to quantity. Yet we are now at a point when nearly everybody makes this "mistake". This has now become acceptable. For the record, I still use "few" and I also still refuse to split the infinitive, which just sounds wrong to me.

The Meaning of Life

1) 5 simple rules for happiness:
   1. Free your heart from hatred.
   2. Free your mind from worries.
   3. Live simply.
   4. Give more
   5. Expect less.

I do think we complicate life too much. Isn't it interesting that we get so much pleasure from giving? What makes us happy is making other people happy.

Yet too often we are too self-centred. The next quotation echoes these sentiments.

2) The best way to cheer yourself up is to cheer someone else. Mark Twain.

3) Real integrity is doing the right thing, knowing that nobody's going to know whether you did it or not. Oprah Winfrey.

Wow! In the end the truth will always come out, if not in this world, then in the next. My mother used to say that a lie is like a two-legged stool; it cannot stand up without another lie, then another … Sir Walter Scott put it this way: "Oh what a tangled web we weave, when first we practise to deceive."

4) The happiest people don't have the best of everything: they just make the best of everything. No author was given.

Right now the Chinese are hell bent on becoming rich, thinking it will make them happy. It won't, although it might make them greedy. We need to appreciate what we have, rather than hanker after what we have not. We have many blessings: it is not a bad idea to count them.

5) Though miles may lie between us, we are never far apart, for friendship doesn't count the miles: it's measured by the heart.

Again I do not know who originally said this, but how true it is. In Chongqing I did not have a lot of friends, but around the world I did, and in this modern age of communications there are many ways to keep in touch. We can still meet as people, even if we cannot hug.

6) When I was five years old, my mother always told me that happiness was the key to life. When I went to school, they asked me what I wanted to be. I wrote down "happy". They told me I didn't understand the assignment, and I told them they didn't understand life. John Lennon.

Do we understand life? I think we are meant to be happy, not just in the next life, and not just tomorrow, but now. If I am happy now, then I will be happy tomorrow. This has become something of a mantra for me, which my students imitate. "Are you happy?" Actually I have been saying *"Ni gaoxing ma?"* but sometimes I would change that to *"Ni kwai le ma?"* since—or so I am told, as I am no expert in Chinese—that *kwai* le is stronger than *gaoxing*. Sometimes too I would say, *"Ni kwai le, wo kwai le":* if you are happy, then I am happy. This gets back to what I was saying earlier, that giving to others makes us happy. "It is better to give than to receive."

Miscellaneous

1) The world will not be destroyed by those who do evil, but by those who watch them and do nothing. Albert Einstein.

This has been stated in different ways by many people, but the one which appeals to me most came, I think, from Dietrich Bonheoffer, when he said something like this: "They came for the Jews, and I did nothing, because I was not a Jew. Then they came for the Gypsies and I did nothing, because I was not a Gypsy. Next they came for the Catholics and I did nothing, because I was not a Catholic. Finally they came for me, but nobody did anything, because there was nobody left." You may remember that he was a Lutheran pastor who died in a concentration camp during the Second World War.

2) Innovation distinguishes between a leader and a follower. Steve Jobs.

He, of course, is speaking from within his own field, where he was very much an innovator and a leader. Many inventors, however, do not develop their inventions: they leave that to others. Edmund Hargreaves, for instance, solved the problem of flight: but he never flew. The Wright brothers did that, using Hargreaves' ideas. Nor is there anything wrong with following; if everybody was a leader, would there be any followers? We depend upon others.

3) Every adversity, every failure, every heartache, carries with it an equal or greater benefit. Napoleon Hill.

It might take a lot of faith and hope to see this, especially at the time of a disaster. I cannot imagine this being of much comfort to someone who has just watched his house burn to the ground in a bushfire, or who has just been told that her son has died in a motor accident. There is the story of Thomas Edison watching his laboratory burn down, destroying years of research. He called his wife and son to witness it. "Isn't this wonderful: there go all my mistakes, so that now I can begin anew." It takes a lot of courage too.

4) Four beautiful thoughts on life:
   1) Look back and get experience.
   2) Look forward and see hope.
   3) Look around and find reality.
   4) Look within and find yourself.

There is that hope again: it just keeps cropping up when we talk about the future. I think the third and fourth of those interact, in that we also find reality within ourselves, and we also find ourselves in our reactions to the world around us, and especially in our relationship with God.

5) Existence would be intolerable if we were never to dream.

Again, no author was given. Dreaming of what could be better goes hand in hand with hoping that it will be.

6) We have to do the best we can; this is our sacred human responsibility. Albert Einstein.

Indeed, the real sin is not failure, but not trying. Jesus too has something to say about this, in his parable of the man who buried his master's talent Lk 19/11-27. The man is condemned because he did nothing with his master's money.

7) I live in a small house: but my window looks out on a large world. Confucius.

It is good to see Confucius getting a guernsey, China's greatest sage. His words really need to be heeded here in China, where too often the attitude is just the opposite: "I live in a large house: but my window looks out on a small world." Too often here, the attitude seems to be that the rest of the world is but an adjunct to China. Often for instance, students will say that their aim is to work for the glory of the motherland, but I have yet to meet one who wants to make the world a better place.

8) People who change after change will survive. People who change with the change will succeed. People who cause the change will lead.

This caption was accompanied by photographs of Mahatma Gandhi, Nelson Mandela, Abraham Lincoln and Margaret Thatcher. What an interesting combination of people. The inclusion of Thatcher is a surprise, at least to me. Gandhi is arguably the greatest figure of the 20th century.

As an aside, at times I would ask my students who were the greatest figures of the 20th century. Invariably I would get Mao Zedong, Zhou Enlai, Deng Xiao Peng etc.: in other words there would not be a single person who was not Chinese.

9) Don't let the noise of other's opinions drive out your own inner voice. And most important, have the courage to follow your heart and intuition. They somehow already know what you truly want to become. Everything else is secondary. Steve Jobs.

I guess this is what Steve Jobs did himself. We still need to listen to others; if we do not, then we are just pig headed.

10) Life is too important to be taken seriously. Oscar Wilde.

This is typical of Wilde, a man who loved the bon mot, and for whom the turn of phrase was more important than the content. There is the story of him at a party where he heard a lady say something very pithy and clever. "Oh I wish I had said that," said Wilde, to which the lady replied, "You will." Consequently a lot of what he wrote is nothing more than light hearted fun and not to be taken seriously. And that is good. I like him. Some of his short stories and plays are really good, but my three favourites are "The Importance of Being Earnest", "Lady Windemere's fan" and "The picture of Dorian Grey". Yet he is not all froth and bubble, as this quote illustrates. We do need to be able to laugh at ourselves. A sense of humour is essential for a realistic view of ourselves and to get a more balanced perspective on life.

You may have noticed that some people have been quoted more than once—like Steve Jobs and Albert Einstein—while other quotes have no known author. My own name—sadly—does not appear even once! One might wonder why these particular people were chosen. Einstein, for instance, was a great scientist, possibly the greatest ever, but does that make him an authority on everything else? The same might be argued with regard to Steve Jobs: a high profile person, yes, but does this mean he knows the secret to life?

My take is that when it comes to living, everyone is an expert, and anyone can come up with a statement based upon his/her own experience of life, a word of wisdom with which others can relate. Now hang on a minute, as I just try to come up with my word of wisdom … I know it is here somewhere … now where did I put it? … Oh well, next time.

In photograph 17, on the far left, one can just see the top of this international building where I was working and where you will find these quotations.

2.5: Upper Campus

2.5.1: Layout

The road from the front eastern gate goes past the Alliance Française building where it begins to climb to the upper campus, first over the railway line. One can walk up the road, or take the more direct route by climbing the more than 300 steps. The route up is lined with accommodation buildings for both staff and students.

Photo 18: Steps leading from the upper to the lower campus

Up top there is the oval, which is used for soccer, athletics and the military. There are tennis and basketball courts next to it, plus many tables for table tennis set up between buildings. There are, of course, plenty of buildings for student accommodation, plus classroom blocks, shops, a dining room, a library and other open areas, including "alphabet park", which is lined by a wall sporting the letters of the (English) alphabet. The stones of this wall have sayings from significant figures in human history, in many different languages. I like it.

From the top of the road, one could look down on the city below and quite a sight it is. I will never forget my first view. The sides of the mountain were bathed in greenery, while down below was a forest, but not a forest of trees: it was a forest of high rise buildings, all around the 25 to 30 storey mark. I had never seen anything like it. This is how you accommodate about 17 million people. Cf. photograph 19. You notice too how the atmosphere is not too clean.

Photo 19: Shapingba from Gele Shan

Meanwhile, construction was ongoing for further development still higher up the mountain. A university town was at this time being built further out along metro line 1 (Da Xue Cheng), with other universities planning to move out, including the Law University next door. The local authorities were keen to retain SISU for economic as well as prestige reasons. Hence they were giving them some financial incentive. Even so, this new development was costing heaps.

2.5.2 The Military

The oval, as I said, was used not only for sport but also for the military. An army base was situated nearby, just the other side of the Law University. Another military base was not far away on the opposite side. Military training is compulsory for all first year students for the first three weeks of the new academic year in September, and the oval is where they train.

I guess all this is necessary, just in case Upper Volta decides to invade. These first year students are all dressed in immaculate, new military uniforms, in contrast to the rather shaggy military shirts worn by the *bang bangs,* the stick carriers on the streets. It seems a little incongruous that underneath their military caps you do not see hardened veterans of many campaigns, but baby faces. They can be seen on the university oval doing their drills, 30 or so squads, of about 50 to 100 in each. The military is held in high esteem, being the means by which the empire has expanded over the millennia: they can do no wrong. They even have their own TV channel.

In 2012 a notice was put up informing us that this training would culminate in a parade on the university oval. It is wonderful that we were actually informed beforehand and that we would be welcome. I went, but I saw only one other overseas teacher present. There were not many students present either, perhaps 200, apart, of course, from the roughly 3,000 first year students on parade.

At 9.00 a.m. the review began, with the troops in serried ranks lined up in two groups. The first group, comprising 20 squads of around 100 cadets in each squad, was in the centre of the oval, while the remaining 10 squads were on the far side. I arrived early and took a place in the stands, below the seats reserved for the bigwigs, until the army arrived, whereupon I moved to the next row. These soldiers had been the instructors over the previous four weeks.

Proceedings began with the playing of the national anthem, everybody standing bolt upright. This was followed by the march-past. Each of the 20 squads on the oval marched past the reviewing stand, breaking into the goose-step for about 50 metres. For me, the goose-step reminds me of Fascism: the march of the dictators, who of course, continue to rule here. The cadets did it quite well, and in fact the whole parade went off very well indeed. Mass performances are a forte of Chinese society.

Photo 20: cadets goose-stepping

The cadets then sat on the running track, while a number of events took place in the centre of the oval. A band played while performing quite a few complicated manoeuvres: it looked great. This was followed by the obligatory Kung-fu, much to the delight of the spectators. Martial arts are really big in this country, featuring in many TV productions and films. Finally, the remaining troops from the side of the oval swung into action. These were all wearing white gloves, which stood out as they performed their various manoeuvres. It looked quite spectacular. Their final manoeuvre spelled out **C H I N A,** which gives a clue as to what all this is really about. I was just surprised that they used the English spelling rather than the Chinese characters.

An awards ceremony completed the proceedings. As the squad numbers were read out those mentioned would clap. Award winners then lined up at the front, before receiving their certificates from the VIPs, just behind me. Then it was dispersal. The whole parade had lasted about 1 ½ hours. But what is it all about?

In this country military training is compulsory. Here we had 3,000 students in one university, in one city. There were no guns involved, apart from side arms, but I imagine it would not take long to learn how to shoot. More importantly, these young people have learnt unquestioning obedience. The armed forces in China number about 5 million, but this is without counting the reserves, and without counting those involved in cyber espionage. This country could conceivably put some 500 million troops into the field. What other country can do that? It was Mao Zedong who remarked that he did not care if he had 3 million casualties in war, as he could simply replace them with 3 million more; and replace these with 3 million more. "America cannot do this." Upper Volta take note. China wants to be a great military power: it already is.

There is, however, another reason for all this training, and it has to do with the internal situation. After the 1989 Tian-an Men Square massacre, military training was increased from one month to three. The idea was to create an obedient population, with no criticism of the status quo. As one local put it, "It is a form of brainwashing." The central authorities are very jealous of their position and will brook no opposition whatsoever. At this time they were a little nervous, with a leadership changeover looming for the following month and a scandal in this particular city of Chongqing. You may know that our erstwhile police chief had just been sentenced to 15 years gaol; amongst other offences he visited the American consulate in Chengdu without permission. Meanwhile, his erstwhile boss, the former secretary of the CP here, Bo Xilai, has been stripped of his membership and was awaiting trial on corruption charges with sexual misconduct thrown in as well. His wife had been sentenced to prison for life for murder. Now Bo Xilai's rival has been appointed emperor for life.

It is all most serious, an attitude reflected in the professional military personnel responsible for training these cadets. In the reviewing stand I was sitting immediately in front of them. They were sitting bolt upright, hands on knees, not a smile amongst the lot of them. I turned around to take a photograph of them. And got away with it. Here it is—photograph 21 showing their ramrod straight postures and the completely serious expression on their faces. Wow! Behind them cadets were receiving awards, so maybe the army thought I was more interested in them.

Photo 21: Life is no joke

We were living not only not in interesting times but also in an interesting city.

2.6: My Apartment

For three years I had been living in somewhat substandard accommodation in Tongren, before coming to SISU. Upon arrival I was shown my new home, a home which would remain so for the next three years. It was situated on the second floor of a building located within a compound reserved for foreign teachers. Part of the reason for this was to limit contact with the locals, especially the students, for fear we would "contaminate" them, which means introduce ideas inimical to Communist Party dominance. Heaven forbid!

As I was shown through the apartment, my guide seemed somewhat anxious that I would be pleased. My goodness: there was no need to worry. It was clean and spacious, without mould on the wall—which I had in my previous apartment in Tongren. I had a TV set which worked, electricity throughout, hot water, a Western toilet, even a bath, none of which I had in Tongren. I even had two verandas, a small one outside the kitchen, and a larger L-shaped one outside my bedroom and lounge room, meaning I had veranda on three sides. The kitchen was spacious and well-appointed with a gas stove, refrigerator and cupboards for pots, pans etc. Wonderful!

For a while my stove was been giving me problems. Two spots were getting really hot, so there must have been some sort of leakage. This could be dangerous. One night, after I had finished cooking, the spark plug which ignites the gas would not stop sparking. I called the workman and he took the stove away to get it fixed. Later he returned with another stove. The lady who lived in the apartment above me complained that she had leaking water and maybe other problems, so she had been shifted, leaving her apartment empty. In came the workman carrying her stove. Wonderful, except that it was too big to fit—not much, mind you, just a smidgeon—but still too big. This did not stop our worthy tradesman from using considerable force, all to no avail; it is a wonder the stove did not break. Next day our second workman turned up with my old stove. Well, we know it fits, but will it work properly? He told me that the two hot spots had been fixed, but that the starter no longer worked. I could still cook, but I needed to light the gas with a match or a lighter, not really a major problem. I am sure our cavemen ancestors had bigger problems in trying to light their cooking fires.

Even though I am not much of a cook, I do enjoy cooking, with my offerings being eminently palatable—well I think so. Nor far away in Lieshimu there is a wet market for buying fruit and vegetables. There are also two supermarkets, so that one can buy the vast majority of one's supplies close by; but not all, not

Western foods such as good cheeses, wines and cereals. There were little things the university was doing to look after us expatriates which I appreciated. One of these was to provide a bus every month or so during the semester to take us to Metro, a German owned supermarket, where we could buy goods we could not buy elsewhere. One spends more money, of course. For Christmas 2012 I treated myself to a bottle of Benedictine to share with friends; that really is a luxury. I wondered if SISU was getting any money from Metro?—perhaps a proportion of what we were spending. One lady was a shopaholic, spending enormous amounts of money on unnecessary goods—and she was using my card. Metro has this curious system, whereby you cannot shop unless you have a membership card, even though we used to swap them around, lending them to people who did not have one. Thank you SISU.

Right opposite my apartment is a tennis court, which I used from time to time. It was in frequent use, necessitating the need to book a timeslot.

Beside the tennis court is a restaurant, called the Teachers' Restaurant for some reason. Here they provided very good meals for a reasonable price, although if one was eating alone you needed to order few dishes as the individual dishes were meant for a group. Upon arrival I was given a number of meal tickets to tide me over until I could buy my own supplies: fantastic. Using just one a day meant they lasted me a week. Formal dinners would also be held in this restaurant, such as when we had guests from outside. We also had birthday celebrations here. All in all the contrast with the niggardly attitude of Tongren University was a stark contrast. I felt that I was truly welcome, not tolerated as an unfortunate but necessary evil.

The veranda, as is common for Chinese apartments, had rails attached to the ceiling. And it was here that I would hang my weekly laundry. The building did have a dryer, but I rarely used it for environmental reasons. Once I was staying in a youth hostel in Phoenix, Arizona. I was talking with the manager, an English lady, when a young American man came up to ask her where the dryer was located. He had found the laundry, but not the dryer. She rolled her eyes in amazement, while pointing above. Goodness, it was so hot and dry that as soon as you hung your clothes on the line it was almost time to bring them in again. I bought some bread for sandwiches, but in no time all the moisture was sucked out of it, so that it simply crumbled. I used these crumbs to cook with eggs. Why do we waste so much electricity, especially when Global Warming is so catastrophic? On rare occasions in Chongqing I did use the dryer, but this was only in the depths of winter, when one's laundry could hang on the line for days and still be wet.

My apartment also boasted a reverse cycle air conditioner—essential in a climate which had some very hot days in summers and very cold days in winter. Even so I would use it as little as possible. Another great boon was that they would give us an allowance of electricity, water and gas; anything over this we would pay ourselves. On one occasion I went to pay my excess over a winter, when I happened to notice the bill for another teacher, residing in the same building: he/she had racked up over 800 Yuan, while my bill came to about 6 Yuan, or just over a dollar; not bad for a whole winter. I managed this by carefully using the heater (in winter) or air conditioning (in summer) only at crucial times during the day. I never heated my bedroom, as I had an electric blanket. Wonderful.

Whenever I had guests staying, they would take the bed, while I would sleep on the couch, which was so small that I could never get a good night's sleep—and I am no giant. Only one guest slept on this couch while I took the bed, and that was one of my beautiful students from Tongren, Erica. She came with me to make sure I was settled in, helping clean the apartment and being invaluable in many other ways. Thank you: she is wonderful. She insisted on taking the couch, telling me in the morning how comfortable it was; admittedly, she is petite in stature.

Photograph 22 shows this couch, where I spent much of my time, eating, preparing classes, and relaxing. It also shows some of my students—April, Amber, Li, Han, Remon and Jerry—relaxing on this couch. I tended to decorate my apartment with some of my photographs plus a reproduction of a Chinese painting, which another student had given to me.

Photo 22: students relaxing in my apartment

In April the weather can be changeable as we come from winter into summer. It could be quite warm during the day, with the temperature in the high twenties, followed by thunderstorms at night even some hail. Whether this was the cause or not, I do not know, but when I got up one Saturday morning, I had no electricity. These days we are so dependent on electric power, especially for my fridge: I did not want my food going bad. I used my gas stove to heat water for my breakfast coffee, so that was not a problem. Mysteriously I seemed to have been the only one affected, so I checked the fuse box, but all seemed to be in order. In any case at 10.00 a.m., the power came back on again—just like that.

Meanwhile, workmen were outside our building attempting to clear a drain. Water had overflowed, flooding the area outside our steps, so that if you wished to leave the building, you would have to wade through a stinking, filthy lake—not very pleasant; or you could leap across, but from a standing start you certainly would create a new world record; and then you would need to get back in again. I remained in my apartment for most of the day, venturing out for my daily walk during the afternoon. To accomplish this, I used the apartment below me, entering from the stairwell, exiting via his front door, away from the smelly lake. Thanks Cyril.

If all of the above seems just a little too simple, let me introduce a complication: Cyril had trouble opening his inside door. There were in fact two locks, one of which could only be opened from the outside while the other could only be opened from the inside. So we had fun throwing and catching his keys from my balcony to him and vice versa. You cannot have life being too simple: where would all the fun be?

This was, however, not the end of the morning's problems, as my shower rose broke. Here I was having my shower, revelling in the one of the simple pleasures of life, when "whooomp"—off shot the shower head, clattering onto the floor. I reattached it—as you would—then another "whooomp" ensued, and off it flew again. I reported this to the maintenance man, who checked it out and away he went. Several hours later he returned with a new shower rose. Wonderful. Everything breaks down eventually. The trick is to get it back up and running again, and in this university they were pretty good at doing that quickly—well, most of the time. Thank you.

I was therefore happy with my apartment. It was a little more luxurious than student dormitories. At this point, let me make myself abundantly clear: I am referring to the male dormitories, because I never set foot in any female dormitory, although I imagine that the standards would be similar. Photograph 23 shows two students—male of course—in their room. There is not a great deal of space. Other dormitories house more students. The student on the left was about six years older than his classmates, because he had been a policeman for some years before enrolling. He was forced to leave the police force after an unfortunate incident. While attempting to arrest a drug dealer he was stabbed several times in the abdomen; he was lucky to survive the attack. He showed me his wounds and they were ghastly. Why do people do these terrible things? Why do people take drugs?

Photo 23: a male dormitory

On a lighter note, at times I would give anagrams to my students to work out. One of my favourites is "dormitory". If you switch the letters around you get "dirty room". In some cases, most apt, although the students always maintained that they kept their rooms clean.

2.7: A Tale of Tongs

In Tongren I had a pair of metal tongs, which was very useful in the kitchen, as they could grasp food, especially hot food, in transferring, for instance, newly cooked food from a saucepan to my plate. The night before I left Tongren, I had everything packed away, including the tongs, when I found that I needed them for my evening meal, so I took them out again and used them, but after washing up, I did not repack them, leaving them in the kitchen. I was assuming that my new apartment in Chongqing would come equipped with kitchen utensils: plates, cups, dishes, pots and pans, frying pans etc.—including tongs—but this was not the case. While indeed my spacious apartment was fully furnished, it contained nothing whatsoever in the kitchen. Apparently what happens is that as soon as someone leaves, the cleaners literally "clean out" the apartment, leaving nothing for the new tenant.

I regretted leaving behind so many of my personal kitchen items, including my tongs, which I had bought myself. Not to worry: this is Chongqing, a much bigger city of some 17 million people, or thereabouts, so I felt sure I could just wander down the road and buy some tongs—and everything else—virtually anywhere. Not so. I did purchase quite a few items, but not tongs. Never mind, as not too far away in Shapingba there is a large French supermarket called Carrefour; surely they would have tongs. They did not.

So I went back to TONG-ren! Mind you, I did not return simply to retrieve my tongs, as I had other unfinished business to attend to. After two days I returned to Chongqing, carrying many items from my old apartment which belonged to me and not to the university—including those precious metal tongs. So now I was happy.

End of story? Well, not quite. You are not going to believe this, but after only a couple of weeks, they broke. Oh no! The pin holding the two arms together came out. You could still use them, except that the two arms no longer met, meaning it was very difficult to pick anything up. They were next to useless.

What a pity, but never fear, as there is another large German supermarket, called Metro, which is even better, and the university lays on a bus for us teachers from overseas to go shopping there on the last Friday of most months. It takes about 35 minutes in the bus to get there. At the end of September, 2011, I checked it out—but sadly, no tongs. Nevertheless I did buy other valuable goods, such as wine and cheese. Life however is never perfect, so you soldier on doing the best you can. There is a saying: "If something is worth doing then it is worth doing well." I will not argue with that. G. K. Chesterton in his usual habit of turning things on their head, declared: "If something is worth doing, then it is worth doing badly." What on earth does he mean? He means that in practice we must settle for the less than perfect. I am not a good cook, but I do the best I can—it is worth trying. If it comes to that, I do not consider myself to be a particularly good teacher either. It is just something that I have been asked to do, and I have done it from year to year, thinking that it is temporary, and I will soon go off and do full time what Melchizedeks do. Yet I ended up spending decades in the classroom, doing the best I could.

At the beginning of October, 2011, I went to Hangzhou in Zhejiang Province for a week, and there visited that city's Metro store, where I bought a few items, but alas no tongs.

At the end of October, we again returned to Metro, the one in Chongqing, and this time I spent even more money buying wine, cheese, cereal, tins of tuna and other sundry items that you cannot get elsewhere. And I found tongs! They were not, however, the metal ones I had been using—they were plastic. But they are tongs. Wonderful—except that they could melt in heat, so you do not use them to take chips out of hot oil. Now I was a happy little Vegemite. All was well—except that I still had to wrestle with my broken metal tongs when dealing with very hot food.

One of the things I have learnt over the years, especially when living overseas, is to appreciate the simple things in life, things we might otherwise take for granted. All things are precious and should be valued. I do like the American idea of Thanksgiving. Maybe we all need something similar in our own cultures. We say Grace before meals, to thank God for the food provided, and we even ask God to bless the cook, but do we ever stop and thank God for the means used to cook that food—such as the fuel and the utensils? Probably not.

On Sundays, we attend Eucharist, a wonderful word which means "thanksgiving", wherein we do thank God for all the gifts given to us, as well as the human contribution. This is the meaning of the Offertory where we bring up bread, wine and make a monetary contribution, representing our work. These gifts are transformed into the Body and Blood of Christ. Notice that I said "Christ" not "Jesus", as it is broader than one man, including as it does the whole of the Body of Christ, the Church. Through this, all these common things in our lives are sanctified. All of Nature is sanctified through Christ. We make a point of this when we talk about "holy water", but it is not only water which is made holy: all creation is.

Now you see just how important and valuable those tongs are. And so is "every-tong" else. Thank you, Lord.

"EXTRA, EXTRA, READ ALL ABOUT IT. LATEST NEWS ON TONGS", as a newsboy may have yelled on a street corner in a previous generation. If you thought the story on tongs was complete, read on.

There were two men deputed by the university to look after the upkeep of our building with an office downstairs. I had occasion to ask them to fix my gas stove, as I have already reported; you do not fool around with leaking gas. While the workmen were doing their job, I asked them if they could also fix my tongs. They examined the tongs closely before getting to work. Their first step surprised me: they took out the second pin which held the tongs together. Now I had two pieces of metal; in fact three, as a ring holding the two together made the third. Now what? For the next 30 minutes, they proceeded to place a single length of metal through the two holes, in place of the two that had been there before. They gave them back to me to inspect.

Well, there were still two problems. Firstly, the third piece would not fit over the end, and secondly, there was no spring to separate the two arms. They took them back and had another look, considering what to do, before getting to work again. It was sometime later before they had solved both problems. Another piece of steel winding around the connecting pin acted as the spring. The job was done, and expertly so. As for the piece that keeps the two arms together, the secret is to put that on first.

Needless to say I was very happy with the result. Now these men are paid by the university to fix appliances etc. belonging to the apartment—like my stove—but I was sure that this did not cover personal items like tongs. Yet they made it plain that they wanted no money for their efforts, even though it took both of them the best part of an hour. I could see moreover that they themselves were mightily pleased with their efforts. There is a degree of satisfaction in working through a problem to a successful conclusion. Nevertheless, I wanted to do something for them, so presented them with a can of beer each. With this, they were delighted. We had a win—win situation here. Not only did I have my tongs fixed, but these men were feeling good and we had established good relations. This is so important.

When I first arrived in August 2011, I had a load of luggage to move up to my apartment, so I asked one of these men to help. This he did, but on that occasion he asked for payment of 10 Yuan, which I duly handed over. I did not argue. Erica was with me and I could see she was not happy, as this was somewhat exorbitant for the service rendered. I have a sneaking suspicion that if this situation were to arise after the tongs incident, he would not be asking for any payment. We had established *guanxi*. In the long term I think that 10 Yuan was well spent. Human relations are more important than money.

2.8: Rudolf

At Christmas time, 2011, my nice comfortable apartment was so attractive, that I found myself with a companion: a rat. No, no, no, this is not a confession, and I did not say "I am a rat"; rather, I had a rat. Or maybe he/she had me. Probably the latter, since—and this is a rather embarrassing admission—this rat was cleverer than I am.

A man living two floors above me had a rat in his apartment, apparently ensconced in his heater: not a bad place to be in winter. He succeeded in getting rid of it. Upon which the little critter decided to take up his/her abode in my apartment. Thanks mate. Rudolf the Rat—we will call him this from now on, even though I do not really know his sex, nor even his rat name, but since he appeared just before Christmas, Rudolf seemed appropriate. He would raid my kitchen during the night, exhibiting a partiality to bananas, meaning that I needed to buy bananas for two. The other Rudolf, of course—you know the reindeer one—finds very few bananas growing at the North Pole, so has to make do with lichen. And my rat's name is definitely not Ben. It might be OK for Michael Jackson to have had a pet rat as his friend, but I draw the line. I doubt if Michael Jackson really had many other true friends.

How was Rudolf getting in? Therein lies the problem; I did say he was cleverer than I am. While Rudolf the reindeer might have a bright nose, Rudolf the rat had a bright mind. I found four holes: three in the kitchen and one in my living room. I blocked off two in the kitchen, the others taking a little more time. Each night I would close my kitchen door, as I am quite sure that the rat could not open doors—or at least I did not think he could. I tried putting my fruit on top of the fridge. Now rats cannot climb up on top of fridges, can they? Rudolf could. He did have a nibble at a persimmon and an apple, but bananas were definitely his preference. How does he get there? Maybe he can climb up the electric lead, so I shifted the fridge away from the wall, as the power point is up high.

He climbed onto my living room table, so I needed to ensure that there were no clothes or anything else nearby that he could use to climb up. Yet I even found his calling cards behind books, high up on my bookcase. How did he get up there? Mystery. I also tied up my rubbish each night, so that he could not drag rubbish over the floor. He might be clever, but he was not very tidy. I must say that he was satisfied with one banana a night. I mean he was not chewing a bit out of this one and a bit out of that one, as birds do with fruit hanging on a tree.

He must have had a good Mummy. "Rudolf, don't be greedy. You are not getting anything else till you finish what is already on your plate!"

Rudolf also had a liking for paper towels. Whenever I inadvertently left a paper towel out, in the morning it was gone. Where did it go? Now I am quite, quite sure that they did not take off by themselves, and I am equally quite, quite sure that Rudolf had a lot to do with it. Was he that hungry that he was eating them?—they probably would not taste very nice without a pinch of salt, and being a Chongqing rat you would think he would like some hot spice as well. Or was he making a comfortable lining for a nest somewhere? Goodness, is Rudolf really Rudolfa?

One kitchen hole was on top of the pipe which takes exhaust fumes from the stove. The opening was small, so our furry friend had been gnawing away at the Styrofoam to make it larger, thus making a mess of my floor as well. Now this flue is high up. He could jump down easily enough, but how did he get back up again? Could he jump vertically into the air to a height of 1 metre? From other evidence I think he could. Not only was he clever, but he was also very athletic. There was an added problem: How did he get into the flue from the outside, as the opening is very high up a tiled wall? I did not think it possible, but there was another hole into the ceiling, his more probable entry point. I blocked this off with a piece of wallpaper.

For six days I was without internet access. I was not getting much help from the university. "Oh it's not just your problem: it's a campus problem. Just wait" I did, then called again. "OK, we'll send someone around but right now they are busy." Again I waited. They arrived eventually and soon had the problem fixed—but what caused this problem? Now I assure you that the answer is no laughing matter. Is everybody the sole of sobriety? Good. Rudolf ate through the cable. Yep. Rats eat plastic—and most everything else, although I still think he prefers bananas.

How could I get rid of him/her/them? What is the address of that Pied Piper? Of course I would have to pay him. It would not be a good idea not to pay him. I wonder how many guilders he would want. He would not have to walk far, as here we are living between the two rivers, with the Yangtze to the south and the Jia Ling much closer to the north, about 20 minutes' walk away, though possibly a little longer if you are playing your flute and waiting for some of the laggards to catch up.

Someone suggested that I use mothballs. I did not know that rats were akin to moths, but I'll try anything. I placed a moth ball at each of the entrance holes, and in cupboards, but they did not appear to be making any difference. If rats are supposed to run away from moth balls, then someone neglected to tell my furry friend. No, I thought that the best option was to seal up all holes so that he could not get in. Then maybe he would go back upstairs. To this end, I sealed up one hole with tough plastic, another hole with wallpaper, while workmen came in to cover another hole with wire gauze, while the fourth and largest hole they sealed with cement. Now I was not rash enough to claim that we had beaten him, bearing in mind how clever and athletic Rudolf was, but at least we were making life a little more challenging for him. I eagerly awaited results.

What happened next? One night I walked into my kitchen and there he was. Now it would have been friendly to get properly acquainted, but it seems Rudolf was not in a friendly mood that night, as he took off like greased lightning, without even saying "Hello". But he made a mistake: my clever friend did something stupid. He bolted straight for the outside kitchen door, which leads onto a small balcony. Ah, ah, so that's how he was getting in. I called the workmen back to attach a plank of wood to the bottom of the door on the outside, but upon inspection I found that the wood was not long enough, leaving a small hole. Once again the workmen came in, and this time fixed another strip of wood to the inside of the door at the bottom.

That night, I deliberately left out a banana, and did not cover my rubbish. Could he still get in? He could. Amazing. So I called the workman again, and this time they made the inside strip of wood lower, all but touching the floor. As well, I rolled up some plastic and pushed it along the underside of the door. We are certainly increasing his challenges.

More than that: we won. No longer did I see Rudolf in my apartment.

One of my neighbours reported the presence of a rat in her apartment. So far, Rudolf had only been frequenting the apartments of male occupants, but now he visited an apartment occupied by a woman. I was happy; she was not. In fact she shrieked, hollered and yelled, demanding that the university give her another apartment, as far away as possible, which they did, and she moved further up the hill. Before you could say "Rudolf the red nosed reindeer", she was gone: not the rat—the woman.

I cannot understand it. I mean, Rudolf was such a friendly rat. He was also very shy, so sorry, but no photograph.

2.9: Christmas

I arrived in Chongqing in August, 2011, but I was not there for Christmas, as I travelled down to Zunyi in Guizhou Province to celebrate Christmas with some of my former students, whom I had taught in Tongren—and that was great. But I was in town for Christmas in 2012. Christmas 2013 would be different, yet wherever you are there is something very special about this feast. It is a time when peace, joy and goodwill are in the air, even in China which does not have a Christian tradition. It really is a world festival, not just Middle Eastern and certainly not just European, although each region has its own mode of celebration. In Australia, of course, it is summer, so we do not have sleigh bells in the snow, and nor do we dream of a white Christmas. Instead we have outside barbecues, with salads, washed down with plenty of liquid amber, and for seaside folk, we like to laze on the beach. It is also very much a family affair: family members will gather from quite long distances to be together, especially for Christmas dinner, in much the same way as Chinese families gather for Spring Festival. So what was it like in Chongqing?

The local Catholic parish got into the spirit by holding a two hour concert on Christmas Eve. Instead of hiring well known international artists, the local parishioners entertained each other, and with great success. Curiously most of the participants were women, with the men prominent by their absence: I have no idea why. The acts consisted of either singing or dancing, sometimes solos, but in this highly gregarious society, mostly in groups. As one would expect the level of talent might not have been the highest, but what they lacked up for in expertise—and frankly you would find more grace in a herd of rhinos than in some of the middle aged women cavorting around the sanctuary—they made up for with panache. Some of the women danced many times, in different costumes. It was great, and truly in the spirit of Christmas. One female dancer was really good, and I could see from the reaction that the congregation was also pleasantly surprised. Another female singer has a wonderful voice: I could have listened to her all afternoon. We did indeed have some quality.

In the evening, some of us were invited to an apartment, belonging to one of the teachers. In all 26 of us mixed, talked, drank, ate and had a good time. Thank you to the organisers. We were certainly an international bunch, with many countries being represented, with yours truly being the only Aussie. Everyone was supposed to bring a gift which was placed in a pile, then at random each person was given a gift. I scored an electric hand warmer. I had not seen them in

Australia but they are popular here. It is basically a hot water bottle, with an electric cord attached, so that all you have to do is plug it into a socket to warm up your water. I found it to be a godsend, not to warm my hands, but to warm my feet while I was sitting at my desk. Thank you to whomever bought it.

When I got back home after the party, I found that I had left my mobile phone behind: not to worry, but as it was very late (read "early"), I thought I would pick it up next day. I didn't. It had walked. I waited a week, thinking surely somebody would return it, but nobody did. What a nuisance: not only had I lost some photos, but I had lost all my contacts, not to mention the 200 Yuan still sitting in my account. The photographs were not all that important, but the phone numbers were.

On the following Monday I received a visit from the lovely Kate, one of my former students from Tongren. She helped me no end, not only in purchasing a new phone, but also in getting my old number back, which therefore meant I still had that 200 Yuan in my account. Thank you Kate. It is remarkable how God works. This new phone, incidentally, was a Nokia, identical to the one which had walked. They are hardy: I dropped my former phone down a mountain side—yet still it worked; it just had a few scratches and possibly a headache.

On Christmas Eve, we celebrated our own liturgy in my apartment, and on Christmas Day, a number of us shared Christmas dinner in the foreign teachers' dining room. The food was very good and quite inexpensive. It was all very enjoyable, especially when washed down with an eminently potable red. We were given a holiday on Christmas Day, but my Tuesday classes had actually finished the week before anyway, so it was immaterial for me. The university did its part by giving us foreign teachers the day off and by putting up decorations. By night the trees were festooned with lights, looking very pretty. There was also a Christmas tree outside our building with flashing lights—as in photograph 24. Last year they also gave us a significant gift, but not this year.

For me personally, Christmas includes Boxing Day, and this means the traditional Boxing Day test. For you ignoramuses out there, this is a cricket match played at the Melbourne Cricket Ground (MCG) over five days, between Australia and some other country. This year it was Sri Lanka. For those interested, Australia won the match inside of three days. This was the second in a three match series. Australia had won the first match, so there was only the third to come. For me, Christmas still means summer, and summer means cricket.

Photo 24: the door to our apartment building at Christmas

2.10: Sport

Sport is an important part of life. In Chapter 8 I have included student writings on this topic.

Sports facilities within the university were excellent. On the lower campus there were basketball, tennis and badminton courts, all of which were in good use. There was also a swimming pool, which was not in good use. In the summer I loved to use it, on occasions even swimming with the swimming squad. I might add that I was not particularly impressed with their standard. On one occasion I was suitably impressed by a girl doing the butterfly with good style—well, for about 30 metres; then she stopped cold, dead in her tracks, finished, not even swimming the length of the pool. Mind you, the butterfly is a most exhausting stroke—at least for me, and presumably for her. Sadly I could not swim during my final summer at the university because they were demolishing the pool! Why? I was most unimpressed. There was a new pool on the upper campus, but only about 20 metres in length, and when I tried to swim there was told that I was not welcome. Goodness.

Photo 25: university pool—before demolition

Every college I have been involved with has its athletics meeting, usually held in November. In 2012 November was too wet, resulting in a transfer of the meeting until the following April when the weather was not only dryer but also warmer. It did rain, but only at night. The sports were held over Thursday, Friday and Saturday of one week. I was still wearing three layers of clothing on Thursday, down to two on Friday, but by Saturday it had become quite hot: shorts and T-shirt.

Some students took part; most did not. Some students watched; most did not. Some classes were cancelled; most were not. As you may gather, these athletic carnivals were not exactly the highlight of the year. I am sure that some of the athletes were taking it seriously and actually trained, but most did not. Consequently this was not likely to be a breeding ground for future Olympic champions, a fact reflected in some of the events. While some of the more traditional Olympic events were included, such as the 100 metres, other events were of a far more casual nature.

The opening ceremony was spectacular and colourful, in the usual manner. Some forty odd groups, representing classes, schools or programmes, paraded around the oval before lining up in the centre. Their clothing consisted of colourful uniforms, different for each group. The group which I was having most to do with wore tracksuits, black and yellow in colour and in an attractive design. At least I thought so. The girls did not agree, and in fact one could not get hers off fast enough after the opening parade. Teams of girls exhibited a display of rhythmic dancing in the centre of the oval after the march past, something you would not find in Australia. Most of the students at this university were in fact girls.

The rest of Thursday was given over to track and field. In usual fashion, there were few events. One can see that little preparation had gone into training; in many cases none whatsoever. It is not at all a serious competition. One often saw the first lap of a race run very fast, with significant slowing down thereafter. Still it is all a good exercise in bonding: not just students with each other, but also with staff, at any rate for those who bothered to attend.

Friday was mostly given over to novelty events. Some of these were a little unusual.

1. Competitors were required to kick a soccer ball into a goal; admittedly the opening was somewhat smaller than the usual, but while I was watching, nobody—but nobody—managed to kick it in.
2. Tennis. No, the participants did not play five set marathons: they just served. Yep, that's it. Nor it did not matter how they did it, so long as they lobbed a tennis ball—and yes, they did in fact use a tennis ball and a tennis racquet—into the service area. If they succeeded they were given a tick and the next "competitor" fronts up.
3. Basketball. Not surprisingly, the aim here is to throw a basketball through a hoop: well, done—another tick.
4. Volleyball. Now we will see how really good you are, as skill is required. A line of people in turn must bump the ball, using their wrists, back to a person standing in front.
5. Skipping, and I must confess that I had never before seen it performed like this. Two students would hold the rope while their classmates would

skip through one by one, do a loop then return. I wondered how long they could keep this up. Other events included basketball, volleyball and badminton.

More track events followed in the afternoon on the oval. I might add that it is about a ten minute walk up the hill to the oval, remembering the university is built on the slopes of Gele Shan, our local mountain. You can either walk up the road, or climb the 300 or so steps. David (from England) and I were particularly interested in our Lancaster students. Most did not bother to compete, but those who did had obviously had no preparation. Still, they tried. The proceedings concluded with the forty odd groups lining up in the middle of the oval, while presentations were made.

All in all it was a great two days. I do like watching athletics. I used to like participating too, but those days are gone. The pace of events was slow with events just happening. The air was damp and misty as befits the climate, but not actually raining. Photograph 26 shows the "athletes" on the oval, not racing but standing in class groups performing co-ordinated activities, which the Chinese are so good at.

Photo 26: sports' day

I like to watch tennis too and I like to play. For all my time in China prior to coming to Chongqing this had not been possible. In Tongren there were no courts available; curiously in Fuzhou there were courts built while I was there, but no equipment: odd. But in at SISU there are many courts, one of them situated right outside my apartment. I would watch the players from my balcony, some good, some not so good. Inevitably these days we had a woman grunter, which I hate. She was not as loud as some of the professionals but still off-putting. On at least one occasion I imitated her. "Ehhh!" she would yell. "Ehhh!" I would echo. She never got the point, strangely enough, yet I suppose she was doing it precisely so that she could win the point.

In September 2012 a new teacher arrived from the U.K and he also liked to play tennis. Beauty: I now had a partner. We just had to buy tennis racquets and balls. The racquets were cheap, costing only 160 Yuan (about $23), but the balls were expensive at about 90 Yuan for three. Then, in another store, we found much cheaper balls, at only 19 Yuan for three—or about one dollar each. Marvellous. You could hire a court at 20 Yuan an hour or part thereof, if you play in the afternoon, or 10 Yuan if you play in the morning.

Thus equipped on one Sunday afternoon John and I faced off with our new racquets and new balls. The former, I found were quite serviceable, so long as you are not playing in a competition, but there was a slight problem with the balls: they didn't bounce! They just sort of went "clunk". Now we knew why they were so cheap. Well, we hit most of them, though I refuse to be drawn on which part of the racquet I actually made contact. Towards the end we decided to see how l long we could extend our rallies, bearing in mind that not long before Djokovic and Murray had quite a few rallies in excess of 30 hits. We made it to 23. Nah, don't think we will join the professional circuit just yet. Fidelis, please note: sorry to have to tell you, that our personal long standing record of a 17 hit rally has been broken. Fidelis is one beautiful person who was my hitting partner when we were living in Chicago. For the past twelve years she had been working in Haiti.

In due course we were joined by two others, one from Korea, one from France. I could not believe how poor my tennis had become: the worst it had been since I was a child. In fact my ten year old self could probably have beaten the current version. That is what happens when you have not played for a while. We scheduled two games a week: Monday afternoon and Wednesday morning, one hour each time. I do so enjoy it when I actually hit a ball in the centre of the racquet, rare though that was at this time. I was hoping that in time I would reach the level of my 12 year old self!

At the end of one academic year I said goodbye to a student, but before doing so he told me that he plays tennis. "I like tennis too," says I. "Oh, what a pity that I have only found this out the day before I leave." He then stopped in some confusion—there's that word again—lots of confusion here. "What's up?"

"Oh, I shouldn't say this, but I thought you were too old!"

Thanks pal; when are you leaving?

Chapter 3: SISU Surrounds

3.1: Gele Shan

I found the district surrounding the university to be very interesting. It is mountain country, which is always interesting. Climbing the 2,000 or so steps to the top of Gele Shan is a popular pastime, especially on weekends, when many locals make the ascent for health reasons, both physical and psychological; it takes about 40 minutes. It is good to stretch one's legs. For the not so vigorous, there is a chair lift which operates on weekends. There is something attractive about mountains: betwixt Heaven and Earth, as it were, one can get a better perspective on life. On the top there is a village, enjoying a climate which is certainly more amenable in summer. There is also a hospital up top for infectious diseases and chest complaints—very suitable in this heavily polluted city.

One of my students invited his class—there were not many in the class—to a restaurant about half way up the mountain in order to celebrate her birthday. I was privileged to have been invited. The main dish was traditional style Chongqing *la zi ji,* or hot chicken. This dish was huge, and was placed in the middle of the table. All you could see was red chilli peppers, but somewhere underneath was chicken. People were digging around for some time before they could find even the minutest piece; the dish was mostly *la jiao,* or chilli, but not chicken. Sorry, but this was too hot for me. Meanwhile our birthday boy was sitting back smoking. He would be all of 18, probably going on 12. Oddly enough he is Japanese. Later I asked him if he wanted to give up smoking, and he replied, "Yes, but it is too hard." It is too, especially when you think it is.

The railway line maintained a fascination for me, becoming a magnet on my afternoon walks. One needed to cross it in order to climb to the upper campus, or one could walk along it. This I did in both directions, being careful as the sleepers were not always evenly spaced, in some places there were iron bars which one needed to step over, and wooden sleepers in particular are apt to get slippery in the wet—and it is nearly always wet. Most of the sleepers are made of cement, and these are easier to step on. One also has to limit one's stride as the sleepers are quite close together, unless you are about 1.2 metres tall, one's stride, being about the same length as one's height. Sometimes you can walk beside the track, but mostly not, either because it is too uneven or overgrown. To the north, the line runs through a tunnel, perhaps 500 metres long, for which a torch is essential. In the middle, due to curvature of the line, you cannot see light in either direction. On a dark, cold, overcast, wintery day it can be quite eerie.

I loved the isolated sections, surrounded by forest, and also the vegetable plots which are quite common even within Chinese cities. When walking south, one passed through the army barracks then a siding on a section of rail still in use. One had to be wary of engines going back and forth. At the siding, a man lived at the end of a platform, objecting to my perambulations, but I would always ignore him—and his guard dog too. I often did a loop, either turning right to climb Gele Shan and re-enter the campus from above, or turning left to walk on trestles over a valley and back onto streets.

Photograph 26 shows part of this trellis section. The pylons are newly built, forming the legs for another metro line.

Photo 27: crossing a valley

There were other hills in the district which I enjoyed climbing. Apart from the exercise, they gave interesting views over the university and its surrounds. They have witnessed interesting history too, as the Americans had a centre here to plan operations during the Second World War.

3.2: Zhazidong Prison

There is a gaol close by SISU built by the Kuomintang for political prisoners. I walked there one Saturday afternoon, surprised at how close it is, being only about 25 minutes' walk. I had thought it was much further away. Today it is no longer a prison, but a museum, a monument to the "martyrs of the revolution". Upon reflection, I am not in the least surprised, as it gives the current regime some legitimacy. There is a garden, even closer to the university, with about a dozen statues of some of those who died. There are four such memorial gardens in the area, the most important being "Lieshimu", meaning "tomb of martyrs", a name now given to this suburb. There are other "Lieshimus" elsewhere in China, one outside Bijie, Guizhou Province, which I had visited.

The site of the prison used to be a coal mine, which closed after its owner died in 1931. In 1943 the site was turned into a gaol, and the opening to the coal pit covered over, and remained covered till a freak rainstorm flooded the area in July 2007, so quite recently. Oddly enough this part of the gaol is built over a ravine, with water gushing down underneath. One would have thought that this would be a possible way out for prisoners, but there is no record of any escapes.

The prison housed some 180 prisoners, both men and women, with 16 dormitories for the men and two for the women, on two levels, which look reasonably respectable. Most had cots, which seemed to be quite comfortable as well, so long as you realise that sleeping on a hard surface may not be considered uncomfortable. I know this is not the way we soft Westerners are accustomed to sleep: we like a nice soft bed, but the average Chinese does not, and a hard bed is the norm. Some rooms had no beds at all, so that the prisoners slept on the floor. I think I prefer the cot. The present buildings were constructed in the early 1960s, as at the end of the war, the old buildings were burnt. The reconstruction, of course, is part of the party's propaganda.

One room was not open, a separate building at the end of a courtyard, abutting an outside wall: the toilet. Now I am not complaining; I did not really have a need to use the toilet, and in any case a new modern structure has been built outside the wall for any visitors who so desire. I expect the gaol's toilet is not unlike many others in China, even today: pretty basic, consisting of just a smelly hole in the ground. What is interesting, however, is that this was probably the only place where prisoners could get some sort of privacy. So this is where they passed messages, plotted escapes, or maybe just called the guards names. Perhaps it should be called the communications room.

Photo 28: grinding rice

At the end of this courtyard there is a basketball ring. I do not know when it was built, but maybe the prisoners were allowed to play basketball for exercise. Nearby is a wheel for grinding rice. Apparently the rice they got was not exactly prime quality, being contaminated by mildew and mixed with sand. I can well believe the mildew in this climate's cool, wet winters. This would also give the prisoners some exercise. You can see the mill in photograph 28, where two men would move the bar back and forth, thus rolling the grinding wheel over the rice.

There is another room, on the side of another courtyard—there are two courtyards altogether—which was probably the non-communications room, and this is where it really gets nasty. Its official name was the interrogation room, but it was really a torture chamber. It is still equipped with instruments of torture, and I have no reason to doubt that this room witnessed much suffering and agony. Why do people do this to other human beings? Homo homini lupus. ("People can act likes wolves to each other," for those whose Latin might be a little rusty.) Now I see why this gaol is no longer in use: it has too much value for propaganda purposes. This is not to say that the current regime does not do the same, as—let's face it—every totalitarian regime has done down through the centuries. Man's inhumanity to man: when will it ever stop? It is barbaric. And it gets worse.

The civil war ended in 1949, with victory going to the Communists, as we all know. On 27th November, 1949, the guards massacred most of the prisoners, according to the account given here. Each dormitory has a plaque outside with the names of the prisoners who were housed there, together with their year of birth and year of death, invariably 1949. Of the 180 prisoners most were shot, with only 15 escaping. Apparently there was a gaping hole in the wall at that time, through which these 15 got out. I have no idea how the gap got there. Perhaps Communist forces were launching an attack at the time, bearing in mind that Chongqing was the capital of China under the Kuomintang, so that forces here held out for longer than elsewhere. The date is certainly late, as victory for the Communists had been hailed in Beijing on 1st October, which is now celebrated as National Day. One would have thought that killing these prisoners was pointless. China's bloody history continues, and will for some time, I think, just as long as power and Nationalism are revered as the supreme virtues, as they still are in China.

This prison visit was most instructive, but perhaps not in quite the way the Communists intended. The Kuomintang were certainly bad, but the Communists are no better.

3.3: Lieshimu

Ge Le Shan lies to the west, on the slopes of which SISU is built. To the east, the land continues to slope down and on this slope is a park. When we say "park", we are not to think of this in Western terms, where we might have trees, grass, ponds and gardens. In China a park very rarely has much grass: it is mainly concrete. There are shrubs and flowers, but usually not planted in the ground; instead they are planted in pots. This system does have one advantage, in that they can be moved around, thus forming different coloured patterns.

This particular park is about 600 metres long and about 50 metres wide, with about 300 steps cascading down the slope. These steps are a little unusual, in that they are wide but have low risers. There is a water feature towards the bottom and areas where people can sit under some trees, generally parents who watch while their children play. Gates close the park off at night—as early as 5.00 p.m.—so one needed to walk through before then. Outside to the left, there is a supermarket, where I would regularly buy my supplies.

One could, however, walk around the park if the gates were closed. The southern side of the park has no steps: it is a road, so that if you do not like climbing steps you could always take this option. The road is lined with trees—so technically it is an avenue. The trees are of some interest to me, because they are part of a very ancient genus, dating from the Permian Era, around 270 million years ago. They belong to the conifer group (gymnosperms), which includes pines, firs etc. They are gingkoes, characterised by triangular shaped leaves with veins coming to a point. This venation is somewhat different from flowering plants (angiosperms), which have either parallel veins in monocotyledons (such as grasses) or the dendritic structures of dicotyledons (such as roses). Western botanists had only seen fossils of this tree, unaware that it was still extant in China. The trees can be large, although the ones lining this street in Lieshimu are quite spindly, to the point where some locals wanted them replaced with larger trees in order to provide more shade during the hot summers. There are two other species of trees in the world, which are just as ancient, viz. the cycad (from around 300 million years ago) and the Wollemi pine (from around 200 million years ago), the latter endemic to the Wollemi National Park in New South Wales, Australia; in spite of the name, they are not pines.

The walk up the northern side of the park is up a gentle slope at first, before you climb more than 100 steps. There are lots of steps to climb in this neck of the woods. I would castigate my students on their laziness because they would be taking the lift up to the ninth floor, whereas I would always walk up the stairs; it is healthier.

The western end of Lieshimu Park has a broad set of steps which form a bridge over the road. Down the centre are different flags used by the Communist Party at one time or another. The steps lead to a large grassy mound, forming the tomb for about 50 of the so called "martyrs". Around the outside are statues of some of those who had been executed. This whole section juts into SISU grounds only about 100 metres from my apartment.

Not far away there are two more monuments to these "martyrs", in the form of two smaller parks. Some of these people even have statues erected in their memory. I wonder if in the future there will be other monuments built to honour those killed by the Communists. What is the difference between a rebel and a revolutionary, between a criminal and a freedom fighter? It depends upon who wins. "Lieshimu" means "cemetery of the martyrs".

Photo 29: new housing estate

The main road winds around the university, runs between the east gate of the university and the park, goes through a tunnel, with that bridge overhead, then swings right to go through the shopping centre. These shops included another supermarket, a wet market, the post office, banks and restaurants. At the end of the shopping district is the underground metro station. When I arrived in August, 2011, this station had yet to open, but metro line 1 was in the process of being extended out from Shapingba. It opened just before Christmas and was a real blessing, thus opening up the entire city to easy travelling.

Beyond the station is housing, with new high rise apartment blocks going up apace. I would watch construction, taking two years from beginning of demolition of the old buildings to completion of the new. These old buildings were of course much smaller—just one or two storeys. Some were still standing when the time came for me to leave Chongqing, but their days were numbered. Much of the new housing is in the form of compounds, surrounded by fences and with guards at the gates. I had no trouble, however, in wandering through: must be my Chinese eyes! Inside there are quite attractive gardens complete with water features.

Photograph 29 shows a garden area in one such estate, the buildings being reflected in a pond.

In my afternoon walks I became very familiar with this suburb of Lieshimu. Apart from these new housing estates there were lots of old ones; how old I do not know, but they were certainly showing their age. The district is also hilly, with lots of steps leading to interesting nooks and crannies. There is an American owned engine factory, which is surprising, flying both the American and Chinese flags—and you do not see that too often.

Markets were seemingly everywhere. Sellers have no problem in displaying their wares on footpaths or wherever they can find space. Photograph 30 shows one such, which you are unlikely to find on any Sydney streets. A man had a number of live chooks in cages. You selected which one you wanted, he would kill it, prepare it for you, and you take it home for that night's meal.

Photo 30: Anyone for a chook?

3.4: The Law University

Next door to SISU is another university, "The Southwest University of Law and Political Science". Some years prior to this a friend of mine was a student here, which is somewhat ironic, as she hated the Communist Party with a passion, because they had persecuted her family. She put up with the propaganda, graduated and is now a lawyer in Beijing. Some of these lawyers are truly heroic, as it is dangerous to attempt to indict CP members; many have been beaten up or worse. The CP, of course, is above the law: this is actually written into the constitution.

The campus is quite large and with beautiful gardens it is a good place to wander around. There is a water feature just inside the front gate in the form of an artificial pond with an island in the middle—ideal for some quiet contemplation. I loved this pond. Cf. photograph 31. Often it would be completely green, with the entire surface covered with a plant, which looked like duckweed to me. Once I saw a man sitting by himself practising on his *erhu*. Some of the buildings are quite grand and look as if they have been here for a good many years. There are smaller gardens and parks, interesting courtyards and of course lots of steps.

The buildings are quite old and in fact the authorities were planning to shift the campus to University Town, further up the railway line—a whole new development. There is a current trend in China to have many tertiary institutions close together.

Photo 31: pond in the Law University

Sometimes, as I wandered through the campus, I would stop to watch students playing badminton or table tennis, their standard being somewhat above mine. One of our English teachers at SISU was brought up on table tennis, which surprised me, as he grew up in England. I know the sport is yet another English

118

invention, but these days the Orient has made it their own. Nevertheless, he was quite good, boasting that he was SISU champion; perhaps.

Next door to the Law University, on the southern side, is an army base. There are many such throughout China, as this country has a massive military. I guess there is a different attitude to individual lives, in that in any conflict Western military forces try to limit their casualties as much as possible. Like all military establishments here—and there is yet another not far away—there is very tight security. I liked to smile at the guards as I walked past. I mean it must be terrible having to stand all day, stiff as a board. I am glad it was not me. In the mornings one could often hear bugles calling the soldiers to their duties.

3.5: Shapingba

Lieshimu is a suburb of the much larger district of Shapingba, which literally means a sandbank, no doubt referring to a feature of the Jialing River, which forms one boundary. This is a major centre, with a large square, called "Three Gorges Square" and many shops, being in fact one the major shopping meccas in Chongqing. Many of these shops are underground, which is not a bad idea in an extreme climate. Canada and north eastern China do the same. One of these shops is Carrefour, a French store, where I would often go to buy supplies one could not get in Chinese shops—like wine. I also bought a computer here and a shaver. In both cases, after looking at the various brands I opted for foreign brands—Hewlett Packard for the computer and a Philips for the shaver. In both cases the Chinese shop assistants who were selling the Chinese brands were livid with anger, and let me know. You do not buy foreign brands if you can possibly help it; this is being unpatriotic. In Australia, we do not have this Nationalism, to the extent where we so not care much if local brands go under, as long as I can get the cheapest price. In fact we would often buy a French champagne, even though a sparkling white from Tasmania is not only much cheaper but is probably better quality.

From time to time we would eat at one of the restaurants in Shapingba, around Three Gorges Square. One of these is Pizza Hut, but not if you want a good pizza. Then, you go to Suzy's. This is a family-run restaurant, very small, initially using the living room of their apartment. Consequently, you need to know how to get there, as it is complicated. They are on the 12th floor of a building, overlooking the square. Word spreads so that the quality of their food and ambience was attracting more customers, necessitating renovations. The family moved out to live elsewhere and tables were added to what had been the bedrooms. Streamers in the Italian colours adorn the roof, while photographs of patrons adorn the walls. She has fed many people from overseas.

Photo 32: Three Gorges Square, Shapingba

Each afternoon I would go for a walk with Shapingba on one of my routes; it would take about 25 minutes to walk into the Three Gorges Square. I always found these walks interesting. As you approach the commercial centre your way is blocked by a major expressway: you would have to be mad to walk across that. But there is another way—partly underground. There is a tunnel, lined with shops, selling many items from clothing to books. I once bought a belt here, asking the proprietor to put in holes for the belt. This she did by using a hammer and nail; it worked. Under Three Gorges Square there is a large shopping mall and I have seen them elsewhere in China, especially in Heilong Jiang Province, where it is bitterly cold in winter. As one emerges from this tunnel, one comes to off-ramps from the expressway, beneath which sellers are again to be found proffering their wares. The entrepreneurial spirit of the Chinese is amazing.

Photo 33: underground shopping, Shapingba

Approaching the square the footpath is not only used for walking on. Groups of tradesmen can be found, sitting on their box of tools, waiting to be hired. Stickmen ("*gang gang*"), with their bamboo poles and thick ropes are ready to carry someone's goods. This, too, is where beggars gather, often exposing some deformity in order to elicit more sympathy. Around the square are pedestrian bridges and on these sellers are displaying various knick-knacks. There is always something happening. Here too there is a bus stop, from which one can catch a bus back to SISU; if you wish to be assured of a seat, you need to go to the other side of the square, to the previous stop.

3.6: Coffee Shops

We Westerners like our coffee; well, this one does. My mother was allergic to coffee, so it never appeared in our household when I was a boy. In later life she developed a liking for cappuccinos, so it was a real treat to take her out to a coffee shop. For the final five years of her life she was in a nursing home not far from a McDonald's; her visitors would often walk up there with her, so that she could enjoy those lovely cappuccinos.

In Tongren, my previous home, coffee shops were few and far between, but in Chongqing we had a selection. It became something of a tradition to go to such a shop after Mass on Sunday mornings. There we would sit and chat for an hour or so, enjoying each other's company even more than the coffee. We would take it in turns to shout, though—since we did not organise a roster—this was always a matter of some debate. "It is my turn to pay this week."

"No, I think it is mine, as I have not paid for some time."

"You are both wrong: it is mine, and you paid two weeks ago." We always managed to sort it out without coming to blows: it was all good fun. First, however, we needed to decide which shop we would go to.

In Shapingba there were initially five options. One choice was Starbucks. The problem here was that one of us was not particularly fond of Starbuck's coffee, so we rarely went there.

A second contender was a bookstore called Sysyphe, or Xi Xi Fu in Chinese. I do not know where its strange name comes from. It may be Chinese or it may be a corruption of Sisyphus, the character in Greek legend, king of Corinth, who is forever pushing a boulder up a hill; as soon as he gets it up there, it rolls down again. Most probably it just sounds like the Chinese Xi Xi. You can also get English books, including the classics; and they are cheap. The room was large, had comfortable chairs, good coffee and a toilet, though sadly, not Western. There was however, a problem. One of our number—no names—just happens to like talking and he has a very loud voice. Even though the shop was closed off from the library proper, nevertheless people were complaining of the noise we were making! What, us? Perish the thought! After that we rarely went to Sysyphe.

A third option was Createa. This is situated on an underground floor of a large building. The coffee was good, the staff was very friendly, it was quiet—as there was hardly anybody else there—so we could talk as loudly as we liked;

or one of us could—and it wasn't me! Sadly this shop disappeared before I left Chongqing.

After a while, a local person introduced me to yet another coffee shop, and I liked it. I promised the others that I would take them to it, but had forgotten where it was. In attempting to lead them to it, I took a wrong turn. Each Sunday I had been saying, "Sorry, but I have been too busy this past week to find it: next week." Well, I finally found it. I was in Shapingba to change renminbi into Aussie dollars. This is, or can be, a difficult process. The government does not want Chinese money leaving the country, so it places restrictions. I can only take out a certain proportion of my salary. This means that I must produce proof of exactly how much I earn. This must be certified by the president of the university for which I work. And of course, I need my passport. You cannot cross the street in this country without your passport. There is a simpler alternative: you just get a local person to make the exchange: all he/she needs is his/her ID. I asked one of our students to help me and she did: wonderful.

On one afternoon, we had been to the bank—and there is only one bank you can go to—and had purchased Aussie dollars at the very high rate of 6.5 Yuan to 1 AUD. The Aussie dollar was too high at this time, while the renminbi was too low. She had time, so I suggested we go search—and we found it— eventually. It is only small. As we walked I remembered details. It is not all that far from the 821 bus stop and is very close to a pedestrian overpass. Right at an overpass, I saw the sign and stairs—you do have to look.

You go up the stairs, wooden and narrow. On the second floor you turn left, not right, to find the stairs continuing upward. On the third floor you come to bat wing doors. Go through and turn right and you find yourself in a cosy, rustic room, bare wooden floor, with six small tables plus a long table at the window. See, you can't miss it. The room is small: perhaps 25 square metres. In front of you are seven large antique clocks affixed to the wall. In the far corner is a London style telephone booth. On shelves are antique knick-knacks, including an old TV set, a large watering can and an antiquated 16 mm film projector, the sort I used to use thirty years ago. The counter on your right is quite large compared with the size of the room, but they do need to prepare the coffees and other drinks and also make cakes. In large letters it has the word "LOVE" on its front. On the long table by the window are the words "LIVE SIMPLY". The room has character. It is the kind of place to go to for a quiet chat with friends, while local students used it to study. And the coffee is good. There is also an outside section on top of the roof, where it would be nice to go in the summer. If you really want a quiet nook, there is also a small mezzanine, which can accommodate maybe six people.

Photo 34: Full Town Cafe

The owner had not advertised her shop, as she wants to keep the atmosphere. Maybe this is one reason for the name: Full Town Cafe—though I understand this was also the name of a popular TV series. The lady, whose name is Helen, also owns a small knick-knack shop nearby, her primary business, and from here she had brought her ornaments. Six years previously she approached the then owner of the cafe, offering to buy the premises. The price asked was very high and she simply could not afford it. So she prayed. There was a fire in the cafe, and a person jumped from a window in order to escape, suffering some injuries, as this room is on the third floor. The owner was afraid of being sued, so she skipped town fast, selling her premises to Helen for a song. Maybe this town became too full for her. God does work in mysterious ways, at least Helen thinks so, as she promptly became a Christian. Interestingly, her Chinese name means "light".

There is another coffee shop quite close to our university in the local shopping area of Lieshimu. This is owned and run by a lady whose English is excellent. This shop is even smaller, sitting perhaps a dozen people. She also sells cakes. Once I had a waffle: very rare in this part of the world, a situation which I think unlikely to change in the near future, at least if this specimen is any indication. It was too doughy and its topping was not nice—a little bitter. The coffee is expensive, but quite good. The shop's main attraction is its location, situated as it is close to the university.

So there you have it: Shapingba coffee shops. Before you pay your next visit, review your options and choose yours. There are other places we frequented elsewhere, and these will be mentioned in chapter 7, "Going to Church".

Chapter 4: Outside the City

Introduction

Whatever country I have been in, I have used every opportunity to explore. One can learn so much, quite apart from taking a break from study or teaching or whatever else one is doing. In Chongqing there were many such opportunities and they were marvellous, as I hope this chapter will testify.

4.1: Dazu

One Saturday in early December, 2011, the university put on an outing for us. This is one facet of this university which I really liked.

We were told to meet at 8.30 a.m. sharp in front of the auditorium. Some of us did. Where are the others? Very few turned up, for one reason or another. I know some people had other engagements; I know one man who did not come because his wife had not been invited—he is a member of staff, while she is not. Maybe the rest were still in bed, recovering from the previous night, when we had been to see a performance of Chuan Opera. Some people did not get the message. A measly twelve of us were gathered for the trip. I was feeling a little sad, in that if the university is going to go to all this trouble for us, we should take advantage of it. If no one is interested, they may think twice about hosting these events in the future.

We left around 8.45 a.m. It was a pleasant trip, or most of it was. On the outskirts of the city we went into a long tunnel, at least 4 km in length, on the other side of which is the countryside. There is a clear demarcation, with the city on one side of this mountain and farmland on the other. You need to know your way, as we were not on the expressway the whole time, with twists and turns once we had turned off. In one town—in China farmland never extends very far before you are into another town—they were doing up the road, resulting in only one lane being open for traffic. The Chinese do not have a sense of fairness, meaning first one side goes and then the other so that you take it in turns, you share. Here it every man for himself. It is odd. On the one hand you have a society where the individual is subservient to the whole, while on the other hand you have this intense selfishness. Yet once you break through into the inner circle, as it were, they can be beautiful thoughtful people. It is the Great Wall Syndrome operating yet again.

At around 11.00 a.m. we arrived at Dazu 167 km from SISU and were immediately ushered into a souvenir shop, in typical fashion. Does anybody want a carved purple and cream jade dragon? I could have got you one for only 1,000 Yuan. Actually I would have paid only 800 Yuan, but there is the commission, you know! Our guide for the day joined us, bought the tickets and in we went. Outside is a large stone statue of one Zhao Zhifeng, which was carved by the guide himself. I will come back to Zhao later. Our guide also carved many of the objects d'art in the souvenir shop. Apparently he is only a guide part time, which is probably a good thing, as his carving is definitely an improvement on his English. I understood about 10 % of what he told us throughout the day.

So what is this place? You may be wondering, since this is now the fifth paragraph and I have not mentioned the raison d'être of the place. It is a V shaped vale, a watercourse at the narrow end. Buddhists came here early in the Tang Dynasty, around A.D. 650 and carved many statues out of the rock, some 50,000 of them over a number of sites, most in bas relief, some almost free standing, representing Buddhist Theology. At Dazu they extend for about 300 metres around the two sides of this vale, cut out of the steep cliff walls. Some are very large, in true Buddhist fashion: one reclining Buddha is more than 30 metres in length, and is interesting in that only half his body is above ground, so to speak. The carvings went on for centuries, being similar to Longmen Grotto in Hubei Province, although not as extensive, and with some colouring. There is no evidence here of the vandalism wrecked by Mao Zedong's Red Guards, so that is good. They did damage Longmen Grotto.

Some depictions I found more interesting than others. There is one of Hell, with people being tortured—as in photograph 35—so there is a parallel here with our Christian belief, not that God tortures anybody, because He/She does not, but people are tortured by themselves and their own choices. Yikes: I must remember to behave myself. There is another of a man carrying his elderly parents in two panniers: not a bad representation of filial piety. They must have been heavy.

Photo 35: Hell in Buddhism

What interested me more than anything was the water. This is a wet place, and indeed it was drizzling on this day. Most people sheltered under umbrellas, while I stood under the overhangs at the cliff face when I could, or sometimes shared Yulia's umbrella, my Russian friend whom I had been sitting next to the previous night; she was teaching Russian at this university. It was not raining heavily, more of a nuisance value. The top of this vale has a small waterfall, which has been ingeniously channelled through a dragon's mouth. There is also a cave here, with more carvings inside. Water comes in from one side, and this too has been diverted through a culvert under the floor.

It took us about two hours to wander at leisure around this site. The vale is known as Baodingshan and is one of many such sites in this area where Buddhist carvings are depicted. Actually, it is broader than Buddhism, as elements of Taoism and Confucianism have also been incorporated, so that the message is eclectic. Many of the carvings were done over a 78 year period from A.D.1174 to 1252 during the Song Dynasty, under the supervision of the Zhao Zhifeng I mentioned earlier. He was a Buddhist monk, of the Tantric school. The idea is to teach people Buddhist doctrines and encourage them to live good lives, in much the same way as religious statues and stained glass windows have done in the

Christian West. It really is a site well worth the visit, and in fact was placed on the World Heritage List in December 1999.

Photo 36: Sheltering under Yuria's umbrella

Having completed our tour, we proceeded to saunter back to our entry point about 500 metres away, and for some a snail's pace would be a more apt description, as they stopped to shop at some of the souvenir stalls lined up on one side of the road. Vendors were pestering us to buy this or that knick-knack, for "only 20 Yuan". You probably know the drill. One young lady was actually looking for a white lion to give to her mother, but the 300 Yuan plus price tag on the jade carvings were way out of her league. She very happily settled for a 20 Yuan version. I felt the weight of it. Sorry, my dear, but this is plastic. I wonder if her mother will realise.

I was with the forward group, and after waiting for some time, our worthy guide expressed some impatience and asked someone to go and fetch the laggards, so I did. I could do with an extra walk. Some in our group were also expressing their cold and hunger, as it was now about 1.30 p.m. Back on the bus we did not go far before stopping at a restaurant, where we were suitably replenished. About 2.15 p.m. we headed for home, arriving back about 4.30 p.m. It was a good day. I am happy, and pleased that the university would put this excursion on for us. Thank you.

4.2: Zunyi

4.2.1: Christmas 2011

Zunyi is a small city about four hours south of Chongqing by bus or 6 1/2 hours by train. When I say "small", I mean by Chinese standards as it is about the size of Adelaide with a population of maybe 1.5 million, although of recent years it has been growing fast. My friend, Greg, spent some years teaching at Zunyi Medical University and I had been there twice before to meet him. Christmas 2011 would be my third visit to meet with Grace, a former student of mine from Tongren, who was teaching there at that time, and Jenna, a young lady I had worked with the previous summer in Meitan. Erica plus three American Peace Corps workers would come up from Tongren.

The university here kindly gave us Christmas Eve off, meaning I did not have to teach for the first two hours of the day. They also gave me a gift certificate to be used at the coffee shop in the building where I was doing most of my teaching, worth some 300 Yuan. One of my classes presented me with a bunch of beautiful flowers, so that my apartment was smelling like roses—and carnations, gerberas etc. I cooked my major meal at lunchtime and packed a sandwich for my evening meal to eat on the train and left at 12.15 p.m., giving me plenty of time to get to the station for departure just after 2.00 p.m. It was a good trip, but—of course—crowded. I read mostly.

Photo 37: countryside

I really enjoy train travel, gazing out the window as beautiful rural scenes flash by, or—to be more precise when one is on a K train—crawl by. These trains are not fast. Photograph 37 shows a typical rural valley, hills on both sides, a river flowing down the centre, a village nestling on the slopes. On the left one can also see a highway on legs, allowing cars to flash by travelling along this beautiful valley.

We arrived in Zunyi on time, just before 8.00 p.m. and there were Grace and Jenna to meet me, standing side by side, which was interesting because they did not know each other, so introductions were made. Jenna had also brought two friends. We went first to my hotel, one of the 7 Days Inn chain, and spent the rest of the evening chatting. It was great. In this active, busy society of ours, just being together and enjoying each other's company is very important. At around 10.00 p.m. we returned to the railway station to meet the Tongren contingent, and waited ... and waited. The train was delayed. Jenna and her friends needed to return to their dormitory, as it closed at 11.30 p.m., which is about the time the train eventually arrived. It was good to meet up with Sky, Kate and Joe, whom I had known and worked with in Tongren for a year, and of course it was a special pleasure to meet Erica again, looking more beautiful than ever with a

131

new hairstyle. It suited her. Needless to say, we had a late night. Even after we finally parted, Erica and Grace would talk well into the early hours of the morning. Women like to talk, you know. Erica was staying with Grace, who was living here.

The next morning we wandered up to the old part of town, not far from my hotel, and visited the "Meeting Hall", which I have written about before as being the place where Mao Zedong, in defiance of the CP central committee in Shanghai, had himself elected as head of one of the two red armies in January 1935. All this was during the Long March. This beautiful building is also where the top leaders slept. It is now a museum, commemorating those times.

Here too we met the three Peace Corps teachers from Tongren and shared lunch. Many Peace Corps workers were gathering here from around the region to celebrate Christmas, and after lunch we met some of them. It was very pleasant wandering through this district: Red Army Street is quite attractive. We climbed a local hill, also dedicated to the CP—such monuments are all over China—and met with Jenna again. She had brought me a present and one from her friend whom I had met the previous night. Strange: I had only just met the girl. Last night I had noticed that she said nothing, keeping herself in the background, so I tried to include her in the conversation, which is really a commonplace thing to do, but apparently for her it was a big deal: somebody actually noticed her. These people are beautiful: really good at showing their appreciation.

For our evening meal, we went to Grace's house, where her family had prepared a truly delicious meal. It was good to meet Grace's parents, even if my Chinese was too poor to sustain much of a conversation.

This Christmas Eve would be memorable. Our plan was to go to the local Catholic church for Mass at 7.30 p.m., but the best laid plans are apt to go awry. Before I left Chongqing, I was told by another person what his experience had been in Zunyi on Christmas Eve, and it was not very pleasant, as he was set upon by gangs of youths, spraying him with a sticky gel. He made a complaint to the media that such behaviour was barbaric, a criticism which strikes at the heart of Chinese culture. This year—probably as a consequence—the police were on the streets to control the crowds and mitigate such instances.

The police may have been out in force, but so were the people, in their tens of thousands, so much so that the whole central district had been blocked off from traffic. Hence it was impossible for us to get either a taxi or a bus to the church. Nor could we walk. We just could not go. In the end we decided to go to the railway station to buy Erica's return ticket. The bus back towards my hotel went only two stops, leaving us a fair distance to walk. One possibility was to find a quiet coffee shop or bar somewhere to sit down for a while until the crowds subsided a little. In the end we opted to walk, even though the streets were awash with people, walking in both directions. Where are they going? Some were wearing masks and many were carrying cans of sticky gel: one had to be careful not to get sprayed. In Tongren one year, my companion was set upon by a mob of young men and sprayed, some of the goo getting into his eye, which was inflamed for weeks afterwards. I have no idea why they do this.

Christmas is a Christian festival, commemorating the birth of Jesus. God has entered human history and is part of our history, showing us that God's way is not ours, that God's weakness is stronger that human strength. The birth of Jesus is the watershed in all of human history. But are the Chinese aware of this? No, they are not; so what is going on? Is it just Jingle Bells and Christmas trees, carols and shopping, or a chance to let your hair down? It may be all of those, but it is much, much more in my opinion.

Jesus is not only a Christian figure. In fact he was a Jew. Nor is Christmas just a private festival for Christians, or even some Western cultural event. Jesus is head of the entire human family. He lived and died for everyone; God does not have favourites. The birth of Jesus is thus of universal significance. I think that this is what the Chinese and everyone else know subliminally. This is why Christmas is such a special time, not only for Christians but for the entire world.

We did make it safely back to my hotel. I had only a little of that sticky spray on my coat, while Erica had some in her hair, but otherwise no problems. There had also been some injuries, with at least one ambulance in attendance, but overall, it was peaceful, the atmosphere was one of revelry, not of violence. Christmas is a time of peace. In fact this may be especially so in China. All along the street you could buy apples dressed up in cellophane for 5 Yuan. If you want just the apple, then it will cost you 1 Yuan. In Mandarin, the word for peace is "*ping an*" whereas the word for apple is "*ping guo*".

My hotel fronts a main road with the river just beyond. Festivities continued well into the night, with lots of noise to boot. Nevertheless I did sleep well—eventually.

Next morning, Christmas Day, Erica arrived about 8.15 a.m. and we went together to the local Catholic church. We had a rough idea of its location, so needed to ask directions. It was surprisingly close, only about ten minutes' walk away. We met the local priest before Mass got under way at about 8.45 a.m. This was the first time that Erica had been to a service, so I did my best to explain what was going on, but I knew it would all be strange to her. At least she could understand the sermon, whereas I could not. I asked her what the priest had said. "It was boring!"—and he spoke for over half an hour. Gosh, are priests the same the world over?

After Mass we headed back to the hotel to pack and check out. Grace, meanwhile, had been at school. Christmas Day is not a holiday here and nor is Sunday. After she arrived we checked out and headed off for a lunch of noodles. You can spend time rushing hither and yon, doing this and that, but I just wanted to spend time with these two beautiful people.

We went back to Grace's apartment and watched a movie I had brought with me on a CD: "Mao's Last Dancer". It is a true story based on the biography of Li Cunxin, who was born in Shandong in 1961, and was chosen to study ballet at Mao's ballet academy in Beijing, from the age of nine to around seventeen. The director of ballet in Houston came and taught for a while, then offered two scholarships for a three month stint in Houston. Li was one of those chosen. His exposure to the West was mind-blowing, having been subjected to communist propaganda all his life. Later he returned for another year, at the end of which he defected, creating an international incident. Later still he married the prima ballerina, an Australian named Mary, became an Australian citizen and settled in Melbourne with his wife and three children. At time of writing I think he is ballet director in Brisbane. The film is Australian. I might add that not all the Australian actors managed to get the American accent right, just as many non-Australians fail to get the Australian accent right, Meryl Streep being an exception. The girls really liked the movie, as did I. I had not seen it before, although I had read the book. I have also met the cinematographer a couple of times, as he is a Randwick parishioner in Sydney, when he is not spending time in Hollywood.

We sat and chatted till it was time to go, as my bus was scheduled to leave at about 5.00 p.m. I took some snacks with me to eat on the way. It was time to say goodbye. Erica would be leaving later that night, taking the train back to Tongren, although actually to Yuping, leaving her a 75 km taxi ride. It was truly fantastic to spend time here in Zunyi for these people. This had been a special Christmas.

The ride back in the bus was smooth, but fast. To "entertain" us, movies were shown, and they were up to their usual standard of unrelenting violence. Being in a generous mood, I would give them a star rating of 1/10. One movie was anti-Japanese. There are many such. China seems determined to maintain the rage, not wanting to bury the past. No apology is ever acceptable. Relationships have never really been "normalised", at least not on China's side. It is a pity and serves nobody any good. It is ironic that here in Zunyi Mao is honoured, although he killed far more Chinese than the Japanese ever did.

By 9.00 p.m. I was back in Chongqing railway station and went looking for the bus stop, in order to catch the 210 bus back to SISU. I could not find it, in spite of asking directions from a number of people. I knew that the 808 bus goes close to SISU, but also noticed that there are two 808 buses. I asked the driver of the first if he went to Lieshimu. No. OK, does he go to Shapingba? Yes. Good, then I can take this to Shapingba then change to the 210. Fine, except that when I got to Shapingba I found that the 210 stops running after 8.30 p.m. Great. So I hopped on the next 808 to take me to Lieshimu and walked the final ten minutes or so. I got home eventually.

Back at SISU, I noticed that lights had been strung up on trees, making a very pretty sight, a pleasant one to come home to.

4.2.2: February 2014

I returned to Zunyi, at Grace's invitation, at the end of the winter holidays at the beginning of 2014. I had actually spent some time with her and some other of my former students in Xishuangbanna, which is situated in southern Yunnan Province, bordering Vietnam. Max, a friend from Australia, whom I had met a couple of years earlier, would also be there.

One Friday just after lunch I left my apartment to take a bus to a train station. Note the use of "a". We have two bus numbers going past our front gate: 821 terminates at the north bus station, while 210 terminates at the central bus station. I took the 210. These buses seem to be about a hundred years old, and make all kinds of complaining noises, especially when straining up hill. It takes about 45 minutes to get to either station, both of which are located, conveniently, next to the north train station and central train station respectively. On each of these routes, the buses leave at about ten minute intervals, maybe a little less. I found myself wondering, since our bus was going so slowly, if the next bus could catch up. Yes, it could. I once saw four buses arrive outside our gates in two minutes: three 821s and one 210.

At the central train station I was surprised by the crowds. I mean, the holidays were now almost over, so I was expecting a diminution of travel; not so. And of course, people were carrying their usual loads of luggage, as photograph 38 suggests.

Photo 38: Chongqing railway station

Boarding began 20 minutes before departure time, and we needed every minute of that to get so many thousand people through only four gates, where railway officials were checking tickets. Once through there was still a walk of several hundred metres to the carriage, as these trains are long. Well, maybe it was supposed to be a walk, but many people run: you have to beat everyone else, you know. My carriage, naturally, was right down the end. All went smoothly, however, so that we left right on time at 2.14 p.m.

The carriage was crowded. You see four people on a seat meant for three, three people on a seat meant for two and still there are people standing. Later I walked through the carriage to use the toilet. It is amazing how some people occupy the aisle, yet make no effort to move out the way when someone wants to get through. Smoking is not allowed on public transport in China now, but hardly anybody takes any notice. It is more important to have the legislation than to enforce it; that is not why it is there. So on this train the end of the carriage was full of smokers; one could smell the smoke as it wafted through the carriage.

About an hour out of Chongqing we passed by a power station. Of recent years these have been shifted out of the city in order to improve air quality. Well, it certainly has resulted in a marked improvement in Chongqing city, but here three smokestacks were belching thick smoke into the atmosphere, while nearby two large cooling towers were emitting broad columns of steam. We have to change this.

The couple opposite me was a surprise. I guess I still have a lot to learn about this society. Public, or indeed, even private exhibition of affection is unusual, yet this pair was all over each other. First love perhaps? Unlikely, as they were about forty years old. Perhaps their relationship is new, or maybe they have been deeply in love for the past twenty years. Who knows? It was good to see, at least as far as I am concerned. Nor were they so wrapped up in each other as to ignore the world around them, as the man noticed my trouble in writing, so made some space on the table between us. *Xie xie* ("Thanks, mate").

Our route took us through country that I am now quite familiar with: lots of tunnels and bridges, lots of steep sided mountain valleys and rugged terrain. Villages occupy every vestige of almost level ground, with farm plots on the steeper slopes. Canola was just beginning to display their bright yellow flowers, which I will always associate with spring in this province. I did live here for three years. One brave peach tree was displaying its pretty pink blossoms, even though the weather was still cold. By contrast, the towns and villages we were passing through were rather drab, with little colour. Even the newer apartment blocks were unexciting, without the more imaginative approach that one sees in the larger cities.

We were supposed to arrive at Zunyi at around 6.00 p.m. but instead it was nearly two hours later by the time we pulled in. These K trains are quite smooth and reasonably comfortable, but they are slow. It is a conundrum that while their arrival times do not seem to matter, departure times are generally spot on. I was supposed to meet Grace at the station, but I was thinking, "Yes, but that was two hours ago." When I emerged I did not see her, but did feel her as she jumped on my back! Now I ask you: "Is it my good looks or magnetic personality that causes pretty girls to jump all over me?" Hard to say. I also met for the first time her boyfriend. He asked me to choose an English name for him and I told him I would think about it.

We took a taxi to the hotel I would be staying in, another of the Home Inn chain. I had two double beds for the price of one. Beds usually are big enough for two, even though I was on my own. After checking in it was time for a late evening meal, which consisted of rather nice goat noodles. I had never even heard of it. I think it was actually called "mutton", but in this country this mostly means goat. Sheep is eaten, at least in the summer, but it is not common, unless you are in Nei Menggu.

It was time to head back to the hotel to retire for the night. It was now getting on towards 10.00 p.m. yet the street life was as energetic as ever. This included some shops fitted with loud speakers, blaring out "music"; well, it may not be real music, but it is certainly real noise. I for one would never shop in such places, but would hurry past to find some quiet shop. They may be attracting some customers, but they are definitely repelling me. They were located on the other side of the street from my hotel, yet their noise was still loud. I was hoping they would shut down soon, as I did not want my sleep disturbed. Goodnight.

The following afternoon we drove about 40 km to Feng Xiang, Grace's home town. The name comes from a sweet smelling wood used for curing bacon, thus giving the bacon a tasty flavour. When it comes to food, the Chinese are past masters. The climate here is cool, meaning that it is rather cold: it snows in winter, and we were now at the end of winter. Tea bushes, which like a cool climate, can be seen on the hillsides. Canola and vines can also be seen. Apparently the planting of vines is a more recent enterprise as more and more Chinese are taking to drinking wine. At the edge of town is an abandoned glass factory; apparently it had become uneconomic.

We visited the home of a cousin, where people were playing mah-jong. The family had bought a table which they were hiring out for 80 Yuan a day, so not a bad side business, as people here love playing this game and indeed love gambling. People can lose thousands of Yuan in a single day. Crazy. I am not in favour of gambling. The stove, around which we huddled, is a very popular design, serving not just as a heater, but also as a cooking stove and table. The flue is interesting, as it comes up from the stove, then turns to disappear into the wall. Now where does it go?—as the wall links with the people next door and this is the ground floor of a four storey building. It must go through the inside of the wall, as it emerges on the outside of the building, overhanging the footpath. I was intrigued to see a bucket depending from the opening, thus catching water droplets.

From here we walked to Graces' family home, no longer occupied. Inside it has a corridor, rather dark, running the length of the building. In the middle is a small courtyard, shared by another household, where rain water could be collected and daily chores undertaken, such as food preparation and laundry. At the back of the house is a sty. It is quite common for rural homes to fatten a pig every year for Spring Festival. The whole complex is now looking somewhat dilapidated and in fact was due for demolition by the government, for which the family will receive some compensation.

Photo 39: Streetscape, Feng Xiang

Photograph 39 shows a street scene, with wares for sale piled onto the footpaths, in typical fashion; you walk on the road. The traffic here in this village is not heavy. I noticed that these wares were mainly household items plus farming needs. You do not find the high fashion clothing items which grace the cities. Whole streets had new buildings which were yet to be occupied. There was one old house still standing with newer buildings on either side. Apparently the elderly owner refused to budge. This says something, as years ago they would not have had a choice, but would simply have been evicted. These houses are about 100 years old. The newer buildings are not the thirty storey affairs we see in Chongqing, being but three storeys in height.

At around 6.00 p.m. we drove back to Zunyi for evening meal, being joined by Shay, his girlfriend, and a Dutchman working here, making a merry party of seven. We had hot pot, and people kept loading up the pot with fresh supplies. As long as you keep eating, more and more food will be added. The idea of not wasting any food is trumped by the loss of face if it is felt that not enough food has been provided. We ate heaps. Once again I lost the battle of who pays. I have seen situations where it seems to be almost on the point of violence, as various parties contend for the privilege of footing the bill. It is cultural, partly due to hospitality, partly due to not being in debt to anybody: far better if the other owes me a favour. People have striven to be the ones beholden to, rather than the other way around.

After this it was back to the hotel.

Sunday is church day. I was up early at 6.40 a.m.—well that is early for me, even if not by much. I was expecting Grace at 7.00. At 7.20 I called her: still in bed. I guessed she was tired. That's OK, as I can probably get to the church by myself, as I have been there before, but where exactly is it in relation to this hotel? The concierge gave me rough directions, as had Grace, so off I went.

After a while, I checked with a lady cooking food on the street. Naturally, I made the mistake of saying *Tian Zhu jiao tang,* whereas I should have said *Tian Zhu jiao tang.* What, you can't see the difference? Well, there's no sense in you trying to learn Chinese! I had used first, first, fourth and second tones, whereas I should have used first, first, second and fourth tones. I mean, be fair: making one tonal mistake is enough to create absolute confusion, so making two is unconscionable.

I walked on, crossing the river over the second bridge, as I had been told. I was close. There was a man on the footpath also selling breakfast, so I thought I would ask him. No response. I asked a second time. No response, so I walked away, whereupon he grunted (and naturally I assume he got his tones right) then vaguely waved his arm. "Thanks, mate, and may God bless you." There were two possible routes, and I wanted to be sure I had the right one.

I had. You walk up a cobbled street, with bollards across its entrance to stop the passage of cars. About 100 metres up there is a small lane off to the left. If you walk up only about 30 metres you come to a dog leg and here you can see the church, just ahead and a little to the right. Easy? It is easy when you know where to go, but otherwise it is hidden. This is often the case with Catholic churches in this country. It raises questions, does it not? Who is hiding from whom?

In I walked, but where are the people? Inside I saw one solitary woman praying, so I ventured to interrupt her orisons to ask her what time Mass would be celebrated. I had been told it was 7.30, but it was now well past that. *"Jiu dian"*, or 9.00 a.m. *"Xiexie"*. Now I do believe in praying, so please don't get me wrong, but I thought, nevertheless, that I would return to the hotel.

There are some attractive parks along the riverside, so I wandered into one of these. Elderly people were doing Tai Chi. There is a walkway below, only just above water level, and here other people had congregated. Then I noticed that four—two men and two women—were wearing only swimming gear. My goodness, it is winter; it is cold; nay, it is frigid. I am wearing three layers, including a heavy coat, with a hood. These people actually entered the water and began swimming. Ya gotta be kidding me! I am glad it was them and not me. There was a slight breeze, but enough to add to the chill factor when they got out. I cannot vouch for the purity of the river either. Years later I met one of these men—in Australia. Life is strange. Photograph 40 shows this swimming spot.

Photo 40: Zunyi river

Back at the hotel I packed up, since I would not have much time later. Soon afterwards I returned to the church. It takes only 12 minutes, if you know where you are going, and by now I was familiar with the route. No, I did not ask either the lady or the gentleman selling their foods; the man was too busy sitting anyway. At 9.00 a.m. the people were saying the rosary. At 9.15 they began choir practice, led by a nun, who was actually wearing full habit. You do not see this in very many places. She has a good voice too.

At 9.30 it was clear there would be no Mass. Then Grace rang. I left the church and proceeded to walk back to the hotel while I was talking with her. She asked me to hail a taxi, and she would give the driver instructions. Now you can spend ages looking for a taxi, but as luck would have it, one drove up right at that moment. Grace was still talking with me when I handed the phone to the driver. It was that immediate. We drove not all that far, where we picked up both Grace and her boyfriend.

Let me interrupt this narrative for a moment. After I arrived two days ago, Chen—Grace's boyfriend—asked me for an English name. I said I would think about it, as it is important to choose a name which both suits the person and which he or she likes. In this case, I chose Will. He likes it; so do I. It also happens to be my second name, and my father's name, and quite a few others in my family.

First we drove to Shay's house to pick up Max, before taking him to a bus depot where he could catch a bus to the airport. He was on his way back to Australia. It had been good to see him again, and no doubt the next time we meet will be in that fair land Down Under. Then it was time for an early lunch—a sticky rice porridge plus corn. It was very nice. Next we piled into another taxi, this time to take me to catch my bus back to Chongqing. We were running short of time and naturally, this is precisely the time when the traffic is heaviest. We crawled along, our driver smoking. The reason for the congestion soon became apparent when we passed an accident: a car and a bus had had a minor disagreement, the vehicles left just as they were at the actual site, as is usual in this country. Once past the accident site—and before—our driver was going like a maniac, weaving in and out of traffic like there was no tomorrow.

We were at the bus station at 11.50 a.m. with my bus due to depart at 12.00 noon. Grace and Will (as he is now called) were not allowed in to see me off as they had no ticket, so we said goodbye outside. "Thank you for a great weekend. See you next time in Chongqing." I saw them afterwards in Australia, too, because after their wedding they came to our beautiful Land Down Under for their honeymoon. Later still Grace would return for a couple of years studying for her masters. It took me a little while to find the correct bus, as there were quite a few of them lined up. We left right on time at 12.00 noon.

It was a fast trip. I was taking some photos of the countryside as we whizzed by, so my travelling companion gave me his seat by the window. *"Xiexie, ni tai hao le";* "Thanks mate, you are most kind." He was an engineer from Chongqing. The ride was a little bumpy, probably because of damage to the road surface caused by overloaded trucks. At 1.30 we had a five minute comfort stop, so I walked around. We were on the side of a hill, and I noticed piles of rubbish simply thrown over the edge: not good.

I read a little, dozed a little and did a sudoku. By 3.20 p.m. we were back in Chongqing. The journey had taken a mere 3 hours and 20 minutes, compared with 5 hours 45 minutes by train: quite a difference. We got off our bus, I collected my luggage from beneath, and walked around to the suburban bus station, got on the 210 bus and left immediately. Wow. I was back in my apartment by 4.15 p.m. So fast.

It truly was a great weekend. What a life—what a great life.

4.3: A Wedding in Qian Xi

One of my former students from Tongren was getting married over National Day, 2013 and very kindly invited me to her wedding. Two other teachers from SISU, John and Anne, expressed an interest in going, and yes, Amy said that they too would be most welcome. Her wedding reception was due to be held on Wednesday night, 3rd October in a country town called Qian Xi in Guizhou Province. I thought we could get there on the Tuesday, thus giving us time to explore the town. How wrong I was.

We were planning to leave by 8.30 a.m. on Tuesday 2nd, which should have given us sufficient time. I did however notice that John was lightly clad. "You might want to consider something warmer, as Guiyang is 1,000 metres above sea level." He went back for more clothing—he would need it, as events were to prove.

The south bus station in Chongqing is right next door to the railway station, which is convenient. We decided to travel to Guiyang by bus as it would be quicker. In Guiyang the long distance bus station is a long way from the railway station and we would need to get to Qian Xi by bus. If we went by train we would still have to get out to the bus station in Guiyang early in the morning for our connection. This is all good reasoning, but life is not always reasonable. This trip was to be—well—interesting.

Getting the 210 local bus from SISU to the bus station was not a problem, but finding the correct ticket office was. Having put our bags through the X-ray machine, and queued for some time, we discovered that we were in the wrong place. Back out we went to find the correct one, a much smaller room and just so crowded. I bought the tickets while the other two waited with the bags. It was 146 Yuan each. Our bus was not scheduled to depart till 10.40 a.m., giving us an hour wait. We went to McDonald's for a coffee. While there we thought we would use the toilet before getting on the bus. Now that is a good idea, is it not?—especially when you do not know how long it will be before the next stop, and we had been drinking coffee. Now McDonald's has a toilet, right?—and half the of the patrons go there to use the toilet, right? Well, it was not so easy to find this one. Listen carefully: you go upstairs, head to the far left, go down a dark, bare, cement corridor till you find a man; pay him 1 Yuan; continue about 40 metres, following the red arrow around corners and eventually you will get there. Piece of cake. *Cesuo* rating 2 (i.e. toilet rating on a scale of 1 to 5).

Back at the bus station, we found that the waiting room had no seats. This small room was wall to wall people—plus luggage. The buses exit from the left hand side, while the ticket counter is at the far end, meaning there is a constant procession of people back and forth. We just stood, pushed this way and that. There were simply too many people. Eventually we moved, with lots of pushing and shoving towards our bus. Thank goodness we had an allocated seat. It was 11.05 a.m. when we finally got under-way: nearly half the day had already gone.

There is a fairly new highway connecting the two cities, so that in theory one just zips along: the journey can be completed in 4 ½ hours. We did not. We crept along, the traffic being so heavy. As there were too many people at the bus station, so there were too many vehicles on the road. The situation was not helped by an accident, which is normal here where more than 300 people are killed every day on the roads.

It became clear that we would not be able to go on to Qian Xi today, so I rang ahead to say that we would find a hotel in Guiyang tonight, then go on to Qian Xi in the morning. We amused ourselves with various puzzles: John and Anne were very good at cryptic crosswords; I am not. For the locals movies were screened on TV monitors, possibly half a dozen throughout the course of the journey, all of them up to the usual standard of maybe 1 out of 10 for the better ones. I am sure China is capable of producing good movies, but not for public buses. The violence is almost unremitting.

The scenery, however, in this mountainous terrain is stunning, with steep sided hills, and consequently not much agriculture. Some sections were looking as if they were farmed in the past, but perhaps the farmers have walked off the land to seek their fortunes in the cities. When we were not crossing valleys on bridges we were piercing mountains through tunnels. There was one toilet stop, with a crowd in the men's, so you can imagine the length of the queue for the women's.

We finally crept into Guiyang at 11.10 p.m., the journey taking nearly three times longer than it should have taken. The first thing we did was to go to the ticket office to book our ticket for the following morning, but alas at this hour it was closed. Oh well, let us just find a hotel. There is one close by, although it did take us a while to locate it. Sadly, it was full. We were told there was another "that way". Fine, but how far "that way"?

"Duo yuan?" Unfortunately, this has little meaning for the average Chinese. I have often been in this situation. You prompt them: "*Yi bai mi? Liang bai mi? San bai mi?*"—they have no idea. Two young men there said it was 300 metres (*san bai mi)*. Fine. Let's walk. Carrying our luggage, we walked the 300 metres: no hotel. At 600 metres we found a high school. Great. At 1,000 metres we waited for the young men who were walking behind us. "It is a little further, but we have booked the last room." Wonderful. Why could they not have told us that back at the first hotel? What would you do now?

We walked back to the bus station, and found a row of deserted shops opposite, where we settled down for what was left of the night. There were still people about, especially a group who took an interest in us, coming up to say hello. There was also a police van. Oh, oh, are these foreign vagrants going to end up spending the night in a cell? Not to worry, as they moved on – the police, that is, not the foreign vagrants.

Photo 41: our Open Air Hotel, Guiyang

We chatted till 2.30 a.m.—or some did. Now we needed those warm clothes as it was getting chilly, though not too cold for the mosquitoes. John also found a piece of Styrofoam, so at least he had a more comfortable seat. Later, Anne found some cardboard; oh, the comforts of home! I love this time of night, when all is quiet, when the frenetic activities of the day have finally stopped. And there are no horns!—oh bliss, oh joy! It is a time when one can enter into oneself and into Nature, and into God—or rather to be more aware of God's presence. There is real wisdom in the contemplative orders of the Catholic Church, as this is the time when these monks and nuns rise to pray. Let us wait in quiet for the dawn.

At 4.30 a.m. on Wednesday in our Open Air Hotel, I got up to walk up and down, being a little cramped, and also to pray. Around 5.00 a.m. we had breakfast: I had brought some cereal and last night bought some coconut milk. Now where is that coffee?—no coffee shop was as yet open, of course. We wandered around to the ticket office, which opened at 6.40, and they do sell coffee. God is good. The counters opened at 7.00. Before that I had asked an attendant at what window I could buy a ticket to Qian Xi: "ershi liu" (26). That saved us some time. We got our tickets, 50 Yuan each, with the bus due to leave "*xianzai*", like right now. We were away by 7.20 a.m.

The scenery along this route is also mountainous, with small valleys and interlocking spurs. The road does wind, but also spans deep gorges on pylons, with perhaps a small stream visible way below us. It is amazing. The rock type is mainly sandstone, which can be seen in its bedding planes not only in road cuttings, but also on cliff faces. Vegetation is scrubby, but with a lovely cream coloured flower adorning the tops of some trees. There was also a red leafed vine, looking attractive against its sandstone backdrops.

The people hereabouts belong to some minority group, evidenced by their distinctive architecture, the roofs of their houses having a ridge along the centre line, with three projections—one in the centre, the other two at either end. Maybe they are Tujia. Rice is a major crop, with paddies having been recently harvested before the coming of winter, which is cold and bleak in these parts. The rice stubble had not yet been stacked in large ricks for the winter, but was still standing in the paddies in small bundles.

The distance to Qian Xi is about 120 km, about half way to Bijie, from where Eric would be coming; she is another of my Tongren students. It is not far. On the open plains of Australia it would take just over an hour to cover this distance, but here the journey takes nearly three hours, so that we arrived a little after 10.00 a.m. Immediately we caught a taxi to our hotel, the Yong Gui Rong He, the taxi driver charging us 10 Yuan, which I thought a little steep for the distance in a country town. Sure enough, when we left the price was lower. Taxi drivers.

The hotel is really nice, and is, I think, the best in the town. The tariff, however, was quite reasonable at 676 Yuan, for two rooms for two nights, or about $30 each a night. A shower and change of clothes was a priority, as our Open Air Hotel of the previous night did not have showers … or a toilet … or water …, though it did have plenty of fresh air. This hotel also had plenty of rules and regulations, which were certainly lacking in our previous abode. They came under the heading of "NOTICETOHOTELGUEST"—all one word. Here are some examples:

1. Puttingup visitor for the night in private or tranefer beds is not allowed. Lodging guests are to inform front desk they should wish to stay out temporarily for the night. (Using an Open Air Hotel perhaps?)
2. Fiercepoison, inflammable, explosive or tadioactive articles are strictly for bidden be taken into hotel; hotel rooms are not allo wed for cooking by mcails by electricity, gasoline or alcohol. (All terrorists, please note.)

3. Guests with guns or weapohs must be accompanied by relevant registered documents. (Nice to know that terrorists are not entirely barred.)
4. Strctly prohibit prlstitaion.
5. Observe sanitary regulations set up by the horel. Poultry, animals and any rottem things detri-mental to hygience and health are not allowed in thehotel.

There were other regulations, but these give you the idea. So if ever you intend to stay at this hotel, remember to behave yourself.

The next priority was to have a nap, before the festivities of the wedding in the evening. That was welcome too, especially in view of the paucity of sleep the night before. Later we went for a walk to explore the town, which appears to have many hardware style shops: no idea why. The weather was cool and drizzly. Then we learnt that the reception would be held in the very hotel we were staying in; now that is convenient, at least for us.

The reception was due to start about 6.00 p.m. and it got under-way a little after that. People sort of arrived, while the bride and groom greeted them in the hotel lobby. It was good to see Amy again, who was looking particularly radiant in her white wedding dress, and to meet her husband for the first time. We chatted for a while and she pressed money into my hands. Unbeknown to me, she had already paid for our hotel rooms, so that we had actually paid twice. She was reimbursed by the hotel and was now passing the money on to me. Should I accept it?—especially considering it is her wedding, and I do not think they have a lot of money. Yes, I did, and readily. You see, we had not yet handed over our *hong baos,* or little red envelopes. At weddings, as the guests arrive they give a red envelope containing money to an attendant sitting at a table, who then records how much each person gives. I hate this, but it is Chinese custom. The amount you give depends upon the location and how well you know the bridal couple. The normal amount here at this time was around 300 Yuan. In Tongren it had been only 100 Yuan. You avoid 400 Yuan, as *"si"* can mean four or death, depending upon the tones. The amount actually increases as your relationship with the couple becomes closer. Thus the bridesmaid is expected to contribute some 2,000 Yuan. Why would anyone want to be a bridesmaid? Another excellent amount is 888 Yuan, as 8 is considered to be a lucky number. I guess it would be lucky for the couple. Is it any wonder that some poorer students dread being invited to weddings? We simply added the money Amy gave me to the money we had already put into these envelopes, so that she got it back again. Simple. This money table also features a pile of cigarettes, as traditionally these are handed out to the guests. The evils of smoking had not yet penetrated this society.

The dining room was upstairs, so soon we were at our allocated places, with close to 200 other guests. Our table included classmates of Amy's plus her mother. The bride and groom appeared to the strains of "Here comes the bride", so that Western influence had reached even here. The meal was really tasty, interspersed with quite a few toasts, especially when the bridal couple did the rounds. The drink used was *baijiu,* literally "white wine", although it is distilled from grains not fermented from grapes. And it is strong, so you just sip from tiny glasses, or at least I did. Some people *gan bei,* or drink it all at once. It could blow your head off.

Photo 42: formal and informal wear

At the end of the meal, the bride and groom went onto a stage, where an MC took over. Now here was something unheard of in a Western wedding. We dress up for weddings, but the Chinese are far more casual, apart from the bridal couple. This MC was wearing a chequered shirt, over blue jeans and sneakers, with no tie or coat. Cf. photograph 42. To me, he looked out of place, especially considering his formal role. The couple said they loved each other and intertwined arms to toast each other. And that was it. The actual wedding officially takes place when they sign a document at the government office.

After the meal, Amy changed her Western white dress for the traditional Chinese red dress, red being the colour of good fortune. Some of us walked to Amy's apartment, not far away, where we settled down to play cards or mah-jong for some hours. We were taught an interesting Chinese card game. It was late by the time we wandered back to our hotel. What a great day, and a memorable one. On the morrow we would be returning to Guiyang.

On Thursday 4th October, it was 8.30 by the time we surfaced, wandering down to the hotel dining room for breakfast, which was included in the tariff. It was the usual Chinese fare of noodles, egg etc., but no coffee. Thank goodness we had our own. A large part of the morning was spent with Erica, just ensuring that anything I had written about her family in a previous book, "A Traveller in China", would not offend, should it ever reach a wider audience. No, it was fine.

At 12.30 p.m. we checked out and went to the bus station to get our tickets, but we were told not to. Why? Later Amy and her husband arrived and he bought our tickets. Oh dear! I tell you, these people are just so generous. We sat down to have lunch al fresco style. We had the four classmates from Tongren University, Amy's husband and niece and we three. Sadly it was time to say goodbye, hoping that we will meet again.

At 1.20 p.m. we left. Initially there was little traffic, but unbelievably the driver was in no hurry: we just crawled along. Later, as the traffic picked up, so did his speed, or at least his attempted speed, as he would try to cut in on other vehicles, or go off onto the verge in order to get ahead. On one occasion he roared through a petrol station then straight out again in order to gain two car lengths. Crazy, but there appears to be a compulsion to get in front. They even go out of their way to get in front of someone, rather than simply go behind. Videos were shown on the bus, depicting the usual violence. I cannot remember a single smiling face from any Chinese movie. What a pity, and what an indictment.

It took us a little over three hours to complete the journey, arriving in Guiyang at 4.20 p.m. The first thing we did was to revisit our Open Air Hotel to take some photos, where we were welcomed like long lost brothers by the same people we had been talking with two days before. It was great. Chinese people can be so friendly.

Our next priority was to get hotel accommodation, or we might find ourselves back there for another night. We took a taxi to the Tong Da Hotel, which is located most conveniently right at the railway station. We had decided to take the train back to Chongqing, as the roads were just too crowded. I paid for our hotel rooms using my bank card. Our next priority was to get a train ticket, except that we needed our passports to do that, and the hotel had them. You need your ID in this country for anything, as the government likes to control the population tightly. We walked the short distance to the railway station to await Grace's arrival, as she would be coming down from Zunyi to spend a couple of days with us. She arrived at around 6.30 p.m. and we went back to the hotel to register her name. After waiting for some time, we noticed that the front desk was also selling train tickets—wonderful—so we bought our tickets there instead of at the railway station; we booked seats for the 7.53 a.m. train on Saturday morning, although Anne would be heading back earlier.

It was time to eat. We headed off towards the city to find a suitable restaurant, which we did in fact find, eventually, after wandering around for about an hour. We were some distance from our hotel so we took a taxi back at around 10.00 p.m. to end a good day. The morrow, Friday, would be spent in this city.

We would be having some very interesting conversations in Guiyang, but here I will refrain from stating with whom. People are thinking and no amount of government crackdowns can prevent people from thinking. Currently the government employs something like 2,000,000 people just to monitor the internet in an effort to track and so control the populace and to hack into overseas companies, governments and other organisations. This is going to really extraordinary lengths. We have a government ruled by fear.

The One Child Policy, when combined with both a preference for boys and with increasing material wealth, is creating unforeseen social problems. Many shops had "help wanted" signs outside because of difficulty in getting labour. Few young people, especially urban males, want to do menial jobs. They turn their noses up at hard work and low pay. As a result, the wages of workers have risen to the point where overseas companies are regaining a competitive edge.

Some American companies, for instance, are returning to the US. Young people who do accept a job as a shop assistant, very often do not last long, some a mere few hours. They do not have financial worries as their parents support them. They have too high expectations of cushy jobs and high pay immediately. In a word, they are spoilt. One wonders what the future will be, especially when this generation is running the country.

Another conversation was with a Communist Party member, who was decrying the iron fisted control exercised over so many by so few. There are something like 80 million members of the party, but only a very few have any say. One person told me he was even blocked from voting within the party. There is a growing sense of powerlessness and frustration. At the moment it is simmering, but when will it explode? I do not know but probably not any time soon.

On Friday morning I wanted to do some shopping and also enjoy a good coffee. There is a coffee shop which I have often been to whenever I am in this city. It is located close to Ren Men Guang Cheng (People's Square), a major square about a kilometre down Zunyi Road from the railway station. An attractive pedestrian bridge leads across the local river to this square. Cf. photograph 43.

Photo 43: pedestrian bridge, Guiyang

The coffee shop is called "Highlands Coffee": I do not know why, as the proprietor is in fact American with a Singaporean wife. So here we went to spend an hour or so relaxing with good coffee and cheesecake. A couple of children outside noticed us, so we had a wonderful time with them, as they made faces at the window.

Photo 44: charming children

After coffee it was back to Ren Men Guang Cheng for supplies. Beneath the square is Wal-Mart's, a good place to buy some chocolate and Bega (Australian) cheese. When I was teaching in Tongren, there was even more reason to shop here, as there was no Western supermarket in that town.

About mid-afternoon we went to catch the 253 bus to head out to R and E's place; they are a lovely family, whom I had known for some years. Where do we get this bus? It originates from somewhere near the station, but exactly where? We wandered up and down for some time, before sharp-eyed Grace spotted its number at one of the bus stops. Good. The bus, however, was prevented from coming into the bus stop because quite a few cars were parked there—illegally, of course—so we were standing out on the street. The situation eased a little after the appearance of traffic police, when a number of cars actually got out of the way. Good: we would have more space at the footpath.

In due course, bus 253 arrived. What followed was the most disgraceful exhibition of sheer selfishness that I have witnessed here in this country. It is normal for people to push and shove, elbowing their way in to get inside the door before as many people as possible. This behaviour is normal, but on this occasion it was violent, with people actually fighting. It was a rough house. Grace was not only pushed aside with some force by one man, but he also kicked her. She kicked him back. It was nasty. Naturally he got on first and got a seat, where he sat for the entire journey, completely ignoring everyone else, eating corn. He did not offer his seat to anybody, including an old man, back bowed by the weight of years and hard work. In this situation I refused to become involved; instead, I just drifted with the crowd till we came to the door, then allowed anybody who so desired to push in front of me. One young girl held back, so I thanked her before I boarded. I thought it important to show by my behaviour that common courtesy and politeness should prevail. Unfortunately these are not common here. It was possibly the most disgraceful exhibition of bad manners that I have witnessed anywhere.

For the next 45 minutes we stood, actually getting a seat for one whole stop. Not to worry. The bus stop where we alighted is only about ten minutes from their apartment. What followed was a most delightful evening with these lovely people. It was good to see that financially their lot was improving. They have a son, who at this time was six years old and is growing up to be a lovely person: I doubt if he is being spoilt. By the time we left, it was getting late, so we eschewed the long bus ride in favour of a taxi, which would take about half the time.

The next morning, Saturday, we made a big mistake. Breakfast was scheduled for 7.00 a.m. at our hotel, so we thought we would have plenty of time to check out afterwards and leave. When we arrived for breakfast at 7.00, we found it was crowded; in other words we could have come at 6.45 a.m. You live and you learn. After breakfast we picked up our bags and proceeded to take the lift down to the lobby. It stopped on nearly every floor, even though nobody could get on because the lift was already full. Once down we found that the reception desk was also crowded. It was a long time before our turn came. Then I had to produce my credit card—again. But I have already paid! Do they want me to pay twice? This had never happened before, not even in this hotel when I have stayed here previously—and what a time to happen, when we had such a tight schedule. Finally we could leave. About time. We rushed to the station; we rushed through security, at least in so far as one can. We rushed to the gate with five minutes remaining, only to be told we were too late. What? I have never missed a train in China before. The gate lady was adamant. B…r.

There was nothing for it but to see if we could get a ticket on another train. Surprisingly we could, due to leave at 10.30 a.m., but no seat. B…r. How would you like to stand up for ten hours? We bought some fruit and yoghurt for lunch then settled down to wait. An announcement was made: our train was delayed until 11.00 a.m. B…r. Meanwhile, the seat next to me had been used as a rubbish dump; ever heard of a rubbish bin? The weather was cool, necessitating warm clothing, and it was also raining, well drizzling. The concourse was full of puddles, no doubt due to cars and trucks driving over it. One conclusion to be derived from this long wait is that our 7.53 a.m. train must have left on time— otherwise we would have had plenty of time to catch it. Another announcement was made: our train has been further delayed till 11.30 a.m. B…r. We were moved to another waiting room, where we stood behind a barrier, like race horses.

Suddenly we were racing. Normally Chinese people walk quite slowly, but not in this situation. Nevertheless they were no match for John who sprinted to the front. At least you are not going to be pushed and shoved when you are out in front. We had been allocated carriage 5, but Grace led us to carriage 8, then later we moved to 9, where there is a counter at the end of the carriage. After some time, an attendant came and we were able to pay 65 Yuan extra in order to upgrade to a sleeper. Wonderful. It was in carriage 17, so we had quite a walk through the train, almost to the front. We would travel now in relative comfort.

For the next three hours we chatted until just before 2.30 p.m. when Grace left us at Zunyi where she was living and working as a teacher. It had been truly wonderful to have been able to spend a couple of days with her. In later years I would be spending more time with her in Australia where she came to study for her Masters.

On the way to Guiyang we had been on the roadway, high up the side of the hills. Now on the train we were down in the valley, following a river, with the roadway high above us on its long legs. We still had plenty of tunnels to go through. We read mainly till it got too dark, when we discovered that there was no electricity in this particular carriage, although other carriages did have light. I went into the next carriage to read, where I got chatting with a man who was teaching Chinese in a middle school. Naturally, he asked me how old I was, and

I asked him to guess. He said, "More than 50." True enough, though I refrained from telling him how much more. Then I asked him how old he was, and he asked me to guess. "45." He roused his wife; he showed me his ID card; he was astonished. He thinks I am a wizard, so I did not tell him that it was just a lucky guess.

We had our evening meal on the train in the dining car. Many of the staff were lounging around, some smoking, would you believe? The menu was not exactly à la carte: it was all the same, basically meat, cabbage and rice, all for 20 Yuan, which is double what it was just a few years ago. I had a beer, 6 Yuan, which used to be 5 Yuan. Inflation.

We got into Chongqing at 9.00 p.m., meaning it took 9 ½ hours, which is considerably shorter than the 12 hours for the road trip to Guiyang. We were back in our apartments by 10.00 p.m. What a wonderful time we had had, in spite of and perhaps partly because of the hiccups. It was especially pleasing to meet those friends again. They truly are wonderful people and knowing them has been one of the highlights of being in China. God is good.

4.4: Daying

Daying is a town 2 ½ hours' drive from SISU, just over the border in Sichuan Province. In June, 2014, I was asked if I would I be interested in joining a bus-load of staff members who would be going there on Sunday night, returning Monday night. "Why?"—wrong question. I should have known by this time that you never know what is going to happen until after it has happened. No, this does not mean that in time all will be revealed; all is never revealed, but maybe just enough. So a better question is, "Why not?" I said I would be glad to go.

5.30 p.m. was the scheduled time for departure, or so I was told, but at 5.15 I received a call to the effect that we would have a simple repast in the dining room before we left. Simple it was not: there were many courses as befitting a Chinese banquet. It was 6.30 before we boarded the university bus. "We" included some of the big-wigs, some Chinese teachers and some from other countries, in all about 30 people. The OS teachers included one each from USA, Spain, Germany, Syria, Armenia and Australia.

Our route took us to Yang Gong Qiao, a major intersection not far away, where we headed west for a short distance before turning off onto another expressway to head north. Initially the terrain is mountainous, with several tunnels taking us through to a less rugged terrain. At the border of Sichuan we were stopped by the local police for a check. It appears that our driver had left one of his documents behind, resulting in some delay. You need your personal ID card, your driver's licence and also some other kind of permit. Bureaucracy!

By 9.00 p.m. we had arrived in Daying, a new looking town on the Xi River. Our hotel is called "Marine Holiday Inn". Marine?—we were a long way from the sea. I gather it gets this name because this town's claim to fame is a salt lake, which they liken to the Dead Sea. It is, however, a little smaller. The Dead Sea is about 600 square kilometres in area, whereas this one is more like one hectare. In Australia there is Lake Eyre, which is usually dry, but is more than 10,000 square kilometres in area. I do not know how salty Daying Lake is, but the Dead Sea is 34.2 ppm, compared with the oceans at around 3.7 ppm. I was expecting to be sharing a room with someone else, but no, we were given individual rooms. Wow, and the university is paying for all of this.

After dropping off our bags, some of us decided to go for a walk. Eric from the US, Antonia from Spain and yours truly from Australia went together. We headed towards the lights, finding a street still under construction, the footpath yet to be laid. There were some small restaurants and noisy bars, including a karaoke: not for me thanks. Eric was hungry and was looking for a place to eat. Notwithstanding the fact that we had eaten a large meal not all that long ago, he is a growing lad—young and big. Having walked completely around the block, we settled on a small restaurant, once we had picked our way across the non-existent footpath. I was looking for a beer. There we sat, drank, ate peanuts and talked, while Eric also devoured some scallops. Life is good. I am not sure what the family thought of our presence. I bet they had never before seen anything like it: not only three *laowai,* but an old one wearing a hat (the head still being bandaged from a crack on the head), the young one wearing a Mohawk.

It was late by the time we got to bed, but not before a lovely hot shower. Our rooms were on the fifth floor, giving us a view of the surrounding countryside. The lift is one of those which travels up and down the outside of the building, so that you can view the surrounds as you ascend or descend; I like these.

Next morning we gathered for breakfast in the hotel dining room on the sixth floor, the top. From here there is an excellent view of the salt lake complex. The menu, of course, was entirely Chinese, so I ate very little—no toast, no bacon and eggs, no cereal, no orange juice, no fruit, and **no coffee**. I returned to my room for my own cup of coffee, which I had brought with me. Never leave home without it. By 8.30 a.m. we were back on the bus, where we waited, for around

15 minutes. Apparently the hotel had billed us for an extra room, which was not used. Negotiations took place—I hesitate to say argument. The goodies won.

We were not on the bus for long—even including our wait—as it is but a short drive to Daying Middle School, our destination. We walked onto the oval, where hundreds of students were massed. A table and chairs had been set up on a raised platform, while below were seats and desks for the teachers, both from the school and the university. Now do you think the students were all standing quietly in their serried ranks, waiting for the show to begin? No way: you will never guess what they were doing: studying! They were reading aloud from their English books. I am amazed at how they do this, even in a classroom where everyone is making such a racket, yet no one seems to be disturbed. This middle school was new, the buildings looking fresh and exciting, the oval bright and inviting: I would have loved to run a few laps.

Now it was becoming clear what this is all about: SISU was trying to attract students. It had embarked upon a most ambitious expansion programme, involving the construction of many large buildings at great expense. If those buildings are not filled with new students, then the university would be in serious financial trouble. This year, there were not enough students. SISU was reaching out to middle schools in order to attract future students. This ceremony is the inauguration of a new programme of co-operation between the school and the university. What does this mean?

Bearing in mind that it is not easy to gather accurate information, this is my understanding. For the two final years of schooling the university will assist in teaching those subjects which are useful for overseas study. Students from Daying will then go to SISU for a further year of preparation before embarking on study overseas. The question arises of how this will be managed in detail. SISU is 2 ½ hours away: you are not going to travel back and forth every day.

Photo 45: looking suitably official?

We sat quietly while speeches were given. Even the students were quiet. The headmaster gave the first speech, but unfortunately he did not know how to use the microphone, so he was not clear. He was followed by Professor Yong, who did know how to use it: she was clear. This was followed by a signing ceremony, with the exchange of red folders—all very impressive looking. Meanwhile photographers were everywhere. In this country, they do not try to be unobtrusive, as in the West. They steal the limelight, meaning that everyone else can hardly see what is going on.

It was all over in about 45 minutes, with the first rank of students trotting off as if it was a true military drill. This society is so highly organised. But the day was not yet over,

At around 10.00 a.m. we walked off to a lecture hall, filled with maybe 200 students and some parents. We overseas teachers were asked to sit at the front desk, facing all those pairs of curious eyes. I wondered how many people from other countries they had actually seen in the flesh before. We were asked to introduce ourselves.

Eric went first. When he told the audience that he was from America, they erupted in applause. This society is amazing in its ability to hold conflicting opinions without a problem. China has a love-hate relationship with the US. On the one hand they resent the fact the US is the world superpower, a position which they think belongs to China and China alone. On the other hand they like so much of American culture.

Antonia was second. She comes from Malaga in Spain, so naturally was teaching Spanish. What was remarkable about her self-introduction was that it was entirely in Chinese: she had spent a year learning full time.

When my turn came, I started in Chinese but the bulk was in English— naturally, as my Chinese is so poor. After me came our German teacher, then the Syrian, who told us that he teaches Business Management or how to make money. That got their attention.

Another who received an enthusiastic applause was a man who teaches Japanese. Why should this meet with approval, considering the hatred which the Chinese have towards the Japanese? It was not because of the language he teaches but his nationality: he is Chinese. The lady born in Armenia, who actually teaches English, completed the introductions.

And that was that. We had expected questions from the students or parents, but nothing, so we filed out. For the next couple of hours we stood at the school gate handing out leaflets to anybody interested. Few were, but they took the leaflets anyway. I noticed that there was just one leaflet on Australia; just one. At the end of the day, we still had just one. There were also some small stuffed koalas which had come from Newcastle University; these we gave out. I gave one to a girl who then told us she wants to study Spanish. Oh well.

Just after 12.00 noon we climbed back aboard our bus. It was starting to rain, and indeed it had been overcast and threatening all morning. In fact for the past couple of months we had seen so much rain, mostly in the form of drizzle. We were taken to another hotel for lunch, yet another sumptuous repast. I do not know what some of the dishes were—one may have been shark, another may have been sea cucumber. One fish dish was really nice, having a smooth texture, unusual in fish. And we drank *baijiu* or white rice wine, which was potent at over 50 % proof.

After the meal we were told that it was a siesta time, as we were being conducted to some very comfortable lounge chairs in the foyer. I mean, they were very comfortable. Most of us made ourselves at home, where we drifted off to sleep: must have been the *baijiu*. Later, very much refreshed, I decided to go for a walk. Nobody else was interested. I did not go far as it was raining ever so slightly. Nearby is the local river, the Xi Jiang, so I walked down one side and up the other. It was quite peaceful. People were sitting along the bank, fishing, with what success I do not know, as I saw no fish. There is a lovely park along the river bank, much more attractive than the muddy, still to be laid footpaths.

Photo 46: fishing in the Xi Jiang

At 3.30 p.m. we climbed back aboard the bus to return to the middle school. This time we did talk with groups of students, something I had been expecting to do in the morning. I had maybe a dozen around me, asking all kinds of questions, mainly about study, but also about Australia and other matters. One young man asked what I thought about China's disagreement with Korea, and China's disagreement with Japan, and China's disagreement with Vietnam and China's disagreement with the Philippines. I ignored the question and addressed another student. Hey, there is a common denominator here, in case he had not noticed; just maybe the problem is China. It reminded me of the mother who was so proud of her son: he was the only one in the army who was in step. We chatted for about 45 minutes before it was time to leave. Naturally, we took the obligatory photographs.

At 4.30 p.m. we were ready to head back to Chongqing. It was a smooth ride back, with no interruptions for licence checks. We were back at SISU by 7.00 p.m., but that was not the end of the day, as the university had arranged for yet another meal for us. Whenever I arrived back in Australia, people always remarked on how much weight I had lost; I was thinking that next time they might remark on how much weight I had gained. At least one young lady declined the meal, in an effort to maintain a slim figure.

It had been an interesting couple of days and I am glad I went. I doubt that I contributed much, but at least I provided one of the foreign faces, which seems to go down well, and I suppose, especially if one is as good looking as me!—with or without a bandaged head!

Chapter 5: Some Happenings

5.1: National Day

The current regime took control on 1st October, 1949. Part of their genius was to declare this as the country's National Day and making it a week long holiday. There are two things to note about this. The first is the length of the holiday, reflecting the intense Nationalism of the people, far greater than I have found anywhere else. In Australia, by contrast, we have a one day holiday and nor is our nationalism nearly as intense. The second is the ability of the Party to equate themselves with the Nation, so that loyalty to the CP is the same as loyalty to the country, and contrariwise, any criticism of the CP tantamount to treason. Louis IV of France had a similar view. "L'estat c'est moi."
"I am the state."

For National Day 2011 we were invited to a meal. Great. This had never happened in Tongren. At 4.45 p.m. about 20 of us from overseas gathered outside the auditorium where we boarded a bus to take us to the Hilton Chongqing, a five star hotel, which—as one might expect—is beautifully furnished. There we were joined by sundry other people from other countries also working in the city, including business people and official representatives. We stood around while being served pre dinner drinks. I chose a beer. Wrong choice: it was terrible, both watery and sour tasting. We were then ushered into a large hall, where a group of eight women and one man began playing lovely music on traditional Chinese stringed instruments, such as the *erhu, qipa* and *zuzhang,* while we chatted and sipped our drinks. The main purpose of our presence was to listen to a propaganda address by the deputy mayor. Amazing, is it not? Many much smaller societies, like Australia with its 25 million people, are represented by a head of state. Here we have 34 million people represented by just a mayor.

Photo 47: playing the *zuzhang*

His address was interesting. He gave us a report on the current state of Chongqing, both economic and social. Naturally, everything in the garden is not only rosy, but positively blooming. Whereas the economy for China as a whole was at this time growing at a staggering 10% per annum, in Chongqing it was reputed to be 30%. The previous year $US 1 billion from overseas was invested in the city, this year it was expected to be $US 10 billion. In a similar way, the city was investing huge amounts of money in acquiring overseas interests, including in Australia. Of the top ten megacities in China, Chongqing, we were told, had the cheapest housing, while in rural areas, much was being done to improve education and narrow the gap between rich and poor. And so it went on. Remember that this is National Day. The CP is doing its level best to convince people what a great job it is doing.

The address was in Chinese, but I might say a word about the translator. He was a young man who stood to the side with a pad, noting down what the deputy mayor was saying, then, when he paused, he would translate it into English. In other words, he is an instantaneous translator. This is just so hard to do: your knowledge of both languages must be well-nigh perfect. It was a most impressive performance.

After the address, we had our meal, which consisted of finger food. You took a plate then mingled, talking to people while juggling plate, fork, and for me a glass of wine, which, I might add, was a lot better than the beer. The food was artistically presented, and quite nice, with many pastries and sweet desserts. They were evidently trying to cater for Western tastes.

At 7.30 p.m. our minder told us it was time to go, so outside we went and climbed back onto the bus for a trip to the local concert hall, called the Opera House or the Great Hall, which is a most impressive building, circular in shape, with three concentric rooves, reminding me of the Temple of Heaven in Beijing. Cf. photograph 6. A wide flight of steps leads up to the colonnaded front entrance. I might add that there are stairs everywhere in this very hilly city. The square shaped wings are also grand in scale. Thus the architecture is a good example of yin yang.

We began with the regulation playing of the National Anthem, with everyone standing and waving their flags, which had been provided for the occasion, and—naturally—we did so with unbounded enthusiasm. The anthem was played by a massed brass band, using—perhaps surprisingly—Western instruments. On a lighter note—no pun intended—the band members were running a little late, literally running in just ahead of us. I was also a little bemused by the leader of a Chinese group, a woman with the voice of a fish monger's wife, who was screaming at her group, "**kwai de, kwai de**" (hurry up, hurry up), accompanied by the sight of portly middle aged women attempting to run up the steps. Their performance was in itself a most amusing act.

The concert consisted of around 20 items, all of them massed choirs plus dancing. In this country the mass comes before the individual. They are past masters at co-ordinated performances. It appears that the individual takes his/her meaning from the whole, rather than the other way around. All were conducted with military precision, those marching off after completion of their acts, were immediately followed by those marching on for the next act, giving a seamless continuity. The acts themselves showed an attention to detail, getting everything just right, in a studied, polished performance. This applied equally to adult and child groups alike. Many of the performers were smiling, but they were not grins of sheer delight, but rather masks worn for the occasion. To sum up, this was not a concert showing a group of people thoroughly enjoying themselves in a relaxed manner, caught up in joi de vivre, apart from some of the children. Rather it was an intense, very serious performance, which says a lot about China. Still I enjoyed the acts, the music, the singing, the dancing, the colour—and especially the sight of portly middle aged women running up the front stairs!

By 9.30 p.m., it was over, having lasted some 90 minutes, which some of our group thought was too long. I disagree. I was enjoying myself. Outside we went, but not in any leisurely manner. When a group of Chinese see a door, it is a bum rush, as a visit to any bus stop will illustrate, where there is pushing and shoving to get on the bus in front of everyone else. On this occasion, I was actually knocked over by a woman rushing out. I fell onto an American teacher from SISU, with whom I was walking. Profuse apologies: from me, that is, not from the woman who knocked me over: she continued her headlong flight down the steps. I wonder if she was one of the women running up the steps a couple of hours earlier.

The journey back to our university did not take long, and we had a good view of the city at night. I like the bridges over the Yangtze, brilliantly lit up, and the reflections of lights off the water. It had been a good day.

5.2: Awards' Night

At the end of December in 2012, I was invited to attend an awards' night. At first I was mystified, having no idea what awards were being referred to, as even our fluent English speakers amongst the staff do have some difficulty in explaining things in English; or maybe I am too dense to understand. There was only one way to find out, so I opted to go, especially as it was free and gave me another opportunity to learn about this city and perhaps this country in general. In Australia awards are given to citizens who have done outstanding work for the community, either throughout the previous year or over a long period of time. Australia Day, 26th January, is the occasion when these awards are announced. I am still waiting for mine!—maybe next year. It turns out that this night would be the Chongqing equivalent.

My companions would be three of the Russian teachers, with whom I had been spending a deal of time. We were driven in a university van to a large imposing building, which, I think, is the studio for a local TV station. First we were issued with ID tags, which we hung around our necks. I do not know if this made us important or what. Next we were ushered into the TV staff canteen for a complimentary meal. We were given quite large helpings, although we had little time to eat. It tasted OK, but unfortunately had repercussions in the early hours of the morning: I got quite sick. From here, with some difficulty, we found our way into the auditorium, large enough to hold about 500 people. We were ushered to our seats, to find that we had a torch and a bunch of flowers on each seat. The flowers were plastic, but even so, mine soon disappeared; not to worry. The torch was heart shaped and came in two colours: yellow and blue; I got the yellow. At the appropriate time in proceedings we were to wave one or other into the air—with great gusto, naturally.

In front of us were three large screens. These were soon filled with images of Chongqing taken from a helicopter as it flew over the city. It was all quite impressive. Next was shown a video of a man walking through difficult terrain, carrying a basket on his back. It transpired that in the basket was an old 16 mm projector together with all the other paraphernalia for showing films. This man would lug his equipment over rivers and mountains to show films in isolated villages. After this short video, the man himself came onto the stage to be presented with a bunch of flowers—real ones, I trust—a certificate and a statuette. This was the format for each successive winner of an award. In all there would be ten.

The second award went to a policeman for many years of service. He seemed to be about 60 years old, but with extremely gnarled hands. The video showed him at work tending to his station, but with flashbacks to his earlier life.

The third award went to a social worker in a village, or at least that would be our Western equivalent to his role.

The fourth went to a young woman born with curvature of the spine, and hence confined to a wheelchair. At this point I was starting to wonder what all this was really about: why this person? Is she the only handicapped person in Chongqing?

The fifth went to a district official, who would travel around on his motorcycle, often on muddy tracks, helping to solve disputes and generally catering to people's needs. In addition to the usual awards he was given a car, as a replacement for his motorcycle.

The sixth went to a man who had opened and subsequently run a library in his village, in order to help improve the literacy of the people. Unfortunately he had recently been killed in a motor accident, so the award was accepted by his daughter. About 300 people were being killed in motor accidents every day in this country: that's right, **every day**.

The seventh went to two boys, brothers who have another brother who is handicapped. They would take turns in carrying him around on their backs. This of course is wonderful, but would it not be better if their brother had a wheelchair? If our worthy district official was given a car, why not give a wheel chair to this person?

The eighth went to a police forensic expert, one who works behind the scenes to help solve crimes.

The ninth went to a worker, employed to maintain the water pipes beneath the streets. This again raised some questions for me: why this particular worker? From the video, it did not appear that he was doing anything outstanding, or indeed different from any other worker. What does it mean?

The tenth and final award was not a surprise in this highly militaristic society. It went to the top graduate of the police special forces unit. The video showed him in combative roles.

At the conclusion, all the winners went onto the stage together—all ten of them. I was thinking, "Just ten?" In Australia, out of our population of 25 million, hundreds of awards are given to individuals each year. Here, however, in this municipality of 33 million, there are only ten. What is going on? And why these particular ten? My take on this—and I may be wrong—is that these are token awards. Sure, these individuals have all done great work, but I am also sure that many others have as well. One must bear in mind that this is a society where the group matters more than the individual. Hence, these ten are a representative selection. The maintenance worker, for instance, represents all maintenance workers. This, however, still raises other questions. I gather that the stories of these particular ten happen to have made it into the public domain.

When one looks at the groups represented, we have three people who had contributed to village life; we have three from the police/military; and two from the handicapped community. There was nobody from the education sphere, nobody from the medical professions, nobody from the arts, and nobody from Science. It is not surprising that there was also nobody from the legal profession or from journalism or from religion. These I would not expect as they are more likely to be brutally persecuted by the regime for opposing its injustices. It is also noteworthy that amongst these ten, there is only one woman, and she is handicapped. I understand that there are other awards given within each profession, voted on in some way by members of that profession, but they did not make it to the municipal stage.

In this life there are many people who do great work, but it is hidden. Very few people get the public recognition which they so richly deserve. What of mothers, struggling to raise their children in poor circumstances, their hearts filled with love for their family? What of poor farmers, living lives of hardships, yet with little to show for their toil in terms of monetary gain? What of rural teachers doing their best with little in the way of resources, to ensure that the next generation will be educated? Some of my former students are doing just that: I am so proud of them.

We do, however, have a God who sees all and will reward all. We are, I think, in for a few surprises in the next life, when the so-called great ones of this world will be surpassed by the hidden "nobodies". Their reward will be to hear the words: "Come you blessed of my Father and receive the kingdom prepared for you from the foundation of the world: for I was hungry and you fed me, thirsty and you gave me a drink; I was a stranger and you received me into your homes; naked and you clothed me; I was sick and you took care of me, in prison and you visited me" Mt. 25/34-36.

5.3: The Intercontinental Hotel

On Easter Sunday 2012, I was invited to the five star Intercontinental Hotel for lunch. I have never been a frequent visitor to five star hotels, which are somewhat out of my league. The general manager was a delightful Kiwi lady whom I had not previously met. I did not know the location of the hotel, except that it is in the Jie Fang Bei district, but thought if I went to the end of the line I could walk back. I had trouble buying my ticket to Chao Tien Men, until the patient staff finally got through to me that the train does not go there. Maybe the station was closed for repairs. So I was advised to get off the station before, Xiao Shi Zi, which I did. Then what? I asked the station attendant where the hotel was located, but he spoke no English, but another man came up to help. He found it on the local map. Great. As we walked out of the station, he asked me where I was from. I asked him to guess. He knew I was Asian, but did not think I was Chinese, probably coming from some nearby country. He was astounded when I told him I was Australian. Goodness, was I becoming more Chinese the longer I stayed? Other people had indeed thought that I was Chinese. I was expecting to wake up any morning and find that my blue eyes had become a very deep brown!

After that it was easy to locate the hotel, only a short walk away. In fact it lies about half way between Jie Fang Bei and Luohan Buddhist temple. Cf. map 3.

We had a truly delightful lunch, one of those buffets where you eat as much as you like of delicious Western food. Even better than the food, however, was the company. There were about a dozen of us from a number of countries. Opposite me was a young couple from Finland, here for one year to establish a direct air link between CQ and Helsinki for Finnair. The manager of Fiat was there, plus the manager of an engine company. Another New Zealand lady was head of the British Council, which runs the IELTS tests. We had one Italian gentleman staunchly supporting Berlusconi. He told us that while Berlusconi might like the ladies, especially if they are pretty, his government had not been corrupt, as have other Italian governments. Under his watch the economy did not improve, but it got no worse either. Their sovereign debt had gone from 100% to 120% of GDP. This gentleman would underline his points by saying, "Pay attention!" Maybe he should have been a teacher. It was a delightful meal.

Photo 48: Easter meal

Photograph 48 shows our group at this meal. The jumper, I am wearing, is very clever. Not many people can work out all its meanings.

Now that I knew where this hotel was located, I could go there on future occasions and did so. On one occasion it was the base for an organised walking tour around the city, as reported in chapter 1.10. Over a couple of years, we

Australians and New Zealanders held our ANZAC Day commemorations here. We had other meals here also.

I learnt, incidentally, that the Intercontinental chain was an offshoot of Pan American Airlines, to provide accommodation for passengers, once they had arrived at their destinations, being the first company to do this. The airline itself folded many years ago, but the hotel chain is still doing well.

5.4: ANZAC Day

Sharon, the New Zealand manager of this Intercontinental Hotel, began inviting Australians and New Zealanders to commemorate this important day in our histories. Sharon's talents extend to combining genuine warmth of personality with organisational skills. In 2012 she experimented with an outside dawn service; only eight people attended, the wet weather not helping. In 2013 she decided to arrange the whole affair inside the hotel.

People who do not have the privilege of coming from the Antipodes, may not be aware of the profound significance of this day. On 25th April, 1915, troops from England and other parts of what was then the British Empire, landed in the Dardanelles with the aim of driving up into Istanbul and forcing Turkey out of the First World War. Australia and New Zealand had only recently acquired nation status (1901 and 1908 respectively), so it is not surprising that they were still very much tied to Britain's apron strings. We fought together and have continued to do so ever since. Our two nations are probably closer than any other two nations on the planet. On one visit to New Zealand, an Australian Prime Minister expressed it well, when she stated, addressing their Parliament in Wellington, that Australia is friends with many nations, but with New Zealand, we are family. Indeed my own grandmother came from New Zealand, with some Māori roots.

Australian and New Zealand troops landed at a place called Gallipoli. It was supposed to be a surprise, but it was anything but, with Turkish troops occupying the high ground, raining fire down upon the disembarking soldiers. In this battle, all combatants suffered heavy casualties. Indeed one Turkish regiment facing the ANZACS suffered losses of 100%. In all some 8,709 Australians and 2,721 New Zealanders would be killed. The allied forces fought on till Christmas then withdrew, so the whole expedition was not exactly a roaring success, yet this baptism of fire forged two nations. Each year we remember. Each year we are inspired to work for a better future. If you have not worked it out yet, **ANZAC** stands for **A**ustralia and **N**ew **Z**ealand **A**rmy **C**orps.

When I lived in Canberra, I loved to hop on my bike and ride down to the National War Memorial for the dawn service. ANZAC Day is also frost day in our nation's capital, as it is around this date each year that the first frosts of the oncoming winter appear. It is so quiet, almost surreal, to ride through the early morning mist, sounds muffled. The most memorable was in 1965, the golden jubilee. I can still see in my mind's eye hundreds of diggers, veterans of Gallipoli, marching up Anzac Parade. It was a stirring sight. All of those men have since died, of course, and in 2015 I travelled up to Canberra from Sydney to commemorate the centenary of the landings. That event too was something special.

I have visited Gallipoli, a visit which has achieved pilgrimage status for all patriotic Aussies and Kiwis. Many things impressed me. One was the way a brotherhood was also forged with the Turks. Out of animosity grew mutual respect. Today, Turks are most co-operative when they find out that one is an Aussie, or presumably a Kiwi. A second was the address given by Kemal Ataturk, the founder of modern secular Turkey, wherein he has Mother Turkey telling foreign mothers that their sons who died here are also Turkey's sons. A third combines a photograph with a statue. Outside the Turkish Memorial is a statue of a Turkish soldier carrying a wounded digger for treatment, while the museum has a photograph of Simpson, an Australian soldier, with his donkey, on which is a Turkish soldier being carried to get treatment. I was privileged to be able to visit Simpson's grave at Gallipoli. ANZAC Day is great and has a lot to teach us.

On Thursday morning, early, three of us from SISU caught a taxi to the hotel, two Australians and one from England; she was the only one there from some other country. As more people arrived, I was astounded to find that there were so many of us here in CQ—something like thirty. The Song Room was decorated with both flags, which are very similar. At around 7.00 a.m., the Australian National Anthem was played, but curiously not New Zealand's; I do not know why. A colonel from New Zealand then gave us an address. He is an interesting man. There was one other ex-serviceman there, Richard, from Australia. An ANZAC poem was read by one of the children, whose father was headmaster of a school. Then it was my turn to don my clergyman's hat and lead the assembly in prayer. This is a role I did not often perform in China. I was wondering if the hat would still fit. Two children laid wreaths, we all recited the Ode, followed by a minute's silence and finally the playing of the Reveille and Last Post completed the proceedings.

I am conscious that not all my readers share our traditions, so let me quote the Ode, which is actually the fourth verse of a poem composed by Laurence Binyon (1869—1943).

"They shall not grow old, as we that are left grow old;

Age shall not weary them, nor the years condemn,

At the going down of the sun, and in the morning,

We will remember them."

The next item on the agenda was breakfast, and what a repast it was, serving as my main meal of the day. Each table was decorated with our two flags, with the order of service at each place, plus a sprig of rosemary for remembrance. We were also sporting a picture of a poppy, another tradition, since this flower grew "on Flanders fields" in Belgium, where many an ANZAC would die later in the war. Breakfast was a good time to talk and make new friends.

Unfortunately I could not linger, as ANZAC Day is not a holiday in this country, and I had classes to teach. Patricia and I headed off fairly quickly, as we were intending to take the train and so would need at least an hour. Instead, however, we opted for a taxi, since we could get this immediately in front of the hotel, so were back at the university in plenty of time. Later in the day, my students asked me the meaning of the poppy. China idolises the military, so have no equivalent remembrance in their culture: they only remember victories; I cannot imagine them turning a defeat into a national day; this would be unthinkable, although they do reinterpret defeats as victories.

Thank you, Sharon, for organising such a wonderful event. In fact it was such a success, that it was repeated the following year.

In 2014, ANZAC Day fell on a Friday. I had planned to meet John, another English teacher, who actually comes from England, at Sun Square—the usual meeting place in this university. I left my apartment with three minutes to spare—ample time. Now—and please do not get me wrong here, as I am in no way trying to denigrate the inestimable character of our worthy John—but let it be said that this particular noble person does indeed have something of a reputation for tardiness. You can count on one hand the number of times he had actually been on time. Therefore, after I left my apartment, I deemed it precautionary to check his apartment. Sure enough, his light was not on. Oh dear!

I went up to his door and knocked. No answer. Oh my goodness, don't tell me he is still in bed! I knocked again: still no answer. I will have to ring. I just hope he has not turned off his mobile phone. Ah, success: his phone is ringing. "Hello," he said, "where are you? I am waiting in Sun Square!" I assure you, miracles do happen.

We were leaving early, with more than ample time, partly because we did not know how long it would take us to find a taxi at such an early hour, but as luck would have it, we hailed one inside the university grounds. Also as luck would have it, our driver was young and inexperienced. No he did not know where the Intercontinental Hotel is located. No he did not know Minzu Lu—a major road. No, he did not know where Yuzhong District is. But all is not lost, as he did know Jie Fang Bei (Liberation Monument). I mean everybody from the age of two onwards knows Jie Fang Bei, whose photograph graces the cover of this book. The hotel is close by, but he did not know precisely where. We drove around, and around and around. "OK, this will do," as I forked out nearly 50 Yuan for the fare. Eventually we found our way there—still very early; in fact we were the first to arrive.

As it turned out, our ceremony did not get under way till 6.50 a.m.: we still had to organise details, as our regular organiser—the manager of this hotel—was still in Beijing, attending a meeting. The ceremony included a welcome, saying the Our Father, reciting of the Ode, playing of the Last Post and Reveille, with a minute's silence in remembrance of those who had fallen. We next sang our two national anthems. My task was to say the final prayer and give a blessing. All of this took place beneath our two flags and a wreath. There were fewer people there than last year, only about fifteen. We missed a family of five who were here last year but had since returned home.

Next followed a truly sumptuous breakfast, at the end of which one of the two soldiers present gave a magnificent address, during which he quoted Paul Keating's great speech at the internment of the Unknown Soldier about twenty years' ago. One of these soldiers came from Australia, the other from New Zealand. The text of this speech is now on a wall at Villers Bretonneux, in France, which I visited in 2018, exactly 100 years since the Australians recaptured this town from the Germans on 25th April 1918, a key battle which marked the beginning of the end for Germany in the First World War.

It was good to mix with each other and chat. Proceedings ended with our two soldiers carrying the wreath of remembrance downstairs to be laid in the lobby.

John and I returned to SISU by train, as by now the metro was operational, beginning as it does from 6.30 a.m.

5.5: Acting

Before coming to Chongqing, I had been teaching in Tongren, a town in Guizhou Province. Over several days, Greg and I were with a television crew from CCTV (Central Chinese Television) for the filming of a documentary. This experience has been related in my previous book on Tongren, but my acting days it seemed were not yet over.

On one Wednesday in November, 2011, four of us from SISU had an interesting time indeed. We were picked up at 2.00 p.m. and driven in two cars to a local TV station. In their studios we were made up so that we would be more or less presentable before the TV cameras. The makeup room had two mirrors, each surrounded by lights so that the make-up artist could see what she was doing. They told us that she was one of the best they had. Now why would they say that? How many do they have anyway? Maybe they thought we were such a terrible looking mob that only a supreme effort on the part of one of their finest could make us look anything like presentable.

Having thus been made presentable—more or less—we were taken to the studio, where we stood, one by one, in a room with a blue coloured curved wall, while we recited two lines, to wit: "Chongqing—a place you must visit. "*Chongqing fei qu bu ke.*" Or at least that is what I said. The others said the same, except that their first line was in Japanese, Spanish and French respectively. I guess I was representing the English speaking world. In other words it was just a promotion to sell the city. It was not easy to get worked up about it, especially as two lines are hardly enough to get into the spirit. We were supposed to smile, which is what the director kept telling me: "*Xiao.*" I don't think I did a good job.

I must confess here that my heart was hardly in it. I guess that when it comes to the advertising industry I am a little biased. I do not have a great respect for the way the truth tends to get stretched to the point of straight out lying. In the real estate business, for instance, "cosy room" really means broom cupboard size, "spacious" means there is nothing in it, and "ocean views" is only correct if you stand on the toilet seat to get a distance view of a tiny patch of blue. An utter dump is called "a renovator's delight". And on it goes. TV advertising is often deplorable. "**AAAAALLLLL AUSTRALIA HAS BEEN WAITING FOR THIS MOST AMAZING EPISODE YET!**" I know one Australian who could not give a stuffed fig. They often misuse the word "ultimate"; they advertise gambling, then have the hypocrisy to state, "And remember to gamble responsibly". Who is being irresponsible?

You find celebrities endorsing this or that product, but are they sincere? Do they really use or even like the products they are supporting? Or are they just doing it for the money? Well, if it comes to that, we got paid too: hardly enough for an overseas holiday, but still something. I did try to be ethical, by changing what they wanted "Chongqing—a place to be" to "Chongqing—a place to visit", then had a rethink to the statement above, where I added "must", albeit a definitely overworked word. This city, incidentally, is certainly worth a visit, although you may not want to live here.

I decided I would stick to teaching.

5.6: Phoning Home

Family is very important and my brother, naturally, especially so.

This is the internet age, is it not? Nowadays, it is easy to contact people all around the world, not only via the internet but also by telephone. I mean, all you have to do is dial, right? If only life was so easy.

My brother, my favourite brother (I only have one) was having a birthday. Actually he tells me that he does not have birthdays any more. Once I told my students that I was 150 years old when I was born, and I have been going backwards ever since. Uh? Sometimes I am really terrible. At any event I wanted to phone my (favourite) brother for his birthday. Let me restate that: I really wanted to phone him. Nah, that's not good enough. Let me say, I REALLY, REALLY wanted to phone him. Clearer? Incidentally, he was not on the internet, so that avenue was ruled out.

Now my mobile phone was fine, but it could only be used within China. I only had to go into Hong Kong and it no longer worked, so I had Buckley's chance of phoning Australia. Nil desperandum, as one could buy a phone card, which could be used from one's fixed phone. Now that is simple enough: you buy the card, hit the right numbers, and hey presto, you are through. Did I mention lifting the receiver first?—yes, more complications.

I bought a card.

It took me ages to find out how it worked, as I kept following the instructions but without any success. "Press 1 for Chinese; press 2 for English." So far so good. Then you are told to key in your code, "followed by the pound". What does that mean? It turns out it means the hash key; where "pound" comes from, I have no idea. Just to make sure you are paying attention, the code is 14 digits long; I kid you not: FOURTEEN! Why do you need so many? I was not phoning outside the galaxy. The next step was to key in yet another number, thankfully only four digits long this time, "followed by the pound". Whew!—I am getting tired. Next come the country code, the area code and finally—finally—the number. Oh no, I forgot "followed by the pound". That surely should get me through. No luck. You repeat the whole process: still no luck. What am I doing wrong? You have to dial 00 before the country code, that's what. Goodness. So in all you have to push a total of no fewer than 40 keys.

Eventually, finally, at long last, I got through—but not to my brother. I needed to ring my bank in Australia first. Well, at least I had completed the practice run, so that from now it should be easy, right? Wrong.

I took my now used phone card to the shop and asked for another, the same kind. I bought it, but was a little surprised that it cost 50 Yuan, instead of 25 Yuan; the first card was marked 50 Yuan but I had paid only 25 Yuan. "Are you sure this is the right card?" Yes, he was sure. It wasn't, but by the time I found out, I had already scratched the numbers, so I could not return it. I was not a happy chappy, so went back to tell him. This time I bought the correct card—from someone else.

Good. Now I can ring my brother. I scratched the card to reveal its secret numbers, only to find that the numbers themselves were scratched away. Oh no. Now I cannot use this card either; it is useless. For the second time I have done my dough. I bought yet another card.

This time I was very careful, like very careful. Then equally carefully I hit all those keys, well the first 26, when I was told that I had an invalid number. What? I took my card to my co-teacher. What am I doing wrong? She examined it carefully. "That is not a 5: it is a 6." Oh my goodness, I had not scratched hard enough. Maybe now—at last—I can phone my brother.

Back in my apartment, very, very carefully, I keyed in all those digits, and hit all those keys—all 40 of them. There was a ringing sound. Wow! Someone picked up the phone at the other end. Miracle!

"Happy birthday, mate."

Photo 49: a SISU walkway

I loved walking around campus for exercise in the afternoons. Photograph 49 shows an interesting path between the upper and lower campuses, even if it does look a little dilapidated.

5.7: A Scungy Mao

I have stated previously that some of us English teachers were working under the umbrella of a Hong Kong based organisation, called AITECE (Association for the Teaching of English and Curriculum Exchange Inc.). Every year someone from Hong Kong, generally the head, would pay a visit to AITECE teachers scattered around China. At the end of 2011, Hugh came to Chongqing, where a number of AITECE teachers were working at various universities. All of these teachers are motivated by more than monetary gain, not that this would be much of a consideration anyway, considering how low the wages are, even if we were getting a little more than the locals. It is good to be backed by an organisation, and not to be swanning off on our own: it does give us a little more clout, so to speak.

Hugh spent two days in Chongqing, enough time to meet with the five AITECE teachers at SISU and also with the administration. This gave both us teachers and the university a chance to look at how things were going. Sometimes there are real concerns which need to be addressed, as indeed there were in Tongren. Most of the time, thankfully, all was well, but there is considerable value in knowing this. Hugh expressed the desire to have a meal with us, so I suggested Monday night, just in case the university decided to host a meal on Tuesday night. As it transpired they opted for Monday night as well, without telling us, of course.

The vice president of the university was our genial host, together with the head of the Foreign Affairs Department and his deputy. While this meal was more social than anything else, it did give the administrators a chance to show their appreciation and was a pointer as to how things were going. It also gave us a chance to have a look at them. I had never met the *waiban* (head of the FAO) until this occasion, and he took the lead in making the appropriate toasts. It is just so important in this culture to say all the right things, even if there is not much substance. The vice president had a lot to say when the topic of conversation got around to earthquakes, as he is, if I am not mistaken, a structural engineer by profession. Only three years earlier there had been a massive earthquake in Sichuan, not all that far away. Shoddy workmanship due to corruption on the part of communist party officials resulted in the deaths of many people, including a lot of children. Meanwhile the *waiban*'s assistant, who is really the one who handles our affairs, had little to say: I was wondering why.

The following day just the AITECE people had a lunch together. Only about 200 metres from our building is the auditorium, which has the Alliance Français office, and on the second floor a café, called "Café Liberthe", thus combining "coffee" with "tea". Here one can get not only good coffees but also Western style meals. I had a pizza, which I thoroughly enjoyed: it was surprisingly good. Even Greg would have thought so, and he is no mean pizza maker.

I invited Hugh to come to one of my classes, and that was good—good for everyone, as it made a pleasant change for the students. I brought a map of the world so that they could see where Ireland is located, as that is where Hugh came from; perhaps surprisingly, some of them even had a rough idea. These particular students were heading off to Lancaster University, which is at least in the same part of the world.

One morning, Hugh and I headed off to the local wet market (fruit and vegetables) for a walk and a talk. There I bought some bananas and other fruit, which cost something like 14 kwai 5 mau, which can also be written 14 Yuan 5 mau, or 14.5 Yuan—about $2.30. There are ten mau to one Yuan. I handed the lady 20.5 Yuan, so that all she had to do was to give me 6 Yuan in change. The 5 mau note I gave her was brand new, yet she refused it. Why? I thought I was making life easier for her. Instead she gave me 5.5 Yuan in change. Fine, so what difference does it make? I noticed that the 5 mau note she gave me was scungy. Let me explain here that unlike Australia, which uses plastic bank notes, China uses paper, and when this paper gets old, it really looks terrible. It not only looks dirty, but begins to come apart, and in fact this particular 5 mau note I was given had been torn then patched up with sticky tape. As I said: it was scungy, which is even worse than grotty. I looked at it and thought: "Will I accept this?" In the past I have refused such notes, but on this occasion, for some reason, I did not. "I will just pass it on to the next person," I was thinking. Not so easy.

Photo 50: John at the wet market entrance

Photograph 50 shows John, another AITECE teacher, standing at the entrance to the local wet market. As can be seen, you need to descend a flight of stairs, not always easy with sellers sitting on the steps displaying their wares. Inside were rows of counters stacked with meat, fish, vegetables, eggs, spices and even various sweets. The floor was generally awash, so one needed to be very careful not to slip. This is where I was handed that scungy mao; now I had to get rid of it.

A couple of days later, I had occasion to visit a supermarket, whereupon I produced my scungy 5 mau note. The check-out chick refused it, as indeed she had every right to do, even though it is still legal tender. "Oh, oh," thinks I. "Am I going to be stuck with this note, with nobody willing to take it?" I was not going to even consider the possibility of hawking it from vendor to vendor over the next few weeks, hoping that somebody would take it, so I thought of another solution. A bus ride in this city was costing 2 Yuan. There was no card system or any electronic system at this time, although it would not be long before this would be introduced. You simply pop your 2 Yuan in the slot when you hop on a bus. So the very next time I boarded a bus, you can guess where that scungy 5 mau went. Now it was a government problem. I suggest it be taken to a bank for destruction: it had well and truly served the community and passed its "use by" date. When are they going to start using plastic bank notes?—probably never as China is moving swiftly to become a cashless society.

After his two-day visit, Hugh headed back to Hong Kong, but not before leaving us with a nice little present each, in the form of a lovely box of Toblerone. Thank you, Hugh: I love chocolate. Is there anybody who does not? Yes, is the answer, as I know one person who does not. Most strange.

5.8: Earthquake

In April 2013 a deadly earthquake occurred in Sichuan Province, which borders Chongqing; the epicentre was at Lushan, near Ya'an, still 500 km away. In contrast to the terror and horror in Sichuan, here the scene was more comic. People were rushing down stairwells and pouring out of buildings, still dressed in pyjamas. Some were even taking the lifts, which is not a good idea: should the power fail, they would experience a very rough landing indeed.

It amazes me how so many people opt for the lift on a regular basis, rather than walking up the stairs, even when they have only one floor to ascend, and especially when they are supposedly fit young adults. A lot of my teaching was done on the ninth floor of what is known as the Hongwen building. In the morning, as we would be going off to class, there would often be a crowd of people waiting for the lift. They never seem to worry about weight limits, and will squeeze more and more people into this small space without a thought. I have even heard the warning siren going off, indicating that they have exceeded the limit, yet nobody will move to get off. Nor do they gain much in time, as those who took the lift would arrive at the ninth floor only slightly ahead of me. I find it curious that there is such an emphasis on gyms and diet regimes, yet some people will not walk up a few stairs.

Getting back to the earthquake, by my clock, the quake struck at 8.03 on a Saturday morning. I was up by then, but not fully dressed. I was not about to dive outside still scantily attired, so the first thing I did was to get dressed, but by then the shaking was all but over: it did not last long. Interestingly, I knew immediately that we were having an earthquake, perhaps having lived in Rabaul, Papua New Guinea, for a number of years contributed to this. Here there were no injuries and no damage that I am aware of, which is far from the case in Lushan and Ya'an, where some 193 lost their lives and something like 11,000 people were injured. There was much structural damage, with also some damage to cultural relics. Ya'an incidentally, is a small provincial city, with a population of around 1.5 million, so about the same size as Adelaide.

5.9: Thrills and Spills

Life is so exciting: you never know what will happen next. Indeed at times one's whole life can change in an instance. I saw plenty of examples of this when working in hospital. One's life might be sailing blithely along, when "bang": one is hit with a heart attack, or a stroke, or a traffic accident. I used to tell the patients in hospital that the difference between us was that today they were horizontal, while I was vertical; tomorrow it could be the reverse.

On a Monday evening in mid-June, 2014 I invited a student to join me for a meal in the students' dining room: my shout. This was at 5.30 p.m.: students do tend to eat early here. You pay for the meal with a card, which is scanned by a machine; sounds simple enough, except that the machine did not like my card. What is my security No.? You mean I have to yell out my number in the middle of the dining room? I told the lady, but it still did not work, so Lucy had to pay for my meal. How embarrassing! I owed her a meal.

"Let's go for a walk," she suggested. Chinese people like to do this after a meal and an excellent practice it is. Actually, I had already been for a fast 50 minute walk before our meal, but a stroll wouldn't hurt—or so I thought. In Sun Square we met up with three other girls, friends of Lucy. They told me that the university pond was being drained. "Oh no! Why?" We decided to have a look, and yes, there was now hardly any water remaining. What have they done with the fish?—and the frogs?—and all the other animals? Even the plants had been cut down. We decided to walk around to the other side to the spot from which photograph 16 was taken.

The next thing I knew I was flat on my back, having slipped on very treacherous wet, slimy ground, my head hitting the ground, hard. I sat up slowly and felt the back of my head; it was muddy and bloody. I sat for a while before getting up carefully, walked gingerly across to a nearby bench and sat down. I just wanted to check on the damage. Do I have concussion? Am I feeling nauseous? Do I have a headache? No on all counts; I felt OK, probably better than the students. Tiffany looked as if she was about to have palpitations; Lucy was on the verge of crying; Elsa was a little more practical. "You need to go to the clinic." She was right, as I could not see the back of my head, so needed the experts to check it out. It was not far.

At the clinic I was told that I needed stitches, but they could not do that there, because at this hour the resident doctor had gone home; I would need to go to a hospital. They patched me up. I walked back to my apartment to get some money—you will not be looked at in a Chinese hospital without money. I remember that young Australian man in Fuzhou who was left to bleed to death on a hospital floor because he had no money. Lucy went back to get her bag, and we met again in Sun Square, which is a favourite meeting place. At the front gate we piled onto a taxi and off we went to the South-west Hospital Emergency Centre. Hey this is not an emergency. In Australia we were calling it "A and E"—Accident and Emergency. At the desk I paid the money, gave them my particulars, all in Chinese, even using my Chinese name. We waited.

Meanwhile I was getting phone calls. It appears that Lucy rang Cyril, who rang everyone else. She also told the dean of an English department, who—promptly notified everyone else. I was sitting peacefully in the waiting room, when Denise turned up. "Hello, what are you doing here?" says me, thinking that she needed some treatment as well. No, she had been contacted and told to look after me, precisely because she was my co-teacher. She remained with me for the rest of the evening, even paying all expenses. It transpired that the university would foot the bill, possibly around 1,000 Yuan. I was wondering who else knew about this. The way things were going I could be on international news by midnight.

I had the stitches put in, with a blue covering over my head during the process, which I am sure looked so fetching, and Lucy holding my hand, the others looking on concernedly. Next the doctor put a mesh over my head to keep everything in place: goodness, I would not want to lose anything. Apparently I look like a pixie, or maybe a nun with a wimple, or maybe a cross between both. The next step was to have a CT scan. There may have been some danger of internal bleeding, and this could be serious. I was sure that everything was OK, as I did not even have a headache. By 9.00 p.m. I had had the CT (Computer Tomography) scan—an interesting process, which was a new experience for me. You lie on your back, perfectly still, while the machine buzzes and X-rays are taken around the head in sections. I lifted my head just a little, as the back of my head was precisely where it got banged. I just had to keep it there without moving.

We were told there would be a two hour wait for the results. At this point it was really not necessary for the students to hang around: they did have exams looming. They went home while Denise and I stayed and chatted, while checking a screen for my name and number to come up. To get the results, you are given a bar code, which is scanned by a machine in the waiting room, and it is this machine which gives you the X-ray sheet. It is all so high tech.

Naturally it was late by the time we got home, and around 12.30 a.m. by the time I got to bed. Next morning, I was reading my Bible, when I came across Ps. 36/23: "The Lord guides the steps of a man and makes safe the path of one He loves. Though he may stumble he shall never fall for the Lord holds him by the hand." Yeah?

Life is full of surprises: sometimes the thrills, sometimes the spills and sometimes both together.

Some of the English teachers at SISU were undergraduates from a certain American University. They were not trained teachers, which itself created some problems. One young man, for instance, would rarely give any mark under 95 %. This is unreal. One young lady only lasted a few weeks before she had to return to the US. Hence I question the rationale behind this policy. This story concerns one of these young teachers, a young man whom we shall call Erwin—

obviously not his real name—a strapping young lad with a very healthy appetite. Unfortunately he also had a mishap, falling through the glass door of his shower, putting out his hand to break his fall. It is not a very good idea to put your hand through glass. Let me illustrate with another story.

Many years ago—1986 to be precise—I was teaching at a boarding school in Australia where I had set up an Astronomical observatory on the roof; I was teaching Science. In March of that year, 1986, I had some year 9 students with me in the early morning in order to watch Halley's Comet, this being the best time to see the tail. After the viewing, as the light began to increase, I told the boys to return to their locker room to prepare for the day, asking just one to stay behind to help me put the telescope away. We had just finished when another lad rushed back to tell me that there had been a fight. Immediately I went down to the locker room, where indeed two lads had been fighting, one a small boy, the other rather big.

It appears that the small boy dashed out of the locker room, and slammed the door shut, gloating at the big boy through the glass: "Nah nah nah nah nah"—as boys do. The big boy promptly punched him: through the glass. I found the smaller boy not only suffering from a smack in the face, but also having some glass in his face. As for the larger of the two, he had cut his wrist. I took a look and could see his partially severed artery pulsing. Oh, oh, this is not good. I lifted his hand as high as it could go, wrapped a towel around his arm and went to get car keys. I piled the boys plus one other into the car before driving very carefully to the local hospital.

The nurse on duty had formerly been a student of mine. She put the lad into a wheel chair before going very carefully upstairs in a lift to one of the wards. Here she gingerly began of take off his clothes—maybe a mistake. The artery burst, sending a fountain of blood skywards. One compact was not enough. She pressed another and another onto the wound: all turned red. With bloody hands she pressed the emergency button to summon help. It took some time for the situation to be brought under control. You will be pleased to know that the boy lived—both of them. The moral of this story is that it is not a good idea to put your hand through glass. Fighting is not a good idea either.

Erwin was not fighting, but he did put his hand through glass. He had been out drinking, so it may not be surprising that he lost his balance in the shower. Luckily he did not sever any arteries, although he did incur considerable damage with several deep cuts. Furthermore, a shard of glass fell onto his foot, cutting that as well. He required many more stitches than my four or five, the whole operation to stitch him up taking some four hours. Yes, folks, most definitely I had been outdone.

Now it just so happened that he had the same co-teacher as I had: Denise. She was the one who looked after me so well, in what turned out to be but a small dress rehearsal for the main event. I cannot begin to tell you how much she needed to do. A couple of days afterwards, some of us visited the patient in the hospital emergency trauma ward, bringing some food, to wit, some soup and a couple of pizzas. Other visitors had also brought him food, none of which, I am sure, went to waste. Erwin's appetite indicated that he was on the road to recovery, although it was going to be a long road. He would not be returning to the States that summer.

Now how do I feel at having been outdone in the injury stakes? Did I feel any burning desire to recapture my crown (if you will excuse the pun, since it was my crown which was injured)? The answer is … no way; not on your nelly; absolutely not; never in a million years. I do trust that is clear. Remember that it is a good idea to look after ourselves and not go falling over, either onto the ground, through glass doors or anything else.

5.10: Daddy

One facet of life in China as a teacher which I really appreciated was building relationships with my students. They are such good people that it was not hard to like them. One could empathise with them in the ups and downs of life, with their struggles, victories, hopes and fears.

On my afternoon walks for exercise students would often accompany me, providing excellent opportunities for talk. On one such walk in Tongren, Erica declared, "I would like you to be my father." I mean she is not an orphan, she does have a father and an extraordinarily good one at that; she has a mother and siblings. I was privileged to have spent an entire week over Chun Jie one year staying with them on their mountain farm.

Something similar happened in Chongqing, with Lucy deciding to adopt me as her father. It was really touching to be walking across campus and to hear a shout behind me from the other side of a square, "Daddy, Daddy". It was curious that she chose to use this form, which in the West tends to be used more by young children, rather than "dad", which adults tend to use. There is something quite special about either form.

In Chinese, it is *baba*, first tone and fourth tone. The word for mother is *mama*, two first tones. In Hebrew dad is *abba*. When I was living in Israel I would hear children using this when calling for their fathers. It is the word used in the Bible by Jesus for God. God is indeed our father. There is a neat part of the Passion Narratives when a murderer, Barabbas, is set free instead of Jesus, who is subsequently crucified. *Barabbas* simply means "son of the father"— which is who Jesus is, and now who we are too.

Yes, being hailed as "daddy" across the campus was something very special.

5.11: Nationalism

If I were to name the most important aspect of the Chinese psyche it would be Nationalism—with a capital "N". I have written about this many times, especially in "China—Behind the Mask" (Austin Macauley 2017) Chapter 14.

It is no big deal in Australia if foreign firms own our buildings, our companies, our mines, our farms or whatever. But this cannot happen in China. Foreign companies must have a Chinese partner. Foreign companies cannot buy Chinese banks, or land or have a stake in Chinese mines. Goodness, even geology maps are considered to be state secrets. Using international credit cards can be a problem too: they must be Chinese.

In Chongqing I bought a shaver and a computer, in both cases opting for overseas brands and in both cases the salespeople for the Chinese brands were really angry. I must buy Chinese.

I decided to download Skype, but it cannot be done, because one can only download TOM.Skype, which is the Chinese version. In this instance, it is not just a question of nationalism, but of control. What I said or wrote could be subject to government eavesdropping and hence censorship. The computer man came to my apartment and I asked him how he felt about this. I was not sure whether the people here took the lack of freedom of speech for granted, so that yet more government control was like water off a duck's back. Just possibly, never in the history of the human race have so many people been so rigidly controlled by such a relatively few number. His reaction surprised me: furious would be an apt description. If that is general, then this government is indeed living on borrowed time, before the people assert themselves. We live in interesting times.

The Chinese national anthem has the line: "Let us build the New Great Wall". Well, they are doing just that—in cyberspace. I find it fascinating that 2,200 years ago, Shi Huangdi built the first section of the Great Wall for two reasons: the first was to keep out the "barbarians", while the second was to keep in the Chinese so that he could control them. That is exactly what is happening today with this new internet Great Wall. It seems that in the last 2,000 years much has changed, yet nothing has changed, at least not in terms of basic human nature. The quest for power remains just as enticing and just as destructive now as it always has been.

On a related topic, although it may not seem to have relevance at first sight, I do not believe in atheism. I do not believe it is possible. I do believe in God, but not just because that is what I was taught from my mother's knee. Philosophically God has to be, to ground everything in Being, to sustain everything in Being. God's presence is all pervasive and dynamic. This is one reason why I like evolution so much. It just fits in so beautifully into God's creative dynamism. As humans, we are made in God's image and likeness; our whole being screams out for God. It is of the essence of who we are to be oriented to God. This is why I say that to purport to be an atheist is a bit like saying that I am water but not H_2O. It is a contradiction. I think we all worship something, but differ in what that something is. Whatever it is, this is our "god".

Now let me explain where this is leading. Communism is ostensibly atheistic. So what in fact did people here in China worship as their "God"? Mao Zedong. He became their God. This is why, even today, you cannot say anything against Mao. I think there is yet another god here: it is China itself. The country is truly worshipped, idolised. There is nothing greater than this empire. That is why China thinks it can do anything with impunity. There is no law outside of itself; it is solipsism. These are strong words, but I think they are true in the main. The people here are wonderful: warm and friendly for the most part; but if you rub just a little you will find rampant nationalism. Religiously, most people are Buddhists, but my feeling is that for most people this is largely surface and does not really satisfy their deepest needs. It is mostly seen doing certain things at important times in your life, such as at weddings or funerals, or when visiting temples. Here people pray fervently "to the god for…" whatever they want. This superficial religion, of course, is not limited to Buddhism; I am sure you will find this with all religions.

Feel free to disagree.

5.12: Miscellaneous

5.12.1: A glowing toe

Early one morning in late autumn, 2012, while it was still dark, I was having a shower, when I noticed that my big toe was glowing. Now that is odd. Now I can understand bright ideas emanating from one's head, but from one's toe? Of course, in Chinese the word for "head" is *"tou"*, first tone, with the same pronunciation as "toe" in English; so what is happening here? I told my students that they are built upside down, with their head at their feet, but maybe I am. Maybe I had been too long in China.

At any rate, I bent down and brushed of ... a something. I turned on the light. It was an insect of sorts. What? It was a firefly in its larval stage: hence no wings. I had seen these in Papua New Guinea it the adult stage—a kind of beetle. At night they would congregate in some tree, their lights flashing on and off—just magical. This might not seem to rank highly in the scheme of things, but to me it was wondrous. It is often the small things in life which can bring so much joy.

5.12.2: Buying wine

From time to time I would buy wine from a French owned supermarket chain called Carrefour, especially Australian wine. The purchasing process is interesting. You don't just waltz in, pick up a bottle and pay for it at the checkout. No, no, no, that would be just too simple. Said bottle has a lock on for one thing. Instead you go to another counter where you pay the money and get your receipt. Carrying this in your hot little hand, you then proceed to the checkout, where you hand over said receipt and present said bottle. The checkout chick then calls her supervisor, while she attends to other customers. You are supposed to stand there patiently and wait. In due course the supervisor arrives; she takes the receipt and goes back to the wine department to ensure that everything is above board. You wait: patiently of course. More customers shove their way past you. Again in due course, the supervisor returns, still clutching the receipt in her hot little hand. Now, you would think, is the time to remove the lock, which is wrapped around the neck of each bottle, so that you can escape. Not a bit of it, as at least this had been removed by this time. Then why not just take your bottle and run? Weird. I never cease to be amazed at the quite unnecessarily complex obfuscations of bureaucracy. Enjoy your wine.

5.12.3: Beggars

Chongqing has its beggars. You find these of course in any society and this one is no exception. One often sees people with a deformity of some kind. We might tend to be a little embarrassed by any deformity we might have. In China, where loss of face is so important, one would think that these people too would not want their deformities paraded in the public domain, but not a bit of it. On the contrary, their clothing is peeled back in order to reveal whatever is ailing them, presumably to enhance their earnings by appealing to people's sympathy. I have seen the most grotesque deformities in the form of tumours, withered frames, or in one case, a man with a massive, misshapen leg. Another man had no hands: these may have been cut off in order to enhance his begging appeal. I have even heard of fathers doing this to their own sons. Horrible; evil. Disabled people do get a government pension, by the way.

Most of the people on the streets are not beggars, but are peddling their wares of one kind or another. Photograph 51 is an example of this. These men are tradesman, seen sitting on their tool boxes, offering their skills.

Photo 51: looking for work

5.12.4: Information

I have mentioned many times that China is not an informational society and have given examples. Often at the beginning of semesters, we would not know our teaching programmes, or when the semester will end, or when holidays will occur and a host of other matters.

In June 2012, for example, I was told during one class that this would be their final week of semester. Really? It is so nice to know these things in advance. Subsequently I was told that one of the classes had not finished and would not do so until 20th June. Later I happened to meet one of the students from this class down the street. She informed me that this was a very busy time for them and that probably nobody would be turning up for class. Wonderful. Nevertheless, I prepared these classes, and I turned up. If they chose not to come, that would be their affair. The administration even continued to pay me.

Nor was David, my colleague in the Lancaster Programme, immune to confusion. He was told before the semester began that he would not be free until 27th July, so he booked his return flight to the UK accordingly. Subsequently he was told that he would be finished by the end of June. Based on this information, he rebooked his flight, paying a penalty of 3,000 Yuan for the privilege. Subsequently it was revealed that the original information he was given was correct. Did anyone know what was going on around here?

Chapter 6: Entertainment

Introduction

Life is to be enjoyed. I believe that this should apply to whatever work one is doing. Indeed the ideal is to be enthusiastic about one's work. I love it when you hear people talking about their work, stating that it is "the best job in the world". Here are some examples:

1. Marine biologist. People love to go on holidays to visit coral reefs, especially the Great Barrier Reef, which is the world's largest. When I was living in Papua New Guinea, I would go snorkelling over a reef three times a week. It was fantastic. Each time I would see something different.
2. Astronomer. To peer back in time, to marvel at the immensity and diversity of the universe, to make new discoveries, is really exciting.
3. Teaching. It is so fulfilling to see the dawning of understanding shine in the eyes of one's students, to be able to inculcate important life principles, to make a difference for the future of people's lives.

These are just examples: every occupation should be enjoyed. Furthermore, any occupation should be undertaken in order to serve the community. A bus driver, for instance, is not just earning a pay packet: he is doing a service to the community, most especially so if he has good public relational skills. In China, students would ask us what courses they should do, especially if they planned to study overseas. We would reply, "Well, what are you interested in? What are your strengths and talents?" These were irrelevant questions. What they wanted to know was what courses would land them the best jobs so that they could earn the most amount of money. China is obsessed with getting rich, no matter how this is achieved.

I am a teacher—a truly fantastic profession, whereby one can influence the lives of young people in most important ways. I think it unfortunate than in Australia we have a tendency to regulate everything. This may be for the best of motives, but the underlying philosophy appears to be that you can legislate for goodness. You cannot. It is tragic that the teaching profession is losing excellent teachers because of unnecessary red tape. For goodness sake, teachers are professionals: let them get on with the job. Have confidence in them.

So we work—in whatever job or profession we are engaged in. Presumably we work hard, as we should, if we are really dedicated. But we need time off; we need relaxation. What did I do in China by way of entertainment?

6.1 Television

I had a television set in Chongqing—and it worked. This had not been the case in Tongren, my previous abode.

I had five English channels. NHK gave me news from Japan, while GW gave me news from Germany. CNN, an American channel, gave a more global perspective. RT, "Russia Today" was not specifically aimed at telling viewers about Russia. Instead it was an intense propaganda channel, aimed squarely at America. Every single item was anti-America. Nothing, absolutely nothing that America did was right. Finally there was CCTV 9, the Chinese channel. This too was heavily biased, not so much anti anybody, but more pro-China. Everything that China does is right. If anybody, anywhere, on any issue disagrees with China, that that person/organisation/country is wrong. There is no shade of grey here. The other person's point of view is not considered. There is no room for negotiation.

As an example of the above, we have China's recent invasion of the South China Sea. The government claims it is open to negotiation, but only on the premise that the entire sea belongs to China, which of course it does not, except by force.

I could sometimes watch a movie, as there was a movie channel. Sometimes the movie was even in English. Curiously, I could barely hear it, even when the volume was turned up to maximum. I know not why. There was not a great selection, and they tended to replay them quite a few times, but I still enjoyed them.

6.2: Alliance Francaise Auditorium

One of the attractions of this university is the first class entertainment. In June, 2012, for the second time in as many months, Alliance Française from the French Department put on a concert.

Alliance Française was set up to promote French culture and the French language around the world, including Australia; indeed other cultures have done much same, such as the Goethe Institute, founded to promote German language and culture. In the middle of the 19th century, Victor Hugo declared that French culture was the only culture, the only civilisation in the entire world, and that the French people were specially chosen by God to promote their civilisation to less fortunate peoples elsewhere. I doubt if anybody would hold such extreme views today, but the French remain intensely proud of their culture and are vigorous in promoting it. Nowadays we have the Chinese version, the Confucian Institute, although this is not primarily cultural but is a propaganda tool of the government, attempting to promote Chinese policy around the world.

Most concerts I have seen at universities have been student productions, but this one involved professional performers in a baroque concert. While this may not be my favourite style—I prefer 19th century classical music—I was most certainly not going to pass up a free concert. And I am so glad I went.

6.2.1: A Baroque Concert

The concert was due to begin at 6.00 p.m., which seemed to me an odd time, as it is right in the middle of evening meal. I would have thought that 8.00 p.m. would have been better, but maybe the group had another engagement. This group consisted of three men playing violins, one woman playing a cello, with another on keyboard. The name of the group is Stradivaria. I wonder if any of their violins is a Stradivarius. They played pieces from Papini, Flamengo, Pedrini and Pergolesi. Teodorico Pedrini is especially of interest. Born in 1674, he became professor of music at the court of the emperor of China from 1711 until his death in 1746. This was during the Qing Dynasty, at a time when a number of European delegations, notably from the Portuguese, were being received in China. This was also a time of Chinese expansionism—although one must admit that China has always been expansionist, seeking to conquer more and more territory. This was the time when Chinese armies conquered both Tibet and the North West (East Turkistan). The Chinese army was however defeated in its attempt to conquer Burma as well.

After a short intermission, Pergolesi's Stabat Mater was played and sung, the instrumentalists being joined by a soprano and a counter tenor. The latter is rarely heard these days, but in the Baroque period they were common. In those days the singers were called castrati, because they were indeed castrated as boys, in order to retain their high pitched voices. Thankfully, this practice no longer takes place, as these male singers can have their voices trained; at least I assume and hope that this is the case. These singers were superb, not only blending in well together, but both possessing such pure voices. They alternated solo pieces with their duets. The soprano was actually Chinese, a lady by the name of Zhang Zhang. Even though one would have thought that the Baroque Period is about as European as one can get, there was nevertheless a strong Chinese element in this concert, and indeed in Pedrini's music. Cultures are not static: they change and part of this is through mutual influence. Nowadays we are seeing more and more Western influence in China and Chinese influence in the West.

It was a short concert, lasting only about 90 minutes, but excellent. I am glad I went.

6.2.2: A Short Film

Oddly enough, on the following evening I found myself back in the auditorium, together with an Irish gentleman and an English lady: yes, we were dressed up, with the gentlemen wearing coat and tie. The occasion was a short film being made by some first year students. We were supposed to be judges in a competition. We sat at a desk in front of the stage while one of the students gave us a rendition on a violin. No doubt our faces betrayed our concentration, pleasure, even awe. Surprisingly there was only one take, so that the whole shoot was all of 30 seconds. I can only conclude that our acting was excellent from the first. This was certainly not the case last year when we were asked to take part in a TV commercial extolling the virtues of Chongqing as a tourist destination. On that occasion I had to do take after take. I do not think I ever got it right. Nevertheless, the commercial was still being played at this time on local TV.

6.2.3: A Ballet

On a Sunday night in September, 2012, we had a concert from a visiting ballet company from North East China, the Huanyang. Communication was as terrible as ever, but I was fortunate in that I happened to find out about this concert while at dinner with fellow teachers at around 6.00 p.m. Naturally, I had no ticket, but not a problem as I simply wandered up to the door and was given one—for free. Wonderful.

The ballet was superb. There were about a dozen items altogether, each one short, as the concert lasted about 1 ½ hours. Some were segments from classical Western ballets; some were from classical Chinese dances; others were modern compositions. There was such grace and poise, such colour and movement. The latter did create a problem for my camera, as it is difficult to capture clear photographs in poor light when combined with rapid movement: you tend to get blurs. But this can also be good, giving a better sense of the vitality of the whole, not just a fixed moment in time. Ain't life interesting: you never know what will happen next.

6.2.4: A 7th Birthday Concert

In this same year, another concert was staged in the Alliance Française concert hall on 12th December. What a great date this is: 12—12—12. We will not see the like again—at least not in my lifetime, as the next time such a conjunction will occur in 01—01—01, or the first of January, 2101, and I for one will not be around at that time. Certainly some people alive now will still be alive then.

This particular concert was staged to celebrate the 7th birthday of Alliance Française in this university. Various French dignitaries were present, including the French ambassadress, who had flown down from Beijing for the occasion.

The concert began at 7.30 p.m. with a professional pianist, playing excerpts from various composers. He was absolutely superb, although I would question his selection of pieces. He was playing to an audience of mainly young Chinese people, not the cream of Parisian society. The pieces were boring, dull. His final two selections were much better, with a bit of life and actually including tunes, whereas his earlier pieces were eminently forgettable.

This was followed by a concert produced by the French students themselves, with two ladies doing the presenting, one Chinese and the other French. All night both French and Mandarin were used. I must confess that my understanding of both is severely limited. The French teacher also joined the performers at one stage, playing the flute. She is a talented lady. She was also my tennis playing partner. The concert consisted of eleven items. I will not give you a detailed description of every item, but some were standouts, at least for me. I must say that the overall standard was amazing. It could easily grace the boards of the

Sydney Opera House, with patrons paying big bucks to attend; for us it was free. This university is certainly a great place to be. The quality came not only from the actual performers, but also from the costuming and from the backdrop scenes, on a large screen, computer controlled. It was all excellently done.

This was illustrated especially well in one item, "La Derniere Classe d'Alphonse Daudet", ("Alphonse Daudet's Final Class"). Daudet was a 19th century novelist. In his early career he was a teacher, a job he detested. Apparently his pupils gave him a hard time: welcome to the classroom jungle. Politically he was a monarchist and—which is not surprising—had an ardent love for his country. The end of the scene shows him going up to the "blackboard" and writing—in actuality, standing in front of the large screen and moving his hand in the air—" Vive La France"—with the lettering appearing simultaneously on the screen. It was very well done.

A scene from Mozart's "The Marriage of Figaro" was one of my favourites. There was such attention to detail in the costumes and also in the backdrops. What I particularly liked was the singer. She is a mezzo soprano, which is comparatively rare in this country, where most female singers tend to be sopranos. Contraltos are even rarer. Indeed, most singing and most musical items tend to have a higher pitch than our Western music, possibly because the language itself, with its tones, tends to be at a higher pitch than English. I have noticed that in past concerts which I have attended, the lower notes had been supplied by Western instruments, such as the cello and double base. This lady could sing; I could have listened to her all night.

In another item, "Concours Hippique", three young women played *erhus*, two stringed instruments. Their piece was Mongolian. You may know that for the Mongol peoples horses are very important, a key component of their culture. The music was onomatopoeic, marvellously fitting the galloping of horses, while the backdrop screen depicted horses racing across the wide Mongolian plains. Cf. photograph 52.The ending was superb, with the *erhus* sounding just like the neighing of horses. The musicians were highly skilled. Most enjoyable.

Photo 52: Concours Hippique

Another item, entitled "Under the Paris Sky" ("Sous le Ciel de Paris"), depicted various scenes of the Paris skyline moving across the screen to the accompaniment of some dancing and music. Curiously there were three instruments: violin, piano accordion and guitar. I wonder what made them put those three together.

Perhaps my favourite item was what really amounted to a fashion parade, with models dressed in Chinese clothing from various dynasties. I am certainly no expert here, but I think they came from the Han, Tang, Ming, Qing, the Republic and the current communist party dynasty. The backdrop screen did tell us which dynasty was being represented when the various models walked on, but I did not get it all. Traditional Chinese clothing can certainly be both sumptuous yet elegant. Of course most of the more lavish clothing was that worn by court officials and other members of the ruling elite, while the poor peasants in the countryside wore much simpler and less colourful clothing. Yet this was not always the case, as one garb from the Tang Dynasty (AD 618—907)—the purple coloured wrap—was worn by the lower classes, yet it is still elegant and beautiful. In photograph 53 she is the one in the middle, with—on her right—the empress' dress, and on her left, a nobility dress. On the wings we have modern dress, which you may just recognise! The Tang represents a high point in Chinese culture.

Photo 53: Chinese clothing

At the end of the performances, a large birthday cake was carried onto the stage, while all the performers gathered around, with the dignitaries also being invited up onto the stage—no, not me. With all their different costumes it was certainly colourful. Congratulations to all those who made this possible, and particularly to the previous head of Alliance Française here at SISU, who was now working in Oslo.

SISU was a great place to be.

6.2.5: Down Town

Yet another concert was organised by the French department where the venue was not SISU but a theatre down town. The theatre was new, in an area refurbished by the now disgraced former leader of CQ, Bo Xilai. It contains a modern complex of shops and restaurants and is probably patronised by the nouveau riche, as the prices were somewhat on the high side. We arrived early and sat in one such establishment, thinking maybe that we would have a cup of tea before the performance began, but not at those prices, thank you. We declined.

The nature of the concert was surprising. There were seven performers and they were all rap dancers, a very modern dance form. The music, however, to which they danced, was classical. What an interesting combination! All music, I suppose, is to some extent onomatopoeic, but some pieces a lot more so than others. Maybe they chose their pieces carefully. One piece they did not choose, but would I think, lend itself to a rap dance interpretation, is The Sorcerer's Apprentice.

Four of us attended the concert, arriving by taxi, which is a good way to travel, firstly when you have a few people, and secondly when you do not know where you are going, both of these conditions being operative in our case. At the end of the concert we returned home by bus, as we found we were on the bus route back to our university, although not the bus that would have dropped us right in front, as that one ceases to run after 8.30 p.m. I have no idea why: trying to encourage students to get home early?

6.3: Chuan Opera

On Friday 16th December, 2011, we overseas teachers were asked to meet at 6.00 p.m. if we wished to see some Chuan Opera, to be staged at the newly constructed Opera House. Would I ever! So after an early meal, I joined a goodly number of other teachers for the half hour or so drive. Oddly enough, we were dropped off around the back, so that we walked through the backstage area, where the artists were getting ready for their performances. It was clear to me that we should not have come in this way. Our guide was uncertain, so that at one point we stopped, went back, stopped again, then continued. She was very uncertain. Once inside, we needed to find seats, but we had no tickets. Where do we sit? Once again, confusion reigned. Some of us found seats, but were then told that these were reserved. "Move up please." Those behind us had already sat down and did not want to move back, so one of the American teachers and I had to squeeze past till we came to the end. Should we sit here? For goodness sake, let us just sit down; they can throw us out if they want to. We were in a good position, to the right of centre stage, six rows back, with the American lady on my right and a Russian lady on my left. From the large banner at the back of the stage, it was evident that this performance was being hosted by the Municipal Government for us people from overseas, not only from SISU but also from other institutions, as a Christmas offering. I think this is fantastic.

These operas can be colourful and dramatic, as photograph 54 illustrates.

Photo 54: Sichuan Opera

18 months previously, I had watched a performance of Sichuan Opera in Chengdu, Sichuan Province. What is the difference between Chuan and Sichuan I wondered? Probably none, as Sichuan simply means "Four Rivers", as apparently there are four major rivers in the province. Chongqing used to belong to Sichuan, and is culturally much the same. Chuan Opera has morphed over the years from early forms dating back to the 3rd century BC, into different styles, five of which were combined early in the 20th century into the present form. We would see three of these forms: Hu harp, Dan opera and Kun tunes. Parts of Sichuan Province tend to favour one or other of these forms, with Hu harp prevalent in the west of the province, Dan opera in the north and Kun tunes in the east, which includes Chongqing .

Proceedings began at 7.30 p.m. with an address by Mrs Chen Yuanchun, Director General of Human Resources and Social Security Bureau for the municipal government. The Chinese like long grandiose sounding titles. They also like to laud themselves to the skies, as once again we were treated to a diatribe of how wonderful the government is, and what great work it is doing, much along the same lines as we had had at an earlier performance at the Great Hall a couple of months back. She concluded by hoping that we foreign experts would have a happy time here; well this one certainly was. We had a host and hostess from the Foreign Experts Bureau plus another hostess from the opera theatre.

The opening act was full of colour and dancing, replete with long whirling ribbons, which I really like. They are so rhythmical. No wonder they are used during gymnastic performances at the Olympic Games. We also got a glimpse of their elaborate masks, and a couple of fire breathing men. I do not know how they do this, but it looks quite spectacular, with a gush of flame heading into the air. It was a short act.

This was followed by another even shorter act, and a humorous one at that, but an unscheduled act. The front of the stage was decorated with pot plants, a very common feature in this country, but one which prevented the people in the front row from seeing the performers clearly. Surreptitiously, two people sneaked up to the stage and started taking down the pot plants. Soon others from the front row joined them, so that one by one these pot plants disappeared, much to the amusement of the audience, who were laughing more at this act that at the formal acts on stage.

The second—formal—act was very long. It depicted an episode from one of the Four Classics in China, called "The Water Margin". A man called Wu Song became a hero for beating off a tiger with his bare hands. These days, the odds are stacked a bit more heavily in favour of humans, with the tigers being outnumbered by about 30 million to one. His sister-in-law, Pan Jinlian, tries to seduce him. Pan's husband, Wu's brother, is a mere cake maker, and she despises him, but Wu sticks up for his brother. She proceeds to attempt to seduce him by using her hands in a lascivious way while she makes cakes in front of him. This cake making involves eight steps and went on for a long time. This is where I became a little puzzled. Now I have seen lascivious dances in other parts of the world, but this one does not even come close. Some of the pelvic thrusts in PNG dances, for example, leave little to the imagination; in comparison, Pan's dancing was somewhat staid. What I did like was the supple movements of her hands. Wu, by the way, is not interested in her advances, and I do not think I would be either. This culture is not sexually explicit, at least not in my book. Nevertheless, it has not stopped them from producing 1.4 billion people!—and just maybe there is a link here. I think there is.

We had a kind of interval next, when six volunteers were invited onto the stage. It was quite a bum rush, with eight making it. My American friend sitting on my right missed out. She was No. 7, but turned back thinking she was too late, while others kept going. They were required to follow the stylised movements of lance fighting, which our hostess kept telling us was "s-w-ord fighting"; gosh English can be difficult. They were pretty hopeless, of course, but each received a stuffed panda toy for their efforts. Other stuffed toys were thrown into the audience, but only as far as the fifth row. We were sitting in the sixth, so sorry, but nothing to bring home to you.

The third act tells the story of two young ladies going for a walk, when they come upon a man, Hua Yun, who kills two eagles with a single arrow shot. Now please do not try this: we need to protect our eagles. One of the young ladies, Hanyan, falls in love with him, and vice versa, though they do not realise it themselves. In one clever scene, the other lady, Tuo, does realise it, ties an invisible string between them and proceeds to pulls the string so that the two lovers move in perfect harmony. It was well done. At the end of the scene our archer fires an arrow off stage; it plopped about 2 metres away. I think our eagles are safe.

The fourth and final act, called Jinshan Temple, tells the story of a white snake who is looking for her husband. The temple denies her access, so she summons up a flood, depicted here by actors carrying boards with painted billowing waves, causing widespread damage. Floods have been common in China, as indeed they are in Australia. What I liked in this act was the acrobats, turning somersaults, and the lifting: the actress portraying the white snake was quite petite, while her counterpart was a much larger male, but they really worked well together, especially when he was lifting her on high. Also in this act we had the face changing, for which Sichuan Opera is famous. A man wears a colourful green mask, but an instant later he is wearing a bright red mask, next a purple mask. What happened to the green and red? I do not know, and I do not know anyone who does: it is a secret.

That was it. It was a very enjoyable evening, and I felt fortunate that the government put it on for us. 18 months previously, as a tourist in Chengdu, I paid a lot of money to see a similar performance; here we were guests. After this wonderful evening it was time to board our bus—after we eventually found it—for the trip home. Some people got off early, as they had not yet eaten, and it was now about 10.00 p.m. They must have been starving. For me it was off to bed, as tomorrow there was yet something else on—a trip to Dazu, as related in chapter 4.1.

6.4: New Year Concerts

Yes, "concerts", as in plural: there were two. In other places where I had worked, putting on a concert over the Christmas-New Year period was traditional. In Fuzhou, Anglo-Chinese College would stage such an event, while the city government would host a dinner for expatriates, which would also include some musical items. Tongren University also had its concert. But here there were two, both under the auspices of the university.

The first one on Monday night, 26th December, 2011, was the longer of the two, from 7.00 p.m. till 10.15 p.m. This was under the wing of the English Department, known as CELL or College of English Language and Literature, which was not my department, as I belonged to the International Department, on the other side of the campus. There would be an amusing repercussion to this. At the end of the concert, Pat—who did belong—was invited up to the stage. I stayed behind, till urged up also by some worthy official, or maybe he was an officious worthy. Photographs were taken with the big wigs, after which the dean of the college spotted me, zoomed over and said—very politely, of course— "Who the hell are you?" I needed to explain myself. Well, I really was an interloper, but I thoroughly enjoyed the concert.

The second concert was under the auspices of the university, so for this one I was not gate crashing. It was shorter, also starting at 7.00 p.m. but finishing before 9.00 p.m.

There is no need to describe these concerts in detail. Instead, let me give some general impressions, and leave you with some photographs of particular acts. Western concerts—depending of course on the genre—often feature individual solo performances, or, when you do have group acts, lead singers or lead musicians. The emphasis here, by contrast, is on the group, with many items featuring co-ordinated movements. It can look quite spectacular.

Synchronised movements, however, are notoriously difficult to perfect. When I look at my photographs, taken in a moment of time, I notice that the actions were not perfectly synchronised, although in the flurry of movement in real time, this was virtually unnoticeable and nor does it really matter. I marvel at the time and effort that goes into these productions, with many hours of practice over many months, plus the hiring of costumes, all for a three minute performance. I for one, really appreciate their efforts.

Another overall effect is the riot of colours. Costuming was exquisite, providing a dazzling visual display. There were vivid blues, reds, yellows and whites, albeit not much in the green part of the spectrum. It is interesting that while green is such a restful colour, and indeed today stands for the whole environmental movement, it is not common in people's apparel. Maybe it does not match many people's skin tones, but I will leave that assessment to the fashion aficionados. The acts were mostly vivacious, with lots of vigorous movement, from swishing sleeves to swirling Spanish skirts, from twirling basketballs to the flashing of long hair. In one act, the girls wore caps initially, which they took off to display long locks and these they shook vigorously in time with the music. I have seen a similar dance in Xishuangbanna in southern Yunnan Province. As for the basketballs, a group of boys appeared on stage carrying basketballs. What is going on here? Are we going to have a basketball match? Not really, but they did twirl those balls most skilfully on their hands, backs, arms, in fact every which way. It was a sight to behold.

The acts were a mixture of Western style—such as the waltz—and Chinese style. One peculiarly Chinese item was a musical ensemble, in the form of a sextet, with two players on *zuzhangs*, two on *pipas,* one on an *erhu* and another on a flute. Briefly, the *zuzhang* is a horizontal stringed instrument, plucked with the fingers, a little like our Western harp. Cf. photograph 47. The *pipa* is similar to the Western lute. The erhu is a two stringed instrument atop a small sounding box, while the flute, in one form or another, appears common to many cultures. All the performers were girls and they gave an exquisite performance.

Photo 55: playing the *pipa*

While indeed most of the acts were in groups, there were a few solo efforts. One girl in a blue dress sang operatic style, and in my humble opinion she should have her voice trained. She needs better breath control, and also needs to be a littler truer on some notes, especially the higher notes, but she has a really good voice. Embarrassingly, my opinion was actually passed on to her, and she replied that it is too hard to become a professional singer and sustain a career. A couple of acts later she was followed by a girl in a red dress, whose voice is even better: she was heavenly. I could have listened to her all night.

One lighter note—so to speak—occurred with the teachers' act, in the form of a waltz. It took three attempts to get started. One could see the performers in the wings, the music would start and they would launch into their routine, only to have it all come to a grinding halt and they had to start all over again. I do not think anybody minded.

Also on a lighter note, the audience was brought into the act, with some dancing on stage, and the distribution of stuffed toys. Believe it or not, yours truly got one, as it was thrown into the audience, but no, I did not catch it. Rather it got me, hitting me in the face, before dropping conveniently into my lap. Anybody want a stuffed toy?—too late. I gave it to the lady next to me.

For the second concert, the area in front of the stage became the orchestra pit, with 5 violinists performing at the start and at various stages throughout proceedings. This too was enjoyable, especially when playing some lively classical music.

So there you have it, a short summary of two wonderful New Year concerts. If you decide to attend one of these next year, do not worry about gate crashing.

6.5: German Boys' Choir

At the risk of seeming to be something of a culture vulture, I must confess that I do like going to concerts. In mid-2012 I was told that there was a German boys' choir singing in the Great Hall, otherwise known as the Opera House. Would I like to go? Indeed I would. My understanding is that this was connected with Children's Day on 1st June.

My contact was a student who gloried in the English name of John; he had the tickets. We agreed to meet at 5.30 p.m., allowing us enough time to get to the concert hall, where the performance was due to begin at 7.00 p.m. At 5.15 p.m. he called me. "I am worried about the traffic; could you come immediately?"

"No, I am still eating my meal. I will see you in ten minutes." We agreed to meet in Sun Square, one of the squares on this campus. Now I did not know John from Adam, but did not think this would present too much of a problem, as all I would have to do was to look for a young man with black hair and deep brown eyes! I arrived and waited. Eventually I rang him. "Where are you?" He was there, but I had walked right passed him. I guess there are just too many people here with brown (grey?) hair and blue eyes. He was a somewhat portly young man of about 20 years old, his physique becoming more common in China, especially amongst the younger generation, as the country becomes wealthier.

Together we walked down the hill to the bus stop. In this city you are either walking uphill or downhill. We caught the 215 bus, although the 265 would have suited equally as well, as they both go to the Great Hall. After we got off, John blithely informed me (a) that the concert would not begin until 7.30 p.m., and (b) that he was hungry. We repaired to a restaurant where John ate while I sat.

Remember that I had already eaten a somewhat early meal. Expect the unexpected, but don't expect a lot of information.

After he had finished, we still had plenty of time, so John suggested a walk; Chinese do like to walk after a meal. There is a large and impressive square between the concert hall and the Three Gorges Museum, so here we strolled. Still early, we entered the hall, after I had paid John the 100 Yuan for the ticket—just a little pricey—to find that hardly anyone else was there. Upon which John wanted to sit in another seat, rather than the one allocated. OK. Later, as more people arrived, we got turfed out of those seats, so ensconced ourselves elsewhere, close to three Westerners. It transpired that they were Germans, and were travelling with the choir. During interval, my companion, being of a rather ebullient nature, not backward in coming forward so to speak, introduced himself and began chatting. The choir, consisting of about 50 boys, came from an area near Nuremburg and were on a six-week tour of some Chinese cities. The following day, in fact, they were going off to Shanghai.

At 7.30 p.m. the concert got underway. The boys lined up in three rows on steps, their ages seeming to range from about 7 to 17. Some of the latter are going to be big boys when they grow up. They were accompanied by four musicians: two on trombones and two on trumpets, although much of the singing was acapella style. Their timing was perfection, their notes exact, but somehow I found it a little too mechanical, lacking heart and warmth. Maybe the audience felt the same way, as there was constant chatter throughout, much to the annoyance of the conductor who asked the audience at one stage to be quiet. Many in the audience were in fact children, and in this city where the One Child Policy was being enforced the little darlings can do nothing wrong. The chatter must have been a little disconcerting to the singers, too. One man behind us was even talking into his mobile phone, to the point when other patrons asked him to stop. You do not have a culture in this country of turning off mobile phones in concerts, in church, in class, and especially not when driving.

There were some 29 items, with the audience clapping politely but hardly enthusiastically at the end of each, and sometimes even before the end. This changed dramatically when two Chinese songs were sung. Suddenly the audience came alive, clapping loudly in appreciation. Nationalism here is extremely strong, but how diplomatic of the Germans to prepare these songs. Each item was short, so that the concert was over before 9.00 p.m.

John was returning home via the metro, so wanted me to do the same, even though it was far more convenient simply to catch the 215 or 265 bus from the other side of the road. The metro station is not a long walk from the concert hall, less than ten minutes, and perhaps not surprisingly in this mountainous terrain, it was not underground, instead being perched on legs above the ground. We took line 2 to Da Ping station, where our paths would part. The station has a good view of the Jia Ling river below us, with the lights from tall buildings being reflected off the water. It looked attractive. I took line 1 just seven stops to Shapingba. This is where it got interesting. One moment we are looking down on the river, while the next moment we are inside a tunnel, having plunged into the side of a mountain. We did not appear to be going downhill to any great degree either, yet at Shapingba there are many steps to climb up before reaching street level. There is a bit of a walk to the bus stop, so all in all it was getting late by the time I got back home, walking the final ten minutes in light drizzle, very common in this climate.

6.6: A Teachers' Concert

This university is so alive. Concerts are common, unlike the previous places where I had lived in China. Having a large concert hall does help and must encourage people to make full use of it. In May, 2013, there was a concert put on by teachers, where many if not most of the performers were teachers. This is wonderful. The students in the audience certainly seemed to appreciate their efforts.

Naturally, nobody told us it was on. One of the other AITECE teachers here found out about it from a student—again, naturally—and rang me at about 6.40 p.m. with the concert due to start at 7.00 p.m. This was actually a big improvement, as recently I had found out about a class photograph, which I was supposed to be in, at 2.15 p.m.—but the photographs had already been taken at 1.30 p.m.—just a tad late!

In I went: no admission charge here. John and I sat close to the front and near the centre, and waited, as the show did not get underway till about 7.30 p.m. Not to worry. The items included comedy acts, dancing, singing and instrumental music. I particularly liked the colourful costumes and especially the effects as these twirled around the stage. On the whole, most performances lacked finesse, being just a little wooden, often with the entertainers not quite sure of their movements, their co-ordination not quite precise, but remember that these are not professional artists. They are to be highly commended for a great night's entertainment.

One musical piece stands out. I had heard it before, the previous December (cf, section 6.2.4), but this in no way detracted from my appreciation and enjoyment. We had three young women playing *erhus,* that traditional two stringed instrument, originating from the north east of China, or possibly from Manchuria. This particular piece, however, comes from Inner Mongolia, on whose sweeping plains the horse is a most important animal. Remember that mounted Mongols conquered China and much else besides in the 13th century.

As an aside here, not long before a student told me that Mongolia belongs to China. "Really? Why?"

"Because we conquered Mongolia." This is interesting, as it implies that might is right, that you have every right to whatever territory you can conquer. Then why were the Chinese so upset when Japan conquered much of China? My reply to this student was, "No you didn't: Mongolia conquered China," much to his surprise. So logically I suppose that China should belong to Mongolia now. But let us get back to the concert.

I like onomatopoeia. I like it in prose, as in "the wind whistling through the trees", or "the buzzing of innumerable bees". I like it in poetry, as in this verse from Henry Lawson's "The Fire at Ross's Farm":

"The cattle tracks between the trees
Were like long dusky aisles,
And on a sudden breeze the fire
Would sweep along for miles;
Like sounds of distant musketry
It crackled through the brakes,
And o'er the flat of silver grass
It hissed like angry snakes."

Above all music lends itself to onomatopoeia. One only has to think of the thunderstorm in the third movement of Beethoven's "Pastoral Symphony", or Paul Dukas' "The Sorcerer's Apprentice", where one can easily imagine the brooms and mops at work. Perhaps the best example is the firing canons in Tchaikovsky's "1812 Overture", or maybe Rimsky-Korsakov's "The Flight of the Bumblebees". This *erhu* piece represented horses, and at the end the performers were able to mimic the neighing of horses amazingly well. I liked it.

One item I did not like particularly well was a military piece, with nine men in military uniform standing ramrod straight and singing in perfect unison, not a smile within cooee, although, unsurprisingly, they were greeted enthusiastically by the audience. As I have said before the army is idolised in this country. I am not sure why, but maybe because the size of the country is largely due to conquests of neighbouring territory. Much of what is now called part of China, was not so in the past. At the end the soldiers saluted and marched off.

One of our French teachers played the flute, which she has done on previous occasions, this time accompanied by a violinist and a singer. They were not bad either. We also had an electric guitar, with the performer certainly not lacking in enthusiasm. In all, it was most enjoyable.

6.7: Towel of Babel

This university is called "Sichuan International Studies University". As you may gather it is all about international outreach. Many students come here because they are planning to go abroad. As an aside, I find this use of terminology interesting; in Australia, we always say "go OS" i.e. go overseas, because our nation is an island, so that one cannot go abroad without going overseas. At this university, students may study international business, or international law or marketing, or other cultures amongst other such studies, and also other languages. Every year a drama night is held, in which students from various language departments put on performances in these other languages. It is a contest.

6.7.1: May, 2013

Over two nights in May, 2013, various language departments showcased their wares and what they had to present was, for the most part, truly excellent. Quite a few presentations were in English, but we also had Spanish, Japanese, Russian, Vietnamese, Arabic, Italian, French, German and Chinese. There were ten items on the first night and eleven on the second, each being given 18 minutes. I have no intention of giving a detailed description of each, but here are some of the highlights.

In my humble opinion, the best performance was the Russian, although I think officially it came in third. It was a presentation of Tolstoy's "Anna

211

Karenina". The costuming was exquisite; I have no idea where they got them. I had been wondering how they would stage the final scene, where Anna throws herself under a train: I mean, how do you get a train onto a stage? They did it brilliantly with a cardboard cut-out of the front of the train, as if it is approaching, with tracks leading from it, accompanied by appropriate sound effects, so that all Anna had to do is step in front of it, as the lighting faded. It is certainly a tragic tale, similar to "Madame Bovary". We need to count our blessings, as often we do not realise and appreciate what we have. The grass always looks greener …

The Italian Department put on a piece from Giuseppe Verdi, again with elaborate costumes. I love this music. The singer was very good, even if a little breathy; perhaps he was nervous, and why wouldn't he be? Once again, the heroine dies so tragically.

Another favourite was "Salome", this one produced by the English department. Here too the costuming was quite good. In this interpretation, Salome falls in love with John the Baptist, and has his head cut off so that she could kiss his lips! You won't find this in the Bible. Her dance, incidentally, was most chaste: no seven veils here. One curious anachronistic detail was John making the Sign of the Cross, thus revealing the producers' rather vague knowledge of Christianity and Judaism. After the show, I saw one of the players still wandering around carrying John's head! This production was also a tragedy.

There were two productions of "Aladdin's Lamp", one in Arabic, the other in English. In the English version, Aladdin becomes greedy and is eventually destroyed by his vice. Thus he is not the hero: yet another tragedy. I must say that I preferred the Arabic version, where Aladdin is the good guy, the drama ending with his wedding. Oddly enough, in this officially atheistic country, he and his bride are married by a priest!—maybe of the Syrian rite? To deepen the mystery, this priest was a woman! Now when is this set?

The performance which got top marks did not get my vote. It was "Don Juan", presented as you may have guessed, by the Spanish Department. I think the principal actor overplayed his part. In the spirit of the night, there was a yet another priest—always identifiable by the large crosses they wear—and the Sign of the Cross. Much be catching. Also in the spirit of the night there was a dead body. Did I say "a"?—there were bodies everywhere, hardly a single actor left standing.

It took the Japanese to restore a little decorum with a traditional Japanese tea ceremony—all very well mannered. Tea drinking, of course, came from China, and the Japanese are very much aware of this, even though they have developed their own traditions. It became very important in Sino-Japanese relations. Even after Japan invaded China last century, they respected Chinese culture and made no effort to destroy anything connected with it. Ironically, it was Mao Zedong who attempted to destroy much of Chinese culture.

A Chinese production depicted a tea house in Beijing, with snapshots of its role at various stages in China's recent history. It opens in 1898 with young dissidents plotting rebellion against the Qing Dynasty. The next scene is in 1918 with disquiet that their revolution was not working. The final scene shows the same people in 1945, now much older, lamenting the destruction that had taken place.

"Chicago", the musical, was another English production. Unfortunately, the songs were dubbed, rather than sung, but the dancing was good, and energetic, as one might expect from young people. Interestingly, the press corps was portrayed as puppets. Now what is this saying? I have no idea: if there is a hidden message here, then I missed it, unless of course the press in China simply echoes government propaganda? Perish the thought! Naturally this musical ends in a death, where one of the inmates is hanged.

One of my favourite items was a story of a *bang bang* or "stick man". These men are easily identifiable by the thick ropes they carry, attached to stout bamboo poles and usually they wear military apparel. These are the carriers who lug anything from fridges to bags of rice, and appear to be a specialty of Chongqing. Many of them are, or have been, migrant workers. This item depicted one such man as hard-working, honest, generous but dirt poor. He is sacrificing everything for the sake of his only child, a daughter, so that she can attend SISU. It was well done, and I liked it. It also has a very important message. Cf. photograph 67.

Unfortunately one item did not make the grade—and it was about Ireland. It was not well produced, the costumes were weird, the English was poor and to make matters worse, the microphones were faulty. One of our teachers hails from Ireland and he went especially to see this production. What a disappointment for him.

We returned to spectacular and wonderful costuming in a French production on the marriage of Louis XVI, who was then the Dauphin, to Marie Antoinette, princess of Austria in 1770. My French is too poor to understand the dialogue, but I did appreciate the sets. In one respect, however, this production was not in keeping with the theme of the night, in that it was set only in 1770 and not 1793. In other words, it did not end with their deaths at the guillotine.

Photo 56: Marie Antoinette

This lacuna was put to rights by the Vietnamese production based on a Chinese fable of "white snake, green snake". The costumes seemed to me to come from the Tang Dynasty, when Vietnam was, of course, part of China—or at least the Chinese thought so: they only won their independence by dint two millennia of struggle. Rain sounds were very effective, in fact too much so, as they drowned out the dialogue, not that this made any difference to me, as I do not understand Vietnamese. At the end the white snake frightens a woman—yes, you guessed it—to death. Our theme was restored.

Photo 57: Asian elegance

Photograph 57 depicts part of one scene illustrating how elegant Asian women can look, whether Chinese, Vietnamese or some other nationality.

The Department of Chinese Language and Literature put on Shakespeare's "King Lear", but in modern English, and set in ancient China during the Warring States Period, about 500 B.C. It too was well done. You know the ending of course: bodies everywhere.

One item which attracted a good deal of attention and appreciation was presented by seven students of Chinese, coming from seven different countries. I listened with envy, as their Chinese was excellent.

I seem to have covered most of the items, so let me finish with a bit of humour. There was a performance of Cinderella from the Spanish Department, with a twist, in that the step-mother also acts as the fairy godmother, and whose aim is to get the prince for herself. At the ball, as the clock strikes 12 midnight, Cinderella rushes from the ballroom, but as you know, loses her shoe in her flight. This particular shoe, however, refused to budge, resulting in Cinderella sitting down to pull it off, before she resumed her flight—much to the mirth of

215

the audience. After so much bloodshed, I thought this would be a good note on which to end.

6.7.2: May, 2014

In 2014 the language departments entertained us once again.

The night's entertainment began with welcoming speeches. Usually the host and hostess had the national costumes of various countries. Each of these also welcomed the audience in the relevant language: Korean, Japanese, Spanish, Italian, Arabic and English amongst others. These are the languages in which the acts would be performed. Each act would last about 15 minutes.

The first of these was an adaptation of King Lear, in English. This Shakespearean play had also been performed the previous year, so it is popular. I think that last year they had done a better job of portraying the central theme in such a short space of time, but this year had a better actor playing King Lear: he was superb, especially when showing Lear's intense emotions. How would you cry, "How, how, how, how"?—when the "how" is a howl of anguish.

The second act was yet another portrayal of "Journey to the West", one of the four Chinese classics. I have seen it performed many times. The most dramatic was in Tongren, when one of my students, a rather portly young lady, took the part of the pig. True to character she wolfed (?) down some watermelon with such gusto that she actually choked. She lived, though not without some concerns. No such dramas here, although the question of who is good and who is evil ("monster") was well presented, as the monkey goes around slaying seemingly good people.

The third act was in Korean, which—needless to say—I understood not at all.

The fourth was in Italian, entitled "E Bello e o Monstro" or Beauty and the Beast. This of course is another favourite, and we do not need the language to know the story. Just what is good and what is evil seemed to be a recurring theme in this concert, and indeed, in life itself it can be difficult at times to distinguish. What appears to be good may be hiding something much darker, while what outwardly seems evil may be genuinely good. "The Scarlet Letter" by Nathaniel Hawthorn, a favourite book for me, pursues this theme.

Item five, "The Phantom of the Opera" also had the same theme. I would have liked to have had more singing in this. There was only one short piece, and the singer was quite good, but maybe he was the only one who could sing well.

This was in English, being presented by the Department of Translation and Interpretation. By the end—as last year—we had bodies everywhere—really tragic. I was taken by the reception that the actors were receiving from the audience when they first appeared. There were gasps of surprise from the girls in particular when they saw their fellow students in a new light. "Really beautiful" was a comment I heard more than once.

We come now to Act 6—another old favourite, and another Shakespearean play, "A Midsummer Night's Dream". I had once produced this at Monivae College in Western Victoria—disastrously—not nearly as successfully as these students from the Department of Sociology. I have a personal interest in this play, as I grew up in Titania St in Randwick, Sydney, a street which forms a T-intersection with Oberon St, while one street further south is Helena St. Some local councillor, many years ago, must also have liked this play. Oberon, of course, was king of the Fairies, while Titania was his queen. This play fits in with the recurring theme of this concert. What is ugly and what is beautiful? We do have a tendency to equate beauty with goodness, and ugliness with evil. Beauty is in the eye of the beholder, at least to some extent, or to put it another way, prettiness is what we see with our eyes, while beauty is seen by the soul.

The seventh act was in Japanese, and the audience was able to follow because the script was projected onto a screen. Goodness, you would not want to fluff your lines, as you could hardly extemporise to bluff your way out of it. I, however, still did not understand.

Act eight was another one in English, entitled "The Gifts of Death". I do not know where it comes from, but it is the story of three brothers who are confronted with death in the form of the Grim Reaper. I wonder where this image comes from. I think it originates from Medieval England, although of course the personification of death comes into many cultures, such as Odin in Norse mythology, or Pluto in Greek mythology. The eldest brother is offered the gift of a magic wand, which he uses effectively till he is murdered for it—and consequently is claimed by Death. The second brother is offered a magic stone which can raise people from the dead, which he accepts. He uses it raise his dead girl-friend back to life. She, however, is none too pleased, which I found to be a most interesting twist, as the usual perception is that life is preferable to death; or maybe being with her boyfriend was a fate worse than death! I wondered too at the underlying theology. The second brother kills himself. The third makes no pact and lives to a ripe old age, eventually welcoming Death. The props were great in this act, as in most of them, although the intonation was often wrong. The acting was a little overdone.

Act nine was called "Blood Wedding", presented by the College of English Language and Literature; you may notice that most acts were in fact in English. This is a story of a young lady being forced to marry a man whom she does not love, and nor does he love her. She is not allowed to marry the man whom she does love, and who in turn loves her. The priest officiating at their wedding again had a cross on the front and again was a woman. Is this being prophetic? After her "marriage", her "husband" turns out to be a philanderer, while the lover wants her to run away with him. Should she or shouldn't she? While she is agonising the young women in the audience around me were saying "No, no": being true to your marriage vows runs deep. I have used inverted commas here, because I believe that love cannot be forced, that such forced marriages are not true marriages. In the play, the husband and lover fight, each stabbing the other. So now the young lady has neither husband nor lover; she kills herself. We had yet another evening littered with corpses.

Act ten was in Spanish, entitled "Amor colera" and it was similar. Here the true paramour was belted up by the husband and his cronies. As he fell his head really did smash into the floor: one could hear the crack. Later, when he got up, he was ruefully rubbing the back of his head. How far should one go in the interests of realism? Later, he shot the husband, before having a fight with his lover, flinging her to the floor. She hit her head and died—but in reality, she too really did hit her head hard on the floor. Goodness. While he now had no rival, he had no lover either: another tragedy, and yet more corpses. What a blood-thirsty night, not to mention two actors with headaches.

The next act was the final one, at least for me, as after three hours I had seen enough. I do not know how many acts there were in total, but I was told there were fifteen altogether, spread over the two nights, thus seven or eight each night. Not so – there were more than this This is not an information society … This act was in Arabic. Certainly the costumes were beautiful.

6.7.3: Conclusion

Why were these concerts placed under the banner of the Tower of Babel?

You would know the Biblical story, but just in case you do not, you will find it in Gen. 11 / 1-9. Within the Theology of the day, God was seen as the cause of everything, including evils such as illness and death. Hence here we are given the picture of God who interferes with human speech, creating many languages, so that the people do not understand each other. This, of course, must be seen within the whole context of the Genesis story. You may remember that the book begins with two stories of Creation, one coming from the Northern tradition of Israel, the other from the Southern tradition of Judah. We then have the story of the Fall, of human sin. Evil then spreads, and it is evil which separates humans from each other, from God and from the environment. Babel is a depiction of human isolation and conflict. Thus evil comes from us and not from God.

In Papua New Guinea, this is well illustrated, with some 800 languages developing within such a small population, and this is due to isolation. The rugged nature of the geography itself isolates people, whether because of mountains, rivers or seas. Past social practices also contributed: killing and eating your neighbour is not exactly conducive to intimate social intercourse.

In our present age of globalisation, we see the opposite trend, with the world needing a lingua franca, and this is English. I think I have been so fortunate in having being born in an English speaking country. Teaching English here in China, was for me, not just a chance to be of some assistance to the Chinese, but also of being a force for unity—albeit small—for the entire world. I am in favour of bringing people together.

Does this mean that we should abolish all languages? In no way. Different languages enrich the human race, bringing out differences in culture, different ways we can express ourselves and the world around us. People are different and true unity does not eradicate differences; rather it respects differences. Unity is not uniformity. We live with a dichotomy: on the one hand we need to acknowledge and express our uniqueness and our value as individuals, while on the other hand we are united with others, with the universe and with God.

6.8: A Tchaikovsky Feast

One of the advantages in living in a large city is the range of cultural activities. Small rural villages do not have much in the way of international opera or orchestral works—or ballet. In January, 2013, a Russian Ballet Troupe paid a visit to Chongqing, performing Swan Lake on a Wednesday night, followed by The Nutcracker Suite the following night, both at the Grand Theatre. Cf. photograph 2. I elected, at first, to go only to the first night, but enjoyed it so much that I doubled up for the second. There was some doubt as to whether I could get a ticket on the second night, since I had not booked in advance, but did manage to buy one at the door. I am so glad I did. The price, at 180 Yuan (about $ 36) per night, was probably a little steep for most locals, but I thought it was worth it. You would pay a lot more at the Sydney Opera House.

Getting there on the first night was something of a rush, as we stopped at a shop first to get something to eat, after which we waited for some time before snaring a taxi, in fact two taxis for our group, so that it was rush, rush but we did get there on time. I hate rushing. Must be old age. Our group consisted of our Chinese organiser, a French lady and two Russian ladies, one of whom had never before been to the ballet, so that she would be seeing her first performance in China. Considering the strength of Russian ballet, that is a little ironic. I told her that she must be Tongan. What? Well, she obviously can't be Russian! I had to point out that Tongans are very large dark people, where she is petite, blond and quite pretty. At the end of the ballet, as we were coming down the stairs, I suggested that she could now contact the Russian embassy." Oh, what for?"

"Because now you are eligible for full Russian citizenship." She laughed.

As for the ballet itself, I loved it. These days I hate violence, whether in films or real life. We have a surfeit. When it comes to stories, I do like happy endings—possibly one reason I like Jane Austin. Since in her life she never married her lover, Fitzroy, she determined that all her characters would "live happily ever after." At the end of this particular version of Swan Lake, the swan does not drown in the lake, and nor does the prince dive in after her. True, it is this proof of enduring love that kills the evil sorcerer, so probably more in tune with our Resurrection story, but I still prefer the version we saw, where the prince slays the sorcerer, thus breaking the evil spell. I am also a little ambivalent about the prince confusing his love for Odette, the swan princess, with Odile, the daughter of the sorcerer. Which version do you prefer?

As for the performance itself, it was absolutely exquisite, as one would expect, and so professional. Whenever you seen a mass display, it seems in real time that all the performers are in perfect synchronisation with each other. At least they do if they are really good. If you notice discrepancies then they are not so good. For this Russian Troupe, I noticed no discrepancies, but when later I examined the photographs I took, I did see that the performers were not completely aligned with each other, as in photograph 58. They were not perfect, but there again, nobody is; life is not perfect.

Photo 58: Swan Lake

The stage settings were well done. I liked the way they used the depth of the stage to create the scenes. Diaphanous curtains gave a sense of haziness, while patterns of trees on them created the lakeside. The backdrop was used effectively to portray the lake, together with the use of dark blue lighting, plus a whiff of smoke to add some mist.

After the performance, it was quite pleasant looking across the Jia Ling River to Chao Tian Men, the lights of the city sparkling off the water. Unfortunately, we could not linger as this concert hall is somewhat isolated from main thoroughfares. There were no suburban buses and no taxis, but there was a fleet of buses to take people down to the main road, about a kilometre away, where one could find regular buses and taxis, but these buses left almost immediately after the performance, so that there was no time to linger. Our Russian friends, meanwhile, wanted to chat with their compatriots; fair enough. In fact on the second night, we left them to do just that, so that they had to find their own way home.

On Thursday night we had The Nutcracker Suite. Somebody asked me which I preferred: Swan Lake or Nutcracker. Upon reflection, I think I prefer the latter. It has more catchy melodies and possibly more to think about. Are we not transformed by love? Does not love make us truly more human? It seems too, that the more human we become the more divine we also become—and vice versa. As regards the melodies, you do have those five dances: Spanish (chocolate), Arabic (coffee), Chinese (tea), Russian and reed pipes. There is also the dance of the Sugar Plum Fairy. The Arabian dancer was superb. I also like the ending. When the little girl wakes from her dream on Christmas morning, I think she still has her tiara, with which she was crowned queen of the sweets during her dream. I say "I think", because I could not see too clearly from where I was sitting. It raises the question of what is dream and what is reality? Perhaps our dreams give us a better picture of the meaning of life than do the mundane happenings of each day.

6.9: Impressionism

When I was studying in Chicago, those of us who came from overseas were called to a meeting, in which, amongst other things, we were asked to state why we were there. Everybody mentioned the courses they were doing and their relevance to their line of work, all of which is of course true. But I added that I was there because of Chicago. What? The city itself had a lot to teach me and I fully intended to take advantage of whatever opportunities arose. These included the Chicago Art Institute (read art gallery).

Every Tuesday afternoon the Art Institute was free and often there was a public lecture held on art. Each Tuesday, if I had no classes, I would hop on the No. 6 bus and go, avidly drinking in whatever I could. Now it just so happens that in the late 19th century, when Chicago was booming, the French impressionist painters were in their prime. Is there any connection? Indeed there is, as some of the nouveau riche from Chicago used to travel to France, where they not only came into contact with Monet, Manet, Renoir, etc., but got to know them as persons and admired their works before the general public was aware of them. These far sighted men snaffled up many an impressionist painting, bought directly from the artists, and brought them back to Chicago. If I am not mistaken, I think that even to this day, Chicago hosts the biggest collection of these paintings found anywhere else in the world.

In November, 2013, an art exhibition of impressionist paintings came to Chongqing and some of us teachers at SISU were anxious to see them. One Sunday, after Mass, Cyril, John (whose initials are JC) and I went hunting. Now our leader, the redoubtable JC (of course he is, with those initials) had sussed out the address, to wit, No. 1111 of a certain street. It is situated a long way from the university, taking the best part of two hours to get there. Once off the train, it was stated that he did not know which side of the street the numbers were. This was no big deal, and we soon established that we were on the correct side of the street, which also happened to be the right side, even if the odd side. Confused?

We walked. We found numbers. Good. 1137 came up. "It can't be far now," we noted as the numbers went down. 1115. Just about there. Then we found that the next address was also 1115, as was the next, and the next… What is going on? We came to a cross street. Surely the building on the corner must be the next. It wasn't. Goodness. The next one? Yes: it is number 1113. Wonderful. The next address was—you guessed it—number 1113; and the next was also 1113, and the next and the next … What is going on?

Now the fun began. Oh, you thought we were having fun already? The next two buildings were new high rise under construction: no number 1111 here, as the road bent around in a curve seemingly going nowhere near any art gallery. Now what? We go home, that's what; we caught a taxi. Now I ask you: what would any reasonable person think of the leadership capabilities of JC?

Once in the taxi, we noticed a sign pointing to the gallery down a side street about 500 metres further along. Ok, let us give some credit to John, if perhaps grudgingly.

Were we defeated? Perish the thought. The following Saturday, we returned, this time a formidable party of nine: two Aussies, two Irish, one English, one American and four students. You take the underground 11 stops to Liang Lu Kou, where you change lines. You then have a further 14 stops to Yuan Yang, which—incidentally—means mandarin duck, a symbol of a couple, because there are always two of them. We stopped off here for some time to have lunch in McDonald's, including a coffee for me. Generous Cyril declared: "McDonald's is American, therefore you are all my guests, so I pay." And he did.

After our meal, we began walking, retracing our steps from the previous Sunday and it was so easy. You just go through and underpass, come out, turn right, cross a road, keep walking, over a bridge, cross a road, go through another underpass, keep walking along the footpath until you come to the first street on the right, then you turn right, walk another 100 metres and hey presto, you are there. What could be easier? Obviously number 1111, although situated maybe a kilometre further on, and on another road, was a minor matter, so why quibble about little details like that?

The entrance fee was 50 Yuan, or 30 Yuan for students, but no concessions to grey hairs. We were expecting an exhibition of impressionist paintings, but it was not. There were some impressionist items, but the vast majority of the 166 art works on display were either sketches or wood cuts. The details are simply amazing, even in this art style, where few strokes are used. While the whole exhibition came under the impressionist umbrella, one could see there were merges with other styles e.g. in Gaugin's work. This, I think, is probably because he was somewhat isolated from the others, working as he did in Tahiti, rather than Paris. There were no examples of Monet's work, although he did get a mention. I took some photographs of some of the art works, but not very successfully, as the glass reflected white panels on the walls. A pity. One thing that was really good was a demonstration, on the floor, of how a wood cut is done. There were also reproductions on sale, and a couple in our party bought some. It is good to decorate one's apartment, but I tend to use my own photographs for this.

There were quite a few impressionists represented, most of them what we might call "the lesser lights", or at least the less well known, e.g. Boudin, Desboutin, Picarro, Rafaelli, Sisley and Steinleu. Of the better known artists represented, we had Toulouse-Lautrec, Manet and Gaugin. Sadly there was nothing of Monet, and only a very little of Renoir, Cezanne, Degas and Van Gogh, who were better at portraying light through colour. We were a little disappointed in this and also because there were so few paintings. Nevertheless it was well worth a visit and I for one am very glad I went. You see, I do av sum culcher!

After we had seen enough, our group separated. Four of us took a taxi back to SISU, a journey which took only 20 minutes, compared with two hours by train. I still had corrections to do. After all, I was in China to teach.

Chapter 7: Going to Church

Introduction

China—as everyone knows—is a police state. Everything and everyone must be under strict Communist Party control, and this includes religion. There is no separation of Church and State so that all worship must be under surveillance. Individual human rights count for very little. The Party can do what it likes, as it is above the Law.

I am a Catholic and made no secret of this. However, I would never push my beliefs on anyone else, not because this is illegal, but because I find this abhorrent. Everyone must find his own way to God. I would tell people what I believe, but what they believe is up to them. Religion, however, is not just a private concern, because it is also social. To this end I would go to Mass every Sunday to the nearest Catholic church, or I did initially.

7.1: Shapingba

This is the nearest large shopping centre to SISU and indeed it is the district to which SISU, which is within the suburb of Lieshimu, belongs. It also has a Catholic church, which had Mass at 8.00 a.m. in summer, 8.30 a.m. in winter. A number of us would go as a group from SISU, either by public transport, which takes about 40 minutes, or by walking, which takes about 45 minutes. Take your pick. I much preferred the walk, except in the hot summer months, because I did not want to arrive for Mass all hot and sweaty. It is an interesting route, but you really need to know it, with some climbing and crossing of gulleys; at times one is walking along a major road, at times walking along back streets, including a block which was being demolished at this time. At the end of this section some ladies would sit at their sewing machines, working away, chatting companionably; I would give them whatever sewing I needed to have done. At one point the road crosses a major expressway, while nearby is a deep gulley with market gardens on its slopes. It is common to find these even within built up areas. Cf. photograph 59.

Photo 59: on the way to church

After Mass, we would walk into Three Gorges Square for a coffee, but more about this in the next section.

I was not in town for Christmas 2011, as I went to Zunyi to visit some of my former students. The next major festival was Holy Week, 2012.

On Holy Thursday night, at 6.00, we had the commemoration of Jesus' Last Supper. Curiously, there was no washing of the feet: a pity, especially as mine were rather dirty and could have done with a wash!

Good Friday was a disappointment, in that the 3.00 p.m. service was not the commemoration of Jesus' death. Instead it was simply the Stations of the Cross. This is not what it should be. There was no other ceremony that day. There were also very few people attending, but bear in mind that this is just another day for most people, so people are at work, and indeed I too had the usual classes in the morning.

On Holy Saturday once again some of us went to church for the Easter Vigil ceremony, which began at 6.00 p.m. This is too early in my book, as it is still light and the initial ceremony of light takes its impact from the surrounding darkness. I was expecting a long ceremony, but it was not. The Exultet was said, not sung. I did like the ringing of the bells at the Gloria, while at the same time the acolyte went around removing the purple cloths from statues and crucifixes. This is better than having these removed before the ceremony begins. We only had three readings from the Old Testament, which is the minimum. I personally like these readings: they have a lot to teach us. There were only two adults for Baptism; I had thought there might be more. Otherwise the ceremony went off as it does all over the world. This is the most important liturgical ceremony of the entire year.

There was one sad note, and indeed one that could have been tragic. David, who was next to me, inadvertently placed his sleeve over his candle. Luckily the lady behind saw it immediately, so that David was able to put out the flames with his hand, burning his hand in the process, but that is better than burning all of him. Immediately after the ceremony, we went to Carrefour, a French owned supermarket in Shapingba, where he bought himself a new coat to replace the one he had just burnt.

We continued to frequent the church at Shapingba until just before Christmas 2012, when cracks were found in a supporting column of the church. The authorities were not slow in declaring it to be unsafe, telling the priest that he could either have it fixed, or the church would be demolished, probably to make way for other buildings. Bear in mind that the Communist Party owns everything in China: private individuals lease their properties. As a result, Mass was being held outside in the rather small courtyard until repairs could be effected. And it was winter. No thanks. At least it had been dry. Whatever were they going to do if it starts raining? They would be in for a rather chilly Christmas, but we did not stick around to find out, and instead opted to frequent the cathedral in the CBD. There was another advantage: in the Shapingba church the sermon on Sundays would go for a long time, between 30 and 40 minutes! It was good sleep time for me! See, I must be a good Catholic! The locals, however, did appreciate the content of these sermons.

7.2: The Cathedral

It would take longer to reach the cathedral, dedicated to St Joseph, being more than an hour away, but it was good. Even though it is situated in the Jiefangbei area, in the heart of the city, you really have to know where you are going. We would walk for about ten minutes down to the local station at Lieshimu, catch the train on line 1, transfer down to line 2, travel one further station, before walking about 15 minutes to the church. In fact one reason I had not gone earlier was that I did not know exactly where it was located. And you need to know. John went looking for it one day, having received prior instructions, yet still walked past it several times without seeing it. How is that possible? How can you hide a large church? Easy: you park it off the main street, with access only via a narrow alley. You can actually see it from the main street, but you need to be looking. Photograph 60 was taken from this alley. As can be seen, the central spire is covered in ivy—unusual for a church.

Photo 60: the cathedral

It was certainly livelier and friendlier then the Shapingba church and the sermons would only go for about ten minutes compared with the thirty minutes and more we had to endure before. Truly.

After Sunday Mass, we would still go to a coffee shop, another Starbucks, situated high up above the Jia Ling River. It is an interesting place, with an open area sporting a model of a Caribbean pirate ship. It also afforded a good vantage point over the river. Nearby a new large bridge was under construction and week by week we could watch its progress. It was so pleasant sitting companionably in comfortable lounge chairs sipping our mochas, or whatever, especially in winter, when mist would be hanging over the river, reducing visibility. In the photographs the distances fade into the mist plus pollution.

Photo 61: model of a pirate ship

In April, 2014 we attended the cathedral for the all-important Holy Week ceremonies.

On Holy Thursday, Mass was at 7.00 p.m., commemorating Jesus' final meal with his disciples. All went well, much the same as everywhere else in the world, except that the washing of the feet was very low key and there was no stripping of the altar. On Friday we returned at 3.00 p.m. for the service commemorating Jesus' death. Again the ceremony is much the same as elsewhere, except that there was a final blessing. This was followed by the Stations of the Cross.

One of the aspects I really like about the Holy Week ceremonies is the endings. On Thursday, the altar is left bare, the Blessed Sacrament is removed to a side altar, while the main tabernacle is left open. The atmosphere is solemn, even sombre. What happened to Jesus was a tragedy, mirroring the tragedies happening all over the world. After the Good Friday ceremony, there is no ending, because the death of Jesus is not the end: there is hope; there is expectation. The third ending, after the Easter Vigil ceremony is all joy, all is well; death has become life. This Easter Vigil service began at 7.00 p.m. Outside our front door a blocked drain had caused a lake to build up, but thankfully by this time, this had dried up, so I was able to exit our building via the exit. No need to jump off balconies. The ceremony itself was beautiful, as it always is—the best of the year—but it seemed to me to be a little hurried. The whole was over by 8.30 p.m. There were no baptisms, and this was a surprise, as there are generally quite a few at this ceremony. Why were they not carried out?—They were forbidden by the government, that's why. The Church here does struggle—and there are government spies at every Mass.

The following day seven of us met in Three Gorges Square, Shapingba, for lunch, not only to celebrate Easter, but also to celebrate Cyril's birthday, which was on Good Friday. We went to a very good pizza restaurant, run by a Christian lady, but you have to know where it is located, as it is on the 12th floor. They are really good pizzas, too, much better than the Pizza Hut variety. After that we went to a coffee shop, also run by a Christian lady. Happy Easter.

The cathedral was always crowded. One rainy Sunday we actually found a vacant pew. Great—but we soon realised why: the roof was leaking. We spent the rest of the ceremony trying to avoid the drips. It was announced that the cathedral would be closed after Easter so that roof repairs could take place. We would have to go somewhere else.

7.3: Our Third Church

At the cathedral we had met a truly delightful young lady called Reine. This is not really her English name, since it is actually French—her second language—and means "Queen". Her English is not bad either. Now I have been told that the bishop's name is Regina. Really? This is Latin, and it too means "Queen". Odd. At any rate, on the Sunday after Easter we met Reine at the cathedral and she kindly took us to the other church, so that now we knew its location. Even so it did take a while for us to work out the best way to get there, without having to detour via the cathedral. We experimented with getting off the train (metro system) at different stations, since the church is located between stops. By trial and error we realised that it is best to get off at a station called Qixinggang, which means "seven stars", referring to the stars of the Big Dipper constellation in the northern sky. I have no idea why. From this station it takes about 12 minutes to reach the church. The route is interesting.

Most of the time the walk is downhill, with just one uphill section. Part of the route would take us beside the old wall of the city, then through a major gateway. This old wall dates back hundreds of years before the First Settlement in Australia. Here there is an interesting diorama, consisting of bronze statues of soldiers, some attacking the wall, while defenders on the top are throwing down great stones. The attackers are using scaling ladders, while firing arrows upward. Perhaps it is referring to one particular assault, but more probably it is general. The gate itself is interesting, in that it is in two parts. If you get through the first, you have a tower above you, open to the sky, so the defenders can pour down fire on all four sides. It looks very effective, although the Mongols did manage to conquer the city in the 13th century.

Photo 62: storming the walls

The church itself is located close to the wall, high up on the ridge overlooking the Yangtze River and this is the church indicated in map 3. Just to remind you of the geomorphology, the Yangtze comes up from the south, while the Jialing comes down from the north, both colliding with a high ridge, which turns both rivers to the east, till they meet where the ridge ends. From the church we get a great view of the Yangtze and adjacent sections of the city. Below is Shanhuba Island, about 1.5 km long, used as an airstrip during the war in order to supply the city which was under constant attack from the Japanese. Cf. photograph 12. Chongqing was the seat of government. As we gazed out upon the scenery, I could not help but regret that the city was so polluted.

The church is built in the basilica style, which is probably the most common style throughout the world, with a row of columns separating the nave from two aisles. The style dates back to the 4th century as being the largest style of building available at that time, when Christianity was no longer being persecuted, within the Roman Empire, of course, as it is still being persecuted today. It actually means "kingly house"; in Greek, "basileia" means king. Prior to this time, Christians needed to meet in secret, using the catacombs in Rome, or house churches. The same is still happening in China today. This church—as are many others—is dedicated to Mary.

When we arrived the first time, an usher directed us upstairs, which—after a complicated route is negotiated—leads to the choir loft. This suited us fine, as we preferred this. We had been going upstairs in the cathedral, where a low wooden railing was all that prevented one from toppling over, but in this church, there is a high thick balustrade. One can barely peer through the railing. The pillars are also thick, of the Ionic order, with plain plinths and acanthus leaves at the top.

In the cathedral the choir was situated down the front left of the church, but here they are up in the choir loft—and they were good. The pianist was particularly good, with a light touch and a feel for the music. On one Sunday he was absent and a woman took his place, not nearly as talented, as she thumped out the notes. She however, was still better than the organist in the Shapingba church; and both were way better than me! Enough said.

There are nuns here, dressed in their habits, not a common sight in this country. It is good to see. They also assist at Communion, one of them actually bringing the hosts up to the choir loft—most convenient. The whole feel of the church was happy and rejoicing, reflected in the music. The congregation was mostly old, not all that surprising considering that there is an old people's home here, but there is a vibrant youth community as well. Reine herself had been a Catholic for not much more than a year. Children are not allowed by the government to attend, being yet another instance of the Communist Party's heavy handed approach.

We had an interesting ex-patriot community, with people coming from England, Ireland, the US, Rwanda, Angola and even Australia. The Rwandan lady generally wore a scarf and on one occasion she showed us why. She belongs to the minority Tutsi tribe, 800,000 of whom were massacred by the predominant Hutu in 1994. She herself suffered from a knife cut to the neck—hence the scarf; she was very lucky to survive. She is a lovely lady and while in China she married another Rwandan who was studying in Beijing; she too was a student.

Photo 63: our group outside the church

We needed to find a new coffee place, which we did eventually, some 20 minutes' walk from the church. It is called Costa, bordering a plaza and belonging to a chain which you can find throughout China. It is good coffee too. So there we would go and chat for another hour or so. This served us for the rest of my time in China. What a delightful way to spend Sunday morning.

Chapter 8: Education

Introduction

I was in China to teach, so perhaps it is time to say something about this aspect of my three years in Chongqing. Elsewhere I have written about my philosophy of education, but perhaps a brief summary is in order here.

Education is more than teaching. Teaching is what the teacher gives to the students. Education is what the students take in and build into their way of life. There is that well known saying, that if you give someone a fish, then you feed him one meal, but if you teach him how to fish, then you feed him for life. Giving the fish is analogous to teaching, whereas education is not only teaching how to fish but also inculcating a desire to fish.

For me, the most important quality of a teacher is to love the students. Students know when their teacher is just doing a job, going through the motions and not really interested in their welfare and they know when you are on their side.

The second most important quality is to know them. This is difficult, especially when they belong to another culture. Where do they come from? What is their socio-economic background? What are their ambitions? What do they do in their free time? Etc. One must make an effort to get to know them—and this goes far beyond remembering their names.

The third most important quality is to be enthusiastic about your subject. I taught Science for many years, where one needs to be captivated by the wonder of new discoveries in this amazing universe we call our home. In teaching English one must love the cadences, the way the language hangs together, the way ideas, especially profound ideas, can be expressed. If you think English is just too prosaic, your students will not be motivated. Loving to read great authors, whether in prose or poetry, is a must.

Finally one must know your subject thoroughly. You really do need to be an expert in your field, whatever you are teaching. For English, one must have an inner feel for the language, so that you know how it works. Over time I taught all four aspects of English: listening, speaking, reading and writing. I will have more to say about these later.

Let us look now at a couple of sample semesters.

8.1: First Semester, Autumn 2011

In my first semester at SISU I did not have a heavy programme—just in case people were thinking I was a hard worker. I was teaching 14 hours a week, or at least that is how it is counted, although actually it is less than that. Classes go for 90 minutes, with a 10 minute break after the first 45 minutes. This is shorter than I had been used to, both in Tongren and in Fuzhou, where classes went for 50 minutes. Nevertheless, in all places these segments are regarded as full hours. Hence my "14 hours" was not really 7 x 2 h½s, but was 7 x 1 1/2 hours. But who's complaining?

With this understanding of "hour" in mind, I was teaching two classes four hours a week each, another two classes two hours a week each, and a third group two hours a week. This meant that I had three different lots of preparation to do.

The bulk of my teaching was conducted in the new International Building, but there were classes in some of the other buildings also, including the upper campus. Behind this International Building lies an old building, somewhat dilapidated where many of my classes were taught. Photograph 64 shows one of these corridors on a wet day. While the day may have been gloomy, the umbrellas brought a touch of colour.

Photo 64: a wet day

The bulk of my time was spent with the two "Lancaster Programme" classes. These are young people who would be going early the following year to study at Lancaster University in England. My job was to prepare them, so that they could have some understanding of England as a country, not just of English as a language. Cultural preparation was therefore important. They had another teacher, Chinese, teaching them Oral English, but her job was specifically to prepare them for the IELTS exam, which they would be sitting for in December. In fact I was taking a liberal interpretation of what constitutes "Oral English", and was striving to improve their overall level. Each week, for example, I would give them an essay to write, with the twofold aim of improving their expression and teaching them about England. This included a series of three essays on English history, the topics centring around some key dates. For interest, I chose: 1) 1066—William the Conqueror; 2) 1215—the signing of the Magna Carta and the rise of Parliament; and 3) 1455—1485—the War of the Roses. I thought the latter would be appropriate since they were going to Lancaster, although of course the war concerned the Lancaster and York families and not Lancaster and York cities. Their following series of three essays centred on culture.

The second group I was teaching was called "Visiting Scholars" divided into two classes, but with only about 10 students in each. As the name suggests, these people were indeed for the most part scholars. Most were university lecturers, research scientists or medical people. Many were going overseas to further their research, and to consult with others in their fields. Quite a few already had their PhDs. One man, for instance, was researching wind turbines to generate electricity, while another was a mathematician. One lady was a geologist, exploring for gas and oil in Tibet, while another was a musician, and incidentally, has a wonderful voice. There were three doctors and one nurse. Two others were specialising in Environmental Engineering. Obviously one's approach to a group of this kind is quite different from dealing with students who are still in their teens.

The third group consisted of only one class and was called "The Beginners", since their level of English was rudimentary. Most of these too were career people, with a travel agent and a doctor amongst them. Oddly enough the best in the class was a young lady of 21, who often got the job of translating for everyone else. As you might surmise, the text book was not overly important, as we were striving to get them to talk as much as possible and to increase their vocabulary, as well as to improve their pronunciation and intonation. It is the sort of group where one can be informal and generally have fun.

Curiously, there was no emphasis on "English Corner". This had been standard practice, not just in Tongren and Fuzhou, but in many other places as well. Basically we would spend one hour per week standing around, talking English to all and sundry—whoever wants to come. This was even less comfortable when one was standing around outside in the winter time, as we did in Tongren. Sometimes the sessions were structured and sometimes we just ad-libbed, but either way this one hour a week had been a regular part of our programme: but not here. I have no idea why, and I was not about to complain bitterly with regards to this lacuna, especially as it had never been a popular pastime with expatriates. One can get a little tired of the same old questions over and over again: "Where do you come from? How old are you? Do you like China? Do you like Chinese food? What is the weather like in Australia?" And so it goes on. Hence, even though my programme may have been light, I was not anxious to bring up the subject with the powers that be. Shshsh.

There was, however, a substitute which I really liked. Each Thursday afternoon, 2.30—4.00, there would be a lecture, with a different presenter each week. In November, for instance, one of our visiting scholars gave a lecture on understanding emotions, which happened to be her PhD thesis. What she had to say was eminently sensible. For example, you may not be able to change your situation, but you can change your attitudes. At the end there was a lively and humorous discussion after one wit asked how he could change his wife. My contribution was to whisper to the person next to me the advice of one sage, to the effect that what is more important than understanding your wife, is simply to love her as she is. My listener promptly told everyone, touting me as being the wise man, and saying, "Never try to understand your wife; just love her," which is not quite what I said. So whether from hereon I was considered to be a wise man or a fool, I know not.

On one Thursday afternoon, the noted scholar was me—or maybe they just wanted a change from noted scholars. I spoke on Old Australia. This was in three parts. The first concerned the land itself, some of which is amongst the oldest land found anywhere on earth, from the original crustal material some 3 billion years ago. The second part concerned ancient life, beginning with stromatolites, again amongst the oldest life forms found anywhere, through to the Wollemi Pine, then onto the animals, especially the monotremes (echidna and platypus) and the marsupials. Some countries have just a few species of mammals found nowhere else on earth, while Australia is blessed with hundreds. The third part of my presentation just touched on the aborigines, the world's oldest continuous civilisation, some ten times older than China's. I think this part went down like a lead balloon, as nothing is older than or better than China.

8.2: The Second Semester, Spring 2012

8.2.1: The first week

The second semester was the spring semester of 2012, from February to July, beginning after Chun Jie, or Spring Festival, so that the beginning date varies from year to year. In this year we began in late February. Beginnings are often chaotic, as one rarely knows in advance what one shall be teaching. This semester proved to be no exception.

While I was away over the holidays, I had left my laundry hanging on the line on my balcony, not exactly swaying in the breeze, since there is very little of that here, the atmosphere generally being quite still, grey and smoggy under leaden skies. Hence there was some concern about this laundry. Each week, before hanging it out, I would clean the line, with the tissue always coming away quite black. And that is after only one week. What would my laundry be like after a full month? As it turned out, it was not too bad: I just made sure I gave it all a good shake before bringing it inside. The balcony itself, however, was covered in thick dust of a brown-grey colour.

Classes officially began on Monday 20th, with my first period at 8.00 a.m. This was a class I had taught the previous semester, so I knew them. In the previous week I had found out more exactly what the course outline would be. Last semester our subject had been Oral English, but this time it was General English. Unusually I had a text book, which included a CD. Previously I had had trouble trying to operate the machine, no doubt due in part to my antediluvian proclivities, but also partly due to the fact that the instructions on the machine were all in Chinese. Even the students had a great deal of difficulty with it, as did other members of staff. Sometimes we had to call the experts.

I got on well with this group of students, and was looking forward to my four hours a week with them. We should have fun—and we did.

At 10.00 a.m. I had my second class, a group I was not familiar with. Furthermore, I had received absolutely no information about them or the course. Truly. I had to say to them: "I know nuttin!" I did not know what course I was teaching, or for how long, or what text book they had—if any—or how many periods a week we would have, or what level they were at. The students had to tell me. For the record, this was a one semester course in Oral English, for students who had completed High School the previous year, and who were hoping to study abroad next semester—mostly in England. There was no text book and we had two hours a week. So it seemed that I could pretty well do as I liked. Their teacher from last semester had not returned, so I gathered he had left. Again nobody had said anything.

Wednesday of this week happened to be Ash Wednesday, but no ashes. At our liturgy the previous Sunday the Melchizedek had told us that the ashes would be distributed on the following Sunday, as people need to work all day Wednesday. Believe it or not I had actually worked out what he said from just a few words. I did have a ceremony in my room, but with only one other person, and no ashes.

On Thursday the week really got interesting. I taught the first two periods, from 8.00 a.m., went to the printer to get some printing done and retired to my apartment. At 11.05 a.m., I got a call. "You have a class now." Do I? News to me. Nobody had said anything to me. Now it is quite common to be told something five minutes beforehand, but this is the first time I was told one hour and five minutes late. Have I mentioned that this is a non-information society?

On Thursday lunchtime, I went into Shapingba to meet a lady who had once been a student at SISU. This was the third time that I had met her over the past six months. The story was that she wished to improve her English, so wanted to spend time with me in conversation. Of course, the real reason was—undoubtedly—that she was captivated by my sparkling personality. Oh well, we all have our illusions. The first two times we had enjoyed a coffee together, but this time we had a meal as well, a pizza from Pizza Hut. Actually I am not a fan of this chain, as in the past I have found their crusts to be too thick and doughy, and their prices too high. This time, however, the pizza was very nice, with a crisp crust. As for the price, my hostess insisted on paying. In this culture, it is understood that you never do anything for nothing, so this is her way of paying for my scintillating conversation.

This Pizza Hut is situated in Three Gorges Square, which I have mentioned above. I like it. One pleasing aspect is the statuary, including this one of the boat haulers. Just below Chongqing on the Yangtze River were the rapids, over which boats had to be hauled by muscle power. There were even paths cut into cliff faces. It must have been extremely hard work. I saw these when I first sailed through the Three Gorges in January of 2005, but these days they are covered by water, backing up behind the Three Gorges Dam.

Photo 65: boat haulers

On Friday afternoon, the university put on a bus for us to go to Metro, a German owned superstore, where we could buy Western goods which we could not get anywhere else. We were doing this about once every two months. In this case I had heard the news on the grapevine, and then on Friday morning a notice was actually put up on a tree outside our apartments. I like these excursions, as I can buy Australian wine and cheeses, amongst other things. Each time there appears to be something different in stock: you never know. One item I wanted was tinned tuna, but found only two tins left. Two people before me had also grabbed two tins each. This time they had muesli in the cereal department, so I grabbed a packet. All in all I ended up spending some 500 Yuan, but that is OK for the first visit of the year: you stock up. Others spent more than I did. I know of one lady who spent 1700 Yuan!

On Friday night I relaxed by watching a movie, the recently released Spielberg production, "War Horse", featuring a horse during World War I, when horses were used extensively, and something like 17 million died. The movie is excellent, but is long, going for some 2 ½ hours. As a result I had a late night. That is OK as Saturday was the one day when I could sleep in, not getting up till 9.30 a.m. Wow!

To end the week I had a quiet Saturday—after I finally emerged from between the sheets: doing laundry, preparing classes, correcting assignments, reading and writing. It had been a good first week and I was happy.

8.2.2: The second week—confusion continues

On Wednesday in the first week I had missed a class, simply because nobody had told me that it was on until one hour and five minutes into the class: just a little late. I thought to myself privately that I would make this class up, after I had seen the students in week 2, when we could work out when they were free. All we would need to do then was to find a spare classroom. I received another phone call, telling me that in week 2 I would be teaching them on Thursday afternoon. Ok, no problems. So in week 2 I did not turn up to teach this class on Wednesday at the previously scheduled time. I got yet another phone call: "You have a class now."

"No I don't: it has been transferred to tomorrow."

"No, you have a class now." It dawned on me that the class on the following day was the make-up class and not a transfer. Great, but I wish this had been made clear to me. Part of the problem was that my informer had very poor English. I did take pains to make sure I had the message clear.

I raced back to the class to find that most of the students had gone: only two remained. So we spent the next hour and a half chatting, improving their English as we went along. I decided not to make up this class. If the students chose to take off at the first opportunity, then that was their problem. I would turn up for the make-up class the following afternoon, which I did. But guess what? I was there but no students! First we had students without a teacher, then a teacher without students. I went down to the office. "Your class is at 4.20 (or as she said, 20.4) not 2.30." Wonderful. Ain't life exciting.

On Wednesday, I went into Shapingba once again to meet that lady who was wanting to improve her English, and again we shared a meal and a coffee. She was late arriving, so I sat on a seat and waited for about 45 minutes, watching the passing parade. There was a young boy who caught my attention. He was kneeling on pads with his hands supported on blocks of wood. In this way he was shuffling up and down Three Gorges Square. In his right hand he held a tin, which he stretched out to people for money. And it worked. I saw many people put money into his tin. When he had acquired a certain amount, he would transfer it to his backpack before continuing his begging. I was impressed by the generosity of many of the passers-by. What is wrong with his legs? I do not know, but certainly nothing obvious. I do know that there are many charlatans in the begging business, so possibly there was nothing wrong with him at all, but I really do not know. Certainly many people were giving him the benefit of the doubt.

Another feature of this week is that I picked up four more hours teaching, giving me 18 hours per week. One of these classes was for beginners, and indeed their level was not very high. The other was an intermediate class. There were few students in the beginners' class. Why? Unbelievably because they chose to watch an NBA basketball match on TV instead. This had not happened before, at least not to my knowledge. I surmised that there may be a little trouble with motivation for this class. Admittedly, they can come and go as they please: they were not studying for any exam. It is just an opportunity for them to improve their English.

The second new class I was given was an intermediate class. There were 22 in the class, on the same basis i.e. they can come and go as they please. Hence, I was expecting many of these not to last the distance. Five of them I had taught last semester in the beginners' class; it was good to see them again. As per usual, when I turned up for class, I had no class list, and not even a text book. The students told me what our text was. Later that day—Friday—I went to the office to collect both the class list and text book. Good.

This dearth of information was echoed by another of our teachers in another city. Apparently she got up early for an 8.00 a.m. class, only to be told that the students would be away, so there would be no class. Fine, but why couldn't the authorities have told her the day before? She could have enjoyed a longer sleep. She needs her beauty sleep! (Thank goodness she is far away: after she reads this she'll want to kill me!)

It was also a good week financially. I asked if the university would reimburse me for my air fare back to Australia. I do not think they have any obligation to do so, as I had not yet been there for a year, but I thought there would be no harm in asking. They agreed to pay half, the equivalent to my fare back home after a year has been completed. Actually it does not work out like that in practice, as the airlines ensure that paying one way is about the same as a return ticket— sometimes it is more. On one occasion, I actually bought a return ticket when I only needed one way because it was cheaper. Nevertheless I was happy to receive half of what I had paid. As well as this I was given more than 1,000 Yuan for some work I had done in the week before the semester properly began. Goodness, I really did only a little. I think they were generous because they knew I had curtailed my holiday in Australia so that I could get back. Here they pay so promptly too: very impressive.

Another bright note in the week—literally this time—was the reappearance of the sun, after its winter hibernation. (Yes, I know, that is a tautology.) Yes you could actually see it, albeit hazily, and for most of the afternoon too. The sky was not exactly a deep blue, and not even a pale blue, but what do you want for nothing? I was happy, and so were a lot of other people. The temperature rose significantly as well. What day was this?—Thursday, 1st March, the first official day of spring. Wonderful.

There you have our second week of this semester. There was a good deal of muddling through, but eventually it ended up being a pretty good week—a bit like life, in fact. A lot of our life is just muddling through, but in the end it all works out. All will be well. All manner of things will be well. Thank God. I was wondering what week three would bring.

8.2.3: The fourth week

Week three was not too bad, with the Confusion Index on a low 1, but in week four it climbed a notch to level 2 (where 5 is utter confusion). There were still classes with hardly any students. In one class only one student turned up, a girl, being joined later by two boys, who—even though they were actually sitting physically in the classroom—did not exactly exhibit heaps of enthusiasm. One boy simply put his head on his arms, possibly trying to make up for lost sleep from the night before when he may have been playing internet games till all hours of the morning. They do that. In spite of such an inauspicious beginning, we actually had a really good class. I ended up teaching them what they really needed, yes, even to the boys, who eventually woke up.

I had indicated to the office what was going on with the three classes that were slack in attendance. Late in the week I was called to the office where—and I kid you not, but this is really true—I was actually given some information. The students in two of these classes were sitting for the IELTS exam while students from the third were sitting for the TOEFL exam. Both of these are English exams to test one's proficiency before travelling overseas. The people who sit for these exams would either be intending to study overseas, or perhaps to take up employment overseas. The previous year I had scientists who would be attending international conferences.

It transpired that most of the students in these three classes had already sat for these exams and had achieved the levels they were seeking. This particular piece of information had been given to me by the students, not the office. So what is the purpose of the classes? In the office I was told that the classes would now be discontinued. Well, that is not a bad idea. I was also told that this programme was only ever intended to be for four weeks. OK, but nobody told me. With this lack of information, there is no chance to sit down and develop a solid, well worked out syllabus for a month's work. You just fly by the seat of your pants. Nor is there any chance to bid a fond farewell to the few students who actually put the seats of their pants on the chairs.

Life can be like that. We cannot see the future. Often things happen unexpectedly, things which can change the course of our lives. I saw plenty of instances of this when working in hospital. People would be living out their lives day by day, doing the things they normally do, perhaps taking it all for granted, when suddenly they get sick, or have an accident, or maybe it happens to their loved ones. I am sure everyone has his/her own personal stories. Here are two from my own life.

In 1992 I was out on a training run in preparation for the Sydney to Surf. For those who are not familiar with this run, it has become a real classic in Sydney. It takes place every August, at the end of winter, when the weather is starting to warm up. Nowadays something like 70,000 people participate, but fewer than that when I ran it. The course begins at Hyde Park in the CBD, heads off down William St to Kings Cross, across the flats as you swing around the bays (Elizabeth, Rushcutters, Rose), then you climb for three kilometres—just to separate the men from the boys—over the top of the ridge, then down the other side, where the hill is steep, to Bondi Beach. The total distance is 14 km, and it is a great run. The leading runners complete the course in about 42 minutes, which I find staggering. They are way out of my league: I managed 60 minutes. But it is all good fun, with many people walking, dressing up in costumes, wheeling prams or anything else. But back to my training run: my knee went on me, meaning I could not run, and later had an operation on it. I have not run since. When I started out on that training run, little did I know that it would be my last.

The second example comes from April of 1995. I had been in Tasmania for a hospital conference, and was returning to Sydney with a friend of mine, in his car. We came across Bass Strait on the ferry, spending some time in Melbourne with my family. The whole of my sister's family gathered for a special memorable lunch beside the Yarra River at Southbank. I did not know it at the time, but this was the last time we did anything like this. Just after this my sister became quite ill, and died in December of that year.

What does this teach me? Treasure each moment as if it is the last. My father once told me that he tried to live each day well so that he would never have regrets. He was a wise man.

Let us get back to the Confusion Index. I had lost three classes, meaning that my teaching load would be reduced to 12 hours a week; I would be given another class, making it 14 hours, which is full time. I would be told later what the schedule would be—and perhaps surprisingly—I was. It would be another class preparing for IELTS, meaning that I needed to find out when the students would be sitting for their exam. How much time would I have? Later again I was told that the class would begin in week 6, not week 5.

Week four was therefore a slack week.

8.3: Third Semester, Autumn 2012

I made a mistake. Oh dear!

My co-teacher—the local teacher assigned to look after me and ensure that everything was going well—gave me a class list and text book for the new classes which I was due to pick up after the National Day holiday, October 2012. I took them, but did not look at them till later, when I realised that something was wrong. I tried to contact her for clarification, but could not reach her. This was when I made my mistake.

I sent a message to the head of department. In due course he clarified the matter; my co-teacher had indeed made a mistake. She was profuse in her apologies. She even climbed up to the 7th floor where I was teaching to hand me the correct class list. What happened? My guess is that she was put on the carpet by the boss. I had embarrassed her; she had lost face. Oh no. Although I had been in China for some years, I was still making basic mistakes through thoughtlessness. Now I am embarrassed. I am sorry.

One of the features of any new academic year, not only in China, but in many universities, is booths or something of their kin, for new students to enrol themselves in university activities. These could include anything from a bike riding club, to a book club, from discussion groups to yoga. Whatever. Photograph 66 shows Sun Square packed with temporary booths for new students to explore and perhaps to choose some activity.

Photo 66: A new academic year

8.4: Fifth Semester, Autumn 2013

Universities are wonderful places. I like the energy and young people have plenty of this—and they are everywhere, full of vitality, full of hopes and dreams, although often lacking in confidence. While they are looking to the future, yet they cannot see very far: passing this semester, getting their degree, obtaining a good job—whatever that might be. Meanwhile, girlfriends/boyfriends are not far away: some have them, most do not, but these do plan to have them in the not too distant future. Later will come marriage. Some have more detailed plans: degree by 23; a good job for 5 years; marriage by 28—at least for the girls. If a girl is not married by 28 she is considered to be a *sheng nu* or "left woman"— left on the shelf that is; big loss of face, especially for the parents.

Holiday time is a different matter. It is strange to walk around a nearly empty campus, without young people rushing hither and yon. It is quiet, the atmosphere oddly subdued. Dormitories close for the holidays, reopening a week or so before the semester officially begins. Many of the stores also closed for the vacation, not opening until the final week; these include small restaurants, supermarkets, printing and photo shops. There are still people around over the holidays, as many people were living at SISU permanently, and many on the staff would still be working. Falling applications for enrolment at this time had the staff working to attract more students. Someone has to pay for the large scale development, which was currently going on up the mountain, with SISU being built on the slopes of a mountain, Ge Le Shan. So if you are looking for a quiet place for a holiday, try a university when the students are away.

Over the holidays demolition of old buildings on the lower campus was underway, creating lots of dust and noise. Some people living close by were having breathing difficulties; my own apartment was several hundred metres away. Two years earlier two other areas were levelled, but at this time no reconstruction had begun, if indeed any had been planned, due to all the development on the upper campus. You never know what is going to happen.

In the final week of holidays students start to return. There is no wholesale arrival en masse: just in dribs and drabs. A few taxis and autos would arrive, or a couple of students would alight from a bus. An auto is a small three wheeled vehicle. More frequently, as the week progresses, you would see students or soon to be students carrying bags, wheeling luggage. They would not have much: two pieces of luggage seemed to be enough for a year.

Photo 67: *bang bang* men

Even so a squad of *bang bangs* would be waiting hopefully outside the university gates. These are men, often wearing military style shirts, who are the carriers. Their badge of office is a short, thick pole, with sturdy ropes attached. For a fee they will carry nearly anything. I have seen them staggering along, knees bent, with really heavy loads, the pole balanced across their shoulders. Another name for them, in fact, is "house movers". Well, the house may be stretching it a bit, but they can manage most loads. I have seen two of them carrying a fridge between them. The ones in the accompanying photographs, however, were not working too hard at the time.

Often parents would be accompanying their offspring, especially the first year students; some of them would remain for a while to ensure that their child was settled. This would include helping with the shopping in order to buy essentials, such as washing materials. Welcome to a new semester.

Teachers too start to return, new ones needing to learn the ropes and settle in, old ones resuming where they left off. This is the time to find out what our schedules will be—if you are lucky. In this week I was told my schedule for one class only, in the Lancaster Programme, but this was all, so that for the first week I taught for four hours only. This is the life!—and they were still paying me!

We got underway officially on Monday, 2nd September with a meeting in one of the auditoriums. This consisted of a video of some of the staff singing a rather catchy Chinese song. It went for some time—and then it was played again, but we should have started by now. I got a phone call: "Where are you? We are waiting to begin."

"But we are here." Sitting in the middle of the auditorium, we were not noticed. They were really waiting for Cyril who was with me, as he was slated to give a speech. There were, I think, four of these, all in Chinese, except for Cyril's, which was in English. He was a new teacher here at SISU, even though he had been in China for some years.

At the beginning of each academic year, we get a new lot of students to teach, often several hundred. In both Fuzhou and Tongren every one of them would adopt—at least temporarily—an English name. It was a little different at SISU, where many of my students were adults with their own careers. Many were doctors, many were teachers from other universities and many were research scientists. This is so pleasant, and far more satisfying—at least for me at this stage of my career—than struggling to teach and discipline teenagers who are not the least bit interested in Maths, Science or whatever the subject may be.

These adults mostly stick with their Chinese names, which did make it a little more difficult for me.

Amongst the undergraduates, however, we have English names. As usual we had the well-known ones we are familiar with, but we also had unusual ones, often made up. I had a Timberlake, which, I believe, is the name of a singer. In the same class there was a Dolores, who is a happy sort, if shy, a Rocey (a boy) and—just to spice up our classes—there was a Clove. Some names come straight from their Chinese names: Hanna from Han, Fanny from Fan, Wing from Wen Wen. I did not think I had taught a Wing before, so I was expecting that these classes should really take off. Aily also comes from Chinese. Ai means "love", while li can mean just about anything, depending upon what character is used. I think here it means "power"—so I have the "Power of Love" in my class. Wow! One girl was called Curly, because her hair truly was curly, very unusual for a Chinese person. I had a Dream, a King and a Dragon (very popular in China). There was a Guest and a Young and a Kairos, which I like, as the Greek word means the proper time. I also had a Kitten, no, not the furry type. What makes this even more interesting is that this was a boy, not a girl. Finally, I had a Justin Huang II; I had taught another Justin Huang in Fuzhou.

The weather bares a mention. For the two weeks I was here at the end of the holidays, generally writing up my experiences, it was hot, with each day hovering around 38 degrees. Then a cool change arrived and stayed. The temperature plunged nearly 20 Celsius degrees, to around 20 degrees Celsius— and stayed that way, accompanied by light rain and drizzle, for the next two weeks. Laundry provided such a contrast. Before the change, my clothes would be dry the same day, whereas after the change they would be hanging up for days, still not dry.

Naturally for some time our schedules remained a mystery. Forget about knowing well in advance exactly what one will be teaching, so that one can plan the semester. Initially, as I have said, I was given only four hours a week. Well, that is not enough. Then I was given another six hours, and it looked as if that would be it: still not enough. I agreed to teach some classes outside of SISU as extra curricula activities—but ssh: nobody knows. I was not sure initially how many extra hours this would entail but certainly in some weeks it would be a further eight hours. That is enough—probably more than enough. SISU then gave me a further eight hours a week, so that for some weeks I ended up having as many as 26 hours. Goodness. Fourteen hours is full time.

Just to make life even more interesting, we no sooner began work than we had a break again for two more holidays: Mid-Autumn Festival and National Day. For Mid-Autumn Festival we had no classes on Thursday or Friday (or Saturday either), but on Sunday we made up Friday's classes, which would mean four hours for me. Yet on my free days, I worked—and did so hard for long hours. Teaching? No. Preparing classes? No.

Over the years, various people have suggested that I publish my writings on my experiences. Initially I rejected the idea, as I had only been writing for private circulation. Then I thought, "Well, maybe, but not till I have left China," because some things I have written have been a little critical, and you just cannot criticise in any way. At this point of time I was preparing this material, and it required a lot of work. The words of Qoheleth came to mind: "Son, there is something else to watch out for. There is no end to the writing of books, and too much study will wear you out." Qoh 12/12. Indeed. Qoheleth is also known as Ecclesiastes.

8.5: Daily Schedule

I was attached to the International Department, which is a little different from other departments in this respect, in that instead of having a predictable intake of students for each undergraduate year, many of our students were only part time. Anybody around town who wants to improve his English can enrol for a full semester or part thereof. You never know how many students this will be, although usually it was only a small number: in one semester only four people enrolled. Teaching a class of fewer than ten students was not economically viable for the university, which actually had massive debts at this time, due to large scale construction. The upshot of all this was that for the first few weeks of my final semester, spring 2014, I taught only four hours each week.

Each day had its schedule. With so few classes at the start of semester, I could afford to get up when I woke up. First would come prayer time then breakfast, after which I would settle down to write for the rest of the morning. At lunch, I watched the news on TV.

The afternoon was also a time to be catching up with e-mails and Australian news. Late afternoon was exercise time: I liked to get about 50 minutes of fast walking each day, varying the route each day. Initially we were still in winter mode, with four layers of clothing, including heavy coat. This soon dropped to three layers, then two. If it was a bit cold at the start of the walk, one soon warmed up, the cold being an encouragement to pick up the pace. This was when I did my shopping as well, swinging by either a supermarket, a fruit stall or bread shop as the need arose. One walk took me to a metro station, two stations up the line from Lieshimu, which had been completed at Christmas 2011, yet this one had still not opened. It had never been used, but was still seemingly operational, even with lights on. It was just closed. The surrounding area was full of derelict, abandoned factories, so I imagine that the plan is to pull all these down and build the usual high rise apartments. That would take years, yet there was no sign that they were about to start.

8.6: The Lancaster and Newcastle Programmes

Of all the programmes I was teaching, the Lancaster and Newcastle Programmes were the major ones. The plan was to prepare students to complete their degrees at Lancaster University in England or Newcastle University in Australia. Instead of the usual three year degree programme, they would complete four years: two at SISU and two at Lancaster or Newcastle. The extra time would largely be spent in getting their English up to standard. The students in these programmes were not forced to attend these two universities, but most did. A significant number, for instance, also went to Robert Gordon University in Aberdeen, Scotland.

The programme was headed by Susan, a truly delightful as well as a competent lady. Photograph 68 shows some of us associated with the programme gathering for a meal. The International Building, where we taught and where the office for the Lancaster Programme is located, also has a café, which hosted many a formal meal. Indeed for a short time, I even held some classes here because there were no spare classrooms. I had been teaching in a classroom set aside for the Goethe Institute and therefore meant for the teaching of German, until the German director objected and I got kicked out. Such is life. David and John, two AITECE teachers are on the right, while on the left is our liaison teacher (Denise), Susan and her daughter Coco.

Photo 68: a café meal

A particular week in April, 2012 was interesting. Indeed I found every week interesting and every day. Life itself is interesting. Some days, however, are more interesting than others—or weeks. As for lives, that is up to the individual.

At the beginning of the week, Joe, the head of AITECE, arrived from Wuhan where he was then teaching, to see all the AITECE teachers at SISU: there were seven of us. Each year every AITECE teacher in China is visited by some representative from the organisation. It is good, as we can share experiences and perhaps express concerns. The university also becomes more aware of us as a group. Joe himself had spent many years in China, so came with a wealth of experience behind him. I had never met him before so it was good to make contact.

In the middle of the week two representatives arrived from Lancaster University, in England. As stated, much of my teaching involved 30 students who were preparing to attend this university the following year. Apart from their Chinese teachers, they had David, who himself comes from England, and yours truly from the Land Down Under. Our Lancaster guests gave a presentation before interviewing the prospective candidates. I have never been to Lancaster and knew nothing about their university, so it was good to fill in some of the blanks, and also to put a human face on where the students were heading. It appeared to be a really good university, so I believed that they would be happy there. Not all of them were going to make it, as some were still struggling and their IELTS scores were still too low. They needed a minimum of 5.5.

We had a clash between these two occurrences, as the Lancaster Programme put on a lunch for the two English visitors and staff at the same time as the Foreign Affairs Department put on a lunch for the AITECE teachers. Not only that, but they were both in the same restaurant, near our building here on campus, but in two different rooms. You could not really combine them, as the interests were different. David and I opted to attend the former, on the grounds that we are the only two overseas teachers in the programme, whereas there are seven IELTS teachers,

On Wednesday afternoon we had a lecture given by a professor from Newcastle University. He spoke on culture and it was excellent, both gelling with my own experiences and expanding my understanding. At the end of his presentation, he also spoke about the Newcastle region and its university. Afterwards I told him that he had omitted a vital component: recently Lonely Planet voted Newcastle as the best city in the world. The problem with this is that my Novocastrian friends, whose heads are already somewhat larger than the average, will be puffing out their chests as well. It certainly does have a lot to recommend it, however, with its climate, beaches, Hunter Valley wine region, lakes, wild life and way of life. Unfortunately, the timing of the lecture coincided with a class. That's OK, as I could make up the class at another time.

There were so many things on that there were bound to be some clashes.

In this programme I gave the students topics to research, write about and give speeches on. One of these topics was Australian literature. The student who had this topic got up and gave his speech on Chinese literature. Well, that's OK, but was not the assigned topic. He explained this by averring that Australia—and the West in general—did not have any worthwhile literature. He claimed that Li Bai was the best known and greatest poet in the entire world. This says volumes about Chinese Nationalism. I said nothing, as the other students gave their comments. Several remarked that that he was only saying that through ignorance, because he knew nothing about Australian literature. True enough. I asked him to comment on the importance of alcohol on the poetry of Li Bai. He could not even do that. Oh dear. He knew that Mo Yan, a Chinese author, had just recently been awarded the Nobel Prize for Literature, but was unaware that an Australian author, Patrick White, had achieved this distinction nearly 40 years before.

There is further sequel, which I found rather amusing. I asked the students if they would like me to read out an Australian story. Yes, they would. So I did and asked them to comment on its literary merits. They were effusive in their praise. The story I read out was my own—and there are one or two Australian authors whose quality is a little above mine!

Towards the end if the following year, once again representatives arrived from Newcastle University and a meal was organised by our university to welcome them. There were quite a few students at this time who would be heading Down Under to that prestigious institute of learning. I was teaching about 100 of them. One programme was preparing students to do their Masters in Australia. Another was the so called 2-2 system, where they spend two years here at SISU, then two years at Newcastle to get their undergraduate degree.

We did have a bit of confusion at the start when the director of the programme rang me, saying he was waiting for me outside of the restaurant, but since I could not see him, I went in. He came in later, wondering how I had eluded him. It was not intentional. I was asked to take a seat, and I noticed a spare seat directly opposite the vice president of our university, so that is where I sat. I knew exactly what I was doing. There is a protocol whereby the most important person—the host—sits opposite the door, the tables, of course, being round. Next to him, on his right, sits the next most important person, while the third sits on his left. Thus it continues; right, left, right, left, around the table till you come to the place directly opposite the host, the position with back to the door, if you will. This is for the least important person, often the host's servant or chauffeur—where I was. Then the organiser came up and said to me, "Friend, go up higher"—or words to that effect. Does this make me humble? Nah, just proud: seeking honour, you see.

The meal itself was of the usual high standard, but I was more interested in how our students from the previous year were doing. When I returned to Australia the following year I went to Newcastle to see for myself. There is always the danger that they could be living in their own Little China, with not much interaction with others, whereas I wanted them to experience Australian culture, which is what I was teaching. Yes, we do have a culture!—many in point of fact.

There was another meal related to this. These students, once they get to Australia, would need to know how to cook, and many of them did not, having been spoilt by their mothers: a consequence of the One Child Policy. To this end

255

I was in the habit of inviting groups of students to my apartment for a meal. No, I was not going to poison them with my cooking: chef I ain't. They would feed me. I invited them in groups of eight, as my apartment could hold that many comfortably. For the first group we met at 4.30 p.m. on a Sunday afternoon in Sun Square on campus, before wandering down to the local shopping centre to purchase whatever supplies were required. They shopped, I paid. Back in my apartment, the fun really started. All eight students were packed into my kitchen. Did I say my apartment could hold eight comfortably? Well, yeh, the apartment could—but not the kitchen. Some were cooking, some were cutting up, some were washing vegetables while some were just getting in the way. Just as well we were not going to have broth. Naturally, it was the girls who came to the fore, rather than the boys. In my second group I had more boys than girls and they were excellent.

We ate in my sitting room, with the food placed on the coffee table. It was, of course, delicious. The idea was to ensure they did have cooking skills so that they could not only look after themselves while abroad, but could also entertain others with Chinese fare. Then we sat around and chatted. I asked each of them to sing a song, discovering one girl with a truly lovely voice. She can also play the guitar and piano, and is in fact the class monitor, which was a bit of a surprise as she was such a quiet person.

Clean up started, which took a while, as they had made such a mess. They usually do not use tea towels here, but instead of putting the plates out to dry, they put them away. After they left, I had to drag them out again to drain, minus one plate, which went walkabout. As for the left-over food, I had enough in my fridge to last a week. Why do we always cook so much? Nevertheless, it was a great exercise, also giving me a chance to get to know them better.

One Sunday, however, I made a big blue with one of these groups. I called one group "gentlemen", upon which one of the "gentlemen" said "I am no gentleman." OK, I thought, maybe he thinks his manners are not good enough. "I am a girl." Oh my goodness. She really looked like a boy. She even had a boy's name. I needed to check my class list to make sure. Oh dear!

On another Sunday I was expecting a group from the Newcastle Programme to come and cook, but no-one turned up. OK, so they are not interested. That is fine, because this was in no way compulsory: just for those interested. For the following Sunday, I organised another group. Guess what?—both groups turned up. What was happening? In class, I told the students "next Sunday". Clear enough?—definitely not, and this is my fault, not theirs. Goodness, I had been in China long enough to know this. Our class was on Monday, and in Chinese, *"xia xingqi tian"* (next Sunday) means what we would call Sunday week. I should have said *"zhege xingqi tian"* (this Sunday). Incidentally, the first day of the week here is counted as Monday, not Sunday. Monday is *xingqi yi*, which literally means "week one", Tuesday is *xingqi er*, or "week two" and so forth. Sunday is *xingqi tian*, or "week heaven", which is not a bad name. Now in an attempt to justify myself, even if only a little, let me point out that if you are on a bus, and you wish to get off at the next stop, you say *xia yi zhan*, or "next one station". So here next means the same as we mean, viz. the one coming up. So "next" can mean both the one coming and the one after next. Confused? Then just to add to the confusion, *xia* also means "down", while *shang* means "up", so that "next week" is *"xia xingqi"*, while last week is called *"shang xinqi"*, indicating that they are thinking vertically. Welcome to China.

Meanwhile my small kitchen was crowded, as one would expect with two groups there; someone was cooking at the two gas ranges; someone else was cutting up the meat; a third person was dicing the garlic; yet another was in the bathroom, washing vegetables in warm water. I do not have hot water in the kitchen. What we would end up eating, I did not know, but I knew it would be great. Two students could cook and it was their job to teach those who could not. I was typing while listening to Christmas music. Life is good.

June 2012 also witnessed some frenetic activity in the Lancaster Programme. 30 students were slated to attend Lancaster University in England in the following semester, but a sizeable number had not fulfilled the requirements, especially in terms of their IELTS score. Part of the problem was that expectations had risen. 5.0 is no longer enough; 5.5 or even 6.0 was now required, not just overall, but in each of the four categories of reading, writing, listening and speaking. The office personnel were running around contacting Lancaster, contacting other universities, contacting parents, meeting with parents, meeting with staff, arranging yet another IELTS test while cramming more crash courses into the students.

Clearly some students needed to put a lot more effort into their study before taking the test again, a course of action that does not come cheaply, as it was costing about 1,500 Yuan for each test. Three of the girls actually flew down to Haikou in Hainan Province, thus making it very expensive for them. Their parents must be loaded.

Regular classes were cancelled two weeks early before the scheduled end of semester so that we could spend more time giving mock tests to those who needed it most, with—thankfully—some noticeable improvement. It was not compulsory for students to turn up for these mocks trials, so it may not be surprising that few took advantage of the opportunity. Indeed, the same few, the really keen ones, would turn up every time. These are the ones who will succeed. I have no doubt about this.

Those who would not make the grade, at least as far as entry into Lancaster University was concerned, were applying to go to other universities. Nine were hoping to get into Robert Gordon University in Aberdeen, which—for those of you who do not have ready access to a map—is about half way up the east coast of Scotland. I am sure it is a lovely city, the third largest in Scotland, but I gather the weather is somewhat bleak: wet, windswept and not real hot. One applied to go to Cardiff University in Wales, one hoped to go to the US, while three others were undecided. Our little group of 30, which had been together for almost a year, was about to get blown apart.

The situation was not helped by one staff member being away, having just delivered a baby. It was a busy time and interesting.

As regards regular classes, during normal times, we did different activities both to improve their English and to prepare them for living in another culture. In class, girls generally sit together, usually down the front, while the boys tend to congregate down the back. For the Lancaster group, in one class I placed each boy with each girl, except that there were more girls than boys, so one of the girls had to take the part of a man. They did a dialogue of an argument between husband and wife over which channel they would watch on TV. It was fascinating. One couple solved their problem quickly and amicably, while for others it was a bit more prolonged and acrimonious. One "wife" wanted a divorce. What was really interesting was that in every single case, it was the "wife" who got her way, not the "husband". Now why would that be? Is that always the case? We had a lot of fun in doing this, but it also provided a platform to talk about marriage and what it means, about values, about love.

I repeated this for the second class. It is really interesting how each class has its own ethos. Here they were doing the same work as class 1, but in a different spirit. The first two students I asked to move were anything but willing. "Why?"

"Because I said so," was my riposte, which is about what any mother would say to her three year old. They moved. In this class, however, we had one girl left over, so naturally, I "married" her. We prepared our dialogues while the other couples were preparing theirs, and I was also going around checking. We did our presentation last. In fact we did two. In the first, we had a violent argument, ending with me storming out to watch my football game with a friend, leaving my wife in possession. In the second, we came to an amicable compromise, agreeing to watch her soap opera, turning over to the football game during the ads, and at the end of her programme. It was the first, however, that the rest of the class appreciated more, giving us a clap at the end. Now why would that be?

Every year representatives from Lancaster University would pay us a visit. This I found to be quite instructive as to how China works. The implications are important for both universities: for Lancaster they want students who can perform adequately, while for SISU it is loss of face if their students are deemed to be not good enough.

On one such visit in June 2012 we met for lunch at the overseas teachers' dining room—although banquet is more like it. In the afternoon Susan, the head of our programme, drove the representatives—let us call them Elise and Tim (not their true names)—plus me down to the nearby ancient town of Ciqikou, where we wandered around for some time. It is one of my favourite places. It was good to relax, and talk. Back at SISU we continued to chat before heading off for yet another meal—another banquet. None of this is aimless and it is very Chinese. Elise was young and had recently come into her job. Basically she was handling the applications for hundreds of applicants from China wanting to study at Lancaster University. These students, however, were just names to her, not people. I also gathered—and this is a purely personal opinion, so I may well be wrong—that she was trying to consolidate her position, especially by being a stickler for the rules. If a student from SISU just failed to meet all the requirements, the lavish treatment she was given might make her much more favourably inclined to allow admittance. In Chinese, it is called *guanxi*. This is fine and nothing wrong at all. We need to have a human connection, but you can see how easily it could turn to bribery. You wine and dine first, maybe give some expensive gifts, then you negotiate a deal. There may also be quantities of wine.

The university certainly pulled out all the stops for this meal. We went to a very fancy restaurant complex, some distance away, necessitating a fleet of cars to drive us all. There were three SISU vice presidents, the dean of our department, the head of the Lancaster Programme, another staff member, David and I, and of course, Elise and Tim from Lancaster. Getting there was not easy as the traffic was heavy and progress slow. As well, our driver did not know the way, relying upon GPS. At one point she called another car, as we had been stuck for some time, and had seen many other cars do U-turns, no doubt in order to try another route. The other car was just 200 metres behind us, which we knew because our GPS told us we were 4.8 km from our starting point, whereas they were at the 4.6 km mark. To make matters even more interesting, we missed the turn and found that getting to our destination involved a lot more than simply driving around the block. But we got there.

The feast was sumptuous. I did not partake of all that was on offer: I did not, for instance, subject my stomach to receiving the stomachs of other animals, and nor did I eat brains, but I did like the seafood: abalones, fish and prawns. The latter—poor creatures—had been skewered, still alive. You plunged them into boiling chicken soup. This was a hot pot, Chongqing style, but instead of having one large dish in the centre of the table, we each had our own smaller dish, some divided into two, one side spicy and the other side mild. I was also given black mushrooms, which I was told were good for old age. Thanks. We drank beer, and I was surprised that there was no toast or *ganbei,* where you drain the cup. The reason was that so many of the people here had driven to the restaurant, so could not drink a lot of alcohol. It is good that this was being taken seriously.

My lunch next day consisted of no more than yoghurt and a cup of coffee—I had been eating so much. There was also no electricity this day.

For some time I had been planning a meal in my apartment for the Lancaster students, as part of the "learn to cook" programme. In Tongren I would do this for my students quite often, but this is not Tongren. These people are not poor, but rich. Possibly as a result, they were not nearly as friendly. In short they were not interested. So I invited others. But day after day went by, with official banquet after banquet, so that we kept postponing our meal. That power cut meant yet another postponement. By the time we could gather, most of the food I had prepared had gone off and had to be thrown out. Not many came: one person had just bought a farm; another had just married a wife etc. You learn. This is one exercise I was loath to repeat.

Surprise surprise: Elise and Tim from Lancaster University turned up again in December; evidently there were still problems which needed to be sorted out. Naturally, I did not know they were coming.

Wednesday at this time was my busiest day, with eight hours of teaching, finishing at 6.00 p.m. I would usually eat in the dining room on this night, rather than start cooking. But something else was in the air, to wit a cruise on the rivers with Elise: yet we would be leaving at 4.30 p.m. I turned up for my class at 4.20 p.m., only to tell my students that I would not be there and to ask the class monitor to arrange another time. I gave him my phone number and also my class timetable, which he simply photographed with his mobile phone: modern technology.

Photo 69: a cruise around Chongqing

We drove down to Chao Tian Men, at the junction of the two rivers on which Chongqing is situated, where we boarded a large four decker boat, for dinner and a cruise. We had plenty of time as dinner was not served until 6.30 p.m., so we wandered around taking in the view of the city lights. Dinner was a buffet style, with the food quite palatable, especially the fish and potatoes, although others thought the quality could have been better. It still beats my cooking.

At 8.15 p.m. we started our cruise, sailing for about 15 minutes up the Yangtze, before turning around. We sailed around the point and up the Jia Ling for about 15 minutes before returning, so that altogether the cruise lasted an hour. It was wonderful. City lights reflecting off the water from beautiful Chinese architecture is a sight not to be missed. Across the Yangtze, buildings had been lit up to look like the sails of ships, while a full moon hovered above: magical. Across the Jia Ling River is the Concert Hall, a square shaped building looking, appropriately, like a ship. On the southern bank there is a whole collection of buildings, including the Hongya Cave Hotel in which I stayed last year, in traditional Chinese style.

Elise's visit, however, had a serious side: it was not just an excuse for sightseeing and good meals. While she was interested in students' standards, I was interested to know how our students from the previous year were faring at Lancaster and what we could learn. How could we do better to prepare young Chinese so that they could live happily and productively in another country? Naturally, the bulk of our preparation was taken up with improving their English, so that they could understand lectures in their chosen discipline, but they also needed to adjust culturally and socially. Some Western university students, for example, have a drinking culture, so how can young Chinese mix in successfully without going to excess? They may need to be aware of the pitfalls. On the academic front, how do they handle all the reading which will be given them? How much is necessary? How do they judge what is important and what is not? Another issue is that far from home, they would not be subject to the strict controls they have in their homeland. They have much more free time. Their study regimen is up to them. They need to be far more responsible in organising their time so that they are not wasting it, but have a healthy mix of work and leisure. Are they mixing with local people, or just living in Chinese enclaves? On these matters, I found Elise's visit to be very useful. It was good to see her again.

8.7: Adult Classes

Not all of my classes were to undergraduate students; in fact many were for adults. Some students came from the general community, some from other universities, some were Scientists and some came from various businesses. Of these not all were voluntary, but had been sent by their companies.

8.7.1: Business English

One of the more interesting classes I was teaching was to a group of students from what are known as SOE's or State Owned Enterprises. These, as the name suggests, are completely managed by the state—read, the Communist Party. Of course, every business owes its allegiance to the party and the bigger it is the more it is subject to party control. Even the nominal head of the university was not the king pin: this was the secretary of the Communist Party. One side effect of this is that of more recent years other countries have been becoming more careful in employing Chinese enterprises. Do they engage in spying? Of course they do. Do they steal secrets from their host country? Of course they do. Does the government admit that all this is going on? Of course not. It seems that the more vehemently the government denies something the more likely it is to be true.

I have always found it to be rather ironic that China calls itself communist, considering that the commercial instinct is strongly embedded in Chinese genes. Under Mao Zedong the party genuinely did strive to be communist, but it failed and this period died with Mao. Deng Xiao Ping turned the state around 180 degrees with his famous—and clever—statement: "It does not matter whether the cat is black or white, so long as it catches mice." The statement was clever in more ways than one. In Chinese, "*mao*" means "cat".

Consequently once the brakes were removed the country raced pell-mell down the capitalist road. The society is governed by a tripartite alliance: business, the military and the party. Together they control everything. The country (or rather "empire", because that it what it really is) is becoming increasingly wealthy and powerful, but as in any purely capitalistic society the rich become very wealthy indeed, while more and more people are sucked into poverty. America is a classic example of this. Still—to give credit where credit is due—hundreds of millions of people have risen out of poverty in China and this is excellent.

The people are hell-bent on becoming rich, with many entrepreneurs springing up and multitudes of people entering business. Reflecting this many university students are studying one or other form of business, such as Business and Law, International Business and Economics. The country has gone business mad. It seems everyone wants to run a business, and indeed many people do, more than in any other country in the world. There is I think a grim irony in this. You may know that there are five stars on the Chinese national flag: the large one stands for the Communist Party, while around it are arranged four smaller ones, the symbolism being that each owes its allegiance to the CP. They stand for four sectors of society, viz. peasants and rural landowners in the countryside, employers and workers in the cities. Where do business people fit into this? Not all of them are employers or employees. So it seems that a large part of Chinese society owes no allegiance to the CP.

Be that as it may—and I admit this is nit-picking—from time to time I have found myself engaged in the business, so to speak, of teaching English to business people, or those who wish to become so. In Fuzhou I taught such a course at Anglo-Chinese College. In April, 2013, I taught a similar course at SISU. And it was interesting.

There were about thirty students all from SOEs. All had been sent by their companies to do this course; I do not think they had much say in the matter, which should come as no surprise. The course was over three months, and I would be involved for just one month, teaching them for five hours a week—so roughly 20 hours in all. In my first class they were addressed at the start by a big wig from the CP.

What would I do?—since the design of the course was entirely up to me. This is one of the things I liked about teaching in China, where we had much more freedom, surprisingly perhaps, than in Australia in terms of course content and teaching methods. We were respected as professionals—and therefore were trusted to get on with the job, without all that unnecessary bureaucracy we find in Australia. My task was made easier by finding that I had a group of adults, who were mature and very co-operative. We got on well. As the course progressed our content became more and more business oriented, as I learnt. Remember that I am in no way a business person.

One highlight was taking an article from the Sydney Morning Herald on the gold market. This worked well, because (a) it was current and (b) it introduced them to quite a few new words. One student had downloaded a BBC programme entitled, "The Chinese are Coming", being a report into the massive involvement of China in Africa, where there are now more than a million Chinese working and making profits. This gave rise to much discussion. Holding discussions in groups was one of the techniques used, as it enabled the students to do most of the talking, always a good idea, especially when the teacher knows little about the subject. But I also used it for a wider purpose. Consider some of the topics:

1. A hungry person's right to food is greater than a rich person's right to more profits.
2. Overseas companies should employ local labour before importing from their own country.
3. Competition or co-operation.
4. The moral principles underlying business.

5. Profit must always come first—or should it?
6. When working in another country, you must consider that country's interests before your own.
7. A company's first responsibility should be to (a) it shareholders, (b) its workers, (c) its customers, (d) its country or (d) the environment.

What I was attempting to do was to introduce some moral principles into business—business ethics, if you will. The temptation is put the priority on making profits—and this is wrong.

In another of my books on China, "China—Behind the Mask" (Austin Macauley, 2017) page 57, we discussed the progression from business dinners to bribery, to *guanxi,* to partnerships and to overseas investments, ending with the purpose of money. There is no need to repeat what I wrote here, except to remark that we had a most fruitful discussion.

At the beginning of our course, I had presented two pieces of writing to them to read and act out. One featured a character called "Jimmy". The man who took this part thereafter became known as Jimmy, and whenever I asked for volunteers, the class would call out "Jimmy". He became quite a hit, as well as adding a touch of light relief. The classes become most enjoyable.

I really relished this opportunity to teach some values. Getting wealthy is not the b-all and end-all of life. Service to others must be paramount. There are obligations to the community, especially to the local community if you are working overseas. Going to another country in order to rip it off and send all the profits back is immoral. Honesty in business, as in every other aspect of life, is the best policy. I have no idea how much any of these principles were taken on board, which is usual with teaching: you never know what the students are really learning. But maybe—just maybe—a little bit of Chinese business in the future will become more imbued with some Christian principles. I hope so.

Fancy finding myself in this position: I remain amazed.

8.7.2: Sinopec

These days I think most people are aware of this company, a major state owned Chinese oil company. Some of their personnel were sent to SISU to improve their English; they did not come of their own volition. Our aim was not only to improve their English, but also to teach them something of Western cultures. There are, of course, many Western cultures, just as there are many

Asian cultures. In particular I focused on Australian culture, perhaps not surprisingly.

There were 17 students in the class. Most of them turned up for most classes, although some were away for part of the time, which is normal, both because of other commitments and because of a lack of motivation. Most of them would not be travelling to any Western country, at least in so far as one could foresee. This was important, as it gave them less incentive and less interest.

Another important factor was their age. Being mature adults their attitudes, assumptions and prejudices had formed, meaning that they were less amenable to ideas which did not coincide with their current perceptions. This was a challenge, not only for the teacher, but for all of us.

Nevertheless, they were good people who in most cases were ready to allow their horizons to be expanded, some more than others. Class participation was a problem, as they were not willing to volunteer: they needed to be specifically asked. I think this was due partly to their perceptions as to how classes are conducted, partly to their lack of confidence in speaking English publicly and partly to lack of interest.

Two of the students, Zhang Jin and Li Bin, I had for extra classes and it was a joy to teach them, as they were keen and co-operative. As a result, they made significant progress in improving their general English level, especially Li Bin. Well done.

8.7.3: Visiting Scholars' Class

Lecturers from other universities, including research scientists, not only from Chongqing but also from further afield, like Hunan Province, would come to SISU to improve their English. I confess that I used this opportunity to learn as well as to teach. For example, one research Scientist from Yunnan Province asked me to check the English of a paper he wrote on air pollution in Yunnan. These too were the people who gave lectures on Thursday afternoons.

From 3.00 to 4.00, there would be an open lecture held in our International Building lecture hall. These were not part of any course, but were simply offered so that we could learn from each other. The bulk of the audience of about 50 was made up of our visiting scholars and university staff. In these lectures they could share their areas of expertise. We would have about half an hour on the presentation, usually of the power point variety, followed by an open discussion.

I really liked them and would do my best to attend every week. Here are some examples.

One lecture was on genetically modified crops. This is a technology I have been deeply suspicious about. It seems to me that often scientific advances are made before the ramifications are clear, especially as regards moral implications. The fact that we can do something does not mean that we should. Obvious examples here concern weapons: the fact that we can produce weapons of mass destruction does not mean that we should use them, and indeed we most definitely we should not. Another example concerns gene editing—or gene tampering if you will. We could be producing Frankensteins; Hitler's eugenics programmes come to mind. In the case of genetically modified crops, a certain company produces insecticides designed to kill everything else—more or less. This upsets the balance of nature, with some species, such as the monarch butterfly, suffering severe depletion in numbers. This same product has been shown to be carcinogenic.

Another lecture was delivered by a Canadian, talking about his own country. I learnt a lot. This man had experience in more than one field. Unfortunately he was not as circumspect on some issues as he could have been, resulting in the university not renewing his contract. Rather than tell him straight out, they hedged and delayed, leaving him in limbo for some time.

On one occasion I gave a lecture on non-verbal communication. I was teaching communication through language, but much of our interaction is in fact non-verbal, sometimes in ways which give us some insight into cultural differences. Let us look at some of these:

1) Counting. We simply go through the fingers, 1 to 10. The Chinese do this for the first four numbers, as all the others have their own hand signs. It is more convenient.

2) Calling. We crook the index finger, palm up, moving the finger towards oneself a number of times. The Chinese turn the palm over and wave all of the fingers. They do this too for hailing a taxi, where we would tend to wave our right arm more vigorously.

3) Indicating oneself. We point to our chests: "Me", whereas the Chinese point to their noses. At this point I told the audience that herein lies the reason for the Chinese having flat noses, as over thousands of years they have pushed them flat! At least it raised a laugh.

4) Holding hands. In the West this tends to be a sign of particular friendship, as between two lovers. If two people of the same sex are holding hands in public it is assumed they are homosexuals. In China it is common for friends to hold hands of either sex. You often see a boy carrying his girlfriend's handbag. I like it, even if it does not quite match his own ensemble!

5) Staring. This is considered to be rude in the West, but here it indicates curiosity. I have often been stared at long and hard. They do not quite know what to make of it, however, if I stare back.

6) Hugging is quite common amongst friends in the West, but less so here. One needs to be careful, as one could embarrass the other person.

7) Intonation. I think this is underestimated, especially here where Chinese is an extonation language. There are several ways, for example, to say "really". It is not what we say but the way we say it which indicates surprise, or stress, or a question, or anger or amazement.

8) Horn blowing. This is meant to be a warning of danger, but here I do not know what it means. It is just part of driving and is just as automatic as turning the steering wheel. I could, for example, be walking along a narrow back road near the university as close to the railing as possible, even with my arm over the rail, since there is no footpath. You can hear the vehicles coming behind for some distance—I am not deaf—and being especially careful. Nevertheless, just as a vehicle draws level, you could get a loud **honk honk**, which just about gives one a heart attack, with grave danger of jumping into the vehicle. Horn blowing is a dangerous practice, yet it persists.

9) "V" sign. This is very common here, but I confess I do not know what it means. In the West, if the palm is held out, it means victory, immortalised by Winston Churchill in the Second World War. Here young people commonly use this when having photographs taken. There is, of course, a similar sign, with the palm turned inward, signifying defiance—or at least it did originally. You may know that it originated at the battle of Agincourt in 1413. The French were confident of victory and threatened to cut off the index and middle fingers on the right hands of the English bowmen, thus disabling them. At the end of the battle the bowmen proudly held up their fingers to the French to show that they still had them.

10) Art—in all its forms. This is a huge field of communication and a subtle one, in that the viewer may perceive something other than what the artist intends—whether in painting, sculpture, dance or whatever. For illustration, I used two Aboriginal paintings.

These are just some examples. One also uses sign language when one's linguistic skills are somewhat limited.

I was also invited on outings. One of these was amazing for its significance, a visit to a village called Diao Yu Cheng, or Fishing Village. I have reported on this visit in greater detail in my first book on China, "A Traveller in China" (Austin Macauley, 2014) pages 243-46. Hence there is no need to repeat details here. The village is situated quite close to the city and within Chongqing Municipality. In the 13th century the town was under siege from the invading Mongols for 36 years, finally surrendering in 1279. Its significance lies in the fact that the Great Khan, Mongke, a grandson of Genghis Khan, was wounded and died in 1259 during the siege, thus necessitating the selection of a new Khan. This meant pulling key leaders from battlefields elsewhere, thus saving Africa and Europe from invasion at this time. The rump of their army left in the Middle East was defeated in the Jezreel Valley in Galilee, Israel in 1260. I wonder how many people in the West have even heard of Diao Yu Cheng, let alone know of its significance.

Photo 70: on top of ramparts, Diao Yu Cheng

On another occasion I was invited to join the class for a meal and in fact all of their teachers had been invited. Alcohol flowed freely: wine, baijiu and beer. One of the dishes was noodles. Even though I had been in China for eight years, I was still no expert in using chopsticks, finding it particularly difficult to extract very long strands of slippery noodles from the central bowl onto my plate. Before long noodles festooned the table, but not as a result of my clumsy efforts: it was the local experts who were having difficulties! If they have trouble, what chance do I have? Why not use a fork and shorter noodles, à la Italian style? After the meal, we repaired to a KTV. Now I thought that the original idea of KTV was for people to sing; not any more. Well, you might be singing, but the music was so loud that nobody could hear you. In my dotage, I cannot abide loud noises. Then I saw the beer. Oh, oh, we have already imbibed more than enough: what is it going to be like after we have downed all of this? I stayed for a respectable length of time, before taking my leave. It was still a great night, and I am so grateful that they invited me.

8.8: Academic Writing

8.8.1: Introduction

One subject I loved teaching was Academic Writing. You could teach this to any group of undergraduate students, as they all need to know how to write essays and research papers, but it is particularly pertinent to Chinese students, for two reasons. The first is that English is not their first language, and it is very difficult for anyone to write in a language other than one's mother tongue. Indeed it is difficult enough if it is your mother tongue. The second reason is that their cultural background is so different. Let me talk about these.

This section is about writing, but it is not one long document from start to finish without subdivisions. Nor is it written in the other extreme, seemingly adopted by many journalists, where nearly every single sentence is a separate paragraph. I hate this. If I downloaded an article from the internet to be used for teaching purposes, I would go through and redo the paragraphing before presenting it to students. It just so happens that Chinese students find paragraphing very difficult; they come to class with very little idea of how to go about it—and herein lies another problem.

This writing course went for four hours each week and I planned a separate topic for each week. The idea was to spend the first two hours on theory with the second two hours given to students practising. The problem is that quite a few students—and yes, you would probably guess that these were the weaker ones—failed to come to class. Consequently, when they wrote an assignment, it was quite clear that they had no idea how to paragraph.

As an aside here, I remember very clearly, as if it was yesterday, one particular class when I was in grade 5. A guest teacher came in to give us a whole class on paragraphing. I learnt a lot, but also became somewhat irritated, as he too seemed to think that nearly every sentence should be a separate paragraph. I disagreed then and still disagree today. This particular paragraph, for instance has seven sentences (including this one!). I would try to get my students to pick out the central idea in any paragraph, often expressed in one key sentence. This also helped in comprehension, presuming that the piece had been well written.

Other problems included their persistence in beginning a sentence with a conjunction and not knowing what punctuation mark to use. Hence very commonly—after repeated efforts to correct—I would still get such writing as "I went to bed. Because I was tired." Another problem—a major one—is plagiarism, but more of this later.

What are we to do, especially with those tardy students? One technique was to mark each student's attendance, a practice I am not comfortable with, as it seems to be treating these young adults as children. Nevertheless it is a requirement in some universities. A further technique was to include attendance as a factor in their final mark, a practice I am even more uncomfortable with, as it seems to me that a person's ability should be what counts, not whether they were in class or not. Unfortunately, life is not so simple. In China marks are everything, so may be seen as an incentive. On this, the really big issue for them is getting a sufficiently high score in IELTS (International English Language Testing System), which is required by overseas universities as a prerequisite for admission, which is fair enough, as it is simply a waste of money and time if a student cannot understand the lectures. Once a student has obtained the magic score of 5.5 or 6.0, depending on the individual university, then they tend to sit back and think they have nothing further to learn. It is the mark that matters, a thinking which goes deep into Chinese history, ever since the Civil Service Examinations were introduced during the Sui Dynasty (AD 581—618).

8.8.2: Plagiarism

Plagiarism is indeed a major issue. At this time President Obama and President Xi Jinping were meeting, with the thorny issue of internet hacking high on the agenda. We have different ways of thinking here. For the Chinese, there is nothing wrong with stealing whatever you can, so long as you can get away with it—or at least that seems to be the case. The only crime is in getting caught. So it is natural for a student to copy whole slabs of material, usually from the internet, without acknowledgement. What to do? Here I am caught in a dilemma. If I let it go, then they will continue to do it, but if I give them a zero mark, then they will not go overseas. It is therefore good policy to schedule the due date for their major assignment a full month before the end of semester, so that they have an opportunity of rewriting it, not if, but when they copy—because they will.

The next chapter in this book is concerned with students' work, but as a taste, I am giving some examples here in order to illustrate plagiarism. The topic for their final assignment was "The Future of the United Nations"—with the emphasis on how they saw it, in an attempt to stop them copying. It didn't work. Is anyone surprised?

1) "When I am the U.N., I always joke that manage the global institutions
2) like trying to manage a 184 chief executive enterprise."

So he is in the U.N.? He did not even get the grammar right.

3) "The end of the Cold War has reached ten years and the Yalta system has collapsed."

It was now 24 years since the collapse of the Berlin Wall and I doubt if this writer has any idea about Yalta.

4) "Currently one "superpower situation" is an undeniable fact. America, for example, pursues unilateralism brazenly due to its strongest power in the world."

A number of students only used Chinese sources, with the result that their bias is heavily anti-American. This also explains how they can copy but still get the grammar wrong.

5) "The concept from the beginning was rooted in atifical (sic) soil ... The U.N. from its start was a collective of countries run by kings, dictators, monopoly-clad political parties (which is what the US has become, under the guise of a two-party system) and moneyed interests. It wasn't some grassroots bonanza. It wasn't some magical butterfly equipped with angelic wings. It was concocted by brutes and tyrants, the bulk of them here in our own paradise of arrogant successors to golden heredidary (sic) thrones."

Did she really write this? I do not think so. She even copied some of the spelling incorrectly.

8.8.3: Independence

One topic I gave them to write about was independence. These students were all going overseas to pursue further studies, either to England or to Australia. They needed to be able to look after themselves, far from family and their normal support group. It is these same students whom I had had cooking in my apartment, so that they could teach each other this vital life skill. It is surprising how few knew how to cook. On one Sunday I had four students only one of whom knew how to cook, and he only knew how to cook one dish: fried rice. All he wanted to put into his rice was four eggs and one shallot—and this was for six people. I persuaded him to add some frozen vegetables and some bacon. The result was quite nice, but just a little bland. "You have no *lajiao* (chilli)," says I, to which all of them replied that they did not like hot spicy food. What? This is Chongqing, home of hotpot. Life is full of surprises.

Compared with their Western contemporaries, they are far more immature. Why should that be? Let the students speak for themselves.

The One Child Policy has meant that parents have tended to spoil their little darlings, especially if that darling is a boy: they do everything for him. This is called "the little emperor syndrome". Parents and grandparents have been too permissive. We have already seen extreme examples of this in society. On one occasion in a supermarket one of these little darlings deliberately ran his trolley into me. Great fun. His mother took no notice. He next proceeded to pull goods off the shelves onto the floor. His mother took no notice. Only when staff came running did she deign to do anything. At an airport we had a passenger running amok, ripping a computer apart and smashing it against a window, all because his flight was delayed. They are used to having their own way.

Students wrote that they were "puppets" of their parents, following them blindly. Even when they enrol for college or university, the parents do it, sometimes with other relatives in tow. I have had to tell students that when they go for a job interview they should go alone, without holding on to their mother's hand. "Parents should be tutors, not dictators," one person wrote. I have taught many students who were studying because their parents had sent them, not because of their own choice, and this includes the subjects they were studying. They are not used to making decisions for themselves.

It is interesting that some students were actually sent to boarding school when they were in primary. This may be because the parents were too busy with their own careers, but had the advantage of having the children learn such basic tasks as how to make their bed and how to wash their clothes. The normal situation is that "children are free of any housework and menial labour". I might add that we are talking about city children here, not the countryside.

One student wrote: "When we go to university, we have to live with ourselves. Washing clothes, cleaning the dormitory, tidying the bed and a lot of things—we have to do these by ourselves—but many students do not know how to do these: they are dependent. What is more, their bad temperament will block them from making friends. Finally they will be lonely." What caught my attention here is the social consequences of being spoilt, how it makes people difficult to get on with.

Exacerbating the problem is the education system, wherein the emphasis is on learning, especially learning by rote, rather than questioning. The powers that be would much rather have a compliant population, toeing the party line and not being troublesome. As a result you get students coming to SISU who did not know how to keep their dormitory clean etc. and what was even more worrying, did not know how to control their moods. There is too much emphasis upon marks and knowledge, and not enough on a more rounded education.

The emphasis is on becoming economically independent, so that they no longer have to rely upon their parents for everything. One student, however, talked about the necessity of becoming independent in mind, rather than becoming an unthinking follower—excellent. I got a giggle out of another student who declared that parents should give more freedom to their children, and then, in the same breath, added: "the government should lay down the law" to make these children more independent! She could not see the contradiction.

One result is a lack of responsibility for their own actions, something we know a lot about in Australia. We have become a litigious society, unfortunately, where we are losing this sense of responsibility. For example, if someone trips over a tree root, the immediate reaction seems to be, "Who can I blame? Who can I sue?" Whatever happened to "Goodness, I should have been looking where I was going, instead of playing with my mobile phone." It is rarely me to blame; it is usually someone else. The same happens if there is a motor accident, where people are actually told by their insurance companies (in Australia) never to admit liability. Why cannot we simply admit our mistakes? "Sorry, I was distracted. It is my fault. I will pay for any damages." We get the same in politics with each party blaming the other. I hate it. I reckon I would vote for the party that admitted the great ideas of the other parties, instead of each party saying "black" if the other said "white".

Many students defined independence as not needing to rely on anybody else—but no one is an island—and nor is any nation. We still need to rely upon others. We are co-dependent.

8.9: Intermediate Class

Some of my classes, as mentioned, were for non-university students from the surrounding community who wanted to improve their English, mainly for personal rather than professional reasons. I enjoyed these classes, as the students had chosen English for itself and not primarily because of some advantage to their careers. At least that was the case for the better students at the intermediate or advanced level, although far less so for the beginners, many of whom were overwhelmed by the enormity of the task.

Photo 71: intermediate class

I was in the habit of photographing the students in class groups in order to facilitate my learning of their names. It even worked. In the photograph above we have Amber, Remon, Jerry (at back), Lily, Hong, yours truly and April (at front).

In one of these classes in November 2011, a new student came into my class 8 weeks into the semester. I watched as she entered the back door and walked down to a seat, well dressed, reasonably tall (1.70 m, as I found out later), thin. She walked well. But the feature I noticed most was her hat: we were coming into winter, yet here she was wearing a broad rimmed summer hat, with the rim falling down over her right eye. I welcomed her, naturally, and asked her to tell us something about herself. It transpired that she was a model but at this time she was a full time student at SISU, yet still doing part time modelling on the weekends. She thought she would just drop in on my class to see what it was like. I took the opportunity to ask her why it was that when models are walking down the catwalk, they place their feet one behind the other, or even cross their right foot over the left and their left over the right while they are walking. She got up, hitched back her jumper and proceeded to sashay down the aisle. "It is to reveal the curves of the hips," she said, as she swung her hips from side to side. Now that is interesting, seeing that so many models are pencil thin: maybe they need to do this as they are not very curvaceous. What interesting classes we have! I was wondering if our model would grace us with her presence next week and if so what would she be wearing? Gosh I so looked forward to classes!

Later in the class, seeing that we had already had one exhibition, I asked another student to dance for us, because this is what she does, and I had told her that one day I would ask for her for a demonstration. She was great, moving so gracefully, with exquisite finger movements. I think she was doing the Peacock Dance, which I had seen on a previous occasion. It is a dance originating from the Dai (Thai) peoples in Yunnan. She told me that the Han people have no dance of their own, so use the dances of the minority groups; this was a surprise. The Indonesians also have a similar dance with subtle hand movements. I have seen them doing this even at Mass, as couples dance down the aisle for the offertory procession. Beautiful.

The following year the topic of fashion came up again. We commented upon each other's fashion sense and even did a couple of catwalks. Our fashion model student was used to this of course. Her clothes were very interesting indeed, with flat gold coloured shoes—she does not need to wear high heels—a gold coloured top, flecked with sparkles, matched by a similar coloured headband. It was the rest of her ensemble, however, which intrigued me, and upon which I made no comment. She was wearing a pair of short shorts, of jean material, thus displaying her long thin legs; she has a willowy physique. Those shorts could not have got any shorter. I do not think they quite matched the rest of her outfit.

Another lady was, in my humble opinion, better dressed. She had a red dress coming down to just below the knee. This was offset beautifully by her gold shoes, thin Cartier gold necklace, gold bracelet and gold wedding ring. She was quite wealthy, with her husband being a successful businessman. We discussed the differences between necessary clothing and accessories, between practicality and appearance.

As to male dress, we had here too some good examples, such as a designed buckle on one man's belt. As to headwear, one man mentioned the British bowler hat, while the American baseball hat came under scrutiny. It appears to have little practical value, and is for the most part for appearances only. It will not protect your head from the sun, nor from the rain. The peak is designed, so I understand, to keep overhead lights out of your eyes. The Australian tennis player, Lleytton Hewitt, used to wear his backwards, which had no practical use but was probably intended to convey a debonair attitude.

Wedding apparel also came in for discussion. In China the red *qipao* is traditional wear for the bride, although nowadays she is more likely to wear a Western style white dress, changing into the *qipao* for the reception. I have seen a bride wearing the white dress, with a pair of jeans underneath. Goodness. What did surprise me was the *hong bao,* or red envelope, which guests give to the couple at the beginning of the reception. One reason it came up, is that one of my students has Bao as his surname—same character. I asked him if Bao Xilai, the former leader in Chongqing, was his cousin. He told me that his name has a different character, meaning "thin". I am sure this is correct, although it also may be that every Bao in the city is trying to distance him/herself from the family of the former now disgraced leader.

Another student in this class told a story connected with her birthday. She went to a party, where she got more than a little drunk. Nevertheless, she decided to drive herself home—not a good idea. As luck would have it, she got pulled over by the police to be breathalysed. She did not want to be caught, as this means loss of licence, so she sped off. This did not go down too well with the local constabulary, who sped off in pursuit. They caught her at traffic lights, when she got hemmed in by other cars. She sat there, and I can imagine her terror as the police officer asked her to wind down her window. She shook her head. They shone a bright light on her with possibly a camera as well. Again they asked her to wind down her window; again a shake of the head. This girl is very pretty, small in stature, with big eyes and pointy chin—somewhat elfin. I can imagine her big staring eyes.

Then she started pleading. "Please let me go: today is my birthday!" The officer asked to see her driving licence, which she refused to hand over, saying that the police would keep it. The officer said he would hand it back. "Do you promise?"

"Yes, I promise." She wound her window down just a fraction, enough to extend her little finger. In China, linking little fingers is like making a promise formal. The officer extended his little finger and the deal was done.

She wound down her window and handed over her driving licence, while another officer breathalysed her, realising that she was way over the legal limit, which I think is 0.05, as it is in Australia. He was about to arrest her, when the first officer intervened. "No, I made her a promise." He obviously realised from reading her driving licence that it was indeed her birthday, and in fact he let her go with a warning, calling "Happy birthday" after her. Whew!

Isn't it good to find people with real heart? It was not necessary in this case to throw the book at this 23 year old young woman. She did something wrong— in fact two things: 1) driving while under the influence and 2) trying to escape. But the whole experience was so terrifying for her that she learnt her lesson. I am quite sure she will not drink and drive again. I wonder how much the officer was influenced by her obvious good looks. Mmm.

I had asked the students to give some news to the class and this is what she had prepared, while the others all talked about the earthquake we had experienced recently. I am glad they all had something, as I was suffering from laryngitis and just could not talk. How do you teach, especially when the subject is Oral English, when you cannot talk? I wrote everything on the blackboard (actually white board) while getting them to do all the talking. It was good for them.

Yet another student had a birthday—I mean we all do, approximately once a year—no big deal you say. This girl's story, however, is very sad. At the age of three, she was abandoned by her own mother. At the age of eight, she was again abandoned, this time by her father, after which she was brought up by her grandmother, but at the age of sixteen, her grandmother also abandoned her. How would you feel? What concept of self-worth would you have? One of our teachers organised a party for her and bought her a cake. Nobody had ever bought her a cake before. How sad; and how important it is to affirm each other—which birthdays can do.

At the beginning of one semester I had been forewarned about one student, who is actually a girl, but whom the staff thought to be a boy: she had short hair, dressed like a boy and sat with the boys. Indeed she looked like a boy. Thankfully

I did not make any faux pas. She was also the only student without an English name. She has one now. She told me that she likes music and sport, so I gave hand her the name "Melody". She likes it. Good. So do I.

It is not uncommon here in China, at least in my experience, to find girls who prefer to be boys. Part of the reason is social, because of the preference for boys, and this is not the only society where this is the case. Possibly too, at least in some instances, the girls have lesbian tendencies.

There is no morality, of course, in being male, female or anything in between. We are what we are, made by God, and what God makes is good—in fact, when it comes to humans, "very good". Nor do I see any problem in two people loving each other, even promising to do so "till death do us part", whether heterosexual or homosexual: where love is, there God is. "Marriage", however, is reserved for heterosexuals, for a man and a woman, who not only pledge exclusive love and fidelity, but it is from their loving relationship that new life comes. Homosexual couples cannot do this, and any attempt to do so becomes artificial and—or so it seems to me—to be more an exercise in selfishness (what I want), rather than genuine love (what is best for the child), who in any case, must of necessity, come from outside the homosexual relationship. The problem is one of nomenclature: we need another term for homosexual relationships.

We live in a society which is against discrimination in all its forms, and this is admirable. But finding another term for homosexual relationships is not discriminatory: it is simply a recognition of differences. I think we have been bending over backwards so much so as not to offend anyone, that we have been destroying the uniqueness of marriage.

8.10: Speech Contests

It seems that every educational institution in China has speech contests. In a previous book, "Teaching in Fuzhou", I described these in some detail, so that here I can be brief. At SISU there were not nearly as many as elsewhere, with just one contest being held at the end of the calendar year.

8.10.1: 2012 Speech Contest

There were not many contestants, just 24, but their standard was truly excellent. The topic was "Life as if it is a Gift". I do not know about the "as if" part, as in my book it certainly is a gift, and a most precious one at that. What are the chances of one particular man meeting and marrying one particular woman? Yet our parents did. What are the chances of an individual person being born from one set of parents? It is a staggering four billion to one; that is 4,000,000,000 : 1. We are precious and unique.

I was asked to kick off proceedings with a short speech. I asked that if life is a gift, then who is the giver?—our parents, obviously, but also God. I just left it at that, since I was on a stage in a non-Christian country to talk about giving speeches, not in a pulpit on a Sunday morning. I was interested, however, to notice that a few of the contestants did suggest that we thank "the God". They invariably use "the". I do not know why, although indeed there is only One.

Many of the speeches spoke of people who had come through great difficulties, but persevered, because life is so precious. One lady mentioned was a dance teacher in Sichuan Province. On 12th May, 2008 an earthquake struck causing enormous damage. The school in which she was teaching collapsed due, it appears, to corruption, resulting in shoddy building practices. Many children lost their lives; she lost both her legs. Undeterred she fought back and now still dances, but in her own unique way, using her arms and torso. On a related issue, the government allowed parents who lost their only child in the disaster to have another child. About 130 did so, while approximately another 70 did not, either because they could not afford a child, or because they were now too old to start again.

Another speaker told of a young boy, whose father had cut off his right hand. This is a horrible practice, the idea being to enhance the boy's begging appeal, so that the family gets more money. Sometimes the child is sold to a begging ring and sometimes both hands are cut off. This is evil.

The most powerful stories, to my mind, came from people who told of their own personal experiences, like the lady who spoke of her post-natal depression. She was dressed exquisitely in a purple *qipau*. It had been her own mother who woke her up. "When are you going to start being a mother?"

"But I am a mother!"

"Then act like one." It worked.

Dressing well creates a good impression, at least as far as I am concerned, a remark which I am sure will cause many a raised eyebrow amongst those who know about my own proclivity to dress somewhat casually. Nevertheless, I think we tend to make the judgement that a well-dressed person knows what he/she is about. The better speakers also dressed well. At the other end of the scale was one of my own students, a boy, who dressed very sloppily indeed. His speech was of the same ilk. Consequently he got the lowest mark, 84.5% I actually gave him 82%. But I was only one of six judges. I might point out the marking system is quite unlike anything you would find in the West. Before anyone even opens his/her mouth he is assure of 80%, as we agreed beforehand that this would be the lowest mark, the highest being 100%, which nobody achieved, some coming reasonably close.

The speeches were interspersed with musical items, just to make sure we had all round entertainment, and perhaps also to allow the judges a break from concentration. I was reminded of a set of stairs in Chongqing, which provide an added note or two to the usually mundane activity of climbing up and down stairs. The steps here are painted to resemble the notes on a piano, and as you step on them, they do indeed play notes: wonderful and most entertaining, as you jump up and down, trying to elicit a tune.

Photo 72: musical stairs

A score of people recited a (Henry Wadsworth) Longfellow poem; they were dressed identically with specially made T-shirts with "Life is a Gift" on the front. Parts of the poem were divided up amongst the group, with sometimes just one, sometimes a few, and sometimes everybody speaking, all the time accompanied by a girl playing the violin. It was very effective. One can but admire the trouble and preparation they had gone to.

One woman sang "My heart will go on" from Titanic. It really is a favourite in this country; I have heard it many times. It is just as well this was not a singing contest, as this brave lady would not have fared very well at all. But she tried.

The third item was very good indeed. One man sang and whistled "Falling Rain", while two couples danced. The men were dressed in evening wear, with top hats and clear umbrellas, while the ladies wore floral dresses with cream-coloured blouses. The dancing was quite stylised and not very graceful, but nevertheless very enjoyable. At the end the singer stole one of the men's hats. He reacted by stealing the other man's hat.. It was a nice touch.

Before the prize giving, David spoke well about how difficult it is to give a speech in one's own language, never mind in a second language, but how very well the contestants did it; they were indeed of a high standard. Among the 24 contestants 20 prizes were given—truly. First prize went to a girl who was excellent. She also happens to be from the Lancaster Programme, where I was teaching, so it must be obvious why she did so well! She scored 94%. While in my opinion, there were others who had better content, she was clearly the best in delivery and general English.

8.10.1: 2013 Speech Contest

In 2103 the title was "As you dream, so you shall become". There was on the screen at the start a quotation from one Langton Hughes: "Hold fast to dreams, for if dreams die, life is a broken-winged bird that cannot fly." It is quite a good image.

There were around 25 contestants and they were excellent. I was one of seven judges, and I think we agreed pretty well on our grading of marks. The system, however, may seem rather strange. When I was at university—admittedly a long time ago now—the grading system went as follows: 50% pass, 65% credit, 75% distinction and 85% high distinction. Might I add that I did in fact distinguish myself, by going through the whole course without a single high distinction? In this particular contest, however, if a speaker so much as made it onto the podium, he or she would automatically get 85%. I kid you not. 85% was the lowest mark, while the highest was supposed to be 95%. That is such a narrow range. We were, however, told that we could give fractions. Great, so competitor C on

88.378259 just shades competitor H, who only got 88.378258! No, we did not go to those lengths; in fact, I gave no fractions.

Denise and Cyril were our gracious hosts. One of the features of these contests, which Cyril pointed out so well, is that speeches are a little like icebergs, in that you do not see the enormous work of preparation which goes into them. This is so not just for the competitors, but also for the presenters, and for those who organise the computer graphics, the prizes and the entertainers.

Yes: the entertainers, since in these contests there are breaks about every five contestants, during which the marks are added up from all the judges and averaged out. At these times we have singers, dancers or whatever. There were seven such acts, beginning with one of my students who is a saxophonist, and a very good one too. He was studying to improve his English before furthering his career in the US. In one dance, performed by women, there was a young girl: very cute; I think she was the daughter of one of the dancers. We had a very good singer too. I never seemed to be amazed at people's talents, maybe because I am not overly blessed in this department.

The speeches too were of very high standard indeed. Quite a few were students of mine, but I hasten to add that that is not why their standards were so high. It is customary that multiple prizes are given, for much the same reason as the high marks, namely, not to discourage people, or indeed not to cause loss of face. It is one of the more endearing traits in this society. So instead of having one winner, there were two, with several second place getters and ditto for third. In my opinion the two winners were clearly better than the others. They gave their speeches without a single hesitation, in fact much more fluently than many native speakers. Their content was also excellent. One of the winners was a student in my class called Lucy—cf. photograph 73.

So sincere congratulations to all who participated: superb performance.

Incidentally, we got extra pay for being judges, although there had been a little problem here. The university had undertaken a massive expansion programme, which is fine if you have the money for it, which apparently, they did not have. Consequently they had been trying to save money left, right and centre. Some staff officers, for example, have had their heating cut off, but not the classrooms, so at least the students could keep warm, and that is good. For some months prior to this our pay was withheld. One consequence was that they needed more enrolments, so we are asked to be especially nice to them, and of course, nobody fails. Being nice to students?—goodness, now that is a challenge!

Photo 73: Lucy giving her speech

Chapter 9: Students' Work

Introduction

As a teacher, it is always interesting to see students' work, in whatever field. I said "interesting". This covers a gamut of reactions: one may be delighted, pleased, puzzled or totally disheartened. "Yikes! Look at all the mistakes!"

In teaching Science I was particularly delighted by the standard of students' work. For example, year 9 students were able to plot accurately the orbits of the four Galilean moons—Io, Europa, Ganymede and Calisto—around Jupiter. Year 11 students could thoroughly analyse a water system, a seaside rock platform or a river.

In teaching English, there are four areas to look at: listening, speaking, reading and writing. The major one I wish to present here is writing, after a brief look at the other three.

9.1: Listening, Speaking, Reading

9.1.1: Listening

The major problem here is for the student to listen at the speed of the speaker. Can they repeat what they have heard, and have they understood? In class one uses what are called concept checking questions to find out what they have understood.

9.1.2: Speaking

The key here is vocabulary, as it is in the learning of any language. This must continually be increased together with understanding the words one uses. To this end, reading is essential, as is listening to other speakers. Then it is a question of practice, practice, practice. If you do not speak a language then you forget it.

The next step is fluency, i.e. being able to speak without hesitancy or repetition. Now we come to a personal bugbear of mine: fill-in words. I would encourage my students not to use them. Young Australians in particular are very bad at this, even though they are speaking their native language. Currently the most popular fill-in word—and undoubtedly the most commonly used word in all speech for many young Australians—is "like". I know not why. You only have to travel on a bus in Sydney to hear this word used ad nauseam. "I went **like** to the library today, and **like** spoke to Jill and **like** she told me **like** that Bill had a **like** new girlfriend **like** …" For me this is totally unnecessary.

Intonation is important in speaking, especially in English which is an intonation language. Chinese, by contrast, is an extonation language. The tones are set and you cannot change them without changing the word. In English, the whole meaning of a sentence can change depending upon the stress. "This **is** a blue book"—as opposed to "It is not."

"This is a **blue** book"—as opposed to it being some other colour.

Connected with this is inflection. Generally our voice goes up at commas, colons and question marks, but down at semi colons and full stops. Again—for some reason I cannot comprehend—some Australians, especially women only use upward inflection. "On Sunday we went to the beach. (voice up). We had a barbecue. (voice up). The kids had a wonderful time (voice up)." And so it goes on. Weird—at least to my ears.

9.1.3: Reading

Here again, has the student understood what he has read?—or more likely "she" since most of my students were young women. Again, concept checking questions comes to the fore. I would tell my students to read meaning, not words. Read to understand. The six questions help here: Why? Where? What? Who? When? How? I would encourage them in all their studies—not just English—to be constantly asking these questions, noting down their conclusions as they read. It helps to read intelligently, with understanding and not just soak up words like a sponge.

Reading also involves pausing at the correct places, correct intonation and of course, correct pronunciation. For the last mentioned, Chinese have difficulties with certain sounds, such as "r", "f" or "v", "e" (as in "egg") and the two "th" sounds.

9.2: Writing

I really enjoyed teaching writing.

Naturally one had to cover the basics of how the English language works. I would begin with the verb "to be" as the centre; other verbs are ways of being. Second come nouns—which are the centre of Chinese. Third are adjectives and adverbs. Fourth we would deal with other parts of speech, such as pronouns, prepositions and gerunds. Step five would be to build these into a sentence. Step six adds adjectival and adverbial phrases. Step seven adds adjectival and adverbial clauses. We would look at how these work in set writing pieces, before giving the students exercises.

Some of the writing they produced was great, on a variety of topics but especially on those which most touched their lives. These topics I would set deliberately. Not only was this a great medium for improving their English, but was also a great way to understand them a little better. In addition it was most helpful for themselves. Let us look at some examples.

Example 1: Marriage

It should come as no surprise that young adults in their early twenties should have marriage on their radar. Hence it became a favourite topic of mine within a number of contexts, including a writing assignment. But people have this wonderful ability to surprise, as I found that some of them had not even considered marriage. I supposed they were too focused on their immediate future at university, and of their life in England the following semester (in autumn 2012), assuming they passed their course. Their answers, nevertheless, are interesting.

The topic was definitely "marriage", yet some of the boys talked about what they would expect of their wives, while some of the girls talked about what they would expect from their husbands. Hey, what about your own contribution to the relationship? Some of the expectations the boys had of their future wives included "filial piety", being virtuous, cute (!) and looking after the house. "The house is the basis of marriage." I wonder if housewives would agree. Some of the expectations the girls had of their future husbands included considerateness, loyalty, being more than 180 cm tall, even being able to play a musical instrument, being a basketball player and being neither handsome nor ugly. I gather the point in having a tall husband is that it gives the woman a greater sense of security. Is that why I never married? This list is actually interesting, as I was expecting other requirements, namely having an apartment, a stable job, and loving the wife's parents. Other qualities mentioned included honesty, truthfulness, forgiveness, tolerance, respect and responsibility.

As regards the marriage, some good points were mentioned, such as the necessity for the couple to be intimate friends, with common interests and the ability to work through problems together. One wanted them to work in the same business, although I personally think that that is not always a good idea. One boy wanted no children, but to spend his leisure time travelling with his wife. I wonder what she would think of that. As regards children, most seemed to want two: a boy and a girl naturally. That has become more possible of late since the One Child Policy operating at this time has now become the Two Child Policy. One girl even went into some detail on how she would raise her children: she would give her son a lot of freedom, but not her daughter, whom she would school very strictly inside the house, while her brother played outside. And this is the girl writing, not the boy. Wow, what does this say about the way girls and boys are considered in this society?

Perhaps not surprisingly, talk of marriage also included the day of the wedding, at least the girls wrote about this, but not the boys. Naturally, they wanted a beautiful white wedding dress. One desire which I had not considered was a seaside wedding: on the beach for one girl, in a church for another. She said the seaside is romantic. Well, I suppose it may be if you have someone to love, but I fail to see how any place can be romantic in itself: I think it depends on whom you are with. I suspect the choice of a church had everything to do with romance and not with religion. Is your church romantic? Upon reflection, I can see (!) why the sea might be considered romantic, as it is such a long way from Chongqing to the sea—close to 2,000 km. There is actually a place in Xin Jiang Province, up in the North West, which is the furthest place from an ocean anywhere on earth. Maybe I might go there one day. No, I probably will not pack my swimmers. One of my students came from there and did in fact invite me to her home, but it never materialised. I just never got around to it.

Still on the topic of the wedding, one girl was adamant that she wanted no MC at the reception. Maybe she has had unfortunate experiences, but her reasoning is that being hired, they are just doing a job, with no concern for who the couple are. They go through their routines with no personal touch, doing the same thing for every wedding. What a pity. Maybe the best MCs are relatives.

So there you have it. One curious lacuna is that nobody ever mentioned the word "love". I would have thought this to be primary, with marriage being the state in which the couple sought the happiness of the other above their own. Happiness was mentioned, with one girl stating that marriage is the source of happiness, where you go to bed happy and wake up happy, but there was no mention of how you achieve that state of bliss.

Example 2: Success

Everybody wants to succeed, but—as I asked my students—what does that mean? Their answers are interesting. Some really thought about the question, while others did not. Some just gave examples of success, while others talked about how to achieve it. Nobody really made the distinction between being a success as a person and being successful in a role. For example, many talked about being a successful businessman, making lots of money and living in a big house. Fine, but what kind of person is he or she? One person stressed achieving what you set out to do. You are a success if you live your life the way you want to. Does this make you a success? Let us look at this.

Just before this, in March 2012, a man called Mohammed went on a rampage in Toulouse, France, killing a number of people, eventually being killed himself by the police. Is he a success? Well, he achieved exactly what he set out to do. His brother, another Muslim Jihadist, sees him as a hero. I doubt very much if the families of his victims share that view. Is he a success as a person? I do not think you must kill innocent people to become a success as a person. Somehow I think he missed the bus, his attitude patently wrong, irrespective of how sincere he may have been. The question of how others see you was mentioned, together with how you see yourself. Personally I think that how God sees one is of most importance.

The students gave examples of successful actions. One girl remembered learning how to ride a bike when she was a small child. One boy had been captain of his basketball team, taking them through to the semi-finals of a city-wide competition. Another was a good soccer player, kicking the winning goal in a key match. One girl in elementary school had been asked to be MC at the annual school New Year party. She put a lot of thought and effort into it over some weeks, with the result that it was a resounding success. She felt really good about it afterwards, and indeed still does. Many talked about the seeming successes in society, such as getting good grades if you are a student, getting a good job, earning lots of money, having a perfect family, being a movie star, or becoming a great tennis player and so having a high status. For these particular students being successful at this point in their lives meant being accepted into Lancaster University in England.

One girl dug a little deeper to write about her grandmother. I often wondered, as I saw old men and women shuffling along the streets, what their lives had been like. What a time for them to be growing up in China! I would love to get their stories. Well, now I have one. This lady is truly someone special. She was intellectually gifted, actually attending university in the 1950's. Not many women did that. This was at the time when the "Great Proletarian Cultural Revolution swept the whole land," she wrote. She graduated as a steel engineer. Now that is a surprising occupation for a woman, you may think, but remember that this was the time when Mao was trying to make China become the No. 1 steel maker in the world. Households were encouraged to build blast furnaces in their backyard. Not only was iron ore used, but existing iron implements were melted down in order to inflate production figures, thus depriving poor people of much needed tools, such as ploughs and cooking pots. What a terrible time to be living. She married and had three children. One of her daughters suffered from epilepsy, but she was unable to have her cared for properly. After a short sad life, her daughter died. I bet she still feels the pain. Where this woman really shines is in her obvious love for her grandchildren, the one who was my student in particular, sharing so much of her wisdom with her.

Many wrote about how to achieve success, stressing hard work, perseverance and trying one's best. I would have liked to have seen this expanded upon. Are you a failure if you do not achieve your goals, but do your best? Maybe one's goals are too high. If I play tennis with Roger Federer and lose, have I failed? Goodness, success might mean winning a single point, although it would probably come from a double fault—not that Roger was doing this very often! But if I enjoy myself, and do my best, then that is good enough. Whether Roger enjoys the match is another matter.

One girl wrote really well. Actually that is not true, as her writing was terrible, but her content was excellent. She was lamenting the way society was heading with money taking over as the No. 1 priority. More and more young people are choosing for their majors subjects related to the economy, such as business management and accountancy. Economic success is stressed to the detriment of other values. Overtime is becoming more common at the expense of time spent with one's family. Power is sought after, rather than interpersonal relations, especially with one's family and friends. I agree with her. When you listen to the news, these days, you get the impression that nothing exists outside the economy. Even sport has now become big business. In rugby league, I am a proud South Sydney supporter. About ten years ago, the league moved to push the club out, all in the name of money, but Souths fought on. Even if they are not much of a success on the field, they are a shining example of local support, of community values. Money is not everything and nor is winning—just as long as the Australian cricket team beats the Poms!

Example 3: Grandparents

Grandparents are important in any society, but probably more so in China than in the West. For us, the base unit of society is the individual. Parents have a child for the sake of the child, and in fact it is often the case that as soon as the child has become an adult, he/she is expected to leave the family home and fend for him/herself. A 30 year old man still living with his parents is somewhat frowned upon. In China, by contrast, the base unit of society is the family. Parents have children so that 1) someone will be able to look after them in their old age, and 2) the family name will be carried on—even if 100 million people are called Chang, or Wang or Chen. For both of these reasons, boys are preferred to girls. The latter are raised by the parents for the sake of their future husband. Thus the girl will leave, whereas the boy will remain. Bride price comes into play here as well.

The next point to note is our definition of family. In the West we usually mean the nuclear family: Mum, Dad and kids. But in China grandparents are included in their understanding of what family means. So many times students have said: "There are five people in our family: my father, my mother, my brother, myself and my grandmother"—or something similar. Uncles, aunts and cousins are not far away either. It is unusual in the West to find elderly people living with their families: we shunt them off into nursing homes. That is rarely the case here, although that is changing.

There is another phenomenon which has emerged of more recent days, where we find both parents working. Here grandparents take the lion's share in the role of raising the child. For these reasons it is understandable that a deep bond grows between grandparents and grandchildren. This is immensely valuable, especially as it enables the wisdom of the old to be passed on to the young.

Photo 74: big loads

As I walked around the streets and saw the faces of the old, I often wondered what their lives had been like, what hardships they had endured, often indelibly printed upon their faces. Even today one can see how hard people work, especially on the land. One has only to see the enormous loads people tote around—as in photograph 74.

The grandparents of most of my students were born between 1935 and 1945. This was a time both of civil war and of war with Japan. After the defeat of Japan, the civil war broke out fiercely, ending in victory for the CP in 1949. The years following can only be described as horrific. Mao's land reforms, together with a long drought, resulted in the deaths of some 20 million people. His attempt to become the No. 1 steel maker in the world, with his backyard furnaces, was a fiasco. This was followed by the 100 Flowers campaign, which resulted in the deaths of about 40,000 intellectuals. At the same time, Mao urged the North Koreans to invade the south, so that America might be drawn in. Then he could say to the USSR: "Help! America is going to invade us. We need the atom bomb!" It worked. As if all this is not bad enough, from 1966 to 1976 the Great Cultural Revolution took place, a time of intense suffering for so many people. It was not until Mao died that the country could breathe again and begin to make progress, and as we know, that progress has been absolutely astonishing.

With all this in mind, I asked my students as an assignment to interview their grandparents over Qing Ming Festival. The results were most interesting. As expected, many of the grandfathers had spent time in one or other of the armies, either the CP or the KMT. In one family one grandfather was in the Red Army, while the other fought for the Kuomintang. Thankfully, they did not have to fight each other. One man had been a food purchasing agent and chef for the army. Another was a CP officer, sent to Chongqing as a spy. Remember that this city was the headquarters of the KMT and the nation's capital during the World War. Another, as a CP cadre, was sent as a representative to other countries.

Many of the families, especially those of the grandmothers, had been farmers, and they too went through very difficult times. After Mao collectivised the farms, the farmers were organised into "production teams" and all the food they produced had to be handed in to the "village communes", in exchange for which they were issued with food vouchers. Up until fairly recently, some farmers were still living in a cashless society. Education was at a premium, with preference, of course, given to boys, so that many of these women attended primary school only, with some being still illiterate. One woman, being the eldest of five sisters, never went to school at all. Another woman, as mentioned, did in fact go to university in the 1950's, when few women had the opportunity, and she later made significant contributions in the field of engineering. She was exceptional. Another woman became a teacher and then a headmistress. I found her philosophy of life poignant: "Don't make any trouble." No doubt this helped her survive the rough times.

One man, a farmer, made a journey to Hong Kong at the age of 19, with just a basket on his back, to visit his aunt; that would have been quite a journey. Later his ancestral farm was expropriated by the government, the land being used as a site for a factory. There is not much one can do about this. He plays the flute and erhu, so maybe this helped him to accept his fate with some equanimity. Another man used to write articles against the government, a very risky business indeed, as one could be punished severely if caught. He was punished—often. He is a brave man. Another man went to university and did well in Chemistry, setting up his own chemical factory.

The poverty of their lives is what also comes through to me. They worked hard for little reward. One set of grandparents had never been on a plane, which is still common, but had also not even travelled by train. Some of their marriages were arranged, which does not appear to have detracted from their happiness. In

Western societies, we are so concerned with "falling in love" that we can forget that love is a choice, which you live out by hard work. I wonder how many of these arranged marriages ended in divorce; probably very few. One student, however, did report that her grandparents fought often and vigorously for over 20 years, with the neighbours sometimes intervening to lend advice! But they still loved each other.

This assignment was set so that I could learn something and I was conscious of the fact that these old people would not be around for much longer, and in fact many had already died. I wanted this present generation to get their stories before it was too late. They lived through what was an extraordinary time in history, not only for China, but for everyone.

Example 4: Friendship

Everybody needs a friend. This is especially so for the younger generation in China, for the simple reason that they have fewer siblings to rely upon. In the countryside you still find multiple siblings, but in the cities the One Child Policy has resulted in just that: many young people having no brothers or sisters. This policy was only intended for one generation, beginning in 1979, and has now become the Two Child Policy—much better.

Quite a few of my students would be heading overseas to study, and in 2012 about 25 first year students headed off to Lancaster University in England. Most of these came from Chongqing itself so have no siblings. Of course another result of the One Child Policy is that people have more money—children are expensive—so can afford the best education. I think some of my students did come from quite wealthy families, unlike those in Tongren, where I last taught. To give an example, two students, who had failed their IELTS exams, flew to Hainan to redo it. But SISU is an exam centre! Her family could afford the extra expense.

Students who have gone abroad are a long way from the support of their families, so it stands to reason that friends become even more important to them. With this in mind, I asked them to write an essay on friendship. Not only did this help their English but it also helped their personal growth—and helped me too to understand them better. Most left it vague, telling us how lovely friendship is, with some of them—predictably—copying from the web. But some wrote of their own experiences and these are always the best. Here are some samples.

One boy told how he was sick in hospital, when his friends not only visited him, but stayed with him for a whole day and a night. "I was sick and you visited me." At other times, when in trouble, his friends have taken him out for a drink and just been with him. This is really appreciated.

Bullying is probably an issue in schools all around the world. One girl related what it was like, until one other girl stood up for her. I showed the students a video of a young Australian man who was born without arms or legs. He tells his own story of not being accepted in kindergarten. At the end of one particularly bad day he had had enough. "If just one more person puts me down, I'm never coming back," he relates. At the end of the day one girl called out to him. "Here it is, the last straw."

"Hey Nick."

"Yes."

"You look really great today." Wow, how that one comment uplifted him. It does not take much to encourage someone.

One boy told of what happened to him when 5 years old. He came to school without his lunch. At lunch time he sat there, alone and hungry while his schoolmates ate. His teacher despised weakness, so did not help him. His best friend ate his own lunch, but did not share it. Imagine how the poor little tyke felt. Finally two boys he did not know gave him a bowl of noodles. I bet it was especially delicious. Those boys became his best friends for some years, till they went their separate ways. Reflecting on this, the writer made a profound comment: "Maybe friends cannot be with you all your life, but their friendship can." I think he is right. When I was in primary school, I had two best friends: Brian Dawson and Keith Hartwig. After primary we separated and I have not seen them since. Yet to me their friendship endures. I would love to meet them again, even though we have not seen each other in more than 60 years.

One girl wrote of her having an argument with her parents and subsequently running away from home. At 1.00 a.m. she phoned her friend, who may not have taken too kindly to being disturbed at such an hour, but it was not a problem, and she immediately came to be with her friend. That is true friendship. Another girl was out shopping when it started to rain, and she had neglected to bring her umbrella. Her phone rang. It was her friend. "Where are you? Stay where you are and I will bring you an umbrella." That's what true friends are for.

Of course in English we have that well known saying: "A friend in need is a friend indeed." In Chinese there is another saying: "Wealth is not a true friend, but a true friend is a treasure."

Most of the students did not give personal stories but gave qualities they were looking for in a friend, such as honesty and belief in each other. Friendship develops kindness and tolerance and takes away loneliness. A friend is someone with whom I can share my feelings and interests. One student put it brilliantly: friendship takes you out of your own little world into the world of another. Friends influence each other, and hence it is vitally important to choose your friends well. These young people subsequently travelled overseas to study, and would, undoubtedly, have made new friends. I hope they chose them wisely.

Sadly, most of the assignments told of how other people had helped them, or what they were looking for in a friend. Very few looked at the other side of the coin, at what they have to do for their friends. The Chinese are beautiful people, but can be so self-centred. In a similar vein, China as a nation is arguably the most self-centred nation on the planet, with Chinese Nationalism one of the great evils facing the world today.

So how do you make a friend?—by being a friend.

On one occasion in my life, I was going through a very difficult time. I went to a good friend, who sat with me for two hours. Oh how precious were those two hours. It was not anything she said that was important, but the being there. Gail, unfortunately, has since died, but I treasure her memory, and the time I had with her not long before she passed away. I do hope I was able to be of some assistance to her.

I would like everyone to have true friends and be a true friend. Thank you to all my friends.

Example 5: Rainbows

The Chinese language can be very flowery, full of picturesque imagery, where we would tend to be more forthright. One sees this on public signs, where, for example, "respect the life underfoot" is the equivalent of our more prosaic expression, "keep off the grass". Similar language can be found in students' writings, as reflected in one assignment I gave them on the topic of rainbows.

How, I wondered, would they approach this topic? Probably most people would concentrate on the physical properties of a rainbow. Certainly I would, especially looking at it from a scientific standpoint, although I would throw in a story as well. Only one student, predictably a boy, took this approach, saying that a rainbow results from reflected light, which is quite true, of course, but he neglected to point out that there are also two refractions, one as light enters a drop of water, the other as it exits, the reflection coming from the inside surface of each drop. The sun is always directly behind you.

That is not, however, the approach taken by most students. They talked about the troubles of life, symbolised by rain and storms, after which the rainbow appears in the sunshine, giving hope of a bright future. It is surprising how many said that a rainbow always appears after rain. No it doesn't. There are no rainbows at night. As well, you may get a rainbow before the rain. You can also get a rainbow from a waterfall.

I conducted a funeral some years ago of a beautiful young lady whom I had known for quite a while, as she had been a long term patient at the Prince of Wales Hospital, where I had worked. For some years, the country had been in the grip of a severe drought. At the cemetery, in the late afternoon, we were bathed in bright sunshine, but a thunderstorm was rolling in from the east. With the sun behind us one could see a brilliant rainbow ahead of the advancing black cloud. In this case, the rainbow came before the rain and the dark clouds were not representing troubles, but rather some relief from drought.

There is one other factor from what the students wrote that struck me. A number of them had never seen a rainbow in Chongqing, while some locals had only seen a rainbow elsewhere. I too never saw a rainbow in this city. They decried the high levels of pollution. What a pity.

Here are some examples of what they wrote, with their English corrected:
Sample 1:

The rainbow is a gift from the sun which gives us a sense of happiness and warmth. Life is like a rainbow which contains all kinds of colours: blue is for sorrow, green is for endless hope, while red is for passion. ... Keep an optimistic attitude, then all things can be joyful, and you will see your own rainbow at last. Betty.
Sample 2:

People always like beautiful things, like pretty girls, pretty clothes, some shining jewellery—and the rainbow is the most beautiful thing in the world. It is colourful and mysterious. When I see a rainbow, I feel warm and happy. Christine.
Sample 3:

The thunderstorm is coming; he feels his life is filled with darkness and fear. The sunshine will come. If you want to appreciate the beauty of the next morning, you must get through the night and overcome the difficulties. So hang on: maybe the next rainbow is just around the corner. Laura.

Sample 4:

In my country, we believe that if someone sees a rainbow, something good will happen to them. I haven't seen a rainbow yet. I imagine that after the rainbow, the skies are blue and dreams will come true. Lois.

Sample 5:

When I was a child, I did not know what a rainbow is. I had only seen it from pictures. I knew the rainbow is very beautiful and appears after rain, but I had never seen it in real life. One day, our whole family went to climb a mountain. We passed a brook. Sunshine shot into the brook. I saw there were a lot of colours under the brook—red, orange, yellow, green and blue. It looked so fantastic. It made me so excited, because it was my first time to see a rainbow. Bob.

Sample 6:

One day, the sunshine was very comfortable. Suddenly, clouds came and there came heavy rain. Thomas told his mother: "Mum, what a bad day! The rain makes me unhappy. I cannot go out to play." His Mum said: "My dear, it may not be a bad thing." The rain did not last a long time. After the rain there appeared a beautiful rainbow. When Thomas saw the rainbow he laughed and jumped. "Mum, how beautiful it is. I have never seen such a rainbow like this. His mother smiled. "Darling, as I said, heavy rain may not be bad because of a rainbow. When you meet trouble, you should consider it as heavy rain. You will see a rainbow after it." Chris.

Sample 7:

A rainbow is a reward: God makes it for those people who are brave and never give up. A rainbow is a reward: angels live there; it is beautiful and amazing. A rainbow is a reward: for those who withstand a thunderstorm. A rainbow is a reward: God says that real beauty is for the really brave. A rainbow is a reward: lots of people spend half of their lives yet fail to see it. Cassiopeia.

You may see from this last entry that this student has a certain flair for writing; she was by far my best student. It is highly unlikely that in her future she will produce seven sons and seven daughters (as Cassiopeia, the queen of Egypt, did in the ancient Greek legend), but she may very well produce much excellent writing. I hope so.

Within our Judeo-Christian tradition, the rainbow appeared after the flood as a sign of a new covenant between God and the human race. It links Heaven and Earth, God and us.

May the troubles in our lives be short-lived and may we too be rewarded with beautiful rainbows.

Example 6: A Touching Moment

Another assignment I gave my writing class was to write an essay on the topic "A Touching Moment". This is their work, although I have taken the liberty of correcting their writing mistakes. Prepare to be impressed.

Owen's story:

"It was a long time ago, when I was only 8 years old.

One day, I found a woman giving dogs to any passers-by who was interested. She told me that her dog gave birth to too many puppies so she had to find people to adopt them. I took away a lovely white dog, because I had been wanting a dog for a long time. I called her "Kimmy".

I played with my dog every day. I taught her many skills. For instance, if I said, "Stretch out your paw," she would (do this) immediately. The best skill she learnt was sitting. If I said, "Sit," she would not move anywhere.

However, she grew fat … bit people, and created many other problems. Worst of all my parents told me: "You must get rid of that trouble maker." I had to do what they ordered. I took Kimmy out, looking for an opportunity to abandon her. I guess she knew my intentions, as she stuck very closely to me. I found it to be really difficult, so I told her "Sit!" She sat still at once, as I started to move away. She continued to sit, but stared at me with her innocent eyes. I felt bad, and ran away fast.

I kept telling myself, "Kimmy will be OK; some good people will keep her. My worry never went away. A week later, I could bear it no longer, and decided to return to the place where I had left her. I felt anxious and called her name. I found my dog moribund; she raised her head, looked at me happily and wagged her tail. Soon her head dropped down, never to move again. A passer-by told me she had neither moved nor eaten, even if people offered her food. I cried.

I knew that the reason Kimmy never moved was my order. I felt touched by her loyalty, but also incredibly guilty, because I had used her loyalty to abandon her to die. I am so sorry."

Carrie's story:

"This is a story about dogs, taken from a movie called "Eight Below", which I saw some years ago. It is set in either Alaska or Northern Canada. A geologist was working in difficult terrain when his partner was injured, needing to be airlifted out to receive medical help. Unfortunately their light plane could not take the dogs, which were left behind. It was 180 days before Jerry was able to return, expecting to find all his dogs dead: they had been chained up. However, they had broken free so they could fend for themselves. "They all believed that their master would return and bring them home. A touching moment which made me cry was the reunion… Dogs regard their masters as their friends and family. Never underestimate their will to survive, especially when surrounded by family."

I have seen this movie myself, and it is indeed very touching. It is set, however, in Antarctica, with the scientists coming from America.

Felicia's story:

"I remember Children's Day (1st June) when I was only 12 years old. My parents took me to visit a local zoo. On the way, I saw a crowd of people watching something: two monkeys putting on an act. It seemed the monkeys were mother and son. I love animals very much, and when I saw them I was very excited. The two monkeys were so serious in their expressions, and the audience applauded them.

Suddenly the young monkey made a mistake. The master was angry and cracked his whip. The monkey was too afraid to jump; I could feel his pain. It was heart wrenching. The master cracked his whip again and again.

Unexpectedly, the mother took her son in her arms and used her body to protect him. She stared at the master. I was moved by that love between mother and son, when she was willing to take his place to receive punishment. In my opinion, mother's love is limitless. It exists not only in us human beings, but in animals too. We should not treat them cruelly. As creatures on this earth, we all have the right to be happy."

Comment: Felicia is right, in that treatment of animals in China can be very cruel. I have seen a woman throw stones at a St Bernard dog. I have seen a wolf cowering from its trainer, wielding a rod which this poor animal must have felt many a time. In Chongqing Zoo we even had a kangaroo injured and another killed by people throwing stones. It is not good: animals are to be respected and treated kindly.

Heather's story:

"I think that touching moments in life are not necessarily great: small things can also warm the heart. On a rainy day, a stranger gives you an umbrella. When you are feeling lonely, your best friend gives you a call. A recent incident certainly touched me.

I was at home on my own, so I cooked a simple rice with egg meal. My father came home, did not say anything, but went into the kitchen. He called me to sit at the table where he told me to eat more. 'Rice on its own is not nutritious; you need to eat vegetables.' He returned to the kitchen. Watching his back, my heart felt warm. After a few minutes, my father put another dish in front of me: fish. I got up and went into the bathroom, because I had tears in my eyes.

I have never heard my parents tell me that they love me, but I know they do, because their love is in their actions."

Comment: This is so with many Chinese families; they are not as verbally expressive as Western families tend to be. Parents would not actually tell their children that they love them.

Zoe's story:

This is another family story, which I will paraphrase, occurring during Spring Festival in 2007, when Zoe was still a child. Her grandfather had asked her to go to his house, some distance away. She refused, because she did not want to leave her own family to sit in an empty house. I am presuming that her grandmother had already died. At this her grandfather was very sad, so set off on his own, without telling his son. He had not gone far when he was robbed. Zoe remarked that both her father and grandfather are stubborn, illustrated by their differing philosophies as regards Zoe's education.

When he found that his father had gone, Zoe's father set off in pursuit, finding him some 15 km down the road. Zoe says she was expecting an argument, but this did not happen. She concludes: "Self-esteem is ridiculous when you are facing family member. Love is everything."

Comment: For me, just reading what the students were revealing about themselves is itself touching. Thank you.

Example 7: A Sunrise

Once again here are the emended versions of what students had written, after corrections, together with some paraphrasing.

Evan's story:

"It happens every day, but not every day do I appreciate it." The first time he was at Erlang Mountain on the Tibetan plateau with his parents. "There was a huge red fireball rising from a brimless mountain range." The second time was at Jiuzhaigou in Sichuan Province, the third at Sanya in Hainan and the fourth on a train to Tibet, and each time he was with his parents. "For me, a sunrise is not just a natural phenomenon: it stands for precious family affection, the love of father and mother. My growing up is always a sunrise in their hearts."

Damer's story:

Damer felt sad and disillusioned because of his low *gaokao* score. This is the big—nay, very big—exam held at the end of secondary school. It is intensely competitive, especially at this time when many parents had only the one child. Results determine the future, not just in terms of whether one can enter college or university, but also as to which university, as they have a pecking order. Only the very brightest students would go to a top university, such as Beijing, Tsinghua or Fudan.

Early one morning, his mother roused him from sleep and together they climbed a mountain. "I saw the sun rise slowly and I found everything coloured with its splendour. It seemed that all things had been reborn. The sun gave me hope and courage and helped me realise that I cannot be defeated by difficulties."

Comment: Many derogatory remarks have been made about this current generation of young people in China, the so called "*Xiao Huandi*" or "Little Emperors", and yes, it is true up to a point. They have been spoilt, and do think that the world revolves around them, particularly the boys. Those who come from wealthy families have everything handed to them on a plate. But many do not; it is still a highly competitive society, especially due to the massive population, and many of these young people know how to work hard—very hard.

Cindy's story:

Cindy, with a group of friends, climbed Emei Mountain, a famous mountain in China, situated in nearby Sichuan Province, some 130 km south west of

Chengdu. Her group made it to the top by 6.00 p.m., whereupon they proceeded to pitch a tent, which Cindy maintains is the hardest thing she had ever done. Goodness. After their evening meal, the group of friends proceeded to talk, sing songs and generally enjoy each other's company. Presumably they got some sleep, but they were up before the sun. "The sky began to lighten; a golden light moved slowly from the clouds. I was awed by the scene."

Heather's story

Heather is a Chongqing native and in this foggy, polluted mountain city there is little sun to be seen. She dreamed of watching the sun rise from the sea. Indeed many people here have never even seen the sea, which is a long way away. She has had many difficulties in her life, with a broken friendship, struggles with studies, failure in exams, all leading to confusion. When others around her seemed to have such charmed lives, she was asking, "Why me?" To counter this she had been reading books and standing on the balcony of her apartment watching the sun rise—in so far as one can in this city. This, however, had been enough to give her hope. "You never forget your dream and are full of hope in your heart. I believe that one day we can get rid of haze and see a beautiful sunrise." This is one student I am really pleased with, as she had developed so much over the past year, improving her English commensurably.

Zoe's story

This one is very different. Instead of speaking of her own experience, Zoe wrote a fairy tale, but she did not say where it comes from. She has a community of goblins, which is attacked by orcs and killed, the slaughter lasting all day. There is no respite till nightfall when the survivors shelter in a cave. They decide that their safety lies in darkness, so remain hidden in their underground sanctuary for generations. One day their cave springs a leak and begins to fill with water, whereupon the king tells his people to accept their fate. Little Bob, a somewhat naughty boy, slips away while no-one is looking and finds the source of the leak. This he follows till he finds an opening, through which he squeezes. He was outside—and saw a beautiful world; he saw the sun rise. He plugged the leak before returning to his people. Years later, as king, he led the goblins out of the cave into the sunshine.

Comment: Like many fairy stories, this one has a message for us. We cannot hide from problems forever.

Felicia's story

Felicia climbed yet another mountain, also famous in China, Huang Shan (Yellow Mountain) in Anhui Province. "The sun slowly rose up, like an old woman carrying a load… I feel so grateful for Nature's gifts. People normally neglect the most important things, like a sunrise and fresh air… Everyone has the responsibility to sustain the environment … thereby saving resources. Life has its ups and downs. Like sunrises and sunsets. People are unlikely to be successful all the time." Felicia is another student I am well pleased with: she has worked hard, with results.

Owen's story

This student went to Sanya, which is a popular tourist destination, especially when one is trying to escape from a cold winter. Here he and his friends got up early, and made themselves comfortable in chairs on the beach. He remarked that modern life gives us few chances to appreciate a sunrise. "The dark sky went deep blue. The eastern horizon was dyed red and the fiery sun rose gradually like some new life coming forth. The red colour became much more dazzling and changed into a semi-circle. It looked like a veiled, shy girl peeping at the earth. Later the sun appeared completely and shone with a dazzling brilliance… It was a wonderful experience."

I do like the use of imagination and imagery these students were displaying. I also like the links to human experience: we are not separate from our environment. In Australia, I love to watch the sunrise from our balcony in Randwick. Some years ago I took some students to Sydney and one morning, I got them up well before dawn and took them down to the clifftop of Northern Coogee, from where we could watch the sun rise seemingly out of the sea. It was an awesome experience. One of the students sat mesmerised for a long time, precisely the one who was grumbling most at being hauled out of bed so early on a cold winter's morn. Perhaps the message for us is to get up and live.

Example 8: Sport

Together with most of my countrymen and women, I like sport very much. It is a most important part of Australian life. I had been teaching Australian culture, so naturally this is an aspect which had to be covered. As a homework assignment, I asked my students to write about it and also to compare the situation in Australia with that in China. What they gave me is illuminating and here are some of their comments. Sometimes I have quoted their actual words, and sometimes paraphrased their meaning.

Sample 1:

In China Olympic athletes are chosen from special sports schools, where sport is more important than academic subjects. Children are often sent unwillingly. They are paid for by the government at 35,000 Yuan per player. (Note: I do not know what period of time is referred to here.) A gold medal at the Olympics costs 700 million Yuan. (Note: this seems to me to be an astronomical figure, so may not be accurate. Nevertheless, I think we can conclude that China spends an enormous amount of money in order to win each gold medal. Other countries, including Australia, also invest money in athletes for the same purpose, even if not to the same degree of fervour.) In Australia, the emphasis is on the children, not on the elite, whereas "our sports system is using tax payers' money to support a small group to win glory for our country."

Sample 2:

"Australian sport is regarded as a form of entertainment. To most Australians, sport is a great way to escape the stress of modern living. They make a bet on matches just for fun. However, Chinese people pay too much attention to the results. They always want to win. Maybe this difference is caused by different national characteristics. Anyway, sport is a good way to relax, so do sport now like the Australian."

Comment: I might add that gambling is illegal in China, notwithstanding the fact that the major centre of gambling in the world is Macau. Australians too like to bet, and in my view, far too much. Gambling is even advertised on TV, and at the end of the add a hypocritical rider is added, "And remember to gamble responsibly." Then don't gamble at all.

Sample 3:

Australian sports are more varied. "Sport makes Australian life more rich and wonderful."

Sample 4:

"Chinese do not like playing sport, especially women. They play sport only for keeping their health and having a good shape." Parents force their children to play sport, which they dislike. "We should play sport from the bottom of our hearts and play sport every day, like Australians."

Comment: Perceptions Chinese have of Australia are not always entirely accurate, although what this girl has said is true in the main. Many parents in China, far from forcing their children to play sport, positively discourage them, viewing this as a distraction from study.

Sample 5:

"The biggest difference between these two countries is consciousness: Chinese people do sport for health, but Australians as a hobby. Chinese choose what they are good at, while Australians choose what they prefer."

Comment: Yes, although just maybe one prefers what one is good at.

Sample 6:

Australia has more space for sport: China has a high population. Students are forced into PE. "In the Olympics, the government pays more attention to winning, while Australians enjoy sport more."

Comment: Well, yes, but Australians also love to win.

Sample 7:

"We pay too much attention to winning medals."

Comment: The Chinese certainly have an obsession with winning at all costs; anything less is considered to be a failure.

Sample 8:

"The National Sports Bureau often chooses little children who seem to have a gift and develop them for competition." Note here that Li Na, a well-known successful tennis player, now retired, was a bit of an embarrassment for the government, in that she did not go through the official system, but went her own way.

Sample 9:

"In most sports events, people just sit in front of the TV set and watch them, cheering for victory and upset at failure. They don't really participate in it."

Sample 10:

"Table tennis, badminton and diving are most popular. You can see people play (these) everywhere, and Chinese are crazy about watching diving."

Comment: This seems to suggest that Chinese do indeed love sport in itself, quite apart from just winning.

Sample 11:

Ancient Chinese played a kind of football called Cutu in the 3rd century BC.

Comment: I had heard this before but know nothing about it. I have also heard people say that the English did not invent soccer: the Chinese did. This view comes out of rampant Nationalism.

Sample 12:

"In Chinese squares you will find boys playing basketball, kids watching and playing table tennis and the elderly dancing."

Comment: In the early mornings you will certainly see older people taking part in Tai chi, but not many young people.

Sample 13:

"Australians pay more attention to the nature of sport, whereas Chinese pay more attention to winning. They win medals, but people do not exercise much."

Sample 14:

The proportion of people who really love sport is lower in China than in Australia.

Sample 15:

Although Chinese athletes are world class, this does not mean that the people are strong. On this point, China has a long way to go.

Sample 16:

"Chinese athletes do sport for their career; Australian athletes do it because they love it."

Comment: As regards what happens to athletes after they have retired from competitive sports, there appears to be a difference of opinion from the students. From what I can gather, there are instances where top class athletes are helped by the government in furthering their education and moving into another career, but this may not always be the case, especially for those of lower profile. They may end up as low paid labourers, having missed their opportunity for higher education.

Sample 17:

"Chinese people like watching games instead of playing, whereas Australians prefer to be involved personally."

Comment: You may notice that there are many general statements, which are OK so far as they go. In Australia we too have our couch potatoes, but I think the general statement remains true enough.

There was criticism of the way China fosters its athletes, because it impedes the development of children. Related to this is that there is so much pressure on children to succeed academically that they have little time for relaxation. On weekends they still have their heads in their books, where their Australian counterparts would be more likely to be out kicking the footy or hitting a ball.

Sample 18:

"China controls some sports in order to win gold medals. Sport belongs to the Party. This results in embezzlement in Chinese soccer. I hope the government can allow sport to be free: then we can enjoy many sports, not just some."

Comment: Chinese soccer is a national embarrassment; corruption and nepotism are rife, with the result that the national team may not be the best team. In spite of China's massive population, their team fares poorly in international competitions.

Sample 19:

"The Chinese sports system can be called a gold medal manufacturing machine, far from ordinary people."

Comment: This appears to be a recurring theme in their writing, so I gather that the students at least, and probably many other people are not happy with it. Perhaps it would be better if medals at Olympic Games were issued to individuals, not to countries, so that there would be no mention of which country the athlete comes from, no playing of national anthems and no flags. We could use the Olympic flag and Olympic song.

Sample 20:

"I regard sports as pressure, which influences my scores (marks?). We are eager to see that athletes gain gold medals… the government is always promoting national sport, so it will gradually become more important."

So there you have it: comments from a selection of 20 students, out of 100 altogether. While there is some repetition this tells us what is important for them. For me it gave a little more insight into the society here.

Example 9: A Thunderstorm

As a final example of students' work, here is a topic I gave them at the end of 2012: "A Thunderstorm", once again hoping that they would use their imagination rather than copy from the internet, which was their usual practice. I thought it was a topic they could relate to personally. Well, predictably, some did copy, but many did not. Some were excellent. Here are some samples of their work. Unlike the samples above I have left these just as they wrote them, so that one can get a better idea of their standard of English. My job was to help them improve. When one gets beyond the obvious grammatical and spelling mistakes, some of the imagery is fantastic—at least in my humble opinion. I am sure that some of these mistakes are but typographical errors.

Sample 1:

When we talk about thunderstorm the first idea appear in my mind is a afternoon in summer of Chongqing. Because this moment is a hightime that a thunderstorm will come. Everyone in Chongqing knows that the summer is very hot. So Chongqing has a nickname, stove. In summer, the sun shines brightly and intolerably. The atmosphere around us is too hot for us to stand. But luckily, a dark cloud hit the sun and the wind begin to blow. All the signs show thunderstorm will come.

Soon we will see the sky is full of dark clouds. And lightnings appear in the black sky. Wind become stronger and stronger and we can hear a big noise of thunder. finally. Heavy rain fell the noise of both the rain and thunder are become bigger and bigger.

Usually, a thunderstorm won't last long. After a while, the rain will stop and the atmosphere will very clean.

Sample 2:

Blue sky disappeared: whilte cloud was gone; thunderstorm coming. Few patches of clouds drifting across the sky and soon become everywhere. Dark clouds seem to fall at any time.

Suddenly, a flash of lightning across the sky. Reach the ears bust of thunder. Some rain came down. The rain the next up.

The rain gets heavier the cars and people on this road are gradually decreasing. Thinder getting louder and louder while lightning like a sharp sword across the sky the clouds were "chop" to pieces.

Rain on the leaves. The leaves will soon be break down. almost falling down. Rain hit the spider web. The scared to leave. The rain stopped and the thunder has gone. The sun came out and lots of pedestrians on the road. The ky became blue again. spider re-climbed the cobwebs. weaving a web start.

Comment: This one reminded me of our nursery rhyme, "Itsy bitsy spider, climbed up the water spout." I like the image of lightning as a sharp sword.

Sample 3:

With the wind is blowing, the lightning is attacking in thunder's threat, the tallest tree of the grassland is fell. Between heaven and earth seems to have nothing to fight with the storm, they can do everything as they wish.

The sky is growing dark, the wind is more and more strong, the lightning is more and more terrible, the thunder is getting louder and louder. The grassland only have a piece of green grass in the resistance to the storm, but they are too small.

The rainrop from the sky dive down heavily in the face of the grass, the grass is bending the waist, but she shake off the rainwater and straight her waist, announcing to the storm—" I will never give up!"

The sky is furious, the thunder is growling in the sky, the lightning likes an angry dagger paddling constantly in the sky. The storm is more severe, and the wind try his best to pull out the roots of the grass, but the grass hold the earth tightly, not surrender any more. The grass believe that the sun is at the back of the dark sky, as long as you stick to it. You can see the sunshine again.

Comment: Wow! I liked the imagery. Chinese culture has the image of the tree which bends in the storm and hence does not break, where rigid structures, which do not bend, may break. This image is applied to any situation of stress.

Sample 4:

Thunderstorm is an enormous natural disater. when a thunderstorm comes, the sky appears lightning followed with a terrifying thuder. Thunderstorm is not only a horrible scene but also a cruel killer. It even can destroy houses and some other facilities like power station. After thunderstorm there always come the flood which will take people's property away even their lives. The flood is as ferocious as a monster. It comes in a very fast speed and strong impetus. People who lives in a very remote and mountainous region are too hurry to do enough preparation for the coming flood. Therefore most of them lost their homes and property. After all of this, what you can see is a vast ocean of wreckage and sadness of people.

Comment: China is such a mountainous country and when this is combined with its high population, such disasters as described by this student are not uncommon.

Sample 5:

Thunderstorms is be defined as storms but coming with lightning, thunder and cloud. However, sometimes when people talks about thunderstorm could happen in a person's life. it usually refers to an unpredictable things happens on people's everday life as the thunderstorm.

On the other side, as the thunderstorm is usually of short duration, seldom over 2 hours. so people always says you will see a rainbow after a thunderstorm. Which means no matter how difficult the ordeal you met. things will get in order as long as you survive this thunderstorm.

For me thunderstorms is full of rainbow as life is full of surprises.

Sample 6:

The sky was dense with cloud not a diffuse light from some fragment of a moon could be seen. The lowing sky was oppressive. This evening, was very quiet. as if you could hear your heart beat.

The weather was so cold and the temperature declined so fast. All of a sudden chilly chilly air spilled over the horizon. Dark cloud was rolling madly across the sky, then a sound of thunder seemed to come from beneath. The whole sky was cleved by thunderbolts wresting.

In a short time, a dramatic downpour of water commenced. It seemed like a water curtain dropped from the sky without warning. Out of nowhere, a forceful gust burst forth. The road became a bubbing and splashing steam, the storm cloaked the city tightly like an enormous and foggy coat.

Also, many people don't think thunderstorm is a good thing. but I think it is! Because it can make people feeling refreshed and giving in a cool.

Comment: I love the vivid imagery this student has used.

Sample 7:

This one is quite different. When I first mooted to the students the writing assignment I had in mind, the suggestion was not exactly met with enthusiasm. By way of encouragement I told them that I would do the same as they did: I too would write about a thunderstorm. What follows here is my offering.

It was 5.00 p.m. on a hot, sultry summer's afternoon. Jimmy and his father were lolling languidly in the living room, watching the cricket on TV, fan on to provide some coolness in the stifling heat. Col, Jimmy' older sister, was reading; she was always reading. Craig, his younger brother, was playing with his toys. His Mum was in the kitchen.

Above the cricket commentary a distant rumble could be heard, or at least it could if you were listening. The rumble registered only in Jimmy's sub consciousness, as he watched the players, with one batsman now into the 80's. Would he get his century? He hoped so: it was always good to beat the Poms. The rumble was repeated, this time louder, this time closer, this time penetrating into Jimmy's consciousness.

"What was that?"

"We might be getting a storm," answered his father. "I think it's been building up."

Indeed, it had been so still: not a breath of air, the atmosphere heavy, as if pregnant, as if waiting with expectant breath for something big to happen.

The thunder was now much louder.

"I think it's coming our way," said Dad.

Jimmy, all languor gone, even forgetting momentarily about any possible, imminent century, leapt off the lounge and ran outside up to the back yard. Their house was built on a hill, commanding excellent views of the surrounding suburbs. One could even see the airport and the Bay. He stopped, mouth agape, as he gazed at the awesome spectacle of an enormous bank of black cloud coming from the South East, straight towards him.

"Wow!" was all he could say.

Just then a jagged bolt of wicked looking forked lightning darted out of the cloud, striking the ground some distance away. There was a noticeable pause before he heard the thunder, beginning as a rumble, building to a loud roar.

"Come on in here," yelled his mother, who had seen the lightning from her kitchen window, and of course, had heard the thunder. "You could get killed."

"Oh, Mum, this is awesome. And it's still a long way away."

"Well, it's about 2 km away, but it is coming up fast, and your mother is right," said his dad. "Up here on our hill we could get hit by lightning."

"How do you know how far away it is?"

"The lightning and the thunder occur at the same time. We see the lightning instantly, but it takes time for the sound to reach us, about three seconds to cover one kilometre. This storm is still about two kilometres away."

"Gee!" Jimmy gazed in wonder at the rapidly approaching, rolling black cloud.

"Look, Dad, the top of the cloud is green," said Craig, who had followed them outside.

"So it is: that's a very good observation, son. It means this storm is going to bring hail, so we had better get inside. Your mother will be having kittens by now."

Crack! There was another bolt of lightning, this time closer, this time brighter, as the thunder swiftly followed.

"Come inside instantly, you three," shouted Mum from the doorway, "you'll be getting yourselves killed."

"Come on."

Just then, they were hit with a sudden burst of cold air, carrying with it a peculiar smell.

"It smells nice," said Craig, but Mr McCready was not waiting any longer, as he grabbed his sons and hustled them inside.

"But what is that smell, Dad?" Jimmy persisted.

It was not until they were safely indoors that his father answered, as they stood at the kitchen window watching.

"It's called ozone, a gas in the upper atmosphere. Thunderstorms go very high, sucking air upwards, so forcing other air downwards. That was why we felt that cold air just now."

Just then a large drop of rain fell on the window, followed by another. Soon the outside world was engulfed in a torrent of large drops, drumming in an increasing roar on the roof. Jimmy watched fascinated. Then he noticed that some drops were white, and were bouncing off the grass.

"Look, Dad," he yelled. "Mum look at this, isn't it wonderful?"

"Yes, that's the hail, and you are right: it is wonderful. Never underestimate Nature."

"I'm going to look out the front." He raced through the house to the front windows, rapidly followed by his brother to get a better look, only to find his sister there already, her book momentarily forgotten. Visibility was reduced as the bright sunny day of such a short time ago was transformed into greyness. In the far distance, to the West and North West, a patch of blue sky could still be seen, ahead of the storm.

BOOM. CRASH. A bolt of lightning flashed close by accompanied by a very loud thunderclap. For the next ten minutes the whole family stood at the front windows watching as the storm crashed about them, thunder roaring, lightning splitting the darkness, rain and hail bouncing off the road and drumming on the roof. It was as if the fury of Nature had been unleashed, aroused to violent activity after the torpor of the day. Gradually the storm receded, the thunder and lightning moving to the North West towards the city, while the rain and hail eased.

"C'mon, Col, let's go and look at the hail." The three children went out the back to find that the rain had ceased as suddenly as it had begun. Everything was dripping wet, with hail covering the back porch and lawn. Jimmy picked some up, small round balls. And they were cold, a blessed relief after the heat of the day. The whole atmosphere was now cool. Quiet too had returned, with the occasional sound of distant thunder to remind them of what had been.

The children played with the hail for some time, before there was a call from inside. "Come here, children, watch this." Jimmy rushed back to his father who was now watching the television, just as one of the batsmen hit a boundary. A roar went up from the crowd at the ground: the batsman had scored his century. Col drifted back to her book, Craig to his toys, while mother was already in the kitchen, finishing her meal preparations. They were back to normal.

Life is good. And sometimes exciting.

9.3: "Mao's Last Dancer"

"If you become a teacher, by your students you'll be taught." How true those words from "The King and I" are. One of the ways I have tried to find out about

315

Chinese culture and how students think is to set them assignments. They can be most revealing. "Mao's Last Dancer" is an autobiography of Li Cunxin, a ballet dancer, and it has been turned into an Australian made film. Li Cunxin is an Australian citizen, although he was born and grew up in China at the time of the Cultural Revolution—a truly terrible time.

I showed this film to some of my students, as did another Australian teacher at SISU with some of her students. Cleverly, she asked her students to imagine that they were young Australians, who had never been to China. What would this film teach them about China? What follows is the result of that assignment.

The first comments refer to the poverty. They were really impressed by just how poor people were, especially in rural areas, under Mao Zedong. They had no idea. All of these students were born in the mid-nineties, after the opening up initiated by Deng Xiao Ping in 1979. Improvement was only possible after Mao's death in 1976. I have discovered myself that young Chinese know little about their own history, as all they are taught is propaganda, designed to show the CP only in the best possible light, to the extent of distorting facts. This same attitude also applies to China as a country, which has never done anything wrong, as it is always other countries which do wrong to China. Really? Their Nationalism is so strong, that it is always China, no matter what. They are just starting to realise how terrible Mao was. One student told me that she did not like Mao's dumping of women; he had four wives and numerous sexual partners. Students did mention that any criticism of Mao while he was alive would result in severe punishments, including death; much the same is still happening today, of course, for any criticism of the CP and Xi Jinping, the current emperor.

Secondly, there is a realisation that freedom was extremely limited. Even thought was strictly controlled—and is still is. Everything was governed by politics, including art. A freer expression of ballet was not allowed: it had to fit into the strictly controlled regimen of the CP. One student said the people "were like robots." Li's teacher wanted a freer expression, but instead found himself imprisoned for two years. In fact, after his release, he was allowed to return to the Ballet Academy, but not as a teacher: his job was to clean the toilets. This particularly shocked the students. They had no idea.

Thirdly, the attitude to capitalism made an impression on them. In those days, China was communist, and hatred for all things Western was instilled into them. The worst countries in the world were capitalist, and their people the most miserable, whereas China had a higher standard of living, and the people were the happiest. When Li went to America, he realised that this was all lies. The students of today can now recognise this. Has anything changed? I found it rather ironic that in the wake of a recent aircraft disaster, when a Malaysian plane MH70 carrying many Chinese passengers, went missing, the Chinese Government accused the Malaysian Government of lack of transparency! What is that saying about a pot and a kettle?

Fourthly, they exhibited a satisfaction with the way China is going now, mentioning how much China has developed over the past thirty years, and indeed it has to an extraordinary degree: the world has never seen anything like it. They mentioned the abrupt turnaround from lambasting capitalism to wholeheartedly embracing it, and indeed today one cannot really call China a communist country nor even socialist. As I have told some of my students, China is more capitalist than Australia, which in turn is more socialist than China.

Fifthly, they mentioned how China has moved from being a feudal society to a democratic society. Now this is a surprise, and is not the first time I have heard people enunciate this belief. Is China democratic?—in what way? I suspect that in their understanding of democracy, it is "democracy" with a very small "d" indeed. There are some elections held within the CP, but of course, the ordinary people have no chance to select their government, while even rank and file CP members have little or no say.

Sixthly they mentioned the paucity of information in Mao's day. True enough, but in this respect not much has changed. Not only does the government keep people in the dark as much as possible, but the whole of society is not in the habit of giving information. In this university, for instance, we are not told what is going on or why. Often we would find out the day before that something was on, but rarely well in advance and sometimes not at all. On one occasion I found out at 2.15 p.m. about an end of semester class photograph which was taken at 1.30 p.m. Thanks.

One positive comment refers to the family as the corner-stone of Chinese society. After Li decided to defect, he was barred from returning to China and from seeing his family, causing great distress both for himself and his parents. I detected some ambivalence here, with students wondering how he could do this. At the time, of course, he was considered to be "a traitor to the motherland". Yet the students were certainly admiring his determination to be free, and to pursue free artistic expression in his dancing. They pointed out the tragedy that his marriage to his American wife lasted barely a year. They did like the fact that

317

eventually, after seven years, he was allowed to return to China to see his family. By that time he had an Australian wife. At time of writing, I think he is living in Brisbane working as a ballet director.

Several of the students looked upon Li as a symbol of China, which is interesting, especially considering that he is no longer a Chinese citizen. China, as you may or may not know, does not recognise dual citizenship, so that if you become a citizen of another country, you are ipso facto no longer a citizen of China. Australia has agreements with a number of countries, whereby immigrants can still remain citizens of their country of origin, but China has no such agreements, mainly because they consider that all Chinese should have the Motherland as their primary allegiance, even if emigrants departed generations ago. From the students' perspective, however, as one put it: "He keeps making progress; so does China. He becomes more and more free; so does China." Another student wrote: "Young Chinese are full of energy, dreams and yearning for freedom."

From what these young people wrote, maybe we can learn more about what they think, what they stand for and what they long for.

Chapter 10: Extra-Curricular Work

Introduction

Sichuan International Studies University was employing me full time, but this did not prevent me from doing other work; many other teachers were doing the same. I was not sure what the official policy was on this, as nothing had been said, but usually it is not a problem, just so long as you do not make a song and dance about it and it in no way interferes with commitments at SISU. I agree. Two of us, for example, had been teaching regularly at the computer firm, Hewlett Packard, but before I started I made it plain to them that SISU would always come first, should there be any clash. There never was. These extra jobs also enabled us to earn a little extra money, which was always handy, especially as our regular wage was so low. Mind you, I was not there to make money. Nor did I go looking for extra work, but if it came along and I could do it, why not help out?

Much of my extra work came via a rather extraordinary person, called Michael, who was what could be called an entrepreneur extraordinaire: he had a finger in many pies. Amongst these was working with a travel agency, which involved, for example, organising sailing trips up and down the Yangtze River. He was also running his own English school. I was taken by the doors on his classrooms, each of which featured the flag of an English speaking country, such as England, Australia and Canada, as can be seen in photograph 75. His own English was excellent.

Photo 75: Michael's school

He was very much a free agent and—most surprisingly—a free thinker. I learnt a lot from him. I am quite sure he would not be voicing his views publicly, but he would vent them to us teachers from overseas. We in turn would respect his confidences. He is a remarkable man and I learnt so much from him. Thank you, Michael.

10.1: Hewlett Packard

In 2013 during the Spring Semester, I was approached with an offer to teach a few staff members at a computer company, Hewlett Packard, just two classes, with five people to each class. At the time, I was not overly committed at SISU.

Hewlett Packard was a rather large computer company and at the time it was selling more computers than any other company, with the Chinese firm of Lenovo catching up fast. Lenovo used to be IBM, but was bought by China. It seems China is buying everything these days. Most HP computers were currently being manufactured here in Chongqing in a large plant employing something like

14,000 people. What its future will be I do not know, since fewer people were buying laptops, which were being superseded by tablets, iPhone and the like.

The plant here, however, was not only a factory, as it had a large building dedicated to the software side of the industry. It is here that I was teaching. They were dealing with overseas clients on a daily basis, thus giving them a practical need to improve their English and hence they were motivated. I generally gave them some passage to read so that we could work on pronunciation, intonation and vocabulary, followed by discussions so that they could do the talking. I enjoyed them.

The staff too was most obliging and attentive. Elaine, one of the secretaries, would prepare in advance any material we needed.

To get there was easy. I would walk ten minutes to Lieshimu railway station on line 1, and take the train five stops to Weidianyuan station, giving me another twelve minute walk up to the HP site. The whole journey would take around 50 minutes, but it did take a little longer sometimes when the train terminated at one of the intermediate stations—Shuangbei—necessitating everybody getting off and waiting for the next train. Trains would arrive about every ten minutes. On one trip one young man was so engrossed in his paper that he missed his stop. Sorry, mate: you will just have to get off at the next station and come back. On the crowded train back in the afternoon, it was not uncommon for people to offer this "old man" a seat, which I would graciously decline. After I had been sitting down most of the day I needed to stretch my legs. Naturally I was in complete denial on the topic of rapidly approaching old age.

This whole Wedianyuan area was just being developed, with lots of bare paddocks—a rare sight indeed in this populous city. Wide roads were already in place, but with little traffic: such a rarity. Near the station, a block containing some 20 buildings was then under construction, with each building at the 25 storey level. Photograph 76 shows Weidianyuan railway station sitting atop pylons—a good idea, because it leaves streets free for vehicular traffic. One can also see the edge of a large open paddock. The railway line is heading for a range of hills, which it traverses by means of a long tunnel, taking about 3 minutes to get through.

In inclement weather I could catch a bus from the station. On one particular day the weather was really hot, the temperature in the high thirties and there was absolutely no shade out here at the edge of the city. Elaine arranged for their driver to take me to the station. On another day it was raining and I had neglected to bring my umbrella. This was no problem for Elaine, who lent me her own, one which had been given to her by the company in recognition for work well done. I made sure I returned it in good condition.

Photo 76: Weidianyuan station

In the Autumn semester I was approached to teach again, but this time teaching ten people on a one-to-one basis, one hour at a time, seeing each person once every two weeks. Again I agreed, on the same conditions. At the time I had only ten hours teaching at SISU, so obviously there was no problem, but then I was given more classes at SISU, then yet more classes, until I was well over the full time limit. I was in a quandary, as I found that I was now very busy indeed. I was asked to do more classes: I said "No—I have enough." Should I give up the extra-curricular HP work? I elected not to, as I had given a commitment and thought I could still handle it, and in fact it was manageable. This also meant extra money, of course, and HP were paying more per hour than SISU was doing—and I was also enjoying it. They were really good people and they looked after me well.

Hence every Wednesday out I would venture. Every second Wednesday I would have three students, but only in the morning, while every alternate Wednesday I would have seven students, which would take all day, at least at the beginning. After a few weeks one student pulled out: (a) he was away a lot, and (b) his level was not high. He was often in Beijing and my first session with him was by phone, as he was still travelling. It was not a very practical arrangement. Other students were away from time to time, or were caught in meetings. One spent some weeks in the United States.

On days when I was there in both morning and afternoon, I would eat lunch in the canteen either with Eileen, who was our liaison officer, or some other staff member. The food was basic, but good, with rice, soup and choices of meat and vegetables. Payment was by card not cash. It was interesting to see people form two queues, one for HP personnel, while the other was for Foxtel employees, the company which was making the computers. I found it interesting that there were two distinct sections for the workers, since the plant was divided into two sections, the larger being the manufacturing section, where most Hewlett Packard computers were made. Indeed my own computer was an HP and I had bought it in Chongqing. The smaller group was the IT section, where I was working, with nearly 1,000 people. In China one must get used to massive numbers.

The rooms I was teaching in had names. In the spring semester the room I was allocated was called Guangzhou, named after a major Chinese city, while the one I was in the following semester was called Lhasa, named after the capital of Tibet.

One of my students actually asked me if I thought Tibet belonged to China. Wow! What would I say? I hesitated, then hedged around for a while, before thinking to myself, "Oh what the heck: if they throw me out now I really do not care, as I would be leaving soon anyway." So I answered, "No it is not. It is a country which China has conquered by military might, which gives China no right whatsoever." Surprisingly, he did not seem too upset, as if he was expecting something like that. Maybe that is what he really thinks too, but of course he cannot say so. Currently, as you would know, China is claiming territories belonging to about a dozen other countries. Everything it seems belongs to China. No other country has any rights.

On another occasion I was teaching a student on a one to one basis, going through news items online with Voice of America Special English section. The news item came up of China's claims in the East China Sea. I asked him what he thought. There was a pause. "I am Chinese, so I have to support the Chinese government." Without saying so explicitly, he nevertheless made it plain that he knew China was wrong, but he could not say that. Indeed he could get into trouble if he did.

In class, it was never my intention to take sides. It is important, however, to let students know that there is another side to any issue. Yet on least one occasion, this was interpreted as criticism of China—and that is not acceptable, especially from a foreigner. Put yourself in their shoes; if a stranger comes to your country and roundly criticises it, how would you feel? This could mean apologising, letting them know that it was never my intention to upset them. I was conscious that I was treading a very fine line here. It is a conundrum: how to educate, but without offending.

Photo 77: attractive courtyard at Hewlett Packard

The work environment at HP was most comfortable, especially with central heating in the winter. Each section had a security door accessed via a card from one side and a button from the other. I was issued with a card upon arrival, which I would hand back before leaving. It was so quiet with employees working away at their computers in cubicles. What surprised me was that so many cubicles were empty. One reason for this is that many employees were preferring to do their work from home. Presumably this is monitored in some way.

This Autumn Semester ended with a presentation from each student in a room called Shanghai. Actually there were only seven presentations, as three pulled out for one reason or another, lacking self-confidence being one of them. They were quite good however. PJ—another teacher working with them—and I did the evaluating. This for me marked the end of the semester, 15th January, as I had already finished work at SISU. Now I could take off for holidays, beginning the following day, heading initially to Kunming.

From March through June we had our final semester. On Tuesday 22nd June, for instance, I had seven hours at Hewlett Packard, with seven students, one hour per student on a one-to-one basis, thus giving time to correct personal mistakes, whether in pronunciation, grammar or whatever. I could also check their final presentations—more about this later. It was a comfortable day, in spite of the hot weather, since the building is air-conditioned. Normally I would walk up from the station, but on this day I took the HP shuttle bus, with the advantage that I did not arrive hot and sweaty. Each day the temperature had been in the high 30s. Classes began at 9.00 a.m. finishing at 5.00 p.m., with an hour meal break from 12.00 noon to 1.00 p.m.

The following Thursday 24th was my final session at Hewlett Packard. At this, each of the ten students was asked to give a 15 minute presentation, to show how fluent they had become. Each topic was different, reflecting their different interests. All were interesting. Allow me to mention some of the more salient ones.

Ron spoke of a weekend he spent in San Francisco. He spoke well, backed up with some very good photographs. He was gob smacked by the city. What struck me was just how complicated we are and how much we operate on different levels. China certainly does have an intense dislike of the US, simply because they have usurped China's right to be the only World superpower. They will stop at nothing to unseat the US. While Chinese citizens share this, they also have a great admiration for the US and they copy much of Western culture. For this man, just to find that his hotel was across the street from Microsoft headquarters was enough to transport him to seventh heaven.

Benny reflected his Chinese bias in his presentation, stating that the "Chinese government is always friendly to other countries." Oh Yeah? Try telling that to the Koreans, or the Japanese, or the Taiwanese, or the Filipinos, or the Vietnamese … the list goes on. He also quoted Xi Jinping, "There is no gene for invasion in our blood." Maybe there is.

Joy spoke of a Chinese academic, Yang Yin-Yu, the first president of a Chinese university, Beijing Women's Normal University, in 1924. This was a period of great political upheaval and she made herself unpopular by forbidding her students to take part in politics, even calling in the police. (Has anything changed?) She was forced to resign in disgrace, as being too dictatorial and returned to her home town of Suzhou, where she continued to teach, especially on a one-to-one basis. After the Japanese invasion she spoke out against Japanese atrocities, for which she was murdered in 1937.

One young man, who glories in the name of Grosso, spoke about an Italian soccer player, Fabio Grosso by name, whom he much admired. As well as this player's claim to fame he also has one claim to infamy. During a quarter final match in the 2006 World Cup, with the score at 0—0, just before full time, he took a dive in the penalty area. Penalty kick, goal, Italy won 1—0, and subsequently went on the win the championship. During the recent Soccer World Cup in Brazil, a Dutch player also took a dive. In these situations, a penalty should indeed be awarded—in my humble opinion—but down the other end. Why should cheats be allowed to prosper? There was a sub story to this. In China a well-known soccer commentator was praising this tactic, urging the Italians on to thrash their opponent. Boy, what a role model: cheating is fine, if you can get away with it. He was forced to resign, and never commented again. Who, you may ask, were the Italians' opponents in that quarter final match? Australia. As a corollary, FIFA did apologise to Australia, but by then the damage was done.

The shortest presentation was only ten minutes, by a young man who considers his English to be good enough. He was difficult to teach, as he would try to talk non-stop and not listen. Consequently he learnt very little and gave the worst presentation.

Possibly the best presentation was given by Michael. He did have some advantage, in that he had given this before to the HP boss when she had visited from the US. What distinguishes a good company from a great one? He was relying upon a book which treated this topic, but he had his own ideas, too, not entirely agreeing with the book's author. I like this; he could think for himself. Well done.

The most impressive presentation, however, was given by a young lady on the topic of "How to Find a Perfect Mate". She was 26 years old and not married. In this country, a woman is considered to be on the shelf (or *sheng nu* an "unwanted woman") if she is not married by 28. There was so much pressure, both from the wider society and from her own family, to get married. Celibacy does not make sense in this culture. I thought this young woman was very courageous to be so outspoken about such a personal topic. I do not know why she is not married, as she is smart, very good looking and with a great personality. Furthermore, she is in a work place which is predominantly male. Maybe this is itself a problem: she used the expression, "too little meat for so many wolves". I do hope she finds her soul mate in the not too distant future.

At the end of the proceedings once again I gave small Australian souvenirs as mementos. Once again many photographs were taken. Then it was time to say goodbye. I do miss this place, as I had thoroughly enjoyed my time here. The pay wasn't bad either! I kept thinking that this could be the last class I will ever take. Who knows? We never know the future, and it is generally best not to. It often turns out to be so very different from what we could ever imagine, and so much better too. God is good.

10.2: Doctors

A second extra campus class I taught was for a single two hour session only. Another teacher, Patricia, had been taking them on a regular basis, but could not make it on one particular day. They all belonged to the medical profession, with some thirteen doctors and a couple of nurses. Their specialised fields are interesting. Morgan and Dragon (true!—must be Chinese) are surgeons, with Johnny a neurosurgeon. Penny works with the brain, Oscar with digestion, Anna in haematology, Xavier in orthopaedics, Cheryl in obstetrics, while Davis, Susan and Thunder (again true!) are cardiologists. Then we have the Chinese medicines, with Catherine in acupuncture and Brenda, Jessica and Lily working in TCM—Traditional Chinese Medicines. The aim here, of course, is to take this to the West and indeed Chinese medicine has been available in the West for some time. You may have noticed that they had chosen some interesting English names, with Xavier having no idea how to pronounce his name. Fair enough: I had trouble pronouncing my Chinese name, Ma Keng Li.

While I taught these people for only two hours, I thoroughly enjoyed them. I got them to work in pairs doing role plays on patient-doctor consultations, so that they could work on diagnosis, treatment and bedside manner in English. Curiously, they had been taught nothing about bedside manner. I wonder what that says.

These doctors were rather special. All had been selected by the Chinese Government as part of Chinese aid abroad, in particular to work at Port Moresby General Hospital in Papua New Guinea—and this I like. It may be true that most of China's involvement with other countries is for China's benefit only, but in this instance—in so far as I can judge—that is not the case, unless you consider this as part of China's "soft power". I applaud the initiative; I applaud these doctors. They would be spending two years away from their homes in a strange land. Fifteen had started the programme, with this reduced to eight by the end, after a final examination.

Before they were to leave, Patricia suggested that perhaps we could have a meal together, and they agreed. Michael, the organiser who had recruited us would also come. He was working in Shapingba at the time, so there we met him. He would be driving his car, which—I was told—was beige. So here we were craning our necks looking for a beige car, when he rings me. He has already parked further down the road, with his lights flashing. Great, and I see the car: dark blue. Oh well, the interior was beige.

Guanyinqiao is the district where we had been having our classes, situated on the northern side of the Jia Ling River. Getting there was not a problem in the car, but finding a parking space was. We passed three underground car parks, all full. On the streets too, cars were everywhere. Some had transgressed too much, to the extent that they were wearing wheels clamps. This is a situation which will only get worse. In Beijing at this time, only half of the registered cars were being allowed on the road at any one time. On odd numbered days the cars whose number plates ended in an odd number were allowed, while on even numbered days, those cars whose number plates ended in an even number were allowed. I could see this trend extending across China. Oddly enough (!), we found a parking spot right outside the restaurant we were going to. Actually it was not really a parking space, but it was a space, and that suffices in this country.

The restaurant was interesting: a throwback to the 1950s, in that it was dedicated to Mao Zedong. As we entered, we were confronted with a large mural of China's erstwhile political leader. The back wall of the room we were in was covered in another mural, starring Mao in the middle holding forth. I had my back to him, so my appetite was unaffected. Other memorabilia decorated the room, and when we were leaving we were presented with a button of Mao, depicting that famous photograph taken by Edgar Snow, American journalist, in

Shaanxi in about 1936, with Mao wearing Edgar's cap. Mao did not like hats. Apparently in days past, this button could be used as currency.

Photo 78: end of semester meal with doctors

The meal was the traditional Chongqing-Sichuan hot pot. This style actually originated with the boat haulers here in Chongqing. They were poor people, often being reduced to eating whatever they could get. This included offal which had been thrown out by others. They would boil it, just to make sure it was fit to eat, and add wild herbs and spices to make it palatable and sustaining for their very heavy work. Today, many foods can be added to the mix. We had various meats, including tripe, rice noodles and wheat noodles, mushrooms, greens, tofu prepared in different ways and potato. Even the tripe was nice, and I remember not liking it as a child. Noodles can be very difficult to pick up with chopsticks, as they are just so slippery. Usually, mine end up on the table rather than on my plate, so I was delighted to see that a couple of the others had the same problem—and they are the experts. The food was all placed in a central dish for cooking. The inner ring had no *lajiao* (hot chilli peppers), while the outer dish did. Take your pick.

At the end of the meal, Patricia and I sang farewell songs: "Old Lang Syne" was Patricia's contribution, while I opted for the Hebrew "Shalom Havarim", which also has an English translation. Patricia and I realised that payment would be an issue. The idea of a farewell meal was ours, meaning that technically we are the hosts, and that means we pay. We had brought a considerable sum of money with us to cover the cost, but I knew that the doctors would probably end up footing the bill, which is exactly what happened. I was hoping they enjoyed the meal, as I doubted if they would find a Sichuan style hot pot restaurant in PNG.

It is great that China has taken the initiative to provide doctors for PNG and other places. True, their motives may not be entirely altruistic, but it is a good move nonetheless, and I do hope these fine people gain a lot from their time overseas in another country.

The following year, Patricia had left, so I took over teaching the doctors on a weekly basis for six months each year.

In the 2014 group we had the following specialists: two radiologists, two oncologists, two urologists, two paediatric surgeons, two orthopaedic surgeons, one neurologist, one morphologist, one oral surgeon and one oral and maxifacial surgeon. I presumed that when these numbers were culled around September, there would be no doubling, except for the two oral surgeons, since facial cancers are not uncommon in PNG where people have a habit of chewing betel-nut, or buai, as the locals call it. This nut is mixed with lime to produce copious amounts of red saliva, which is spat out—anywhere. Be careful.

One criterion for their selection was their proficiency in English, and in this area there were a couple who were very weak. They could speak well enough, but haltingly and with limited vocabulary and their listening was not up to par. This can be critical when they are listening to Papua New Guineans, trying to determine what is wrong with them. I placed some emphasis on listening.

Apart from teaching English, I would tell them about PNG culture, based upon my own experiences: I lived there for three years. It is so very different from what these doctors have been used to here in their own country. It will really broaden their horizons, or at least I was hoping it would. It is perhaps a little unfortunate that they would have limited opportunities, as the Chinese government is most protective. They will not have much opportunity to travel to other parts of PNG, nor even to get out much at night-time, as they would be living within a compound. They really would be living within the Great Wall. A reason for this is that there are well founded safety fears, due to the "rascals", the name given to criminal gangs. PNG does have a law and order issue, where the government does not exercise the extraordinarily strict controls that the Chinese government does. In fact one of our doctors was robbed in Port Moresby, just outside the Chinese enclosure. They were living behind a high fence and a locked gate. I am sure that another reason was fear of the doctors themselves being "infected" with "foreign" ideas, such as democracy.

In one class I got them to read a story—actually coming from Australia— illustrating the different perspectives one can get from different cultures. There is more than one way to look at something. When I first went to PNG, I was struck by the number of people just sitting; not doing anything—just sitting. In my culture, we are forever doing things. I can imagine how the Chinese would view this, as they work so much harder than we do. We have our forty hour week, or most people do, whereas the Chinese work for much longer. I was trying to impress the importance of not judging. Who is to say that PNG culture has a more balanced view of what it means to be human, than we do, with our work ethic?

In 1998 there were riots in Indonesia targeting Chinese businesses. The Chinese were richer than other people and this was resented. Yes, they had worked hard for their wealth, but is there no obligation to share what they have? As Christians, of course, the obligation comes from charity.

In class we had also been dealing with medical issues; after all they are doctors. We concentrated on what medical conditions they would most likely be encountering, diseases such as hepatitis, malaria, dengue fever and facial cancers from chewing buai. You do not find these in Chongqing. One discussion concerned the most important role. of a doctor and their responses were interesting. They came up with what I had been expecting—curing illnesses, saving lives—but I have a different perspective. I think a doctor's role can be summarised under three heads: diagnosis, treatment and "bedside manner". All are important, but I think a lot of attention needs to be placed upon the third, which can often be overlooked. I was drawing upon my experiences when working for nine years at the Prince of Wales Hospital in Randwick. As an addendum, I do not think doctors "save" lives, anyway, although they do prolong life, and can cure some illnesses.

These classes were not held on campus. Initially the venue was to the north, involving crossing the Jia Ling River. The route is fairly straight forward, walking down to Lieshimu station to the metro line 1, changing later to line 3, before a short walk across a square: piece of cake.

331

Just as I got used to this, they decided to change the venue, to a place a long way off to the south. Getting to this new venue is rather complicated, so pay attention. This is what you do.

You need to take the train, so you can either walk down to the local station (10 minutes) or take the bus (5 minutes—though you may have to wait for it). There are two factors here: 1) how lazy you are and 2) how impatient you are. You take the train eleven stops to Lianglukou, which is a major intersection. It is easy to count—you know—1, 2, 3 … etc. if you cannot understand the Chinese. In any case the announcer gives the station in English as well as Chinese. Liang-lu-kou, incidentally, means "two streets mouth", as when two streets intersect, it looks like the Chinese character for "mouth".

Well done. Now change to line 3. This entails crossing the mighty Yangtze (or Chang Jiang). For the months of March, April and May the river is very low indeed. Not only is there not much rain at this time, but the headwaters are located in Tibet, which gets rather cold in the winter, locking up these waters in ice and snow. In spring these waters are just beginning to melt and it also starts to rain, as the monsoon season sets in. It takes time, however, before the flow reaches us from higher up. As I crossed the river on the train, I would notice that most of the river bottom was exposed, leaving sand flats. The channel was on the southern side and quite narrow. In the first week of June all this changed. Suddenly there were no sand flats. Suddenly the width of the river extended all the way between the banks, perhaps 500 metres wide at this point. Surprisingly perhaps, the river was not flowing rapidly. Hence the level had risen quietly, without drawing attention to itself. If you did not look closely you could cross without noticing the changes.

You alight from the train at Sigongli (which means 4 km). The following station is called Wugongli (5 km) and the one after that is liugongli (6 km).

Now the fun starts, as the location is still about 7 km away from Sigongli station, but how do you get there? I hailed a taxi and eventually one came along. *"Nali?"* asked the driver, which roughly translates as "Where you wanna go, mate?" to which I replied. *"Wo bu zhidao."* (Dunno!") She looked at me as if I belonged in the funny farm, so I handed her my mobile phone, having just called Michael, who does know the location and could speak the lingo. They chat. Sometime later she handed me back the phone. *"Keyi?"*

"Keyi." We were on our way, with me observing our route closely for future reference.

This is just as well, because even after you have arrived in the locality, the actual building is still hard to find. On later trips the driver might tell me that while he knew the district he did not know the precise location. *"Mei guanxi, wo gei ni,"* an extraordinarily accurate translation of which would be, "Keep your shirt on mate; I'll show you." It was real fun.

On one occasion I had a female driver, with two other women in the car. Wasn't I lucky? We followed the correct route, till we came close to where we should turn off—to the right—but before we got there she pulled out onto the left hand lane—there are three lanes on this road. *"Bushi, you bian, you bian."* Now women drivers are indeed excellent, as I am sure you will all agree, but this one accelerated past a great big truck and screamed around on front of it, by which time we were roaring past the intersection; so I told her again, *"you bian"*, though by now pointing back over my shoulder. Upon which she hit the brakes, with a screeching of tyres behind us and a blaring of horn as that truck driver went very close to ramming us up the backside. I was in the back seat. Wheh! "Thank you very much; it's OK; I can walk from here." She would not hear of it, doing a U-turn in front of oncoming traffic, to drive the 200 metres down the correct road. We survived. And she only charged 25 Yuan: the extra thrills were all free. Do you wish to come to China? Are you feeling lucky? Ah, it's good to be alive. Next time I'll go by bus.

There is a bus too: No. 345 from Sigongli station. One of the doctors showed me a large building and said—or at least I thought he did—that you catch the bus in there. The following week I went inside: nothing. Eventually I did find a bus stop, but it is for long distance, intercity travel, not for suburban. I found a policeman, who must have been all of 18 years old, and asked him. He did not know either, but asked his colleague. "Up there." That's useful. *"Duo yuan?"*— you need to know how far it is. Silly question: they never know. Forget it. I'll take a taxi. Now where is a taxi rank? My young friend led me over a safety barrier—this is a policeman, mind you—down a ramp and voila, there you have it. Not satisfied with this, he went up to taxi after taxi, but either no-one knew where to go, or they did not want to take me. Whatever. Meanwhile, a gentleman (?) came along and barged in front of several ladies to claim a taxi. I got one eventually.

Later, on the way home, one of the doctors gave me more precise directions, but I had had a busy day, I was tired and just wanted to go home, so I did not follow him to the actual bus stop. We only went part way down into an underpass. Water was leaking from a pipe, pouring down the steps, so someone had thoughtfully placed bricks to tread on, meaning one person at a time. I do not know what was in the water, but it certainly stank. I thought it would be easy to follow directions to the other side of the road. It wasn't.

The following week I followed his directions, but could not see the bus stop. I asked. No-one knew, or not those I asked. I walked in the opposite direction and yes, there is a bus stop, but there is no 345 bus. I caught a taxi. On the return journey, I went with that doctor to the actual bus stop, and do you know what? I had been there. I just did not recognise the tiny sign, which I had been looking at end on; there is no shelter, furthermore, as there usually is at bus stops in Chongqing, and it is off the main street. Next week. You may gather I would go once a week. Maybe, just maybe, I will have it all down pat by the end of semester.

The following week—surprise, surprise—everything went like clockwork. The authorities had even fixed that leaking pipe. I did not even have to wait for the bus, as it was already at the bus stop. I was wondering how often it runs: every 10 minutes? Every 20 minutes? I guessed I would find out. This section of the journey takes more than 20 minutes, as we wind up into a mountain, and yes, we go through it, via two tunnels, which are reasonably long, maybe 2 km. And we rattled along with the road desperately needing maintenance, while the bus had been around since the 20th century—maybe the 19th. For the first 15 minutes of the journey, there is no stop because it is all mountainous terrain. Then we have three stops in five minutes. I would get off at the third, leaving me a walk of only a few minutes.

On one occasion, I sat next to a man who was occupying two seats: one for himself, the other for his luggage. When another man wanted to sit down, as there was a shortage of seats, he did not to want to shift. Once again, it is the Great Wall syndrome operating.

Admittedly the taxi gives a smoother ride, and it is faster, but the bus definitely has an advantage. It costs 22 to 25 Yuan for the taxi, while the bus is free. Truly. Chongqing has this great system, whereby if you use a bus soon after getting off a train, it is free. Otherwise it costs 2 Yuan or 1.8 Yuan if you use a card.

This Spring Semester of 2014 had been a light one, thus giving me time to teach these extra classes. Furthermore, I enjoyed working with these good people.

On Wednesday, 23rd June, I undertook the 1 ½ hour journey—assuming one can get good bus and train connections—for my final class with the doctors, from 2.00 to 4.00 p.m. It was a good final class, with each student giving a speech, followed by comments. I gave them each a small Australian souvenir as a memento. Many photographs followed. I wish them well. I have not only enjoyed the classes, but have also enjoyed getting there. I hope you too have enjoyed the journey.

Photo 79: second group of doctors

One night a number of us gathered to have a meal with this same Michael in order to celebrate his birthday. He paid, of course: Chinese custom dictates that the birthday person foots the bill, unlike our Western tradition. Whenever we had a meal, Michael usually paid on one pretext or another. In this way, we are beholden to him and are thus more likely to do some teaching for him. This is very Chinese.

10.3: IELTS

Anyone wishing to go overseas to study, work or settle in an English speaking country needs to show that they have sufficient command of the English language. Perhaps the principal test for this proficiency comes via IELTS. This is an acronym for International English Language Testing System and comes under the aegis of the English Council. Scores are accorded in increments of 0.5 up to a maximum of 9, which is expected to be the level of a native speaker. I know of no non English speaker who has scored more than an

8. There are four areas to be tested: reading, writing, listening and speaking, with each being marked out of 9.

The level of proficiency required varies depending upon one's reason for travelling to an English speaking country or depending upon the university one wishes to attend and the course one wishes to study. This is sensible, as it is not much use listening to a lecture on, say International Business, in English, if you do not understand what the lecturer is saying. There is also generally a requirement that the lowest score be not below a certain standard. For example, one might have and an average score of 6.5, but the listening section scored only a 5, which may be too low.

If a student fails i.e. has not reached the required level, then there is no option but to sit the exam again—but not straightaway: perhaps six months later, thus giving them time to improve markedly. Some students are not prepared to do this, resulting in many failures. And it is expensive, costing at this time some 1,500 Yuan for each exam. Add to this the cost of travelling to the exam centre, and it adds up. Sichuan International Studies University is itself an exam centre, making it most convenient.

Listening, incidentally, is often the most difficult section. When you are speaking, you choose your own vocabulary and speed, but when another is speaking it is the speaker who chooses these. The temptation is to stop mentally, when you miss a word; "what does that mean?"—and while you are figuring it out, the speaker has moved on. Thus you may miss ten words trying to understand one. I would tell my students that they must listen at the speed of the speaker. There could be an added difficulty here due to accent. If your examiner comes from New Zealand or Scotland or Wales, you may struggle. I would tell my students not to be afraid to ask, "Would you mind repeating that?"

The reading section could also be difficult, especially if the section chosen has a lexicology specific to some discipline. Readings could be extremely difficult to understand, even for a native speaker. Questions, of course, are concerned with ones' comprehension.

The writing section can also be a trap in that one is given a certain amount of time to write a passage of say, 150 words, or 300 words. The trap is to keep writing after the suggested time limit has expired. The danger here is that one does not have enough time to complete the paper. I would tell my students that there is no point in chasing after that one extra mark at the expense of losing ten marks because one did not finish the paper.

The speaking section is the one I was most involved with. The perennial temptation for Chinese people is learn off great slabs by heart. Yes, fine, but do they understand? At the beginning of the speaking section I would not allow the student to sprout forth, but would interrupt and ask questions, or apply what they were saying to a different context. In preparing them, I would suggest that they extend their vocabulary—always impressive.

So much for the structure of the IELTS exam, but how does this fit into this section? While indeed I was employed full time at SISU and was teaching students to prepare for their IELTS exam, I was also doing this at a number of other institutions in Chongqing. Most of my extra-curricular work was organised by a most impressive man, called Michael, whom I have mentioned. Often he would pick me up from SISU and drive me to some other educational institution, generally another university but perhaps a middle school to coach students to prepare for their IELTS exams. Often too we would have a meal together. I enjoyed the work and his company. It also gave me further opportunities to explore this city.

10.4: Cambridge Cup

As the name suggests, the "Cambridge Cup English Star Competition" is a speech competition under the auspices of Cambridge University, which is probably the principal university in the world when it comes to English. I did my training in teaching English with Cambridge at a Sydney campus. Here in Chongqing, it is SISU which is the umbrella organisation, so that helping out with this public speaking contest is considered to be under the aegis of the university, even though the contest was not always held on campus, but in another part of town.

Being judges in this competition is very hard work. We would be going all day, with only a short break for lunch. My main gripe, however, is that the judging criteria were unrealistic, with up to twelve categories for each contestant, and you have only a couple of minutes to do it all. I refused to do so many, and told the organisers. It was physically impossible, especially considering the hundreds of contestants of primary and middle school level.

Photo 80: a serious little contestant

They had a choice as to how they would perform; at least I assume they did: maybe they were told. They could sing, tell a story, talk about animals, remember vocabulary, dub a section of some movie, or listen to a passage and answer three questions. There were around five competitors in each batch, and three judges, so I found myself with two Chinese teachers. They were good and we got on well.

On the singing side we were entertained (?) with some old favourites:

1) "There was a farmer had a dog-er, Bingo was his nam-er, B-I-N-G-O (X3), Bingo was his namer…" This is it, but is repeated about ten times. They all said "dog-er" and "nam-er".

2) "Twinkle, twinkle little star, how I wonder what you are, up above the sky so bright, like a diamond in the night. Twinkle, twinkle little star,

how I wonder what you are." This is also repeated about ten times. At the end of each performance, we asked a question or two, like "What is a star?" Silence. We even resorted to telling them in Chinese: *xing*. Silence. Oh well.

3) "Edelweiss". I think you know the words, but we had one little boy who did not, leaving two of us judges to begin singing…Nobody marked us: probably just as well.

4) "I'm a big, big, girl in a big, big world …" except that he was a boy and a rather rugged sort at that.

Some of the voices were quite good, but in marking we had to remember that it is the English we were marking, not primarily the singing.

Some of the story telling was also quite good. In this country people are so good at memorising, especially children. "Little Red Riding Hood" came up a few times, with one variant, "Little Red Hat", where the child was wearing a red hat. I asked her what a red hat was: she did not know. As I said, they can memorise, but with little understanding.

We had a few choosing to talk about animals, their favourites being the panda—naturally—followed by the koala, then cats and dogs. I told them that the koala is NOT a bear; it is just a koala—which they had trouble pronouncing. I wonder how the aborigines pronounced it.

In each batch a certificate was awarded to the best performer, allowing them to progress to the next round. Sometimes we gave two certificates, including one group where there were only two contestants. They were both very happy. They really do take all of this very seriously, an attitude which extends to how they dress. One little girl, maybe nine years old, was wearing eye shadow. I do not like this and would prefer if this is left to adulthood. Let the children be children: it does not last long.

Even though this was hard work, I enjoyed being part of it. Some of those kids were adorable and great fun.

Chapter 11: Farewells

Introduction

In time all things begin and all things must end. It is always sad to say "goodbye": each is a little death. How often, I wonder, are people, at the beginning of some enterprise, are so anxious to get on with and see it through to completion, yet at the end are so regretful, perhaps even wondering why. Maybe this is because it is the journey that matters, at least as much as the destination. This journey involves people, and this is where it can become difficult.

I was with Greg on two occasions when it came for him to say "goodbye", the first when he left Anglo-Chinese College in Fuzhou in 2003, and the second when he left Tongren University in 2010. On both occasions there were oceans of tears. I told him not to come to me looking for sympathy, as it was entirely his own fault. Truly. You see the problem was that he loved his students so much. Hence the solution is easy: just don't love people and they may even rejoice to see you go!

11.1: End of Semesters

The academic year concludes at the end of June. At this time everybody says goodbye till after the long summer break and they return at the end of August. For graduating students, however, there will be no returning. This is a time of mixed emotions. There is relief that their exams are over and that all their studies over the years have finally come to an end. There is a sense of achievement, but also disappointment if one has not reached one's expectations—or their parents'. There is excitement in taking on new ventures as the future stretches before them with all its possibilities. And there is sadness. People who have been living so closely with each other over some years, sharing a dormitory, sharing lectures, sharing work and sharing lives, suddenly find that they are going to miss each other a lot. They will also miss the lifestyle with its securities as a chasm opens

340

before them, with all its unknowns. Over the years I have shared a number of farewell parties with graduating students, sharing this mixed atmosphere.

In June, 2013, for example, we had a party to farewell students in the Lancaster/Robert Gordon programmes i.e. students who would be heading either to Lancaster University in England or to Robert Gordon University in Aberdeen, Scotland. Much of my teaching had been for them. One night we went out to a restaurant, students and staff both. It was interesting to see how they seated themselves—according to their friendship groups, usually coinciding with their dormitories; there were four to a dormitory. This is not a bad thing in itself, and is usually very good, but sometimes it can lead to cliques, and unfortunately that is what happened with this crowd. Having a group of friends is fine, but not when it becomes exclusive. One girl was sitting at our staff table, more or less having been ostracised. This is not good. She was a nice girl, too, very keen and obliging.

Then there was the "infamous four", a group of four girls characterised by a less than co-operative attitude and—at least as far as two of them were concerned—considerable underachievement. They were often late for class, traipsing in together after the rest of the class had settled down to the work in hand. They shared a dorm and—not surprisingly—were on the same table for this final meal. At the end of the meal they came over in a body to have their photograph taken with David, the other overseas teacher, and me. It was all very lovey-dovey. Next semester, three of them would be at Lancaster, while the fourth was going to another university in England. My fear was that they would continue to drag each other down, rather than spur each other on. I also feared they would stick so much together that they would fail to take advantage of all that the university has to offer, especially as regards intercultural exchange. They may continue living in their own Little China. I hope I was wrong.

Photo 81: farewell meal for Lancaster students

In photograph 81 you may notice one of the students making the V sign with their fingers. I do not know why they do it, but it is common; maybe it is "cool". It is interesting that what is considered to be "cool" today used to called "hot" a generation ago.

Another farewell meal was with my Intermediate class. They had a really good spirit and we had a lot of fun throughout the semester, so I was delighted when they invited me to join them in a meal. Afterwards we gathered in my apartment to continue the festivities over a liqueur: most enjoyable.

Sometimes the university would host a staff dinner to mark the end of a semester. In January this would also mark the beginning of a new year. One such was held in the staff dining room on Friday night, 11th January. About 150 members of staff attended including just four from overseas: two from England, one from France and one from Australia. We were told we would be on table 17, so naturally we were on another table. Our places were assigned with name tags, mine declaring, in beautiful lettering "Ennally". Now my name means "son of the poor man". So I guess now I am the poor man, having lost the "son of" bit. There were surprisingly few speeches; I had thought this would be a major feature of the night, but it was minor. Entertainment was more important, with some talented staff members getting up and either singing or playing some musical instrument. This included our Spanish teacher, who plays the flute very well. Sorry, I was not invited to showcase my enormous talent.

The main feature of the night, as one might expect, was the meal. In this staff dining room the meals are normally of a buffet style, but not tonight, as we all stayed in our places and were served. The dishes were the usual blend in any Chinese banquet: fish, various meats and tofu came in first, followed by soups, then vegetables, rice and finally fruit. It was all very nice. But this was not the centrepiece. This moniker would have to go to the toasting. There was toast after toast, mainly to the New Year. There was a toast for the whole room. There were many toasts on one's own table during the meal. Towards the end of the meal, there were many people wandering around from table to table. By this time, not surprisingly, some people were not sure what they were, or maybe even who they were. These toasts were all of the *ganbei*—or "dry cup" style, meaning you drained the glass.

Some of the staff were also finishing their contracts at this time, so that each year there is turnover, with some leaving and new ones arriving. Those leaving in June, 2013 included my three Russian friends so I had a final meal with them. All are young and all have been teaching Russian. One had been here some years ago as a student, learning Chinese, so she will be able to find a job in her home town teaching both Russian and Chinese. Her husband is a navigator on a ship, so is away a lot of the time. Another has Spanish as her second language—but her English too is excellent. I marvel.

Photograph 82 shows four of us outside the teacher's restaurant after a farewell meal to our Russian teachers—Yulia, Anna and Ilyana—in June, 2013.

Photo 82: farewell to Russians

Farewells do not always take the form of meals. We also had a concert—yes, another one—to farewell a graduating class. Two of the students formed the backbone, one playing the violin, the other on the piano, and they were good. I am amazed at how talented people are, in so many different fields. The first half of the concert was just these two, Li on the violin, and Tan on the piano. They played a variety of pieces, European, Russian and Chinese.

The second half of the concert enabled quite a few performers to illustrate their talents, with such of variety of instruments included. A small boy played the piano—very good. Even the dean played a piece. There were several singers, one a small slightly built girl with a powerful voice. There was a piano accordion, a guitar and a violin: I cannot recall ever seeing these instruments juxtaposed before, but they worked quite harmoniously. Li, the violinist, even had her parents present, and justifiably proud they were too. All in all it was a most enjoyable concert and a great way to say "goodbye".

For myself, I had said goodbye in Fuzhou after 4 /2 years and in Tongren after three years; now it was time to say good bye to Chongqing after another three years. I left Fuzhou in order to help settle my 95 year old mother into a nursing home. I left Tongren because I was asked to leave: too old, after they had dropped their age limit to 60 years old. Leaving Chongqing, however, would be particularly poignant in that I would also be saying goodbye to China. I had not planned to stay so long; indeed I had taken each year as it came, but was privileged to have remained for more than a decade.

Thirty years ago nearly any native speaker could have got a job teaching English in China, but as time passed more requirements were added, as follows: you needed

1) To be a qualified teacher
2) With at least two years teaching experience
3) A university degree
4) A TESOL certificate i.e. Teaching English to Speakers of Other Languages.
5) Under a certain age. Initially there was almost no limit here, before it became under 80, then under 75, under 70 and finally under 65. In Guizhou Province, however, it was under 60. In August 2010, at the end of the summer holidays, I had called in at the dean of studies office at Tongren University, where I was teaching, to pay a courtesy call at the

beginning of a new academic year. I was greeted with. "You're leaving!" They were kicking me out because I was over 60. In the event I stayed one more year—because our contracts had already been signed—before moving to SISU, where requirements were not as stringent: we could stay till we were 68. I was 67. I was expecting a one year tenure, but, to my surprise, my contract was renewed for another year. In 2013 I renewed my contract for a third year, but told the director of the Foreign Affairs Office that this would be my final year. I was 70 when I left.

As of writing, in 2020, China has introduced more requirements:

6) Teachers would not be allowed to mention anything concerning religion and this would be monitored within the classroom.
7) Foreign teachers would be required to undergo 20 hours of propaganda—effectively brainwashing sessions. I think I got out at the right time.

Why all these requirements? China likes to be self-sufficient. The rest of the world needs China, not the other way around. But they needed English, the international language, so they needed us. In time we did our job to the point where we had done ourselves out of a job: there were now sufficient numbers of English teachers in China, so that they could teach the language themselves, albeit imperfectly. Many of my students are now themselves English teachers. There are now more English speakers in China than there are in the United States, where many people grow up with Spanish.

Another farewell was for our tennis group. Four of us used to play, albeit irregularly, and during the rainy season, which comes at the beginning of summer, not very often. We learnt not to book the court too soon, as we could find the surface unplayable. It can be treacherous in the wet, as two of us found out, crashing hard onto the ground chasing balls, and no, I was not one of them, in spite of my recent slipping over in the wet and banging my head. Afternoons are usually drier than the mornings. One Saturday morning Han booked the court for 8.00 a.m. I thought there would be a fat chance of playing, but most surprisingly the court was dry and it was not raining. We played for the final time. Han was returning to South Korea, John to England, Ellinore to France and yours truly to the Land Down Under. So we had a final match and also a final meal.

Cyril was also leaving in the summer of 2014 and he too had made that awful mistake of loving his students, one in particular! She is a Tibetan girl—we had several Tibetan students at SISU—whom he had been helping with her English. I must say that under his tutelage her progress was remarkable. In his case the tears were not only in English, but in Tibetan too. He did not however lose contact with her, but continued to be of immense assistance, even after he had returned to the United States.

A number of teachers here belong to the AITECE organisation, a Columban Hong Kong based group, whose aim is to send English teachers into China as Christian witnesses. I think it has been hugely successful. One of the effects of this is that the AITECE teachers in any one institution became very close. Such was the case here at SISU. Every Tuesday night four of us—plus sundry other people—would meet for prayer and a meal in my apartment. These were very special occasions. The same four—again plus sundry other people—would go to Mass on Sundays to one of the local churches, then linger over a coffee afterwards. Naturally we had our own farewell meal with those AITECE teachers who would be leaving—including me.

11.2: Farewell to Fujian

11.2.1: To Luo Yuan

Towards the end of 2013, I was invited to visit one of my former students, whom I had taught in Fuzhou. Unfortunately that was a particularly busy semester for me, as I was teaching on average 26 hours per week, where 14 hours is full time; it was not possible to take time off. We did have the holidays, of course, but I had already made plans for them, viz. to visit Xishuangbanna in Yunnan Province, then Vietnam. When could I get back to Fuzhou? I really wanted to go in order to say goodbye before I left China for good. The answer came in March, 2014, when so few people signed up for courses that some classes were cancelled, thus leaving me with a light load.

On Thursday morning, 20th March, off I set, waking up early in order to be on time for my 8.45 a.m. flight. It takes two hours to get to the airport via the metro, meaning I would need to leave my apartment at around 5.30. Unfortunately the metro does not run at such an early hour, not opening until 6.30 a.m. and it stops running around 11.00 p.m. I would need to catch a taxi.

As luck would have it, as I approached the university gates a taxi came by, saw me and waited. This was fortuitous, as it was raining. He was a good driver, not driving too fast, in fact slowing down at certain points where speed cameras had been installed. Something is happening here: the government is actually beginning to enforce speed limits, a real first. As we neared the airport, he turned and said something. Naturally, I understood nothing, but I took a guess. Now what would he be likely to be asking?—What did I eat for breakfast? How far is it to Timbuctoo? What is the price of eggs in Inner Mongolia? I replied: "*Zhongguo; wo qu le Wuhan*"; "China; I am going to Wuhan." I guessed that he wanted to know what terminal I wanted to go to, domestic or international, but since I did not know the terms for either, I gave him my destination. He was happy. When we arrived, the fare was only 63 Yuan: I was happy. In point of fact I was not going to Wuhan but to Fuzhou, but it would land first at Changsha en route, and on the return journey it would land at Wuhan. I got them mixed. Not to worry.

At the ticket counter I was told that my flight would be delayed. That's OK, no big deal; it often happens in this country. "For how long?" I asked, thinking maybe half an hour or an hour. "*Wo bu zhidao*", or "Dunno, mate." I would just have to check the monitor. I did; frequently. There was never any indication as to what time the flight would depart. The monitor kept showing "delayed" and would do so right up till the time it did in fact depart. The monitor also showed that many other flights were delayed or cancelled. My boarding pass said 2.10 p.m. Maybe. I rang Fiona in Fuzhou to let her know of the delay: she was intending to meet me at the airport.

Time passed. I wandered around the terminal, many times, at least getting some exercise. I checked out the merchandise for sale in shops. I sat for an hour in a coffee shop, sipping a latte. I read. I did a crossword (solved it). I did a sidoku (did not solve it, at least not till later). I did a word puzzle (got 40 words which makes me "genius". Oh yeah?). And I waited. Did I mention praying?— a very good way to pass the time—and of course one prays for humility and patience.

At midday I racked up to the Xiamen Airlines counter to ask if they would be supplying lunch. Well, no not really, but since I asked they said they would, and indeed made good their promise with a very nice repast. It was not their fault I am sure, since so many other flights were affected. Perhaps there was turbulent weather somewhere. There was never any announcement as to the reason. As I have stated many a time, this is not an information society.

Eventually I went through security to find my boarding gate. I was not there long when I discovered that it had been changed—no announcement was made, which is strange, as I had heard of changed gates being announced for other flights. I found the new gate, some distance away, but nobody was boarding. I asked and was told that yes, I could board now. Great. Boarding meant climbing onto a bus to drive to our aircraft parked some distance off. Once on board, I found that everybody else was already there. Had they been sitting there all day?

At 3.40 p.m. we finally took off, seven hours late, and after I had spent 8 ½ hours at the airport. Oh dear!—my glasses case had been left behind—somewhere at the airport. Am I going to go back? "Excuse me, but I have left my glasses case somewhere in the airport. Would you mind delaying the flight while I go and look for them?" Goodness; no way. The crew kept repeating the safety instructions. Whatever for?—surely once is enough.

It took about seven minutes to get into the sunshine as we climbed through two distinct layers of cloud, settling just below a third, filmy wispy layer, contrasting with the sodden, grey sea of clouds below. It was beautiful. I always ask for a window seat; the downside is that you need to plan your toilet breaks, especially if a fat person is sitting next to you.

We stopped off at Changsha, where I phoned Fiona to tell her that we were actually on our way and should be in Fuzhou about 7.00 p.m. Her house was about 75 minutes' drive from the airport, so she needed plenty of notice. Changsha too was wet. There was water in the river, water in the creeks, water in ponds, water in rice paddies, not to mention the water in the skies. And it was cold. We had about a 45 minute stopover, time to stretch the legs. I had been doing a lot of walking today, albeit not getting very far. Getting back on the plane, a woman barged in front of me. "Hey lady, the flight won't leave without you." Meanwhile the man behind me was **shouting** into his mobile phone, to the point of being painful. I call this "The Great Wall Syndrome". Each person acts as if there is a great wall surrounding them; nobody else exists. It is the same for their own group—guanxi—and the same for the nation. China is the only country on the planet. That is why it is normal to claim territory of other countries as belonging to China: the claims of other nations are not even considered.

We were late taking off from Changsha, at 5.45 p.m. instead of 5.20—the story of the day. The plane announcer kept telling us "Your comfort and satisfaction is our forever goal." That is nice to know: there are only two English mistakes, and I make no comment about the actuality. Back in the air we were given a meal. Great: rice, vegetables, a bun with gherkins, a cake and a bottle of water—and a coffee; wonderful.

Finally, finally we arrived at Chang Le airport, Fuzhou just before 7.00 p.m., when we should have landed at 12.15 p.m. Poor Fiona was there waiting with her brother-in-law. It was a smooth ride of just over an hour to her house in Luo Yuan. At her mother's house we had a meal—yes another—and met other members of her family. They had gone to a lot of trouble to prepare this meal, comprising various kinds of seafood, since we are close to the coast here, washed down with both *baijiu* and red wine. There was also a very tasty rabbit stew. We should eat this more in Australia as I used to in my younger days. In fact we used to go out to catch our own rabbits.

At 10.00 p.m. I was taken to my very comfortable hotel for the night, the Jia Fu Da Fan Dian. It was well after 11.00 by the time I hit the sack. What a day. What will tomorrow bring?

11.2.2: Luo Yuan

Next morning, Friday, I surfaced around 8.00, although for some reason I had had a restless night. Breakfast was part of the tariff, so I headed for the hotel dining room, to find the usual Chinese style breakfast: various vegetables and spices, eggs, rice porridge, tofu, tofu crust and bean curd drink—but sadly, no coffee. Luckily I had my own in my room. Never leave home without it.

At 10.00 a.m. I accompanied Fiona and some members of her family to the local Catholic church, which is dedicated to Mary, as indeed many are, especially here in China, where the locals sometimes call the Church the "Mary Church", as distinct from the Protestant variety. There is a sizeable Catholic population in this area. This particular town is called Nan Men, or South Gate. The local priest does not live at the church, but in an apartment in the town, so the church was opened for us by a sister. There is a depiction of Da Vinci's Last Supper on the altar and another at the back of the church, and indeed there is one in Fiona's house, so I guess it is rather popular hereabouts, and it is exquisite. Paintings of St Dominic and St Catherine are on either side of the sanctuary; I do not know why these particular two are so favoured. The church is airy and clean.

Photo 83: Buddhist shrine and Catholic church

The weather on the day was perfect, fine and sunny, fresh with a slight cool breeze. Together we walked to a local Buddhist shrine on Sheng Shui Jie, or Holy Water St. I guess the Catholics are not the only ones to have holy water. There is also a *lieshimu* here, or shrine to "martyrs" = Communists killed by the Kuomintang. They were killing each other, and a battle took place here during the civil war. The shrine is built on a hillside, overlooking the town. There are quite a few steps to climb, and I was surprised that Fiona was taking it all in her stride. She is quite agile, given that she was eight months pregnant. I was just hoping she was not doing too much. I have to admire her and her husband, as they were determined to have a second child, even though they knew this would incur penalties and the displeasure of the authorities. It makes me wonder what this child will become; something very special I think. More of this later.

From here we picked up Joanne, a friend of Fiona and an English teacher, and drove to a nearby bay. This bay is quite large but with a bottle neck opening.

It contains a fishing village and a base for the Chinese navy. The plan was to have lunch here at a floating restaurant; there are many floating platforms in this bay, on which people live. Our party arrived in several vehicles, before embarking on speed boats for the short trip to the restaurant. When I saw it I realised that I had actually been here before, about ten years' previously, on a teachers' excursion from Anglo-Chinese College in Fuzhou, where I had taught for 4 ½ years. Life is amazing.

Photo 84: floating village

Naturally our meal was full of many different varieties of sea foods; two species of crayfish, oysters, pippies, octopus, fish—naturally—dumplings and soup, all washed down with coconut juice, which is something of a favourite in this country. We really ate well. Outside on the deck were tanks holding all this food, so that you pick what you want. Goodness, I think we picked everything. I tried to take the owner aside to tell him to give the bill to me, but all to no avail. My hosts forestalled me and would not hear of any contribution. This is very Chinese: they are past masters when it comes to hospitality. I think this village is called Ji Tou Cun.

From here we drove to a new city currently being built, called Luo Yuan Bay New City. Construction in China is nothing short of mind boggling. In Australia we erect a building here and another there, but nothing on this scale. In just one area I counted no fewer than 50 cranes at work. Whole blocks, whole streets are built at once. I must say that these new buildings look very smart indeed, neat and clean. I noticed that quite a few of them are in fact three storey houses, bespeaking lots of money, as these would be expensive. I believe that in the evening a large musical fountain operates, but we did not see it.

From here it is but a short drive to the home of William's parents, Fiona's in-laws. Many of the family had been with us all day, although William himself had been detained on business in another city. We spent quite some time preparing for the evening, which would be something special. We ate yet again at around 6.00 p.m., and once again it was mainly seafood. I guess my hosts were conscious that Chongqing is a long way from the sea, so does not have as much seafood.

That evening around 20 people gathered, both family and friends, for a liturgy. I thought this would be one way in which I could repay their hospitality. In the past I had been rather loath to do this, but now that I was soon to leave, I no longer cared. I do what I think is best and priesthood is for others, never for oneself. How can we serve the needs of the community? We had a truly wonderful evening. I had brought with me a statue, actually Korean, of Our Lady of the Sacred Heart, which I presented to Fiona at the end. I pray that Mary will guard this special family, especially Fiona's sons. My Chinese, of course, is terrible, so we had a mixture of Chinese and English. There were blessings all round at the conclusion of our service.

Afterwards, as we relaxed, the children played hide and seek. The living room is quite a spacious 25 square metres, and in fact the whole apartment is quite large, having three bedrooms plus balconies. It transpired that I would be staying here for the next two nights. This had truly been a wonderful day, and the morrow too would be special.

11.2.3: Final visit to Fuzhou

Fiona and I left her house at 9.10 a.m. and walked a considerable distance. We were going to catch a train into Fuzhou, so were walking towards the railway station. I of course had no idea where it was; I kept asking and kept being assured that it was not far. We were walking along a dusty cement road in bright sunshine, with trucks going in each direction, honking their horns of course. This road is a major link to a new city, which is very much a construction site. I was a little worried about all this walking, considering Fiona's pregnant condition. She seemed in no way concerned.

Eventually a bus approached so we flagged it down and hopped on, paying 1 kwai (Yuan) each for the privilege. In this neck of the woods there were no designated bus stops: passengers get on or off anywhere. Not many people were aboard, a far cry from Chongqing. We did not in fact have far to go before we arrived at the railway station.

The station itself is quite imposing: large and spacious. I was told it had been constructed with all this current development in mind. Soon many people will live out this way. Fiona had already booked our tickets on line, so we just needed to pick them up. They cost 50 Yuan for the approximately 40 minute trip—but what a trip.

This was a fast train, reaching speeds of 200 kph, yet very smooth and comfortable. I have now been on a number of these trains and they are wonderful. We did not have contiguous seats, so Fiona sat in the first one while I moved to the next carriage, where I found a woman occupying my designated seat. I showed her my ticket and she duly vacated it—no problems. I was, however, surprised that so many people were standing. On every other fast train I had been on, there was no standing; everyone had to have a seat, which makes eminent sense: I would not want to be standing in the event of an accident. I would not want to be sitting either, but it would be preferable.

We arrived at Fuzhou railway station, which I am very familiar with, at 10.35, but of course we were separated. As it turned out we were both at the exit, but missed each other in the crowds. Mobile phones come in handy. Next was a quick visit to the toilet, but where is it? You need to go into the terminal, go upstairs, walk along a corridor, pass through a security check, enter one of the waiting rooms, and there you are: simple.

Back outside we were met by Vickie, another of my former students. I had brought both her and Fiona to Australia in 2008 for World Youth Day. Her brother came with her to pick us up, providing transport in the form of a bronze coloured car, which the ladies said was "golden". Vickie's Mum was running a restaurant, and here we met other members of her family, whom I had met before. Last year I had stayed with them for a couple of days.

After a short rest we were off again, meeting with two other of my former students, Sandy and Nancy. It was good to see them again. Fiona is the only one of this group who was married; I assumed the others were still looking. Because of the preference in this culture for boys, there is quite a sex imbalance, so in theory it is easier for a girl than for a boy to find a partner. Next step was lunch, not only to eat, but also to talk and catch up. The meal was once again seafood, including a very tasty fish, cooked in a sweet sauce. There were also pigs trotters: Greg, eat your heart out! (They are his favourites.) These were very fatty, so why is it that the tastiest foods may not be the healthiest?

Not far away is the beautiful Hot Springs Park. It was here we spent the rest of the afternoon, casually wandering around, enjoying the park, the weather and each other. It was idyllic, especially on this warm, sunny day, temperature around 23 degrees. It is just so soothing to the spirit to see people relaxing and enjoying themselves. Children were playing in a sand pit or by the water of a small lake. Elderly people were dancing. People were strolling around. The little girl in our party loved the flowers, so kept looking at them up close, even picking them, which of course you are not supposed to do. What am I to do when she runs up to give me a flower? *"Xiexie ni, zhege hua tai mei li."* ("Thank you so much: this flower is really beautiful.")

Photo 85: farewell to Fuzhou friends

Photograph 85 shows us outside the Vickie's family restaurant: author, Vicky, Nancy, Fiona, Sandy—plus bub.

Late afternoon we went to a cafe for a coffee, at least for me, the others having various other drinks; and we shared a waffle, which I think is best with genuine maple syrup. Covering one wall is a reproduction of a French painting, "A Sunday Afternoon on the Island of La Grand Jatte" (1884-85) by Georges Seurat, a pointillist painter. It happens to be one of my favourites. The original resides in the Chicago Art Institute, where I got to know it. There is just so much in it. Let me explain a little of what I saw. We had ourselves spent a Saturday afternoon strolling in a park, and it was idyllic. This painting also seems idyllic. But all is not what it seems. Society is awry, punning on the French "pecher" to fish and "pecher" to sin. There is something odd about each item in the painting: a prostitute has an umbrella coming out of her back; the wind is blowing in different directions; the sun is casting shadows at different angles; there is not a single family unit in the whole painting. And so it goes on. I wonder what the future will bring to the people here in China—and elsewhere?

It was time to bid a sad farewell to these lovely people. Thank you for taking the trouble to come and see me. We went our separate directions. Fiona and I headed for the bus station for the trip back to Luo Yuan. We could not get a train seat as it was already booked; a pity, but there is the advantage that the bus depot in Luo Yuan is very close to Fiona's house, so less walking for her. We left just before 6.00 p.m., arriving at Luo Yuan just after 7.00, so quite fast.

A meal had already been prepared for us, and they had taken pains to prepare some of my favourite foods, such as *jiaozi* (dumplings) and *yuwan* (fish balls), plus red wine. Perforce we ate in haste, as we were going to Mass at a local Catholic church and it was due to begin at 7.15 p.m. We got there just after 7.30, so that is not too bad. This church is large, seating, I estimate about 1,000 people, yet it is still too small, as it was difficult to get a seat. Hence they are currently extending the church, making it longer by a further 25 metres. Wow! I guess in this part of the world the faith is alive and well. When the Communist Party took over the Christian population of China was a meagre 1%; now it is 3%; 4 million then, but 50 million now. After Mass I went to meet the priest but he was busy.

Back home to Fiona's house it was time for bed after yet another wonderful day. God is good. No doubt we would all drop into a deep sleep: not quite.

11.2.4: Return to Chongqing

The day began a little earlier than I had anticipated. There was considerable household movement in the early hours of the morning, which woke me up. At 2.30 a.m. there was a knock on my bedroom door: Fiona wanted to see me. She was still in bed, so I sat on her bed and we talked. Her waters had broken, so she needed to go immediately to hospital as her baby would be arriving very soon. We spoke briefly and prayed for both baby and mother, and she was off, leaving just Paul (her first born), the grandparents and me. I went back to bed. Later on in the day her baby was born, another boy. Although a month premature, both were doing well.

I cannot help but ask myself, "Was I in any way responsible for the baby's early arrival?" I think yes, I was. We had done a lot of running around over the past two days, and I had been anxious that Fiona may have been doing too much. She had invited me last year, and I had thought this would be the last opportunity to see her for some time to come. Was it too late? Thank God both mother and child were doing well. I say "for some time to come", because after the birth of a baby, the mother retires for a full month: does not go out, does not even wash. And I was leaving China.

At 7.30 I got up. Granddad prepared breakfast. It did not take me long to pack, after which I sat in the living room praying then writing. Junior (Paul) surfaced around 8.30, proceeding to drive his car back and forth; truly. He is not yet three years old, yet already he has a car, admittedly small, but it goes. It is fitted with a smooth electric motor, with two gears—one forward and one reverse—and... and...—this last item is absolutely essential for any Chinese car—a horn. So he drives back and forth, quite skilfully I might add, blowing his horn.

The living room also has a shrine: a picture of the Holy Family in the centre, surrounded by other pictures, plus candles etc. On another wall is a wedding photo, where the couple has been so airbrushed that they could be any couple in China. This is a pity, I think, as I like them as they are. Prettiness, like tinsel, is on the outside, whereas real beauty is on the inside.

Just before 9.00, Fiona's brother-in-law returned to drive me to the airport, but unfortunately with little conversation due to the language barrier. He is a careful driver, a fact I had noted earlier. We had not gone far when he pulled over to check the tyres: they needed some air. We were not speeding, especially when in the vicinity of speed cameras and when going through tunnels. We passed one truck on its side, its load spilling out over the roadway; maybe that driver had been speeding. The longer we travelled, however, the faster we got, as I surmised my driver was starting to worry about the time. I told him it was OK, as we had sufficient time, and we did. When we came off the expressway, I noticed that the cost was 58 Yuan, which, of course, I was not allowed to pay. Roughly that works out at about 1 Yuan per minute.

At the airport I was a little surprised that he drove to the arrivals' terminal, not up the ramp to the departures terminal. He explained that he had been given strict instructions by Fiona, not to drop me off, but to come with me to ensure that all the procedures went smoothly. In fact he was very helpful indeed. Thank you.

My airline was called "West Air": never heard of them, in spite of the fact that by this time I had probably travelled on most Chinese airlines. Surprisingly perhaps, our flight was only a little late in departing, but we were delayed in Wuhan, where we had a stopover, so that we did not get to Chongqing till about 4.00 p.m. As we took off from Wuhan airport, I took a look out the window: the air pollution was appalling in that you could hardly see anything.

Six years later, Wuhan would be a household name, due to fact that this is where the novel covid-19 virus originated, causing millions of deaths, a world-wide lockdown and an economic recession.

We had left Fuzhou at 11.30 a.m. I must confess that at this hour I was expecting to be served a full meal. But we were not, only a small portion of noodles and some water: no buns, no fruit, no other drinks and especially no coffee, which I actually requested. During the flight the crew was busy promoting merchandise: goodness, is there any end to the Chinese commercial spirit? Train crews do this too. Please, can we just have a quiet flight? This airline, in my book, is definitely not going to get the gong for the best airline of the year, at least not this year; maybe next year, if they look after their passengers a little better.

At Chongqing airport I began wondering what I would have for my evening meal, realising that I had little in my apartment, so decided to eat at the airport. It was a little early, but I was hungry. I went to Dicos, a Taiwanese copy of McDonald's; very rarely do I visit this kind of restaurant. The food was palatable, definitely better than cardboard, but there is good reason why I am not a frequent customer. At least they had coffee, but no milk. Instead they had that artificial "creamer".

The suburban metro system terminates at Jiangbei Airport, so it is very convenient. By boarding here one is also assured of a seat, before the train begins filling up further down the line. I used the time to write in my diary, but with some difficulty. I could not help but compare the roughness of this ride with the smoothness of that fast train to Fuzhou. I found that I could really only write when we came to stations. Not to worry. At Lianglukou (literally "two road mouth"—an intersection, in other words), you transfer to line 1 for the trip out to Lieshimu. There was no sitting on this leg, not that I needed it, as I had been sitting long enough. It is good to stand. Young people these days do not often stand for elderly people; sometimes they do, but they generally have their heads buried in their mobile phones, playing games or whatever.

By 6.30 p.m. I was back in my apartment. What a fantastic weekend it had been: had it only been one weekend? We had done so much. Many thanks to Fiona, her family, and my former students for their hospitality.

11.3: Farewell to Guizhou

I would be leaving China for good at the end of August 2014 and there were a lot of people I wished to say goodbye to. May Day is a public holiday, and not just for one day, but for three. It used to be five days, plus the weekend made it a full week—one of the three "golden weeks", designed to encourage spending and thus contribute towards a consumer based economy. It did not work—and nor did the people. For us at SISU we had Thursday off (May 1st) as well as Friday and Saturday; I was not teaching on Saturday anyway. Sunday became Friday. I did have a Friday class, at 8.00 a.m., but told the authorities I would not be teaching, because I go to church. I transferred my class to the previous Tuesday, thereby giving me the whole weekend off. Thus I was able to travel to Guizhou Province, where I had lived for three years, to say goodbye.

11.3.1: Guiyang

Guiyang, the capital of Guizhou Province, is a city I had been to many a time. Greg was now back there at this time for a short teaching stint. So on Thursday morning, off I went, leaving at 7.30 even though my train was not due to depart until 9.24: better early than late. The 210 bus goes from SISU front door right to the train station, which is also the bus terminal: so convenient. I had been advised to leave at this time, bearing in mind peak hour traffic. Now let me clarify this: I mean, Heaven forbid that I should ever listen to any advice from John—in spite of his initials (JC)—but it just so happened that I was ready to leave by 7.30 a.m.

I did get to the railway station in plenty of time, so walked around, getting some exercise. We began boarding procedures a half hour early, as it takes that long. We still left ten minutes late. As we boarded I noticed that a young man was sitting in my seat, a fact I gently (truly) pointed out to him. Peremptorily he pointed to another seat. Is that his? Is it someone else's? I showed him my ticket, as I was riled by his attitude. With bad grace he shifted. I settled in to a window seat, which is what I prefer, as I can both look at the scenery and take photographs.

No sooner had I ensconced myself than a young lady asked me—nicely this time—if I would mind swapping seats, so that she could sit with her friends. Not a problem, so I moved, and as luck would have it, she too had a window seat. You can attract more flies with honey than with vinegar. This, however, is not the end of the story, as a railway official came and asked me why I was sitting in this seat. The other passengers explained. OK, no problems. Then more railway officials came checking our tickets. In this country the government keeps strict watch over everybody.

It was a slow trip: K trains always are, making such a contrast with the new 300 kph trains. I read, wrote, did crosswords and looked at the scenery. For lunch I ate a Vegemite sandwich, and no, I did not buy it on the train, but had brought it with me—from Australia no less—(the Vegemite, i.e., not the bread). The Chinese do not eat Vegemite: they are not **that** civilised!

It was a bright sunny day, something of a rarity. It was so nice sitting at the window in the warm sunshine. The carriage was crowded, as usual, but at least everyone had a seat, unlike some of the trains I had been on. On a number of trips, I had been without a seat—not the most comfortable. It may not be too comfortable either when one has a seat, with the fat man beside me digging his elbow into my ribs as he played a game on his tablet. On this journey a young couple was sitting opposite me, obviously very much in love. He was quite handsome, but she was really beautiful. While I was admiring the scenery (which, naturally, included them), they had eyes only for each other. Meanwhile a gentleman across the aisle kept staring at me. Goodness, I must be more handsome than the Adonis opposite.

On such a long trip, the occasional visit to the loo is required; notice that I did say "occasional". It is the usual hole in the train floor. Goodness knows what the tracks must look like, or smell like. The one for our carriage was particularly dirty with rubbish strewn about. The person who had used it before me had not even bothered to flush. Outside the toilet men were smoking, even though this is technically not allowed. The sign even says so. What sign? Indeed.

The countryside we were passing through is very mountainous in this province, yet wherever there is some reasonably level stretch of ground there is habitation, such is the population in this country. New towns were being built, the buildings all alike. New express-ways carry vehicles rapidly across the countryside, sometime as much as 70 metres above it, at other time boring through tunnels.

At 6.30 p.m. we arrived in Guiyang, actually on time, in spite of having been parked outside the city for some time, waiting for another train to pass. I left my travelling companions, who were probably going on to Kunming, which is where this train was terminating.

Outside of the train station there is an open plaza. You have to walk a bit to find the buses, and even further to find taxis. I eventually got one, and showed the driver the address which I had on my mobile phone. Off we went, for some considerable distance, until we came to the gates of a technical university. No one is allowed in, and a discussion took place between the driver and the security guards. Eventually, up went the bar, and in we went, albeit not far, only about 200 metres. Now what? I rang Greg and soon Damian came to meet me. Ironically, we walked back outside the gates before veering to the right. I did not need to come in at all.

Damian took us to his place, where his family was having an Easter meal, together with some members of the local clergy, including the bishop—the old one, that is. At 92 he was still active, but a younger man was running the diocese. Damian, incidentally, was a pillar of the church here. Every parish has these committed lay men and women, without whom we would be considerably poorer. They are essential. Greg was also there and it was good to see him again, the last time being in Australia some 15 months before.

After the meal we were driven to the cathedral where Greg was residing, as he was working for the diocese. I would be staying with him, sleeping on his couch. We drove to the cathedral via a back entrance, which I never knew existed, as I had always come in the front. There is a plaza here which people use for tai chi and roller skating amongst other things. The back of the cathedral looks really attractive, even in the dark. Most churches in China use European style architecture, so it is good to see a more Chinese style used here.

Greg and I chatted for a while before bunking down for the night. On the morrow we would have a long drive ahead of us.

11.3.2: Zhen Yuan

Next morning, Friday, we had breakfast in Greg's room. At 9.15 we left for Shiqian. I sat in the back of the car, centre, before being asked to move to the right hand side: no problems. Fr. P was in the centre, Cicilia, our translator was back left hand side, Greg in the front, with Fr. M driving. The previous occasion we had done this journey, some years ago, also with Fr. M driving, it had taken us 12 hours. In the intervening period a new expressway had been built, so that this time the actual driving time would be only 4 ½ hours: what a difference.

As we set off, our driver put a sign on his dashboard giving us priority: there is some government influence here. As it was we found that the expressway was free today, because of the public holiday. Goodness, I cannot imagine that happening in Australia. It was a lovely day, warm and sunny, with light wispy clouds high up. I looked up and saw a halo around the sun.

Further along we came across something not nearly as nice, as we entered a hazy area. Some suggested it might be mist, but no way. I said it was smoke and in fact I could smell pungent sulphur. At least one person was finding this very unpleasant, interfering with breathing. Soon we came to its source: a coal fired power plant. We were out in the countryside, but the government had deliberately located these plants outside of cities in order to reduce pollution—but of course all it did was to relocate the pollution. It was not pleasant.

This is mountain country, yet this expressway makes light work of the terrain. We would go through many tunnels and cross many bridges. It would be interesting to know what percentage of our journey was actually spent up in the air or underground. Another feature is the contrast between the old and the new, the ancient farm dwellings and the new roads above them.

We were asked if we would like to make a short detour to see an ancient town. We looked at each other; yes, well, heck, why not? This is so Chinese. Our companions were planning to stop off at this town anyway, not only to have lunch but also for our translator to catch up with some of her relatives who were living there. Out of courtesy, however, they asked us. Lord knows what would have happened if we had said "Noo way: we need to get to Shiqian quickly." We would have been the poorer, as this town is well worth the visit. It is really beautiful. In this culture one needs to learn to go with the flow. There is saying in Chinese which roughly expresses this: "*sui da liu*" (or *sui bo zui liu*), although these have an overtone of fate, which I would not subscribe to.

Photo 86: Zhen Yuan

We were told that this town was built during the Ming Dynasty (AD 1368—1644). It is narrow, hemmed in by hills on two sides and bestriding a green 50 metre wide river winding through. There is a walkway beside the river, lined with restaurants and also with weeping willows, arching down to greet the life giving waters. People were walking up and down, enjoying this magical place. A lovely arched bridge crosses the river. Cf. photograph 86.

We arrived at 12.45 p.m., so definitely time for lunch. We walked past restaurant after restaurant, as we wondered which one our guides would choose. There was no hesitation at all: the one chosen was part owned by Cecilia's cousin, Simone, who was there to greet us. We had a choice whether to eat inside or al fresco: the latter, of course. We were asked again; perhaps we did not like the soot in the air. What soot? We really did prefer outside, so stuck with our decision. Once again our hosts were being polite, but they did not want us to choose outside. Why? The canopy we were under was broken, so much so that it actually started to collapse after some clumsy person (no names here, as I do get awfully embarrassed) bumped into it.

We had a lovely meal, the fish in particular being a surprise, consisting of big chunks with no bones. This is the fish I like. Greg and I paid for the meal,

362

and also for the petrol. After all, three other people are taking the trouble to bring us to Shiqian. Many photographs were taken in this photogenic village. It is that sort of place; just so beautiful. It bears comparison with Fenghuan, another ancient town in Hunan Province, which also has a river running through it. They are similar.

After our meal we walked to the house of Cicilia's grandfather, where she would often come as a girl, although the current house is modern, only twelve years old at this time, the previous one having burnt down. There is a well here, which has very nice water, a little flat with a slight metallic taste. Here we were given two wonderful, detailed maps of the town, a project organised by Simone, Cicilia's cousin, a talented young lady. The street was being planted with trees encased in decorated stone boxes, looking quite attractive.

We left Zhen Yuan at 2.45 p.m., stopping at a lookout atop a hill overlooking the town. You do get a wondrous view from here, so we took yet more photographs—naturally. Here we were approached by a group of girls who wanted their photographs taken with us—again, naturally. Why do you wonder? Autographs later.

From here it is only about an hour's drive to Shiqian, so that we were there by 4.00 p.m. We had thought that we might stay in a hotel attached to some hot springs, for which the town is noted, but that was not to be, as we were ushered into another hotel, one in which we had stayed at before. Why? Why indeed, as there was a lot going on here.

Photo 87: Zhen Yuan from lookout

11.3.3: Shiqian

Why were we shunted into this particular hotel? True, it is convenient, being located immediately behind the church, and in fact on what used to be church ground before being confiscated by the government. This, however, was not the main reason. On the previous occasion we were here, the heavies from the security police paid us a visit. Now wasn't that nice of them? Maybe. I have reported on this visit before, so let me just say here that this was not exactly a social call. It just so happens that this hotel belongs to the CP. In other words, the authorities could keep an eye on us. On the other hand, our hosts paid for our accommodation; life in China is never simple. What lies behind the obvious? This is why I chose "China—Behind the Mask" as a title for my second book on China.

Fr. M, our driver, was wearing a T-shirt with the words: "GOD LOVE YOU", together with the Chinese characters for Tien Zhu (God, or literally, Lord of Heaven). Actually, I would like to make a slight alteration and change it to: God loves you.

Having dropped our bags in our room we headed for the presbytery, where we found Bishop W. What a surprise. Fr T was also present, plus a sister from Shanghai and a lady from Guiyang who was looking at the diocese prior to taking up an appointment. Here Greg was able to copy some photographs and indeed we took our own. This is a major reason we had come. Seven years ago the MSCs donated a sum of money to fix the roof of this church. We needed to see the results and provide some photographic evidence to the General in Rome. The work had now been done, cracks repaired and the whole repainted. It was looking good. The facade is particularly pleasing, and one would like to preserve it if at all possible. This church is historically important, having been erected by the German MSC province in the 1920s. Shiqian had been the centre of an MSC diocese before they were expelled after the CP took over in 1949. We had also wanted to see the graves of those who died here: we think there are seven, plus another who died on the Long March due to ill treatment by the communists. Every time we made this request we had been confronted with a wall. This occasion was no exception, when we were told that the graves were destroyed by the communists thirty years ago. Maybe.

This Fr. M was in fact a communist plant, spying for the government and later he would leave the priesthood. This is what happens when the Communist Party meddles in Church affairs. On the other hand, the Church in the West has not always chosen the correct candidates for priesthood either. In the 1960's and 1970's some paedophiles were attracted to the Catholic Priesthood, although admittedly at this time the horrors of paedophilia were not appreciated. There were even publicly accepted paedophilia associations.

Over the previous seven years or more Greg had been supporting an orphan, Amy. This little girl, whom I had first met six years before, was now 19: very much a young adult. We also met another of Greg's protégés, a young man of 20, to whom we gave the name Francis, since he asked for an English name. He is a fine young man.

Next door to the church is a building, which had been the convent of the MSC sisters; it has its own courtyard containing a wonderful, German built well. This convent had been taken over by the government and turned into a museum to the CP. It has since been handed back to the church, so that is good, but it was still a museum, the difference being that now the government actually pays rent. How extraordinary is that? There are many layers in Chinese society. On the other side of the convent is a building which used to be the mission hospital. Here we went for our evening meal.

Photograph 88 sows a well built by these German missionaries in the courtyard of the convent, with the church in the background. It was certainly well built!

Photo 88: German built well in convent

As I have explained before, where you sit in formal banquets is important. On this occasion, the bishop occupied the seat of honour, opposite the door. The seat on his immediate right is the first place of honour. Who was sitting here?— the government representative. This says a lot. The next most important person was Greg, sitting on the bishop's immediate left. Then you go right, left, right, left around the table. This is how we panned out: 4—Fr. M; 5—me; 6—Fr. T; 7—Sister M; 8—Fr. P; 9—our translator; 10—a local man; 11—the lady from Guiyang; 12 and 13 were government security personnel. Are they the least important? Cf. diagram 1.

The meal, of course, was excellent; they do not do things by halves. Beforehand our hosts had opened a bottle of *bai jiu,* which they had made themselves from broom corn; eminently palatable. They also opened a bottle of home-made wine, which I actually preferred. This brew was made by a Korean priest who was working nearby amongst people suffering from a contagious disease. They did not tell us what this disease is; it could be AIDS, or possibly tuberculosis; or something else. Tuberculosis, of course is more of an infectious disease. During the meal there were the usual toasts and speeches. After Greg had his say, I suggested to him that for his next birthday I should give him a trowel: he really knows how to lay it on. The facade is just so important and he outdoes the locals.

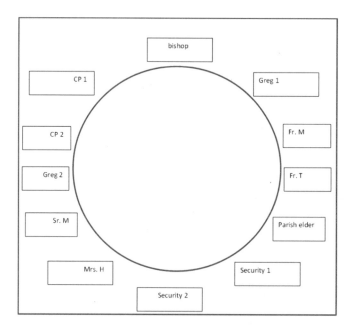

Diagram 1: Seating Positions

After the meal we went for a walk to get some exercise, and also to do some shopping. Greg wanted to buy a dress for Amy. She duly selected a blue dress and a pink. We all agreed that the pink was the one, and she is indeed "pretty in pink." I also wanted to buy a USB memory stick. We went into a shop where we found a 16 GB one at 110 Yuan. That is OK. But the man in charge saw us *laowai,* came over and told us that the price was 150 Yuan. If anyone ever tells you that there is no discrimination in this country, don't believe it; there definitely is. We walked out. Later, Francis offered to go on his own, so I gave him the money and off he went, going to another shop. He came back with the required item; and the price? ¬ 80 Yuan. What a difference! That was about $16.

This town certainly looks pretty at night, with lights reflecting off the river. So many towns in China are built on rivers; there are so many rivers. You can even see lights winding up to the top of a nearby mountain. We went to a bar to have a beer—or two … It was a great time. Spending time with people is so important and one of the great joys in life. I could even carry on a conversation with Amy, as her English had improved out of sight.

It was time to head back to our respective beds.

11.3.4: Sinan, De Jiang, Guiyang, Chongqing

The next morning, Saturday, we got up at 7.30, even though in fact we were awake well before this—no, not because we did not sleep well, but because we could not sleep any more. A man down the hallway was banging on someone's door, and yelling out. This was followed by someone in the car park persistently blowing his horn. This of course is the Great Wall Syndrome again, so powerful in this country. Nobody else exists; they are shut in. Consideration for others is not a factor, unless you are in the inner circle—*guanxi.*

Then the second disaster of the day occurred as it dawned on us that we had neglected to bring coffee. Oh no! How can I exist without my morning coffee?

The phone rang to say that we would be leaving at 8.30. That's fine and we wandered down in plenty of time. We had only just left the hotel when we were met by officers of the Security Bureau, who were here to make sure we were run out of town—but not yet: breakfast first, consisting of rice noodles. You can of course make noodles out of almost anything. The security guys joined us; now wasn't that nice of them? Meanwhile, Fr. M was in the driver's seat, waiting for us. It seemed he could not get out of here soon enough. We bid a sad farewell to Amy and Francis and off we went, getting under way about 9.00 a.m. It is highly unlikely that either of us will ever return.

We drove first to another town, called Sinan, where I used to work some years ago. When I was teaching in Tongren, I would occasionally come to Sinan to assist a young couple, D and A, who were running their own English teaching establishment. They are a great couple, and it is a pity that I would not be meeting them here. There again, we did not know that we would be coming, or at least I did not. This is not an information society, as I have said umpteen times before.

Sinan is yet another town built on the banks of a river, in this case the Wu Jiang, reputedly the fastest running river in China, and I have seen it fairly belting along. It joins the Yangtze at Fuling, just downstream of Chongqing. The mountainside on which Sinan is built is steep, so that the roads switch back and forth to gain altitude. Each level is connected by long flights of steps for the pedestrians. Like so many other towns in China, this too is undergoing profound changes, especially with the development of infrastructure. There is, for instance, a high bridge spanning the river, which was not there the last time I was here.

The reason for our visit became apparent when we drove a long way up the sides of the mountain, negotiating a very narrow concrete road, to a new church. The government had taken over the previous church, turning it into a school, so they were building, at government expense, a new church as a replacement. How about that! This country is just so full of contradictions. At about this time, in another part of the country, I heard of another Catholic church which had been in the process of being built for ten years. The government waited until it was finished, then bulldozed it. Their excuse?—no planning permit!

Photo 89: Catholic church of the Sacred Heart, Sinan

This new church in Sinan, was not at this time quite complete: there were no furnishings for instance. There was no bulldozer in sight either. The cost had been about 4 million Yuan, with around half a million still needed. The front facade is ornamented with a statue of the Sacred Heart—and the reason is interesting. The bishop told us that the parish was being dedicated to the Sacred Heart in honour of the MSC (Missionaries of the Sacred Heart) who had worked here. Great. Greg has suggested to the General that we might like to donate a statue of Our Lady of the Sacred Heart to go into the church. To this he has agreed, although suggesting, wisely, that the statue should be made here in Chinese style. It could be a lovely church, although the problem of access has to be addressed. We took lots of photographs, before saying goodbye to the other vehicle, containing the bishop, Sr. M and others, as they were heading off to climb Fan Jin Shan, a famous mountain not all that far away. I did climb it once, albeit via the cable car, apart from the final 1,000 steps.

Back on the road we headed for yet another town, De Jiang, for lunch. First we headed for the church, where we met another priest, Fr. B, whom we had met in Guiyang. He had been conducting a funeral here; apparently he is known for his excellent funeral services. One might say that people were dying to have him celebrate for them! We sat down eating fruit, while nothing much seemed to be happening. That is often the case in this country, where there is often a lot going on behind the scenes. In this instance, lunch was being organised.

Soon we piled into two cars and headed for town, where we "parked" in a narrow street. I have mentioned before the saying that people do not park their cars in this country: they simply abandon them. Such was the case here. Luckily, no one banged into us, even though the rear was sticking out into this narrow lane.

The meal, surprisingly, was hot pot. They were obviously being influenced by their northern neighbours. It also included pigs' trotters, in Greg's honour because I think everybody from here to the South Pole now knows that this is his favourite dish. It was very nice, but I did not eat too much as I knew there would be another meal in the evening. By 1.00 p.m. we were back on the road.

Once again we were on a new expressway and for a while all went smoothly. We flashed past Meitan, another town where I had spent some time teaching. I rang D, the man I had been working with, but he was away at the time. What a pity.

Our luck held until 3.45 p.m., when we joined a traffic jam. There had been a bingle where two vehicles had had a slight altercation. Undeterred, our noble driver drove down the emergency lane. Truly! He was noble enough, however, to nose his way into the queue when an emergency vehicle came chasing us. After passing the scene of the accident, the traffic increased speed again and thinned out. Good. We had our own minor altercation in the car as we tried to estimate our arrival in Guiyang, the more pessimistic opting for a late time. I am not going to tell you who the pessimist was—and no, it was not me.

Our good fortune did not last as we headed into another traffic jam. This time our inventive driver instituted yet another tactic. He headed off the road altogether, so that for quite some time we negotiated rough roads, bumping along every which way, till eventually we re-joined the expressway—well, it used to be express. How much did we gain? The answer was ... nothing. We were behind vehicles we had been in front of before. I am reminded of switching queues at an airport or wherever. You want to know which queue is the fastest? It is the one you just got out of.

The next thing that happened truly was a surprise. A motorcyclist weaved dangerously in front us—not wearing a helmet either. As we drove past him we saw that he was all of twelve years old if that. Goodness.

Further along we once again headed off the highway, taking all kinds of back roads, but this time in the city of Guiyang itself. We finally reached the cathedral at 5.45 p.m., one hour later than expected—expected by me, that is, but still earlier than our most pessimistic forecast. Nevertheless our 6.00 dinner appointment was postponed to 6.30 p.m.

One of Greg's former students lives in this city, together with her husband and son. We gathered at a Thai restaurant, reputedly the best in the city, and yes, the food was really excellent, especially the curry. It was good to see Echo again. Cicilia also joined us, and later a friend of hers, bringing her three year old son. We had a great night. Years later, Cicilia brought her own three year old son to visit us in Australia, but the less said about this, the better.

Next morning, Sunday, we were up at 7.00 because we wanted to get to 7.30 a.m. Mass. In Chongqing, the Mass begins at 8.30, but we need to leave our university in Lieshimu at 7.00 since the church is located some distance away, requiring a train journey plus a good deal of walking. So I really need to get up around 6.00. Here in Guiyang the church was about 10 metres away! We left straight after Communion to ensure I would have adequate time to get to the railway station, and we wanted breakfast first, especially that cup of coffee. Biscuits, cheese and marmalade plus some fruit made up the rest: quite a bit different from a Chinese breakfast. Greg and I walked out the back way to the main road so that I could catch a taxi to the railway station. We said goodbye, probably for the final time here in China. Next time I saw him was at Christmas, back in Australia.

I got to the station at 9.30, in plenty of time for the 10.26 scheduled departure time. Security was tight, especially after Muslims massacred people at Kunming railway station earlier in the year. Outside were two soldiers, one of them toting an automatic weapon. I entered the station, where ticket plus passport were checked: you cannot go in without a ticket and in this country you cannot go anywhere without your ID card, or passport if you are a foreigner. Thirdly, bags were sent through an X-ray scanner. Fourthly, each person was checked individually with a metal detector. It is now the same procedure you find at an airport. I was in plenty of time, giving me an opportunity to stretch my legs, since I would be sitting for the next nine hours. I also bought another cup of coffee: yes, they do have coffee. It seems civilisation has arrived. It was very nice and surprisingly cheap, at only 15 Yuan, or about $ 2.50.

The train left almost on time, at 10.30, but it was a K train, so we just chugged along. It took us three hours to get to Zunyi, only 170 km up the track. Here I had a talk with Grace, who lives there. I was sitting with a group of five young ladies, who all got off here, as did most other people on the train, at least in the carriage I was in. This meant it was largely empty, a rather rare occurrence in this overcrowded society. I enjoyed it. I was able to stretch my legs, and appreciate the quietness, without people shouting. I have no idea why there were so few people.

The countryside, as I have mentioned before, is fascinating. We would dive out of a tunnel, to find a steep sided valley, perhaps a village at the bottom and cloud covered mountains in the distance. Sorry, I have few photographs to illustrate the scene: I would dive for my camera, but by the time it was turned on ... it is all too late, as we plunged into yet one more tunnel. You get just tantalising glimpses. I did take some photographs, although my best are the ones I did not take! In any case it is difficult to take really good photographs, both because of the train's movement, but mostly due to the dirty windows.

It was a long journey, made to feel more so because these K trains stop for everything. We were actually sitting stationary, and I am not including station stops, for close on two hours: unbelievable! One mystery to me is why railway stations do not have their names prominently displayed. Most appear to have the station name on only one board, which is difficult to locate. Sometimes you only see it as you are leaving the station. Goodness, it really does make it difficult to know where you are.

We pulled into Chongqing on time at around 8.30 p.m., so that I was back in my apartment by 10.00. It had been a great weekend. It had been good to return to Shiqian and to see that our funds had been spent adequately. It was a pleasant surprise to visit that ancient town of Zhen Yuan. It was refreshing to see the new church at Sinan, and to know it was being dedicated to the Sacred Heart. It was wonderful to meet some marvellous people and to renew some long-standing friendships. In particular it was heart-warming to spend some time with Greg, whose contribution to China has been immense.

As for the seeming downside—being hassled by the security police—I think it is rather funny. We are not Muslims intending to slaughter people or blow up installations. We are in fact no threat to the government. All their posturing is rather futile, because in spite of—or perhaps because of—their persecutions, God's work will be done. When we are being persecuted I rejoice, because it means we are doing something right. It is when we are sailing along that we are more likely to lose direction.

11.4: Farewell to Erica, Sunny and Amy

You grow close to your students—some more than others. Those I taught for three years in Tongren, Guizhou Province, were and remain very special to me. Amongst these is Erica—and she was getting married. I call her my "adoptive daughter" because she calls me "Dad"; she had even visited Australia in 2009. The wedding was set for 13th August, partly so that I could be there before returning to Australia. I was hoping she was marrying the right man at the right time.

11.4.1: Chongqing to Na Yong

Erica was getting married on Tuesday. Sort of. She was getting married on Wednesday. Sort of. Confused? Wait: all will be revealed.

On Tuesday morning I set out for the journey to Na Yong, and what a journey it would prove to be. Those who have travelled with me vicariously over many a journey might think that everything had been experienced that could possibly be experienced: not so.

I set my alarm for 6.20 a.m. to give me plenty of time; I do hate rushing. I left my apartment at 7.30, still a little early for public transport, also bearing in mind that it takes two hours to get to the airport. I caught a taxi instead of the train. The traffic was heavy, so that it took nearly an hour to reach the airport. I told the driver which airline I was using so that he could drop me at the correct door: it is about 500 metres from one end of the terminal to the other, and each carrier has its assigned location. Everything went smoothly, so that I had plenty of time to check in and wander around.

My China Southern flight took off only slightly behind time, a little after 10.30 a.m. I had a window seat—as usual—over the wing—again as usual—but it was too cloudy to see anything anyway. We landed at Guiyang airport at 11.30 a.m. The problem now was to get out to the long distance bus station at Jing Yang; both the airport and bus station are a long way from town, but in different directions. I thought there may be a connecting bus, but there wasn't, so I just had to settle for a taxi. It took 50 minutes costing 81 Yuan (about $16).

At the long distance bus station the first thing to do was to find out which window I needed in order to buy my ticket for Na Yong, as there are about 30 windows: you could waste a lot of time if you went to the wrong one. Miraculously, everything went like clockwork: I found the right window, lined up, bought the ticket for 125 Yuan, all by 1.00 p.m. Then I looked at the ticket. Yikes! The bus leaves at 1.10. I hurried to the other end of the ticket office, went through security, and out through the gates to face dozens of buses. Goodness, which one is mine? In these situations, the Good Lord has come to the rescue by providing us with … tongues. I asked. I found it. I was on. Whew!

I sat back to relax and enjoy the ride, even though first indications were not good. This bus was old and dirty. By the time I had boarded there were few seats left, which is not surprising, considering that I had only just made it. The seat I first went to had a stain on it which looked very much as if someone had been sick. Yuck! I took a seat further back, only to discover that this ride was going to be very bumpy and noisy as everything seemed to be rattling. We left at 1.20 p.m. with a toilet stop at 3.30. This was good as I had not had time to go since leaving Chongqing, and one never knows when the next stop will be. You learn to take opportunities as they arise—one of the essential practicalities of travel.

From Guiyang to Na Yong is not far, at least not as the proverbial crow flies: only about 170 km. Yet we went on and on. Mind you we were not travelling all that fast, especially when one considers both how mountainous the terrain is and how closely settled it is. We were no sooner out of one village than we were into another. I was told we would arrive at 7.30 p.m. Wow! six hours for such a short distance. We did not, but proceeded to go on and on. I got a call from Amy, one of my former students, who was going to meet me at the bus station. "Where are you?" Blowed if I know.

We finally arrived at Na Yong at 9.10 p.m., nearly eight hours after leaving Guiyang. The bus stopped at the edge of town and we all got off. Strange. Is this the bus station? No it was not. The station was another kilometre further on. I should have stayed on board. Oh dear! Amy and I spent the next hour looking for each other, but without success. I rang Erica, and she told me what hotel she had booked for me, so I hailed a taxi to take me there, the Wen Zhou—and that is where Amy and I finally met. What a shemozzle!

I dumped my bags then all four us—Amy, her husband, a work colleague and I—went off to have a meal. For some reason this taxi driver refused to take payment from me, even though it was only 3 Yuan. I do not know why. It was 10.30 by now so everyone was hungry. In fact we were lucky to find a restaurant still open. The meal was hotpot and in fact was too hot for me. I was offered a choice of chicken or bacon. "Bacon, please."

"Sorry, we have no bacon." Then why offer it? They hope that you will choose chicken so that they do not lose face. During the meal someone—no, not me—knocked over my beer, spilling it over my trousers. And these were the only trousers I had brought.

It was around midnight by the time I hit the sack. What a day. I had travelled in one plane, one bus and four taxis. I was tired, but the people next door were carrying on a conversation in loud voices. Later on someone started yelling out on the street. It is the Great Wall Syndrome operating again. Nevertheless, I did manage to get some sleep. See you in the morning.

11.4.2: The wedding

I slept reasonably well but not long enough, and in fact had a slight headache. It disappeared later, no doubt helped by my Western breakfast, especially that coffee. I looked out the hotel window, to get a better look at this town in daylight.

Not all streets were paved, so there was a bit of mud around. Nevertheless the ubiquitous high rise buildings were going up and up.

At 8.30 a.m. Amy, her husband and a friend arrived. I had already packed and was waiting in the foyer. I had eaten breakfast in my room, but they had not eaten at all, so I gave them my two meal tickets which I had not used. They produced two others from somewhere, so the four of us went into the dining room. This was my second breakfast; maybe I am a Hobbit from the Shire.

The groom's brother soon arrived with a car and we all piled in, all six of us. We really were squashed, bearing in mind that we were also carrying food for the celebrations. I noticed that some of this food was making a noise. What is that? It was live fish flapping around inside a plastic bag. Poor fish. Maybe there were a lot of fish, as we were packed in like sardines. Amy was sitting on someone's lap—no it was not mine—and she was six months pregnant. Did anybody mention seat belts? How on earth am I going to settle back into Australia after this kind of life?

This drive was interesting in more ways than one. Apart from the fish, including the sardines, we were on the wrong side of the road as often as not, driving over double yellow lines. What on earth are they for? Meanwhile, our intrepid driver was blowing his horn at anything which moved, or which he thought was maybe about to move. One road was closed to trucks, with rocks across the road, leaving just enough room for our car to squeeze through. Do not be surprised at anything. After about 40 minutes, we arrived at the house of the groom's parents.

Now I was able to meet Erica, the beautiful bride, and she certainly was looking radiant on this day, in spite of not having had much sleep the night before. If I might put on my fashion hat, she was wearing a red dress, yellow coat and red high heeled shoes. I asked her if this was the first time she had worn high heeled shoes. No, it is the second: the first time being for her wedding photographs. Red is the colour of luck, very important for weddings; red and yellow are the national colours. Her hair was done up, in two braids. She was wearing make-up and false eyelashes. She was quite a picture—beautiful.

I had been to a number of weddings in China, and each one had been different. In this case, they had spent Tuesday at the bride's parents' home, feasting all day. They were living a fair distance from here, so Erica and her friend Sunny had left at midnight, to travel all night, only arriving at 5.40 on Wednesday morning. Yet she looked as fresh as a daisy. Oh the resilience of youth. I gathered that what was going to happen today was more or less a repeat of what had happened yesterday, but with the groom's family, not the bride's. I was pleased though that Erica's two brothers had both been present at the family home. Hence the wedding took place over two days, both Tuesday and Wednesday.

The day went as follows. There is courtyard of about 100 square metres, surrounded by houses. This was partly covered by canvas sheeting, billowing in the breeze. Round tables, each seating about ten people, were deployed in the courtyard and in two rooms of one house. People ate in sessions, so that as one lot finished, another would begin. All day a group of women—naturally—were kept busy, cooking, setting up, serving the food, clearing up, washing up, then doing it all again. Breakfast was soon followed by lunch, which in turn was soon followed by dinner. There was hardly a break between the meals, with some 150 people or so to be fed.

There is a small extension on the side of the house, perhaps two square metres in size, built of stone, with a slate roof. It is on two levels, the bottom is enclosed, while the top has a low doorway. This is the toilet. The floor is built of stone slabs, with two slits, and these are very narrow, so your aim had better be good. I noticed that for some people, their aim obviously needed some improving. Paper is dropped down the hole, or simply thrown into the corner. That's it. Water is elsewhere.

Meanwhile, the role of the bridal couple was simply to mix and talk. Consequently I spent a large part of the day in a bedroom with Erica, Sunny and Amy, all former students. I had actually been to Amy's wedding over National Day last year: cf. section 4.3. We also chatted with anybody else who happened to come in, or wandered around outside. And of course we ate. This bedroom was piled with bedding and suit cases, the latter being filled not with clothes, but with sunflower seeds and sweets. Enormous quantities of sunflower seeds were consumed, the floor being covered with the husks, later being swept up. The children present preferred the sweets.

What did not happen was the taking of vows: "I, Adonis, take you, Aphrodite …" In fact there was no formal ceremony at all: no wedding march, no grand entrance, no toasts, no speeches, no dancing, and—surprise, surprise—there were no little red envelops (*hong bao*), in which the guests give money to the young couple. This is one way to give the funds which many young married couples desperately need to set up house. I was told that it was not the custom in

377

this village. This was the only wedding I had been to in China where there had been no *hong baos*.

There are, it seems, three stages in the wedding ceremony. The first is the taking of photographs, perhaps months in advance, with the couple dressed in about six different outfits, these photographs being mounted in heavy albums with some enlarged to decorate the walls. This is expensive, costing 4,000 to 8,000 Yuan. The better ones are enlarged and placed on the wall: you can see two of them in photograph 90.The second stage is the wedding banquet, which we were having, and in this instance, there were two banquets in each of the parental homes. The third stage is to register the marriage with the state authorities, a step yet to be accomplished in this case, yet this is the official moment when the couple become married, at least in the eyes of the state.

Photo 90: author with Erica and Sunny

At this wedding, I was not the celebrant; nor did I have any other role. I was simply there, yet it was such an honour. We live in a society dominated by "doing", whereas it is more important to be simply "being", in this case being with Erica and her husband at this most important occasion in their lives. I am sensible of the privilege of being welcomed by this family. Thank you. I do hope this marriage is successful and that they do "live happily ever after". He certainly seems to be very much in love with her, which is good, and I have no doubt that he will benefit from her practical thrifty sense. I have never known Erica to waste a yuan. She is the best bargainer I have ever known, being past master at haggling prices down to get the cheapest deal.

For most of this day of Erica's wedding, I sat in a bedroom chatting, mostly with Erica, Sunny and Amy. I do appreciate that they took this time to spend with me. God alone knows when I would be seeing them again—if ever.

As we drove in I had noticed a waterfall not too far away, so determined to find an opportunity to visit it. After lunch the house quieted down for a while, as some people enjoyed their siesta. I sneaked out, so to speak, walking with one of the young men. The falls are only about a kilometre away and are quite spectacular. I estimated the height to be about 60 metres, and with a fair volume of water coming over they were magnetic in their attractiveness. Cf. photograph 91. A road runs around the head of this vale close to the falls, and many a motorist would stop and gaze before continuing on. We humans really like water.

Photo 91: waterfall

The water falls into a pool, which overflows to gurgle down the vale. Beside the stream a cow was grazing contentedly. The hillside is steep, and—as you find in so many places in this highly settled country—terraced. I am amazed at the amount of work which has gone into building these, no doubt over many generations, hundreds or even thousands of years ago.

Sunny had a sleep in the afternoon, a well needed one, after being on the go for two days' straight. Erica collapsed in the evening, sitting up in a chair, not in or on a bed. She slept deeply too, until awoken by some children coming in to look for lollies. Late in the evening, she began to remove her make-up, which she had been literally itching to do. This is just not her scene. First to come off were the false eyelashes, then the ear-rings. She rarely wears any jewellery and never make-up. Next she washed her face and hair. Ah, that's better. The high heels stayed on till bedtime. One reason why women wear these is to increase their height, and Erica is of small stature—and of course, they are elegant. Oddly enough, this footwear did not originate with women, but with men. Truly. Not that men were trying to increase their height or to appear elegant, but for an entirely different reason. High heels were part of one's riding gear, enabling the foot to grip the stirrup more firmly, when riding a horse.

After the evening meal I went for another walk, this time a little shorter, and this time with Erica and Sunny. We met an elderly gentleman who wanted to know where we were going. "wo*men qu sanbu le,"* I replied: we are just going for a walk. I asked the others if he was one of the guests. No, he was the host, the father of the groom! Oh dear. I had not recognised him.

At around 10.30 p.m. we called it a night, somewhat earlier than I had anticipated. I think a number of people was very tired. I was given a room to myself, on the other side of the courtyard, or in other words, in the house of one of the neighbours. It had a largish size bed, so I asked if we should not have two people here, but no, they insisted that I have it all to myself. They are generous people. I hope somebody was not too inconvenienced. Erica and Sunny shared a bed. That's right—not the bride and groom. I made sure I had my torch with me—another essential travelling item. I knew I would need it if I got up in the middle of the night answering a call of Nature, not that there is the slightest chance, mind you, of falling down the cracks.

Not everyone went to bed, as some began playing the ever popular mah-jong, which they continued to do until 2.00 a.m. The room was right next to where Erica and Sunny were sleeping, but I think it would have taken an earthquake to rouse them. I heard that one lady made a lot of money. I actually do not believe in gambling, which is one reason why I never learnt to play this game, even though I had opportunities.

The next morning I arose around 7.00. The household and guests were already astir. There is a large vat of water in the courtyard which is used for one's morning ablutions; there is no sink, so the waste simply goes onto the ground. Soon breakfast was being prepared, with the first shift at 8.00 a.m., which is when Erica and Sunny finally emerged. We were wearing the same clothes as yesterday, since there were no showers: I had only a wash the night before.

Clean up began last night, but continued today. The tarpaulin cover forming a temporary shelter had gone. Empty beer bottles were put into a large sack and other rubbish collected. A cow in its stall was bellowing; maybe she needed milking. The pig near the toilet was grunting away, adding to this bucolic cacophony. It was nice.

Meanwhile two boys dropped in for a chat, albeit with some language problems, as the one in high school had very little English, while the one in middle school had none. This surprised me, as I had thought that everyone would be studying English these days, but we are somewhat out in the sticks here, a long way from the capital, Guiyang.

11.4.3: Na Yong

It was peaceful in this country district. I liked the sounds of the animals in the morning. Some rubbish was being burnt, the smoke wafting over the courtyard, giving it an ethereal quality in the early morning light. In one corner, there was still a table set up, people sitting around eating breakfast. Cf. photograph 92. After breakfast, as we were getting ready to leave, eight men came huffing and puffing into the courtyard, carrying some heavy steel equipment. I still do not know what it was, but it looked like a thresher.

Photo 92: courtyard

We left the house at 9.45 a.m., walking down the road into the valley, across the stream just below that waterfall, then up to the main road. It was a lovely walk with Erica and Sunny on this most pleasant, cool morning, the sky cloudy, the sun peeping through from time to time. It took about 25 minutes to reach the main road. Erica was still wearing her high heel shoes, which was a bit of a surprise; Sunny's footwear was more suitable for walking. No sooner had we reached this road, than Erica hailed a passing ten seater minibus, and in we hopped. Is this a public bus?—if that is not something of a tautology, since "bus" is short for "omnibus", meaning "for all". It had no markings of any description, but the driver took us into Na Yong for 10 Yuan each, and as we travelled other people got on or got off, so obviously it was a bus. The locals knew.

We drove back along the same route we had used on the way out, through a gap in those concrete blocks preventing trucks and other large vehicles using a particular section of road. Yet how different was this drive from the first. This driver was slow and careful; he gave way to others and kept off his horn. He cannot be Chinese, surely!

By 10.30 we were back in Na Yong, getting off near the bus station—yes, I knew where it was now, after the debacle of my arrival. Here we booked our tickets for departure on the morrow. Just ten minutes up the road, we booked into a hotel, the Tian He Jiu Dian, which just happens to be directly across the road from Erica's apartment. The name of this hotel means "Heavenly Rest"; well it was certainly adequate for my needs, even if not quite the standard of the first hotel I had used in this town.

The apartment being rented by Erica and her husband was reasonably large, consisting, however, or just two rooms, one being the bedroom and the other being for everything else. For cooking they were using a small electric stove; there was no gas. If you wished to use the bathroom, or toilet, or laundry, you used the communal facilities across the hall; no, there was no en suite. For this they were paying 300 Yuan per month, or about $50, which includes electricity and water. Yes, this was very cheap indeed by Australian standards, but Australia is just so expensive.

We had a lunch of noodles at a nearby restaurant. There are plenty of these small family owned eateries. One feature I like is that one could add the amount of *lajiao* wanted, according to taste. Having lived in Chongqing for three years, I do like some chilli in my food. I did say "some": Sunny's bowl was red with chillies'!

After lunch, Sunny made use of my hotel room to have a lovely hot shower. I would have mine in the evening. This hotel did not have that warning which I had noticed in the Wen Zhou hotel: "Be careful landslip." Goodness, is the hotel about to slide down the hill? After the shower it was time for a rest, including a nap, especially for the ladies, as no day is complete without the afternoon siesta.

In the late afternoon I went for an hour's walk around the town, exploring this way and that. One can discover all sorts of interesting things, such as a small park, with a statue of two scholars from a bygone age playing chess. It is nice. The streets are a little hilly and windy, with no footpaths, so people walk on the road. Goods from shops spill out onto the roadway, while the people carry all kinds of goods—even children—often in baskets strapped to their backs.

Erica, Sunny and Amy joined me at 6.15 p.m., when we all went off to have our evening meal—hotpot, plus a beer for me. Hotpot is a favourite meal in this part of China, including Sichuan, Chongqing and Guizhou. The inner person filled we walked to Erica's school, where she was teaching English. The road outside is actually called Zhong Xue Lu, or Middle School Road. Now this town is not the largest city you ever did come across, yet this middle school is the largest in the province, boasting some 8,000 students. Goodness, it is a small town in itself. I have no idea why it is so big, though of course there is no competition from Catholic schools or other private enterprises. I did not get a good look at it, since it was so dark at this time of night.

Our walk back was leisurely with many stops—at shops of course. Women love to shop. Soon it dawned on me that Erica was trying to find something to buy for me. While I really appreciated the intention, it was not necessary and in fact I did not need anything. It was 9.45 by the time we got back to my hotel: time for bed. I had done a lot of walking today, and I was feeling tired. I had a shower before hitting the sack. Tomorrow I would be heading back to Guiyang, where I intended to stay a night before flying back to Chongqing on Saturday. I had just drifted off to sleep when I was awoken by the TV in the next room, sounding as if it was on full volume. Yes, that is right: it is the Great Wall Syndrome operating again. Consideration for others is not part of this culture, unless *guanxi* comes into it. I had trouble getting back to sleep. Goodnight.

11.4.4: Return to Chongqing

On Friday morning I set my alarm for 7.00, but in fact was already up by then. I had my usual breakfast in my room, packed, checked out and was ready to meet the ladies by 7.50. I crossed the road to meet them outside Erica's apartment. Erica and Sunny went off to buy their breakfast, giving me an opportunity to give a *hong bao* to Amy, who could then pass it on to Erica after we had left. Last October I had been to Amy's wedding and had given her a *hong bao*, so it was no problem. I did not want a scene with Erica, as she would probably refuse to accept any gift.

We walked to the bus station, only about ten minutes away, but instead of walking around the front and going through the gate as any normal passengers would do, Erica led us in by the back gate, which is the exit gate for the buses. We had to duck under the barrier. This meant we were immediately in the bus parking area, which was crowded with both buses and people. How the buses managed to manoeuvre in such a confined space is a minor miracle, especially with people milling around. Naturally all this was accompanied by much blaring of horns.

I stashed my backpack underneath and hopped aboard. It was a sad farewell to Erica, as I did not know if I would see her again, but one never knows. Maybe she will come to Australia one day. We had seats 3 and 4 allocated to us, but found they were not together. Sunny managed to persuade a young man to swap so that we could sit together. By 8.45 a.m. we were on our way.

Na Yong is situated in a valley, resulting in a climb of perhaps 600 metres over steep escarpments, which contained some delightful waterfalls. A roadside sign reads; "Love life, no drugs", so I gather that drugs is something of a problem here, as it is in the West. It is a scourge accompanying greater wealth. You do not buy drugs if you need every cent just to survive.

Our journey was slow, as we negotiated roadside markets. I could have put my hand out the window to do my shopping. As usual at these markets, not only food but many household items were on sale. I liked the colourful cloths. One shoemaker was working his trade. You could even get your hair cut, should you so desire, sitting by the side of the road. Judging from what I saw it was more like shearing than cutting. Cf. photograph 93. The road was rough too. As for the inward journey, our speed was slow as we eased our way through town after town, village after village. For the first hour I rested and read, while Sunny slept.

At 10.00 a.m. we had our first stop at a small town, close to the public facilities, for those whose necessity outweighed their squeamishness. It was tiny, with just two holes, meaning it took time if there was any sort of queue, although some did not bother about the holes in the ground, but simply used the corner. There was no water, definitely a *cesuo* 1 rating (toilet rating of 1 out of 5). Below the holes, about two metres away is a small stream. Boy, I do not think I would like to drink that water. Above it two boys were playing: I would not want to fall in either.

Photo 93: roadside hair cutting

385

You may recall that it took almost eight hours to cover the distance from Guiyang to Na Yong, even though it is only about 170 kilometres. This return journey would be even longer, not because our bus was worse: in fact it was bigger and much more comfortable. No, it was because there was a damaged bridge which had to be circumvented. This meant heading north close to Bijie city, then veering east, before approaching Guiyang from the north, rather than from the west, adding a further 200 kilometres to the length of the trip, although only two hours on the clock, giving us a ten hour journey.

4.45 p.m. we had a petrol stop. It may be of interest to see how the prices here compared with Australia—or elsewhere. We filled up, taking a massive 127.8 litres, which cost 945.8 Yuan. This works out at 7.4 Yuan per litre, or about $1.20. This made it cheaper than Australia, but when you factor in PPP, where the purchasing power of I Yuan and $1 are about the same, petrol is much dearer here in China.

We had been climbing towards Bijie, which has an altitude of 1700 metres, but once we started swinging east, we began to descend towards Guiyang, which is just over 1,000 metres above sea level. We crossed lots of rivers, and in photograph 94 one can see what the scenery is like. I was surprised to find a woman walking across this bridge on the open highway—no footpath. I guess one is never far from habitation.

Photo 94: bridge over another gorge

We finally arrived in Guiyang at 7.15 p.m. The bus station is a long way out of town, so we joined a queue for a local bus, which would take us to the railway. It was a half hour wait. No. 224 bus got us to the railway by 9.00 p.m. where the first priority was for Sunny to buy her rail ticket for the following day, or at least pick it up, as she had already bought it on line. The machine spat it out in no time. I already had my air ticket.

The second priority was to find accommodation. We tried Home Inn first, but it was full, so we marched down to the Railway Hotel instead, where I had stayed several times before. I was surprised that Sunny had never been to Guiyang, even though she was not that far away in Tongren. That is like living in Bathurst but never having visited Sydney. We booked our two rooms at around 275 Yuan per room.

The third priority was to eat. This turned out to be an extraordinary experience. We found a noodle place, not far from our hotel; while it did not have a lot of variety, it was good food and inexpensive. Sunny had tonnes of *lajiao,* while I added only a little—and I had a beer. The proprietor wandered across to have a chat, and turned out to be a most genial mein host. There was something different about him. Is he Chinese? He told us he is Tibetan, and then I noticed the prayer beads wrapped around his wrist. His wife is Chinese, and comes from Chengdu. They have two sons and two daughters: that is unusual. He is quite religious, talking a lot about the Potala Palace.

As we were finishing, he offered us roast lamb as an extra. How could we refuse? These turned up on skewers. To go with them, he opened no less than four bottles of beer. I had already drunk one bottle. His wife joined us, as we proceeded to drink and chat some more; he does speak English. We had a great time. When travelling, one can meet some extraordinary people. Time to head back to our hotel for a shower and bed.

The next morning I awoke early, with plenty of time to get organised. In this hotel breakfast is included in the tariff, providing the usual Chinese fare, except that they had hot milk. I ate little, but with the restaurant situated on the 19th floor I got a good view of the city; our rooms were on the 16th. When I say "good view", this city does not appear to have a lot to commend it, as it is largely drab, crowded and noisy. The locals, however, are really proud of their city, as indeed most people are about their own. The hotel has a central hub, from which radiate three wings, so 120 degrees apart. It is very attractive.

Photograph 95 shows the railway station taken from this hotel. There is a pleasing concourse out the front, with lots of buses on the left hand side. The traffic is channelled rather narrowly, and if you want a taxi, you must walk for some distance down the road. I am sure it could be organised better. The other thing to notice is the sea of people, and this was just a normal day. You should see it during one of the public holidays, especially Spring Festival.

Photo 95: Guiyang railway station

Sunny had a train to catch at 9.00 a.m.; I walked with her to the station. One of the things one notices these days at major Chinese railway stations is the heavy military presence, since Muslim terrorists had been indiscriminately killing people at stations. China is a particular target because it has taken over the Muslim region in the north west. It was time to say goodbye to Sunny, and a sad goodbye it is, since she is a truly delightful person, and I enjoy her company so much. Maybe some time in the future she too may come to Australia. Back in my hotel room, I had a "proper" Western breakfast, including coffee.

At 9.15 a.m. I checked out of the hotel and walked down the street a little till I could hail a taxi. The trip out to the airport took about 45 minutes, but what a journey it was. First we had a detour to pick up another passenger, a businessman, and we were off. There was a lot of traffic, and in fact this city is notorious for its traffic congestion. Our driver was all over the place, trying to get through, darting into any possible space, with no thought of signalling of course. Once we got onto the freeway, the foot went down and off we shot. We were still darting in and out of traffic, changing lanes frequently, but at greater speed. The driver was young, and his skills were limited. Speed + youth +

inexperience = disaster. We survived. Our guardian angels were really working overtime.

At the airport, announcements were flagging flight delays, which is normal. I had a second cup of coffee at the terminal, and was preparing to wander around for a while, expecting that my flight too would be delayed. Imagine my surprise when boarding began at 11.45 a.m., 35 minutes before we were due to take off. We began to taxi from the terminal 10 minutes early, and I do not think this has ever happened before. Life is full of surprises. We were even served lunch. It was a most pleasant flight, with me at the window, as usual: I do like to see, not that there is much to see usually, especially due to the heavy air pollution. On this occasion, we flew over the Yangtze River, so I had a good view. It was rather murky looking at this point and narrow; elsewhere it broadens considerably. I had been living close to this mighty river for the past three years, but now it was time to say "goodbye".

Photo 96: flying over the Yangtze River

We landed in Chongqing 10 minutes early too at 1.00 p.m. Everything was going so smoothly, and this continued on the CRT (Chongqing Rail Transport) or metro, so that I was back in my apartment by 3.20 p.m. Wow!

These past four days had been magical. From a travelling perspective it ran the gamut from smooth and efficient to rough with problems. This would also be my final journey in China, after so many. All things come to an end. There would be one more trip, but this would be within Chongqing city, after which I would return to Australia. In the meantime, I had a few days to pack, which turned out to be a slow process, considering that I had ten years' of accumulated possessions.

11.5: Farewell to Chongqing

11.5.1: End of Semester

It was time for me to say goodbye.

Naturally I said goodbye to the students class by class. We also needed to say goodbye to the other AITECE teachers, with whom we had formed a wonderful group. We had been meeting twice a week, sharing prayer and a meal in my apartment on Tuesday nights and going to Mass together on Sundays. We had our final Mass together, our final meal together and our final coffee together. Other people were also included, especially people we had met at church, like Reine. Cyril was the first to leave, returning to the US, then John and Anne returned to England, Michael returned to Australia, leaving just me. John too would not be returning to China, as he had work needing to be done back home. My flight back to Australia did not leave until 26th August. Why so late?

There were a number of reasons for this. I wanted to do some travel for the last time, intending to visit Neimenggu, or Inner Mongolia. China, of course, is a massive empire and there was plenty I had not seen. There will always be plenty I will never see of course and nor is it desirable to see everything. What is important is what you gain from the places you do see.

The second reason was that I was still teaching the doctors and staff at Hewlett Packard, not finishing until 24th July.

The third reason was that Erica, was getting married on 13th August and I had been invited. Cf. section 11.4.

The final reason for my late departure is that I wanted to get my MS finished, "A Traveller in China". This was a long process. For one whole week it had been head down and tail up as I made corrections and changes to the final proofs, before sending the manuscript to the publisher. It was finally finished, at least as far as I was concerned. I found that every time I went over it I would make yet more changes. I was never satisfied, as I saw more and more problem areas, some minor, some more important.

Meanwhile, the clouds had cleared, the rains had gone—after several months—and it was hot. People were sick of all the rain, and it was good to see the sun again, but the heat is the downside. Each day the temperature was into the high 30s, approaching 40 degrees. I would have loved to be able to swim, but the university pool was closed for demolition. What a pity.

11.5.2: Expo Gardens

My final week in China. For the young, time seems to stretch endlessly into the future, but this is an illusion. All things come to an end. My ten years in China were now over, but what wonderful years they were, ones that I will always treasure. I have been so fortunate.

In my final week, I packed, slowly, leaving most things behind, to be put aside for whomever would come after me. These included not only clothes, but kitchenware, bedding and teaching resources. Much had to be thrown out. I was conscious of the fact that I had too much "stuff"—far too much—but I have always been a bit of a magpie.

It was also a time to say "goodbye" to special people. There is one young couple who are very special. They are actively involved on the local church, and are so faith filled. We had a farewell meal in a very nice restaurant indeed. The ambience was truly beautiful, indeed palatial. Naturally, they paid: it is so difficult to pay such is the generosity of many Chinese. Reine lives in Ciqikou, an old village not far from our university, which is Chongqing's premier tourist attraction, and on weekends is excessively crowded.

I really wanted to visit Expo Garden in the city before I left, but each day was drizzling—not the best circumstances—so we waited, until the very last day, when the sun shone. Before I left I needed to see our *waiban*, the one looking after our affairs, but day after day she did not appear. Finally she said she would be in on Monday, 25th. What a pity, as that day the weather was fine, and it would be ideal to go to the gardens and would be my final day. I waited. She was not in her office. "Oh, I'll be in at 3.00 p.m." I was not waiting till then. I left with a friend at 10.40 a.m., catching the train to Lianglukou on line 1 then transferring to line 3, heading north towards the airport. We arrived at 12.00 noon, surprised that the entrance fee was only 20 Yuan: I had thought it would be more.

For the next three hours, we wandered around this park, in warm sunshine, soaking up the beauty of well-kept gardens, a large lake, fountains, beautiful stone bridges and pavilions. This park is large, at 2.2 square kilometres, with the lake in the middle occupying some 0.53 square kilometres. Not many cities in the world would have anything as large, although Sydney does have its Centennial Parklands in the east of the city, where I ride my bike. These comprise 3.6 square kilometres. Expo Gardens is situated in a valley, with full use being made of the natural contours of the land. The scenery is truly delightful.

Photo 97: beautiful Expo Gardens

It is hard for me to express my emotions concerning this very special day. Not only was it my final day in China, but it was also my farewell to Bernadette, who had been with me on many a journey, and a more delightful companion you could not find. Thank you.

Some six bridges, in that traditional Chinese design, which I admire so much, cross the central lake at narrow points. There are pavilions scattered around, in which one can sit and admire the scenery—or have lunch, which is what we did in one of them, from where we could view three of these bridges. At one location there is a large waterwheel, not being used for any practical purpose, except to decorate the landscape. The same could be said for a very large yellow duck, floating in the lake; I thought it was a little tacky. There are a couple of small fountains to add their beautifying effect. Around the lake are sections set aside as gardens, representing cities in China or overseas. Each one is delightful, apart from the propaganda aspect of some. Flowers abound, adding to the beauty. So if you ever go to Chongqing, I would highly recommend a visit to this delightful place, somewhere to get away from the rat race without needing to go too far, somewhere to stroll around surrounded by beauty yet without danger of being run over or deafened by traffic noise. This was such a perfect, yet poignant day.

As we walked I took lots of photographs—naturally. It did seem just a little incongruous that behind this rural style landscape one could see the tall skyscrapers of the city, as in photograph 98. Anywhere in this highly populous country you are never far from people, and we were in a large city here.

Photo 98: a perfect spot

I wanted to get back home in time to see Luo Xiao, our *waiban,* so I rang her to ask her what time she would leave the office: 5.00 p.m. It was time to turn back, although unfortunately I took a wrong road, which seemed initially to be heading in the right direction, but which was taking us further away. Oh dear. My delightful and charitable companion refrained from saying, "I told you so!"

We came by train, but I thought it might be faster if we went back by bus, so that I could be there before 5.00 p.m. We should have taken the train, as I had not factored in peak hour traffic. I missed her. Oh well, I would just have to see her in the morning before I left. That night I relaxed and even watched a movie.

11.5.3: Return to Australia. 26th August

At 10.30 a.m. on Tuesday the university car plus driver, arrived to take Bernadette and me to the airport. It was a large Audi, so it had plenty of room. I told him to drive us to the domestic terminal, not international, since I would be flying to Shanghai first, where I would change planes for the flight to Australia. At Chongqing airport, I said "goodbye" to Bernadette, who would be flying to Nanchang with Sichuan Airlines, while I was going to Sydney via Shanghai with Air China. Both flights were delayed, which is normal, but we would not have it any differently for my final trip, now would we? Our time together had been very special indeed.

Yesterday's beautiful weather was gone, to be replaced by the usual leaden skies. How fortunate we were that we had that absolutely gorgeous day for my final day in China, visiting that idyllic park.

It took an hour to get through the traffic. At Chongqing airport, I could only book my luggage as far as Shanghai, meaning I would have to re-book them at Pudong Airport. This was a nuisance: Air China still left a lot to be desired, but they were improving. Reine and her boyfriend, Michael, also drove to the airport to say goodbye. We had a light meal together, before exchanging farewell gifts. I also blessed their engagement rings, which is really asking God to bless them. He already has and will continue to do so. All too soon, at 12.30 p.m., it was time to bid a sad farewell.

At 2.30 p.m. my plane took off, arriving at Pudong Airport at 4.30 p.m., after an uneventful flight. Coming in to land at Shanghai one got a very good view of the pollution, meaning that one got very poor view of anything else. In the terminal I noticed a most interesting sign at a drinks machine: "This facility does not work because of its malfunction." Really? Whoever would have thought that!

I needed to pick up my bags at the domestic terminal and cart them across to the international terminal, where they needed to be booked through to Sydney. No sooner had I done that that I was accosted by a young woman wanting money. I wasn't born yesterday. "Why do you want money?"

"I'm hungry." Perhaps. I took her to an eatery and bought her something to eat: she had only a little. It was money that she was after.

By 5.45 p.m. I was through customs and had found my way to the correct boarding gate. Here I sat down and proceeded to ring as many people as I possibly could to say goodbye. This took a good deal of time. Finally, I got through to everybody and was actually on the final call when my phone ran out of money, so I had judged the amount I needed to a nicety. I had done the same with my transport card in Chongqing: by the time I left it had less than 1 Yuan left on it. We boarded at 7.00 p.m., and sat for some time on the tarmac, just to ensure that we would keep up the standards by not leaving on time. I was not in a hurry. While we waited safety instructions were given to us, then again, then again ... Goodness, is this plane safe? Or is this the epitome of the entertainment they are offering? We finally took off at 8.40 p.m., having sat for nearly an hour on the tarmac. No explanation was given, but you can bet your bottom Yuan that it was because of crowded skies, not helped by the fact that around 90% of China's airspace is reserved for the military. China is obsessed with its military. We began our 7,874 km flight to Sydney.

At 9.30 p.m. the drinks cart arrived. I asked for a bloody Mary. The flight attendant (air hostess) did not know what it was, so I explained. *"Mei you."* OK, what about a white wine. Yes, they had that, but only with meals. I settled for a tomato juice—sort of half a bloody Mary. When the meal (fish for me), did arrive, alas there was no white wine to go with it. This is served after the meal. Goodness. Did I say this airline was improving? Yet there are weightier problems in the world. At 10.10 p.m. the wine finally arrived, a flat white, which tasted terrible, more like turps. I asked to see the label. Yes, it was a Chinese wine, called Dragon ... something or other. I had deliberately asked for a white, rather than a red, as being safer, as I had sampled Chinese red before. However, I was surprised at the bread and butter at the meal: really delicious. I looked at the label: Australian. Of course.

It was a beautiful night, with a clear view of Orion, Canis Major, Jupiter and Venus. I found I could not get to sleep, so watched a movie instead: "Noah", starring Russel Crowe and Emma Thomson, both of whom were excellent, although the movie itself was just a little fanciful. It does pose the basic need for humankind to love and care for the earth. The sun rose as we were passing Cairns, and it was spectacular, beginning with bright Venus hanging low in the eastern sky as a red glow lit up the horizon in a thin line. Welcome to Australia, on this new day at 6.15 a.m.

Soon breakfast arrived. I chose Western, with eggs, sausages, a croissant and coffee. I generally get a window seat, as I really enjoy looking at the scenery and for this flight I had selected the eastern side (left hand or port) of the plane, down the back so that the wing would not obscure my view. We crossed the Australian coast around Cape Yorke, tracking down the coast as far as Townsville, continuing south as the coastline swung further to the east. I could not find my mobile phone. I searched and searched. I am one of those people who can put an apple in a plastic bag, then cannot find it. I called a flight attendant, and soon two of them were burrowing around. They found it, lodged into the seat. Good. *Xiexie.* This airline is not too bad after all.

In due course we came into Sydney under cloudy skies. As we flew past the CBD, I was struck at just how small it is. Chinese cities are forests of high rise, 30 storeys and more, but Sydney had only this one little island in the middle, the rest of the city being flat. This is now changing as the population continues to swell and other high rise hubs are spurting up elsewhere, like Parramatta. One day Sydney's population will also be huge, with high rise everywhere, but not yet—thank God. The lovely Michelle met me at the airport to drive me to Kensington. She is a true friend, whom I had met many years ago in CICU, Sydney Children's Hospital where she was working as a nurse. Thank you Michelle.

Now I needed to readjust to Australian society, knowing that it would take time. In spite of all my criticisms I loved China and the Chinese people. My time there had been truly blessed. *Zaijian*—maybe, as this literally means "again see".

Photo 99: a reminder of Chongqing